EMBEDDED SYSTEMS

AN INTRODUCTION USING THE
RENESAS RX62N MICROCONTROLLER

James M. Conrad
University of North Carolina at Charlotte

Alexander G. Dean
North Carolina State University

Micriµm Press
1290 Weston Road, Suite 306
Weston, FL 33326
USA

www.micrium.com

Library of Congress subject headings:

1. Embedded computer systems
2. Real-time data processing
3. Computer software—Development

For bulk orders, please contact Micrium Press at: +1 954 217 2036

ISBN: 978-1-935772-99-6

Please report errors or forward any comments and suggestions to jmconrad@uncc.edu.

Preface

This book is the results of a long relationship the authors have enjoyed with Renesas Electronics America, Inc. (and one of its predecessors, Mitsubishi Electronics). We originally worked with this company because of their commitment to providing a low-cost evaluation board and free development software that students could purchase and use in classes and senior design projects. Over the years the boards have remained as affordable (and popular) as ever, and the software development tools available have added more functionality while still remaining available for free to our students.

We have been teaching embedded systems courses for over twelve years (and working in the field even longer). We had not been able to find a book suitable for using in an undergraduate course that would lend itself to the theoretical and applied nature of embedded systems design. Renesas had been asking us to create a book for several years, and the introduction of the new RX62N microcontroller offered a wonderful opportunity to work with this powerful device and integrate it into our classes.

This book also has a radical feature not seen in many books currently on the market (if any). It is freely available for download and is also provided with the Renesas RX62N evaluation board. It is also available for purchase in hardcopy form for a modest price.

This book can be used on its own for an Introduction to Embedded Systems class or an Introduction to Microprocessors/Microcontrollers. It can also be used as a supplement in many different types of classes.

This book would not have been possible had it not been for the assistance of numerous people. Several students and educators contributed to some of the chapters, including: Adam Harris (1, 2), Suganya Jebasingh (2, 6), Vikram Gill (3,4), Archana Subramanian (4), Onkar Raut (5, 7), Steven Erdmanczyk (8,9), Sunil Gurram (8,11), Aswin Ramakrishnan (11), Vivek Srikantan (12), and Paul Mohan Das (12). Stephanie Conrad heavily edited versions of the chapters. Michael McLain helped create the solutions for the homework assignments. Thanks go to the compositor, Linda Foegen, and especially to June Hay-Harris, Rob Dautel, and Todd DeBoer of Renesas for their help in getting this book produced and published (and for their patience!). Many, many thanks go to the reviewers who offered valuable suggestions to make this book better, especially Jerry Zacharias, Mitch Ferguson, Mike Wilkinson, and students from my UNC Charlotte Embedded Systems course.

Jim Conrad: I would like to personally thank my parents, the Conrads, and my in-laws, the Warrens, for their continued assistance and guidance through the years while I worked on this and other books. Also, I would especially like to thank my children, Jay, Mary Beth, and Caroline, and my wife Stephanie, for their understanding when I needed to spend more time on the book than I spent with them.

Alex Dean: I would like to thank Bill Trosky and Phil Koopman for opening the doors into so many embedded systems through in-depth design reviews. I would like to thank my students in my NCSU embedded systems courses for bringing their imagination, excitement, and persistence to class projects. I would also like to thank my wife Sonya for sharing her passion of seeking out and seizing opportunities, and our daughters Katherine and Jacqueline for making me smile every time I leave work to head home.

James M. Conrad and Alexander G. Dean
September 2011

Foreword

The world of MCU-based embedded designs can be divided into those that take advantage of existing code and MCUs, and those that require leading edge MCU architectures and implementations. Dr. Conrad, with assistance from Dr. Dean, spent more than a year internalizing the inner workings and surrounding ecosystem of the newly-developed RX architecture, and have generated a book showcasing the RX line which has a level of peripheral integration that has not been seen before. Indeed, by taking the best DNA of both CISC and RISC architectures, and combining them into a new breed of MCU, the RX line enables design approaches that were previously spread across the CISC and RISC camps and inaccessible in one device line.

The authors leverage the capabilities of the RX and demonstrate their own expert grasp of all the dynamics that differentiate successful end solutions from those of the "me-too" variety. They recognize that successful embedded systems require more than just good hardware and software engineering. Jim and Alex have masterfully applied RX capabilities to real world challenges using examples, applications, and approaches that will surely empower individuals and teams of designers.

Readers aspire to find books that have the right balance between depth and breadth. Where there is too much detail, the relevance can be obscured; while a broad brush approach may trivialize the essence of key topics. This is especially true of books relating to embedded designs that must achieve a utilitarian purpose. Here, Jim and Alex skillfully navigate from topic to topic, knowing exactly when to throttle for maximum utility.

Whether you are a university student preparing for the real world, a design engineer looking for leading edge approaches to time-critical processes, or a manager attempting to further your risk management techniques, you will find their approach to embedded systems to be stimulating and compelling.

Ali Sebt
Renesas
September 8, 2011

Contents

CHAPTER THREE

Organization and Architecture of the Renesas
RX62N Microcontroller Board   35

CHAPTER FIVE

Software Engineering for Embedded Systems   141

CHAPTER SEVEN

Serial Communications   193

CHAPTER EIGHT

Event Counters, Timers, and the Real Time Clock   301

CHAPTER TEN

Floating Point Unit and Operations   391

CHAPTER ELEVEN

Watchdog Timer and Brown-Out Detector   425

CHAPTER TWELVE

Designing Responsive and Real-Time Systems

Chapter One

Introduction to Embedded Systems

1.1 LEARNING OBJECTIVES

In this chapter the reader will learn:

- What an embedded system is
- Why to embed a computer
- What functions and attributes embedded systems need to provide
- What constraints embedded systems have

1.2 CONCEPTS

An embedded system is an application-specific computer system which is built into a larger system or device. Using a computer system rather than other control methods (such as non-programmable logic circuits, electro-mechanical controls, and hydraulic control) offers many benefits such as sophisticated control, precise timing, low unit cost, low development cost, high flexibility, small size, and low weight. These basic characteristics can be used to improve the overall system or device in various ways:

- Improved performance
- More functions and features
- Reduced cost
- Increased dependability

Because of these benefits, billions of microcontrollers are sold each year to create embedded systems for a wide range of products.

1.2.1 Economics and Microcontrollers

Microcontrollers are remarkably inexpensive yet offer tremendous performance. The microprocessor for a personal computer may cost $100 or more, while microcontrollers typically cost far less, starting at under $0.25. Why is this so?

1

Microcontrollers provide extremely inexpensive processing because they can leverage **economies of scale.** MCUs are programmable in software, so a chipmaker can design a single type of MCU which will satisfy the needs of many customers (when combined with their application-specific software). This reduces the per-chip cost by amortizing the design costs over many millions of units.

The cost of an integrated circuit (such as a microcontroller or a microprocessor) depends on two factors: non-recurring engineering (**NRE**) cost and **recurring** cost. The **NRE** cost includes paying engineers to design the integrated circuit (IC) and verify through simulation and prototyping that it will work properly. The **recurring cost** is incurred by making each additional IC, and includes raw materials, processing, testing, and packaging.

The IC's area is the major factor determining this recurring cost. The smaller the IC, the more will fit onto a silicon wafer and the lower the recurring cost. Microcontrollers are much smaller than microprocessors for personal computers, so they will cost less (given the same number of ICs sold). The NRE cost must be divided across each IC sold. As the number of ICs sold rises, the NRE adder falls, and so each IC's price falls as well. Low-volume chips are more expensive than high-volume chips.

1.2.2   Embedded Networks

Some embedded systems consist of **multiple embedded computers** communicating across an **embedded network,** and offer further benefits. Each computer on the network uses a communication protocol to share the same set of wires to communicate, rather than dedicating one set for each possible communication route. Several advantages come from having fewer wires:

- Lower parts cost, as fewer wires are needed
- Lower labor costs, as it is faster to assemble
- Greater reliability, as it has fewer connections to fail

Other advantages come from allowing separate nodes to share information. New features may be possible, or the system efficiency may be improved through better coordination of activities among different nodes.

1.3   TYPICAL BENEFITS OF EMBEDDED SYSTEMS

As an example, let's examine how embedded systems have affected automobiles. A typical modern car has dozens of microcontrollers embedded within it. Let's see why.

1.3.1 Greater Performance and Efficiency

Computer control of automobile engines lowers pollution and increases fuel efficiency, reducing operating costs.

Burning gasoline with air in spark ignition engines is a tricky business if we want to maximize efficiency, yet minimize pollution. The main factor affecting emissions is the ratio of air mass to fuel mass. The ideal ratio is 14.7 to 1, and the catalytic converter is designed to operate most efficiently at this ratio. If there is too little air (a rich mix), then excessive carbon monoxide (CO) and hydrocarbons (HC) will be produced. If there is too much air (a lean mix), then large amounts of oxides of nitrogen (called NO_x) will be created. So we would like for each fuel injector to add just the right amount of fuel. This depends on the mass of the air inside the cylinder, which depends on factors such as air temperature and air pressure. These in turn depend on altitude and weather, as well as whether the engine is warmed up or not.

Another factor is the timing of the sparkplug firing. If it fires early, then there is more time for combustion within the cylinder before the exhaust valve opens. This raises the average temperature within the cylinder and changes the combustion process, affecting CO, HC, and NO_x concentrations.

It would be quite impractical to design a mechanical control system to consider all of these factors and squirt the fuel injectors at just the right instant for the right amount of time. Thankfully, an inexpensive microcontroller is quite effective at these kinds of calculations and control.

1.3.2 Lower Costs

There are various ways in which an embedded system can reduce the costs associated with a device.

- **Component costs:** Embedded software can compensate for poor signal quality, allowing the use of less-expensive components. For example, a low-cost pressure sensor may be very temperature-dependent. If ambient temperature information is already available, then it is a simple matter to compensate for the temperature-induced error.
- **Manufacturing costs:** Many vehicles use the Control Area Network (CAN) protocol to communicate across an in-car network. The embedded network reduces assembly and parts costs because of the simpler wiring harness.
- **Operating costs:** As mentioned above, an embedded system enables automobile engines to operate more efficiently, reducing the amount of gasoline needed and hence lowering operating costs.
- **Maintenance costs:** Some vehicles predict oil life by monitoring engine use history, notifying the driver when an oil change is needed.

1.3.3   More Features

An MCU running application-specific software offers tremendous opportunities for features and customization. These features can make your company's products stand out from the competition.

- **Cruise control** keeps the car running at the same speed regardless of hills, wind, and other external factors.
- **Smart airbags** reduce injuries by adjusting inflation speed based on passenger weight.
- **Power seats** move to each driver's preferred position automatically, based on whose keyless entry fob was used to open the car.
- **Headlights and interior lights** shut off automatically after a time delay if the car is not running and prevents the lights from draining the battery.

1.3.4   Better Dependability

Embedded systems and networks offer many opportunities to improve dependability.

- An engine controller (and other controllers) can provide various "limp-home modes" to keep the car running even if one or more sensors or other devices fail.
- A warning of an impending failure can be provided.
- Diagnostic information can be provided to the driver or service personnel, saving valuable trouble-shooting time.

1.4   EMBEDDED SYSTEM FUNCTIONS ———————————————————

There are several common functions which embedded systems typically provide.

- **Control systems** monitor a process and adjust an output variable to keep the process running at the desired set point. For example, a cruise control system may increase the throttle setting if the car's speed is lower than the desired speed, and reduce it if the car is too fast.
- There is often **sequencing** among multiple states. For example, a car engine goes through multiple states or control modes when started. During **Crank and Start,** the fuel/air mix is lean and depends on the engine coolant temperature. Once the engine has started, the controller switches to the **Warm-Up** mode, in order to raise the engine and exhaust system temperatures to their ideal levels. Here the fuel/air

mixture and ignition timing are adjusted, again based in part on the engine coolant temperature. When the engine has warmed up it can switch into **Idle** mode. In this mode the controller seeks to minimize the engine's speed, yet still run smoothly and efficiently despite changes in loads due to air conditioning, power steering, and the electrical system.

▪ **Signal processing** modifies input signals to eliminate noise, emphasize signal components of interest, and compensate for other factors. For example, a hands-free speakerphone interface may use multiple microphones, beam-forming, and active noise cancellation to filter out low-frequency road noise. Other sensors may have spark-plug noise filtered out.

▪ **Communications and networking** enable different devices on the same network to exchange information. For example, the engine controller may need to send a message indicating speed. To do this, the speed value must be formatted according to the communication protocol and then loaded into the network interface peripheral for transmission.

1.5   ATTRIBUTES OF EMBEDDED SYSTEMS

Embedded systems are designed so that the resulting device behaves in certain desirable ways.

▪ Embedded systems need to **respond to events** which occur in the environment, whether a user presses a button or a motor overheats. A system which is not sufficiently responsive is not likely to be a successful product. For example, when we press a channel select button for the radio, we would like for it to respond within some reasonable time.

▪ For **real-time systems,** the timing of the responses is **critical** because late answers are wrong answers. Igniting the fuel in a cylinder is time-critical because bad timing can damage or destroy engine components (to say nothing of reducing power, or the efficiency and pollution concerns mentioned previously).

▪ Embedded systems typically require sophisticated **fault handling and diagnostics** to enable safe and reliable operation. Often the fault handling code is larger and more complex than the normal operation code. It is easy to design for the "everything goes right and works fine" case. It is far more difficult to determine methods to handle the exceptional cases. What is likely to fail? Which failures can lead to dangerous conditions? How should the system handle failures? How will you test that the system handles the failures correctly?

▪ Embedded systems may be expected to **operate independently** for years without operator attention such as adjustment or resetting. The system is expected to operate robustly and always work. Given that it is very difficult and expensive to write perfect, bug-free software, developers build in mechanisms to detect faulty behavior and respond, perhaps by restarting the system.

1.6   CONSTRAINTS ON EMBEDDED SYSTEMS

Embedded systems often have **constraints** which limit the designer's options, and can lead to creative and elegant solutions. These constraints are typically different from those for general-purpose computers.

- **Cost** is a common constraint. Many applications which use embedded systems are sold in very competitive markets, in which price is a major factor. Often a manufacturer will hire subcontractors to design and build individual sub-systems. This allows the manufacturer to pit potential subcontractors against each other, keeping prices down.
- There may be **size** and **weight** limits for portable and mobile applications. An embedded system for an automotive remote keyless entry transmitter must fit into a small fob on a key ring which fits easily into a pocket. Similarly, the receiver must not be too heavy. A heavier car will have worse acceleration, braking, cornering, and fuel efficiency. Aircraft and spacecraft are especially sensitive to weight since a heavier craft requires more fuel to achieve the same range.
- There may be limited **power** or **energy** available. For example, a battery has a limited amount of energy, while a solar cell generates a limited amount of power. High temperatures may limit the amount of cooling available, which will limit the power which can be used.
- The **environment** may be harsh. Automotive electronics under the hood of a car need to operate across a wide range of temperatures ($-40°C$ to $125°C$, or $-40°F$ to $193°F$), while withstanding vibrations, physical impact, and corroding salt spray. Spark plugs generate broadband radio frequency energy which can interfere with electronics.

1.7   DESIGNING AND MANUFACTURING EMBEDDED SYSTEMS

Embedded systems are designed with a central microcontroller and other supporting electronic components mounted on a printed circuit board (PCB). PCBs provide the means to connect these integrated circuits to each other to make an operational system. The PCB provides structural support and the wiring of the circuit. The individual wires on the PCB are called traces and are made from a flat copper foil. While many circuit designs may use the same standard components, the PCB is often a custom component for a given design.

Designing a PCB requires a completed schematic for the circuit. This schematic is sometimes different than the schematic seen in textbooks. It often contains extra informa-

Figure 1.1   EIN GreenEval Zigbee Module.

tion about the components and construction of the board. For example, a textbook schematic may only show a battery for the power supply, while the production schematic would show the battery case, the number of cells, the rating of the battery, and the manufacturers of the components.

From the schematic, a designer will use their computer-aided design tools to identify the size of the PCB, and then place the electronic components on their board drawing. The designer will also place the wiring between the components on the PCB.

The physical PCB is manufactured from a fiberglass-resin material that is lightweight and inexpensive. A manufacturer will add copper wiring traces to the surfaces of the board and the appropriate insulation and white silk screening. The final manufacturing steps are applying solder, placing the components, and heating/cooling the solder. Figure 1.1 shows an example of a finished board.

The completed boards are electrically tested for functionality. Any board failing the test is inspected in more detail to find the problems. These boards are repaired to increase the passing rate acceptable to the manufacturer. The boards are wrapped in anti-static materials and shipped to the next location for the next stage of production, or immediately installed in a mechanical enclosure (like the mechanical shell of a mobile phone).

1.8   AN EXAMPLE OF AN EMBEDDED SYSTEM: THE EIN GREENEVAL ZIGBEE MODULE

The EIN GreenEval Zigbee (Envisionnovation, http://www.eininc.net/products.html) module is one example of a Renesas MCU-based embedded system. This device has thirty-four digital I/O lines that are controlled by a Zigbee radio.

Figure 1.1 shows the main board of the EIN GreenEval Zigbee Module. As seen in this example, taking off the shielding provides a good look at the internal circuitry. Six of the main components are visible. Starting from left to right; the large cylindrical device hanging off the left edge of the board is an antenna for the 2.4 GHz radio.

The chip labeled 5PE20V (http://www.micron.com//get-document/?documentId= 5965&file=M25PE20_10.pdf) (the small 8-pin chip at the top left of the image) is a page-erasable serial FLASH chip. This chip communicates with the Renesas MCU through the SPI bus. This chip is also used to hold more data than the MCU. Since the MCU can only handle 8 k of data, it is quickly filled. This extra FLASH chip can hold an additional 2 Mbits.

The square chip on the lower left is a Skyworks 2.4 GHz Front-End Module (FEM) (SKYWORKS Solutions, Inc., http://www.skyworksinc.com/Product.aspx?ProductID=752), which simply boosts radio signals sent from the MCU. It is controlled by three output pins of the MCU. One pin controls putting the FEM to sleep to save power, another pin selects whether the FEM will send or receive data, and the last pin actually transmits and receives data to and from the FEM.

The large chip in the center is a Renesas R5FF36B3 from the M16C family of chips with 256 K + 24 K of ROM, 20 k RAM, and 8 k of data (Renesas Electronics America, Inc., *RENESAS MCU: M16C Family/M16C/60 SERIES,* http://am.renesas.com/products/ mpumcu/m16c/m16c60/m16c6b/m16c6b_root.jsp). Thirty-four I/O pins are used to interface with external pins on the module. This processor is running at 4 MHz (controlled by the small metal chip which is actually a temperature compensated crystal oscillator). This chip has an RF radio built in.

The pins at the far right are a programming and interface header. They are used to communicate with and program the Renesas MCU.

1.9 SUMMARY OF BOOK CONTENTS _____

This book is structured as follows:

- Chapters 2 and 3 present basic microcontroller concepts and the specifics of the RX62N.
- Chapters 4 and 5 show how software is built. At the low level they show how programs are compiled and downloaded. At the high level they show software engineering concepts and practices.
- Chapters 6 through 8 present how to use peripherals to interface with the environment and simplify programs.
- Chapter 9 presents how to use interrupts to improve response times and program structure.

- Chapter 10 presents how to use the floating-point math support in the RX62N.
- Chapter 11 presents how to increase system robustness using the watchdog timer and voltage brownout detector.
- Chapter 12 presents how to structure multi-threaded software so the resulting system is predictably responsive.

1.10 RECAP

An embedded system is an application-specific computer system which is built into a larger system or device. Using a computer system enables improved performance, more functions and features, lower cost, and greater dependability. With embedded computer systems, manufacturers can add sophisticated control and monitoring to devices and other systems, while leveraging the low-cost microcontrollers running custom software.

1.11 REFERENCES

Envisionnovation. *EININC Products*. Ontario: Envisionnovation, 2010. Web. Accessed at http://www.eininc. net/products.html

Numonyx MP25PE20 datasheet http://www.micron.com//get-document/?documentId=5965&file=M25PE20_10.pdf

RENESAS MCU: M16C Family/M16C/60 SERIES. Renesas Electronics America, Inc., 2010. Web. Accessed at http://am.renesas.com/products/mpumcu/m16c/m16c60/m16c6b/m16c6b_root.jsp

SKYWORKS Solutions, Inc. *SKYWORKS Products: SKY65352-11*. Woburn, MA: SKYWORKS Solutions, Inc., 2009. Web. Accessed at http://www.skyworksinc.com/Product.aspx?ProductID=752

Chapter Two

Concepts of Microcontrollers

2.1 LEARNING OBJECTIVES

Embedded systems consist of computers embedded in larger systems. Additional circuitry such as power supplies, clock generators, and reset circuits, is required for the computer to work. Transducers (devices that convert one type of energy into another) are also used to connect microcontrollers to the outside world. There are two classes of transducers: inputs and outputs. Inputs are also known as "sensors" and contain such things as switches, keypads, and buttons. Output transducers include devices such as LEDs, motors, and coils.

In this chapter the reader will learn general information about:

- Connecting LEDs
- Connecting motors and coils
- Connecting switches and buttons
- Connecting keypads
- Analog to digital conversion
- Digital to analog conversion
- Power supplies for embedded systems
- Clock generation options
- Reset circuitry

2.2 INTERFACING WITH DIGITAL SIGNALS

2.2.1 General Purpose Digital I/O

Embedded systems consist of computers embedded in larger systems. The processor needs to sense the state of the larger system and environment, and control output devices. The most basic way to do this is through one or more discrete signals, each of which which can be in one of two states (on or off). General purpose digital I/O **ports** are the hardware which can be used to read from or write to the system outside the microcontroller.

The RX62N has eleven I/O ports (Port 0 to 5, A to E). Each port has eight pins, and on most ports all eight pins can be selected as inputs or outputs. However, on some ports some pins are reserved. The reserved pins cannot be configured as I/O pins. Each port has a Data Direction Register (DDR), Data Register (DR), Port Register (PORT), and Input Buffer Control Register (ICR). The pins of a port may serve several purposes; for example, Port 4 pin 0 can be used as a general purpose I/O pin, as an A/D converter input, or as an interrupt input. Depending on the purposes these pins serve, they might have extra registers. Ports A through E have an extra register called the Pull-up MOS Control Register (PCR), and Ports 0 to 3 (P30 to P34) and C have Open Drain Control Register (ODR). All of these registers are 8 bits long.

Certain other registers called Port Function Registers are also present. These registers are associated with special features of the RX62N board such as USB, CAN, etc.

Data Direction Register (DDR)

This register, as the name suggests, is used to set the data direction (input or output) of a pin. DDR is a read/write register. Each bit of the Data Direction Register represents a pin.

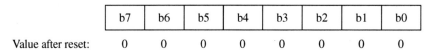

b7	b6	b5	b4	b3	b2	b1	b0

Value after reset: 0   0   0   0   0   0   0   0

Figure 2.1   Data Direction Register. Source: Kuphaldt, T. R. "Successive Approximation ADC," in *All about Circuits,* page 765.

The 'iodefine_RX62N.h' file has C code constructs that make it easy to access each port with C code. Each port is defined as a *structure* and each register of the port is defined as a *union* of variables within that structure. An example of how the DDR is defined inside a port *structure* follows:

```
1. struct st_port4 {
2.    union {
3.       unsigned char BYTE;
4.       struct {
5.          unsigned char B7:1;
6.          unsigned char B6:1;
7.          unsigned char B5:1;
8.          unsigned char B4:1;
```

```
9.              unsigned char B3:1;
10.             unsigned char B2:1;
11.             unsigned char B1:1;
12.             unsigned char B0:1;
13.         } BIT;
14.     } DDR;
15. }
```

Line 1 shows that port0 has been defined as a *structure*. Lines 2 to 14 suggest that Data Direction Register (DDR) has been defined as a *union* with the variable BYTE and a structure called BIT. This organization helps in easy access of the bits of the DDR. Unsigned char $Bn:1(n = 0$ to 7) indicates that the character variable is assigned one bit.

To select a particular pin as the input pin, the corresponding bit of the DDR has to be set to '0'; and to select a pin as output, the corresponding bit of the DDR has to be set to '1.' The general syntax to set a bit of the DDR is PORTx.DDR.BIT.Bn ($x = 0$ to 5, A to E; and $n = 0$ to 7) since ports are defined as *structures* and accessing structure *members* is done so this way. To configure multiple pins at the same time, the *char* variable BYTE can be used. All pins are configured as inputs at reset, by default.

EXAMPLE 1

Set Switch 1 (Port 4 bit 0) as Input

```
PORT4.DDR.BIT.B1 = 0;
```

When a pin is selected as an input from a peripheral, the Input Buffer Control Register (ICR) has to be enabled. The ICR will be explained a little later.

Selecting a pin as an output involves setting the Data Register (DR) and the Data Direction Register (DDR).

Data Register (DR)

The Data Register is used to store data for pins that have been configured as output pins. This register is similar to the DDR in that each bit of the register represents a pin and certain bits of certain ports are reserved.

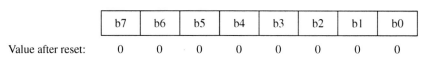

b7	b6	b5	b4	b3	b2	b1	b0

Value after reset: 0   0   0   0   0   0   0   0

Figure 2.2   Data Register.

The Data Register (DR) is also defined as a *union* of variables inside the port *structure,* in the 'iodefine_RX62N.h' file. It is presented just like the DDR. Unsigned char: 1 is used to represent reserved pins.

The syntax to access the bits of the Data Register (DR) is PORTx.DR.BIT.Bn ($x = 0$ to 5, A to E; and $n = 0$ to 7). To select a pin as an output pin, first set the Data Register (DR) to a known value, preferably 0, so that changes in the output can be easily observed. The *char* variable BYTE can be used to set multiple pins as output at the same time.

EXAMPLE 2

Set LED1 (Port D bit 0) as Output

```
1. PORTD.DDR.BIT.B0 = 1;
2. PORTD.DR.BIT.B0 = 0;
```

Line 1 sets LED1 as an output and line 2 switches on the LED.

Sets LEDs 1, 2, and 3 (Port D bit 0, 1, and 2) as Outputs

```
1. PORTD.DDR.BYTE = 0x07;
2. PORTD.DR.BYTE = 0xF8;
```

Line 1 sets LED1, 2, and 3 as outputs and line 2 switches on the LEDs.

Port Register (PORT)

Port register is also defined as a *union* of variables inside the port *structure* in the 'iodefine_RX62N.h' file. PORTx.PORT.BIT.Bn ($x = 0$ to 5, A to E; and $n = 0$ to 7) is used to read the state of a pin and the state is stored in the Port Register regardless of the value in the Input Buffer Control Register (ICR). This register also has some reserved bits. These bits are read as 1 and cannot be modified.

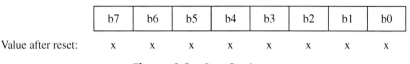

b7	b6	b5	b4	b3	b2	b1	b0

Value after reset: x   x   x   x   x   x   x   x

Figure 2.3   Port Register.

Check State of Switch1 (Port 4 bit 0) and Turn On LED1 (Port D bit 0)

```
1. if(PORT4.PORT.BIT.B0 == 1){
2.    PORTD.DR.BIT.B0 = 1;
3. }
```

Input Buffer Control Register (ICR)

This register is used to buffer the input values for pins that have been configured as input from peripheral modules.

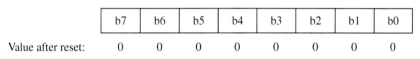

b7	b6	b5	b4	b3	b2	b1	b0

Value after reset: 0   0   0   0   0   0   0   0

Figure 2.4   Input Buffer Control Register.

Before configuring a pin as an input from a peripheral, the ICR must be enabled. To enable the ICR set PORTx.ICR.BIT.Bn (x = 0 to 5, A to E; and n = 0 to 7) to 1. If a pin has to be configured as an output pin, set PORTx.ICR.BIT.Bn (x = 0 to 5, A to E; and n = 0 to 7) to 0. Setting ICR to 0 disables the ICR. While setting the ICR, make sure that the corresponding pin is not in use. For example, when setting IRQi (i = 0 to 15) as input, first disable the interrupts, next enable ICR and then enable interrupts. It is necessary to follow the above steps to avoid unintended operations from taking place.

Open Drain Control Register (ODR)

Most output pins function as CMOS but some output pins can operate as CMOS or NMOS open-drain pins. Since NMOS circuits are faster compared to the CMOS circuits, which consist of the slower p-channel transistors, using NMOS open-drain pins as outputs would be similar to a wired-OR connection. All of the pins of port 0, 1, 2, C and pins 0 to 4 of port 3 are capable of functioning as NMOS open-drain output pins. Setting PORTx.ODR.BIT.Bn (x = 0 to 5, A to E; and n = 0 to 7) to 1, selects the pin as an NMOS open-drain pin.

Pull-Up MOS Control Register (PCR)

Some devices have limited signal swing. When such a device is interfaced with the RX62N board, the signal from the device has to be pulled up so that it is in the valid voltage range of the board (this is not the typical usage, the typical usage is the external device is only capable of pulling down; or there is nothing attached and you do not want the port to float). To simplify this kind of interfacing, pull-up MOS circuitry is available for ports A to E. To enable pull-up MOS for a particular pin of a port, set PORTx.PCR.BIT.Bn ($x = 0$ to 5, A to E; and $n = 0$ to 7) to 1. To disable pull-up MOS, set PORTx.PCR.BIT.Bn ($x = 0$ to 5, A to E; and $n = 0$ to 7) to 0. The PCR is automatically disabled for pins configured as outputs. To enable or disable pull-up MOS for multiple pins use PORTx.PCR.BYTE command. The value of the PCR after reset is 0x00.

2.2.2   Example 1: Reading Switches to Control LEDs

Using LEDs as Outputs

LEDs require a current-limiting resistor so that they do not draw too much current from the I/O pin to which they are connected. Most microcontrollers can sink more current than they can supply, so generally LEDs are connected with the cathode to the microcontroller pin, and a current-limiting resistor between the anode and supply voltage. Formula 2.1 shows how to calculate the value of the current limiting resistor. Figure 2.5 shows the two ways of connecting LEDs to a microprocessor.

$$R = (V_{\text{Output}} - V_{\text{LED}})/I_{\text{LED}} \qquad\qquad \textbf{Formula 2.1}$$

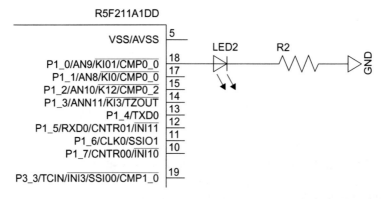

Figure 2.5A   The microprocessor is sourcing current to an LED. Turning on this LED requires a logical HIGH signal on the output pin. If the LED is attached to Port D, Pin 0, and that pin is set to an output; then the code needed to turn the LED on would be: `PORTD.DR.BIT.B0 = 1;`

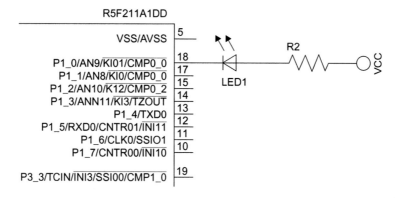

Figure 2.5B The microprocessor is sinking current from the LED. Turning on the LED requires a logical LOW on the output pin. If the LED is attached to Port D, Pin 0, and that pin is set to an output; then the code needed to turn the LED on would be: PORTD.DR.BIT.B0 = 0;

Using Switches as Inputs

A simple interfacing design can include using a pull-up resistor on a pin that is also connected to ground through a button or switch. The resistor will pull the voltage on that pin to logic HIGH until the button connects to ground. When the button is pressed, the voltage at that pin will drop to zero (logic LOW). Figure 2.6 shows a schematic of this approach. If the switch in Figure 2.6 is connected to Port D pin 0, the code to check this switch would be:

```
1. if(PORTD.PORT.BIT.B0 == 0){
2.    //Conditional code goes here
3. }
```

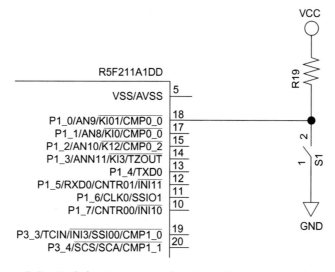

Figure 2.6 Basic button connection to a microprocessor input pin.

Contact bounce is a worry with any mechanical switch. When the switch is closed, the mechanical properties of the metals in the switch cause the contacts to literally bounce off of one another. This can cause false signals to be read as inputs. Your design should take this into account with either a hardware or software *debouncing* solution. Hardware debouncing circuits often require digital logic as well as some resistors and capacitors. Hardware debouncing circuits are very useful for interrupt pins. Software debouncing is accomplished by setting up a timer to check the state of the switch at a set interval, such as every 1 ms. If the value of the input has been the same for the duration of the timer (1 ms in this case) the input can be considered valid. This method helps to ignore false input values.

To better understand configuring I/O pins let us look at an example. The RX62N board has three push buttons and twelve LEDs (six red and six green). Switches and LEDs are simple I/Os and in the following program we will see how to set up switches as inputs and LEDs as outputs. According to this program, when switch1 is pressed, green LEDs will glow, when switch2 is pressed, red LEDs will glow, and when switch3 is pressed, all the LEDs will glow.

```
1.  #include "iodefine_RX62N.h"
2.  #ifdef YRD_RX62N
3.  #define LED1    PORTD.DR.BIT.B0
4.  #define LED2    PORTD.DR.BIT.B1
5.  #define LED3    PORTD.DR.BIT.B2
6.  #define LED4    PORTD.DR.BIT.B3
7.  #define LED5    PORTD.DR.BIT.B4
8.  #define LED6    PORTD.DR.BIT.B5
9.  #define LED7    PORTD.DR.BIT.B6
10. #define LED8    PORTD.DR.BIT.B7
11. #define LED9    PORTE.DR.BIT.B0
12. #define LED10   PORTE.DR.BIT.B1
13. #define LED11   PORTE.DR.BIT.B2
14. #define LED12   PORTE.DR.BIT.B3
15. #define LED1_DDR    PORTD.DDR.BIT.B0
16. #define LED2_DDR    PORTD.DDR.BIT.B1
17. #define LED3_DDR    PORTD.DDR.BIT.B2
18. #define LED4_DDR    PORTD.DDR.BIT.B3
19. #define LED5_DDR    PORTD.DDR.BIT.B4
20. #define LED6_DDR    PORTD.DDR.BIT.B5
21. #define LED7_DDR    PORTD.DDR.BIT.B6
22. #define LED8_DDR    PORTD.DDR.BIT.B7
23. #define LED9_DDR    PORTE.DDR.BIT.B0
24. #define LED10_DDR   PORTE.DDR.BIT.B1
```

```
25. #define LED11_DDR    PORTE.DDR.BIT.B2
26. #define LED12_DDR    PORTE.DDR.BIT.B3
27. #define LED_ON    1
28. #define LED_OFF    0
29. #define ALL_LEDS_ON    { LED1 = LED2 = LED3 = LED4 = LED5 = LED6 =
      LED7 = LED8 = LED9 = LED10 = LED11 = LED12 = LED_ON;}
30. #define ALL_LEDS_OFF    { LED1 = LED2 = LED3 = LED4 = LED5 = LED6 =
      LED7 = LED8 = LED9 = LED10 = LED11 = LED12 = LED_OFF;}
31. #define ENABLE_LEDS    { LED1_DDR = LED2_DDR = LED3_DDR = LED4_DDR =
      LED5_DDR = LED6_DDR = LED7_DDR = LED8_DDR = LED9_DDR =
      LED10_DDR = LED11_DDR = LED12_DDR = 1;}
32. #endif
33. #define SW1    PORT4.PORT.BIT.B0
34. #define SW2    PORT4.PORT.BIT.B1
35. #define SW3    PORT4.PORT.BIT.B2
36. #define ENABLE_SWITCHES    { PORT4.DDR.BIT.B0 = PORT4.DDR.BIT.B1 =
      PORT4.DDR.BIT.B2 = 0;}
37. void main(void){
38.    ENABLE_LEDS;
39.    ENABLE_SWITCHES;
40.    while(1){
41.       if(SW1 == 0){
42.          LED12 = LED11 = LED10 = LED6 = LED5 = LED4 = LED_ON;
43.       } else if(SW2 == 0){
44.          LED9 = LED8 = LED7 = LED3 = LED2 = LED1 = LED_ON;
45.       } else if(SW3 == 0){
46.          ALL_LEDS_ON;
47.       } else {
48.          ALL_LEDS_OFF;
49.       }
50.    }
51. }
```

In line 1, the file 'iodefine_RX62N.h' has been included. It is a custom header file created by Renesas for easy access and manipulation of data. The RX62N board has two sets of LEDs: RSK_RX62N LEDs which are used to indicate basic functions like power on, and YRD RX62N LEDs which are used to simulate a motor. This program uses the YRD RX62N LEDs to demonstrate the use of digital I/O pins. Line 2 and line 32 are used to indicate that the statements between them should be executed only for YRD RX62N LEDs. All pins of Port D and pins 0 to 3 of Port E are the LED pins. The three switches are at Port 4 bits 0 to 2.

In main, first the LEDs have been enabled (line 38). ENABLE_LEDS is a macro defined earlier in the program (line 31) to set the Data Direction Register (DDR) of the LEDs to 1; i.e., set up the LED pins as output pins.

Next, the switches have been enabled (line 39). ENABLE_SWITCHES is another macro defined earlier (line 36) to set the Data Direction Register (DDR) of the switches to 0; i.e., set up the switch pins as output pins.

The next part of the program is an important part of many embedded systems—the while (1) loop (line 40). This loop makes the microcontroller execute all the statements within the loop repeatedly until the microcontroller is stopped by an external force (e.g., power off). In this program, the conditions for LED operation are given within the while (1) loop using if-else statements (lines 41 to 47). Even though use of the switch statement will result in much better code, the if-else statement has been used for easy understanding.

- If switch 1 is pressed (state of switch 1 is low), all the green LEDs are turned on (line 42). The state of the switch is checked using the macro defined in line 33 using the PORT register. From the schematic of the board it can be seen that green LEDs are LED 12, 11, 10, 6, 5, and 4. They are turned on by setting the Data Register (DR) of the LED pins to 1 (active high) which has been defined using the macro LED_ON in line 27.
- If switch 2 is pressed (state of switch 2 is low), all the red LEDs are turned on (line 44). The state of the switch is checked using the macro defined in line 34 using the PORT register. From the schematic of the board it can be seen that red LEDs are LED 9, 8, 7, 3, 2, and 1. They are turned on by setting the Data Register (DR) of the LED pins to 1 (active high) which has been defined using the macro LED_ON.
- If switch 3 is pressed (state of switch 3 is low), all the LEDs are turned on (line 46) using the macro LED_ON.
- If none of the switches are pressed (line 47) all the LEDs are turned off using the macro LED_OFF (line 48).

2.2.3   Driving Motors and Coils

Input/Output (I/O) pins on a microcontroller have specific limits to the amount of current each pin can sink or source. These limits are found in the datasheet. Voltage levels can also be different between sensors and the microcontroller. Both of these constraints must be taken into account when designing interfaces for the actuator.

Because of their large coils, motors draw a lot of current. For Direct Current (DC) motors, simple transistor drivers or H-bridges (shown in Figure 2.7) can be used to interface them with a microcontroller. If the left input of the circuit in Figure 2.7 is connected to

Port D pin 0 and the right input of this circuit is connected to Port D pin 1, the code to turn the motor one direction would be:

```
1. PORTD.DDR.BYTE = 0x03;   //Sets pins 0 and 1 on Port D as outputs
2. PORTD.DR.BYTE = 0x02;    //Sets one pin as HIGH and the other as LOW
```

Stepper motors can use transistors or stepper motor driver ICs. Some ICs such as the L293 or the 754410 are specifically designed to drive the DC motors and interface directly with a microcontroller. Servos are gearboxes that have motor control circuitry built in. These devices can often connect their control pins directly to a microprocessor as their internal circuitry handles driving the motor itself. Other large coils such as relay coils should be treated similarly to motors. Figure 2.8 shows a basic coil driving circuit. Code to drive the coil is the same as it is to drive an LED.

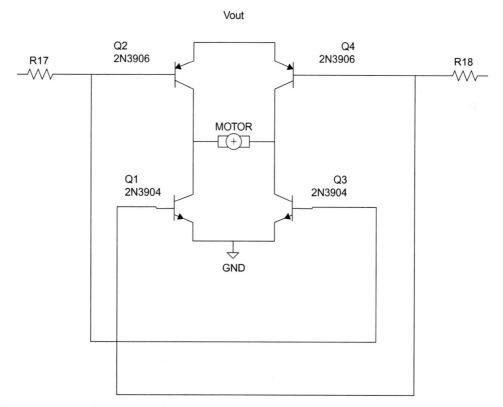

Figure 2.7 H-bridge motor driver. Two if the microprocessor's outputs are connected to the resistors. *Note: Both inputs should not be the same value for the motor to turn.*

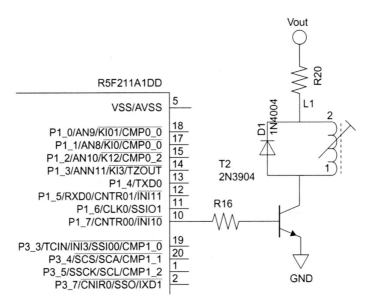

Figure 2.8   A simple coil driver.

There are other methods of controlling large loads with a microprocessor, such as using relays or triacs. The overall concept with all load driving circuits is to keep the source and sink currents of the microprocessor within the manufacturer's recommendations.

Some sensors may require different voltages than what the microprocessor requires. Care should be taken when interfacing these sensors. If the microprocessor runs at 5 V and the sensor runs at 1.8 V, the microprocessor will not be able to read a HIGH logic signal on the sensor output. Circuits for interfacing with higher voltage sensors can be designed using transistors or by using level converter ICs, which convert the signals between the microcontroller and the sensor either uni-directionally or bi-directionally (in case the microprocessor needs to communicate to the sensor.) The use of a flyback diode is very important when interfacing inductive loads, to safely dissipate the voltage spike when the voltage to the load is removed.

2.2.4   Scanning Matrix Keypads

Keypads work as a matrix of buttons. For instance, Figure 2.9 shows an example keypad matrix. The top three output pins are used as the columns of the matrix. The three pins connected as the rows of the matrix are all input pins. A button is placed in the circuit at each intersection of a column and row. One at a time, the output pins turn on and each of the input pins is read. If an input is detected, the microprocessor can determine which button on the keypad had been pressed. For example, if the microprocessor noted an input on the middle row pin at the time in which the middle output was logic HIGH, then the center button must have been pressed. If the columns in Figure 2.9 are connected to Port D bits 0, 1, and 2 respectively, and the rows are connected to Port E bits 0, 1, and 2 respectively; code to read the keypad values of the first column would be:

```
1. PORTD.DR.BIT.B0 = 1;    //Set the output of the first column to 1
2. PORTD.DR.BIT.B1 = 0;    //Set the output of the second column to 0
3. PORTD.DR.BIT.B2 = 0;    //Set the output of the third column to 0
4.
5. if(PORTE.PORT.BIT.B0 == 0){
6.    //Conditional code for Row 0
7. }
8.
9. if(PORTE.PORT.BIT.B0 == 0){
10.    //Conditional code for Row 1
11. }
12.
13. if(PORTE.PORT.BIT.B0 == 0){
14.    //Conditional code for Row 2
15. }
```

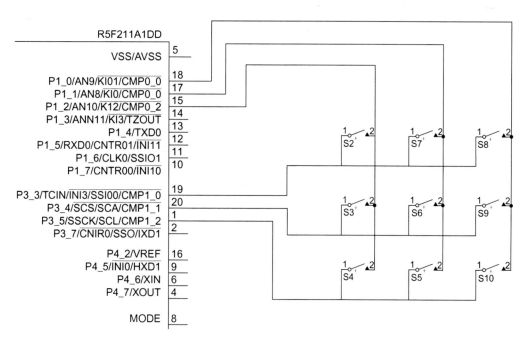

Figure 2.9 Keypad button matrix.

2.3   INTERFACING WITH ANALOG SIGNALS

The world is not digital; it is analog. Microphones, thermometers, speakers, light sensors, and even video cameras are all analog sensors. As a result, the signals from these sensors must be converted to digital values so that the microcontrollers can process them.

2.3.1   Analog to Digital Converters

To read the value of an analog sensor, *Analog to Digital Converters* (also referred to as ADC, A/D, A-to-D, and A2D) are used. This circuit produces a multi-bit binary number based on a voltage scale. The number of bits in the multi-bit binary number helps determine the resolution or precision of the reading; 8-bit, 10-bit, and 12-bit converters are commonly used. ADCs also require a reference voltage. This is a stable voltage to which the current reading will be compared to produce the binary output. The analog reference voltage is scaled by the resolution. Most ADCs use linear scales, so converting the values is straightforward. Figure 2.10 shows the transfer function which is used to convert an analog voltage (measured on the horizontal axis) to its digital output code representation (on the vertical axis). Each step on the transfer function represents one least-significant bit. Figure 2.11 shows an example input analog voltage which is sampled over time.

The resolution of the conversion is determined by Formula 2.2.

$$\text{Resolution} = V_{\text{LSB}} = V_{\text{ref}}/2^{N\text{bits}} \qquad\qquad \textbf{Formula 2.2}$$

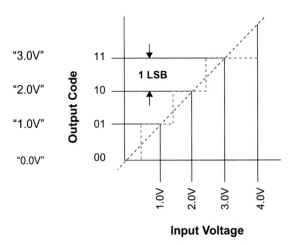

Figure 2.10   2-bit ADC conversion chart. The stair step line shows the ADC's output code.

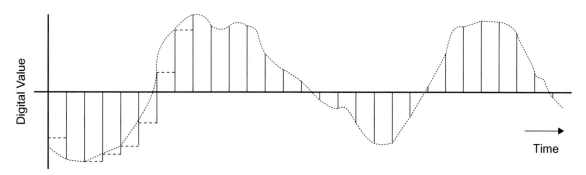

Figure 2.11   ADC readings over time.

If V_{ref} = 5 V, and there is an 8-bit resolution, the volts per ADC raw value step = 5 V/256 = 0.01953 V/step.

To determine the value of the conversion, Formula 2.3 can be used:

$$\text{ADC output code} = \text{int} (((2^{Nbits} - 1) * (V_{in}/V_{ref})) + 1/2) \qquad \textbf{Formula 2.3}$$

For example:

$$V_{ref} = 5 \text{ V}, V_{in} = 2.26295 \text{ V, with a 10-bit resolution;}$$
$$\text{int} ((1023 * (2.26295 \text{ V}/5 \text{ V})) + 1/2) = 463 \text{ ADC raw value steps.}$$

Once the raw ADC value is known, the application software should reverse the formula to calculate the actual voltage on that pin. Since the datasheet for most sensors provides a formula for converting the voltage to the unit the sensor is measuring (be it degrees Celsius, distance in centimeters, pressure in kilopascals, etc.), this formula can be inserted into the firmware to make sense of the data.

More advanced sensors use a communication protocol such as RS-232, RS-485, I^2C, and SPI. These sensors generally take an analog value, convert it to digital, and then send it to the microcontroller for processing using a communication protocol. These protocols sometimes allow for multiple sensors to be connected to the same pins of the microcontroller.

2.3.2   Analog Comparator

Some microcontrollers may contain one or more comparator circuits. This circuit can be thought of as a simple 1-bit analog to digital converter. It compares an analog voltage input with an analog reference voltage, and then determines which is larger.

2.3.3   Digital to Analog Conversion

Just as we must convert analog signals to digital to process them, sometimes there is a need to convert digital signals to analog. In systems that control audio, speed, or even light levels; digital output from a microprocessor must be converted into an analog signal. There are several different methods for converting digital signals to analog.

Resistor Networks

Resistor networks allow a very simple solution for converting digital signals to analog. There are many methods of using resistor networks for DACs, but two designs are predominantly used.

Binary Weighted DACs

Resistor networks are another simple method for DAC conversion. Several different methods are available for using resistor networks, and again it is up to the designer to

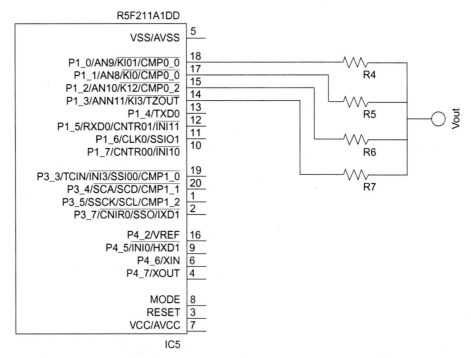

Figure 2.12   4-bit binary weighted network DAC design. Source: Kester, W. A., and Analog Devices, Inc., *Data Conversion Handbook*, 2005, page 153–159.

decide which method is best for a particular design. *Voltage-Mode Binary Weighted DACs* are commonly used with microcontroller circuits. In this design, resistors are connected together on one end (the analog output), and the other ends are connected directly to the pins of a microcontroller port. The values of the resistors are based on binary bit place-values (R, 2R, 4R, 8R, etc.; with R being the least significant bit or LSB). When the pins of the microcontroller are set to HIGH, then the sum voltage of the analog output are related to the value on that port. Figure 2.12 shows an example of a 4-bit Binary Weighted DAC.

R-2R DAC

Another method of using resistor networks to design a DAC is called the *R-2R* or *R/2-R Network*. It consists of resistors of only two values. One value is twice the value of the other. For instance, if the R resistors are one kilo-ohm, then the 2R resistors must equal two kilo-ohms. Figure 2.13 shows an example R-2R network (Kuphaldt, T. R., "The R2-R,").

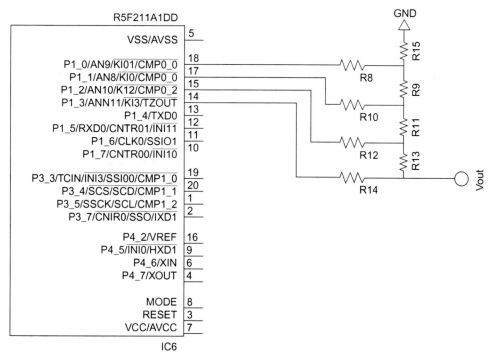

Figure 2.13   R-2R network. R9, R11, and R13 are considered "R" resistors and all = 1kohm while R8, R10, R12, R14, and R15 are considered "2R" and all = 2kohm. Source: "The R2-R," in Kuphaldt, T. R., *All about Circuits*, http://www.allaboutcircuits.com/vol_4/chpt_13/2.html

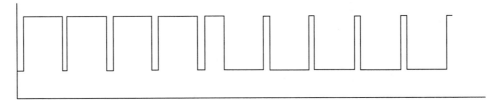

Figure 2.14 An example PWM signal. If this were controlling an active-high LED, the LED would be brighter during the first half of the graph, and dimmer over the second half.

As with the binary weighted DAC, the output voltage corresponds to the binary value on the port. The following example is valid for both R-2R as well as Binary Weighted DACs:

If the V_{ref} is 5 V and there is a 4-bit binary value 1001 (decimal number 9) on the microcontroller pins, we would expect the output voltage to be:

$$V_{out} = (V_{ref}/(2^N)) * \text{(binary value of microcontroller output)} \qquad \textbf{Formula 2.4}$$

For example:
$$(5 \text{ V} / 16 \text{ bits}) * (9) = 2.8125 \text{ V}.$$

Pulse Width Modulation

A common method for controlling the speed of a simple DC motor or the brightness of an LED is *Pulse Width Modulation*. Pulse Width Modulation works as a DAC by changing the duty cycle of an oscillating digital output as shown in Figure 2.14. In the case of an LED, the more time the duty cycle is HIGH, the brighter the LED. This method works in cases where the oscillating frequency is so fast that the resulting output seems smooth. The LED is actually turning on and off several times per second; however, the human eye cannot detect the independent flashes of the LED due to their speed. Motor speed can be controlled this way because the inertia of the spinning armature carries the motor forward through the moments when no power is applied.

2.4   INFRASTRUCTURE: POWER, CLOCK, AND RESET

2.4.1   Power Supply

When designing the power supply for an embedded system, the designer must determine how to power peripherals and whether or not they will use a separate supply. This decision will affect the overall design requirements of the power supply. This chapter only addresses the power supply for the microprocessor itself.

Voltage and current ratings for the microprocessor can be found in the manufacturer's datasheet for the chip, often under the title of *Recommended Operating Conditions* or *Electrical Characteristics.* Another section in the datasheet also shows *Absolute Maximum Ratings,* which should be considered but not confused with the *recommended values.* To be assured that the chip will operate as expected, a system should never be designed to operate too close to the absolute maximum or minimum power ratings. Fluctuations in the power supply may cause the values to go over the absolute maximum ratings of the chip, which can damage the microprocessor. The power supply should be designed with a safety factor to account for these fluctuations, hence the recommended values.

Once the requirements are determined, the source of the power must be determined. Whether the design plugs into the wall or if it uses batteries will determine the type of power supply circuit.

If the design uses mains power, then a standard design method for a power supply circuit can be used. This design will require a transformer to drop the voltage to an acceptable range for a voltage regulator chip. Capacitors will be required to smooth out any ripple or noise.

If batteries are to be used, then the type of battery (NiCad, NiMH, LiPo, etc.) must be selected based on the current rating each battery type can supply, and whether the design will need to be rechargeable.

The length of time a battery will last can be calculated based on the capacity of the battery and the amount of current the circuit uses using Formula 2.5.

Battery Life (hours) = Capacity (amp-hours) / current (amps)   **Formula 2.5**

An 800 mAh battery will power a device that draws 200 mA for;

800 mAh / 200 mA = **4 hours**

Putting batteries in parallel adds their current capacities. Putting them in series adds their voltages.

For two batteries with each 1.5 V and 2000 mAh:

Series: 1.5 V + 1.5 V = **3.0 V** at 2000 mAh
Parallel: 2000 mAh + 2000 mAh = 1.5 V at **4000 mAh**

If the batteries need to be recharged, then a battery charging circuit as well as battery level monitor will also need to be designed.

Regardless of which batteries are chosen, a voltage regulator of some type is generally required. The use of linear or switch-mode voltage regulator integrated circuits (ICs) is a standard practice.

2.4.2   Clock Signal Generation

Microprocessors are synchronous circuits that require a clock to work. This clock allows data to be pushed through the stages of the instruction pipeline and helps the microprocessor coordinate tasks. When selecting a clock generator, the microcontroller datasheet must be used. This datasheet gives the values of the different clocks that a particular microprocessor can accept.

There are two major types of clock signal generators: those that work on purely electrical principles, and those that work on mechanical vibration (resonance of a quartz element). The signal generators for the electrical driven clock can be simple resistor-capacitor (RC) or inductor-capacitor (LC) circuits. Generally, these clocks aren't very accurate on their own, and their design can become quite complicated when precision is required. Many microprocessors offer signal generators with an internal clock that consists of an RC circuit inside the chip, which can be configured. These clocks should not be used when precision is required. Figure 2.15 shows the connection of an RC oscillator to the clock input of a microprocessor.

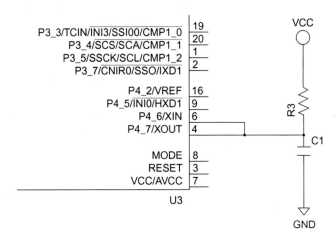

Figure 2.15   RC clock generator.

Clock signal generators that are mechanically driven use a quartz crystal to produce a steady signal. These oscillators rely on the piezoelectric effect of the crystal. This method of clocking is accurate (around 30 parts per million or about 0.003% error), cheap, and widely available. Generally, two small load capacitors are required between each lead of the crystal and ground. The values of these capacitors are based on the crystal characteristics and are listed in the crystal's datasheet.

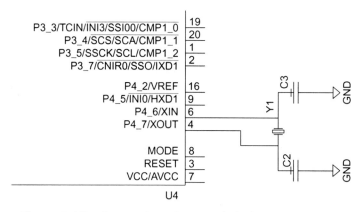

Figure 2.16   Connection of a crystal clock generator chip.

Ceramic resonators are growing in popularity for use as a clock generator. The resonators use a piezoelectric ceramic element that is not as accurate as quartz, yet more accurate than RC circuits. They also contain the appropriate load capacitors built in so they do not require any additional components to work.

External clock generator integrated circuit chips can also be used. These clocks use a quartz or RC circuit as a resonant oscillator, but also contain an amplifier. The frequency can be changed by reprogramming the clock generator. The duty cycle is also selectable for use in cases where a 50 percent duty cycle cannot be used. These circuits are usually more expensive when compared to other oscillators.

2.4.3   Reset Circuit

Resetting a microprocessor starts the processor off in a predictable state. When a reset is detected, the microprocessor loads predefined values into the system control registers. These registers are useful in case of a catastrophic event, such as if the power supply were to drop below a certain threshold. All microprocessors designate a pin that is solely used for resetting the chip. A reset circuit controls this pin to assure a reset is valid if it is used. The requirements of a reset circuit is specific to the microprocessor being used and can be found in the manufacturer's datasheet. Some microcontrollers contain reset logic internally; however, the manufacturer's datasheet should be consulted to make sure it meets the specifications for your application. Alternatively, reset controller chips can be used which contain all the parts necessary for the circuit. Even though they are generally more expensive in some cases, such as low-volume productions, it may be best to use reset controller chips.

2.5   RECAP

It should now be easier to understand how the embedded systems you encounter in your everyday life actually operate and communicate with the outside world. It should also be easier to break some of these systems down into their component parts, given the knowledge of sensor and actuator interfacing presented in this chapter.

2.6   REFERENCES

Kester, W. A., and Analog Devices, Inc. *Data Conversion Handbook.* Lawrence, KS: Newnes, 2005: pp. 153–159. Print.

Kuphaldt, T. R. "Successive Approximation ADC," in *All about Circuits.* Electronic publication. Accessed at http://www.allaboutcircuits.com/vol_4/chpt_13/6.html

"The R2-R," in Kuphaldt, T. R., All about Circuits. Electronic publication. Accessed at http://www. allaboutcircuits.com/vol_4/chpt_13/2.html

2.7   EXERCISES

1. Name ten devices that use an embedded system.
2. Write the C code to set port 4, bits 0 through 3 to be input pins, and port 4, bits 4 through 7 to be output pins.
3. Write the C code to read the data on port 4, bits 0 through 3 and write the read data to port 4, bits 4 through 7.
4. How long will a 2500 mAh battery last if the circuit using it runs at 600 mA?
5. You have a wireless sensor node whose current drain is 50 mA for one minute every one hour and 0.001 mA the rest of the time. I am using a single 5000 mAh cell as the power supply for this device. How long will my device run in hours, days, and years?
6. What are the different kinds of clock generators? Define their base technologies.
7. What resistor value should be used to connect an LED with a forward voltage of 3.1 volts and a forward current of 20 mA to the input pin of a microcontroller that outputs 5 volts?
8. Is it generally safe to connect a coil or motor directly to a microcontroller I/O pin? Why or why not?
9. Is it generally safe to connect a servo control input directly to a microcontroller I/O pin? Why or why not?

10. How many volts per ADC step are in a system with an ADC resolution of 10-bits, and a reference voltage of 3.3 V?

11. How many volts per ADC step are in a system with an ADC resolution of 12-bits, and a reference of 5 V?

12. An analog input has a voltage of 1.37860. What value will the ADC return if it has an 8-bit resolution and a reference of 4.25 volts?

13. An analog input has a voltage of 7.61245. What value will the ADC return if it has a 12-bit resolution and a reference of 10 volts?

14. Using a binary-weighted DAC, using 8 bits and a reference of 4.35 volts, what is the voltage of the output if the 8-bit value is 01011010?

Chapter Three

Organization and Architecture of the Renesas RX62N Microcontroller Board

3.1 LEARNING OBJECTIVES

In this chapter the reader will learn about:

- Basic organization of computers
- Architecture of the Renesas RX62N board
- Endianness, data arrangement, and bus specification in RX62N CPU
- Date types, operating modes, and memory map of RX62N CPU

3.2 BASIC CONCEPTS

3.2.1 Introduction to Computer Organization & Architecture

A computer is a complex digital system. The best way to look at it is by looking at its hierarchical nature. Hierarchical systems are best described as a series of subsystems that are interconnected at various levels to form a complete computer system. At each level is a set of components whose behavior depends on the characteristics and functions of the next lower level. A designer focuses on structure and function within each level. The computer has four basic functions to perform (see Figure 3.1):

1. Data processing
2. Data storage
3. Data movement
4. Data control

Computers process data with the help of the data processing facility. During and after processing, storage is required for this data. During processing, the data needs a temporary or short term storage area. After processing, the data will be stored in long-term storage area. The Data Movement Block provides a data path between the outside environment and the computer. This block is also responsible for the data flow between various subcomponents

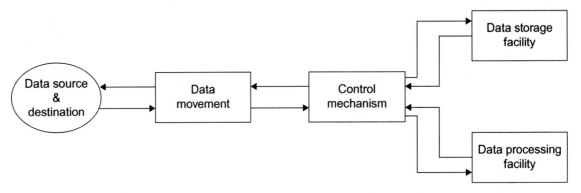

Figure 3.1   A generalized view: Building blocks of a computer.

within the computer. The Control Mechanism takes care of controlling and managing various subcomponents and their interactions with each other.

Computers have four basic structural components (See Figure 3.2):

1. CPU: Processes the data and controls the operation of computer.
2. Memory: Stores data.
3. I/O: Moves the data between the computer and the external environment.
4. System Interconnection: Provides a mechanism for transferring data or communicating between components such as the CPU, main memory, and I/O.

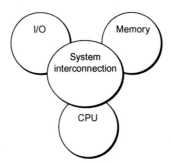

Figure 3.2   A top level view of a computer.

The Central Processing Unit (CPU) is the most complex component out of the four basic components. The structure of the CPU is illustrated in Figure 3.3. The components that make up a CPU are:

1. Control Unit: Controls the operation of the CPU.
2. Arithmetic and Logic Unit (ALU): Performs the computer's data processing functions.
3. Registers: Provides internal storage for the CPU. They store ALU operands.
4. Interconnections: Provides a mechanism for transferring data or communicating between components such as the Control Unit, ALU, and registers.

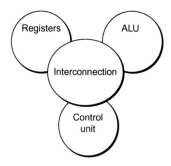

Figure 3.3   A top level view of a CPU.

The IAS[*] computer, which is a prototype of general-purpose computers, is based on the stored-program concept. This idea was developed by John von Neumann and is known as the von Neumann Machine. As shown in Figure 3.4, the von Neumann machine has a main

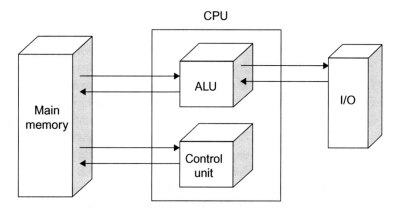

Figure 3.4   Structure of a von Neumann machine.

---

[*] Institute for Advanced Study, Princeton, NJ

memory for storing the instructions and data the same as an IAS computer. It also has an ALU, which processes the binary data. A control unit decodes the instructions and forwards them to the ALU for execution. The Input/Output unit interacts with the external environment and is controlled by the Control Unit.

3.2.2   Architecture of the Renesas RX62N

The RX62N microcontroller architecture has the following components:

1. **CPU:** The CPU contains two main modules or functions:
   - CPU: It is a 32-bit RX CPU with maximum operating frequency of 100 MHz.
   - Floating Point Unit (FPU): This unit is a single precision (32-bit) floating point unit which supports data types and floating-point exceptions in conformance with IEEE 754 standard.
2. **Memory:** The Memory contains three main modules:
   - ROM: Its capacity is 512 Kbytes (max) and it supports two on-chip programming modes and one off-chip programming mode.
   - RAM: Its capacity is 96 Kbytes (max).
   - Data Flash: Its capacity is 32 Kbytes.
3. **Clock generation circuit:** The clock generation circuit consists of two circuits, namely a main clock oscillator and a sub clock oscillator. The CPU and other bus masters run in synchronization with the system clock (ICLK): 8 to 100 MHz; the peripheral modules run in synchronization with the peripheral module clock (PCLK): 8 to 50 MHz; while devices connected to the external bus run in synchronization with the external bus clock (BCLK): 8 to 50 MHz.
4. **Reset:** There are various reset sources available for different modules in the MCU such as pin reset, power-on reset, voltage-monitoring reset, watchdog timer reset, independent watchdog timer reset, and deep software standby reset.
5. **Voltage detection circuit:** When the voltage available on VCC falls below the voltage detection level (V_{det}), an internal reset or internal interrupt is generated.
6. **External bus extension:** The external address space is divided into nine areas: CS0 to CS7 and SDCS. The capacity of each area from CS0 to CS7 is 16 Mbytes, and for SDCS the capacity is 128 Mbytes. A chip-select signal (CS0# to CS7#, SDCS#) can be output for each area. Each area is specifiable as an 8-, 16-, or 32-bit bus space; however, only 176-pin versions support 32-bit bus spaces.
7. **Direct Memory Access (DMA):** The DMA system consists of three different controllers which are explained below. The activation sources for all three controllers are software trigger, external interrupts, and interrupt requests from peripheral functions:
   - DMA controller: It has four channels and three transfer modes. These modes are normal transfer, repeat transfer, and block transfer.

- EXDMA controller: It has two channels and four transfer modes. These modes are normal transfer, repeat transfer, block transfer, and cluster transfer.
- Data transfer controller: It has three transfer modes. These modes are normal transfer, repeat transfer, and block transfer.

8. **I/O ports:** The main modules of I/O ports are programmable I/O ports. There are several I/O ports available on the 176-pin LFBGA, 145-pin TFLGA, 144-pin LQFP, 100-pin LQFP, and 85-pin TFLGA packages.

9. **Timers:** There are seven timer units available for controlling the sequence of an events or processes.
   - Multi-function timer pulse unit: It has two units each supporting six channels and each channel has 16 bits. It provides time bases for the twelve 16-bit timer channels by way of up to 32 pulse-input/output lines and six pulse-input lines.
   - Port output enable: It controls the high-impedance state of the MTU's waveform output pins.
   - Programmable pulse generator: It has two units, each supporting four groups and each group has four bits. It outputs MTU pulse as a trigger. The maximum output possible is 32-bit pulse output.
   - 8-bit timers: It has two units, each supporting two channels and each channel has 8 bits. The clock signal can be selected from seven internal clock signals (PCLK, PCLK/2, PCLK/8, PCLK/32, PCLK/64, PCLK/1024, and PCLK/8192) and one external clock signal. These are capable of outputting pulse trains with desired duty cycles or of PWM signals.
   - Compare match timer: It has two units, each supporting two channels and each channel has 16 bits.
   - The clock signal can be selected from four internal clock signals (PCLK/8, PCLK/32, PCLK/128, and PCLK/512).
   - Watchdog timer: It has one channel of 8 bits. The clock signal can be selected from eight counter-input clock signals (PCLK/4, PCLK/64, PCLK/128, PCLK/512, PCLK/2048, PCLK/8192, PCLK/32768, and PCLK/131072). It is switchable between watchdog timer mode and interval timer mode.
   - Independent watchdog timer: It has one channel of 14 bits. It requires counter-input clock which is available from dedicated on-chip oscillator.

10. **Communication function:** For communicating with the outside world, the MCU provides several controllers:
    - Ethernet controller: The data rate it supports is either 10 or 100 Mbps. It supports both full and half duplex modes.
    - DMA controller for Ethernet: It supports transmission and reception FIFO of 2 Kbytes each.
    - USB 2.0 host/function module: It includes a USB device controller and transceiver for USB 2.0. It incorporates 2 Kbytes of RAM as a transfer buffer and supports data rate of 12 Mbps.

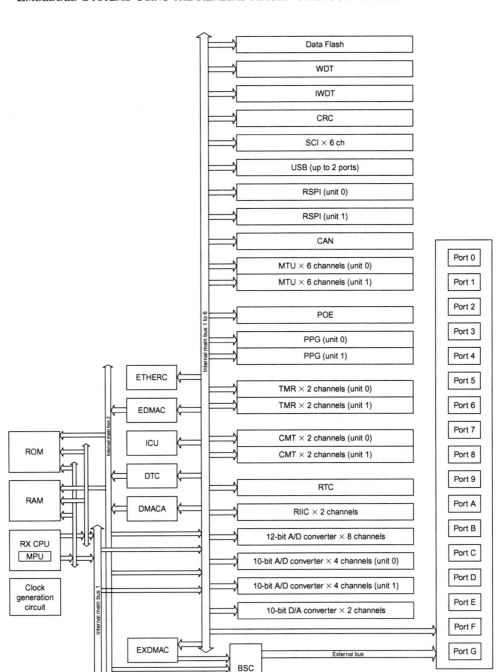

Figure 3.5 Block diagram. Source: *Hardware Manual, Renesas 32-Bit Microcomputer, RX Family/RX600 Series,* Renesas Electronics America, Inc., 2010, Figure 1.2, page 1–12.

■ Serial communication interfaces: It has six channels and supports several serial communication modes such as asynchronous, clock synchronous, and smart-card interface. The desired baud rate is selected by on-chip baud rate generator.

■ I^2C bus interfaces: The communication formats supported are I^2C bus format/SMBus format and Master/slave selectable.

■ CAN module: It supports one channel and 32 mailboxes.

■ Serial peripheral interfaces: It supports two channels and MOSI (master out, slave in), MISO (master in, slave out), SSL (slave select), and RSPI clock (RSPCK) signals. They enable serial transfer through SPI operation (four lines) or clock-synchronous operation (three lines). It is capable of handling serial transfer as a master or slave.

11. **A/D converter:** MCU supports two A/D converters, specifically 12-bit and 10-bit. The conversion time is 1.0 μs per channel. The selectable operating modes are single mode and scan mode.

12. **D/A converter:** It supports two channels and 10-bit resolution. The output voltage ranges from 0V to V_{ref}.

13. **CRC calculator:** CRC code generator generates code for arbitrary amount of data in 8-bit units. It is capable of selecting any of three generating polynomials:

$$X8 + X2 + X + 1, X16 + X15 + X2 + 1, \text{ or } X16 + X12 + X5 + 1.$$

One can also generate CRC codes for use with either LSB-first or MSB-first communications.

DEFINITION OF TERMS:			
ETHERC:	Ethernet Controller	WDT:	Watchdog timer
EDMAC:	DMA controller for Ethernet controller	IWDT:	Independent watchdog timer
ICU:	Interrupt control unit	CRC:	Cyclic redundancy check calculator
DTC:	Data transfer controller	MPU:	Memory-protection unit
DMACA:	DMA controller	SCI:	Serial communications interfaces
EXDMAC:	EXDMA controller	USB:	USB 2.0 host/function module
BSC:	Bus controller	RSPI:	Serial peripheral interfaces

DEFINITION OF TERMS:			
CAN:	CAN module	TMR:	8-bit timer
MTU:	Multi-function timer pulse unit	CMT:	Compare match timer
POE:	Port output enable	RTC:	Real time clock
PPG:	Programmable pulse generator	RIIC:	I^2C bus interface

CPU

The RX CPU being used in RX62N/RX621 group of MCU's supports high-speed and high-performance.

The instruction set architecture (ISA) of RX CPU has a variable-length instruction format. The most commonly used instructions have been allocated shorter instruction lengths, making it possible to develop efficient programs that occupy less memory. The ISA of RX62N/RX621 group has ninety instructions, out of which seventy-three are basic instructions, eight are floating-point operation instructions, and nine are DSP instructions. It achieves high-speed operation by executing instructions in a single cycle. It includes an internal multiplier and divider for high speed multiplication and division. These operations now take less time and hence add to the efficiency of the processor. The RX CPU has a five-stage pipeline for processing instructions.

1. Instruction fetching stage
2. Instruction decoding stage
3. Execution stage
4. Memory access stage
5. Write-back stage

In cases where pipeline processing is drawn-out by memory access, subsequent operations may in fact be executed earlier. By adopting "out-of-order completion" of this kind, the execution of instructions is completed in fewer clock cycles.

Register Set

The RX CPU has sixteen general-purpose registers, nine control registers, and one accumulator used for DSP instructions.

General-Purpose Registers (R0 to R15): The RX CPU has sixteen general-purpose registers (R0 to R15). R0 can function as a stack pointer (SP) and R1 to R15 can be used as data or address registers. The stack pointer can be made to operate either as an Interrupt

TABLE 3.1 Features of CPU.

FEATURES	DESCRIPTION
High instruction execution rate	One instruction in one clock cycle.
Address space	4-Gbyte linear address space.
Register set of the CPU	There are sixteen 32-bit general purpose registers and nine 32-bit control registers. It has a 64-bit register accumulator.
Basic instructions	It has seventy-three basic instructions such as arithmetic/logic instructions, data-transfer instructions, branch instructions, bit-manipulation instructions, string-manipulation instructions, and system-manipulation instructions.
Floating-point operation instructions	It is an optional function that can be used. There are eight such operations.
DSP instructions	It is an optional function that can be used. There are nine such instructions. It supports 16-bit × 16-bit multiplication and multiply-and-accumulate operations. It rounds the data in the accumulator.
Addressing modes	There are ten addressing modes.
Five-stage pipeline	It has a five-stage pipeline and allows out-of-order completion.
Processor modes	A supervisor mode and a user mode are supported.
Floating-point operation unit	It supports single-precision (32-bit) floating point operations and supports data types and exceptions in conformance with the IEEE 754 standard.
Data arrangement	The data can be selected either as little endian or big endian.

stack pointer (ISP) or user stack pointer (USP). The required stack pointer can be selected by the value of the stack pointer select bit (U) in the processor status word (PSW).

Control Registers: This CPU has the following nine control registers:

1. Interrupt stack pointer (ISP)
2. User stack pointer (USP)

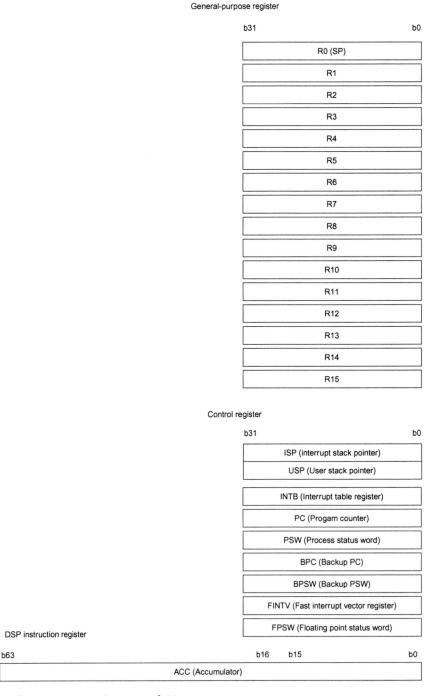

Figure 3.6 Register set of CPU. Source: *Hardware Manual,* Figure 2.1, page 2–2.

3. Interrupt table register (INTB)
4. Program counter (PC)
5. Processor status word (PSW)
6. Backup PC (BPC)
7. Backup PSW (BPSW)
8. Fast interrupt vector register (FINTV)
9. Floating-point status word (FPSW)

The section below explains each control register briefly. It mainly focuses on the bit configuration and the functionality of each register.

1. **Interrupt Stack Pointer (ISP)/User Stack Pointer (USP):** After reset, all the bits of the register hold the value zero. The register is configured with 32 bits. The register can be made to operate either as Interrupt stack pointer (ISP) or user stack pointer (USP). The decision is made by the value of the stack pointer select bit (U) in the processor status word (PSW). Depending on the value of the bit, the stack pointer operates either as ISP or USP. Setting the value of ISP or USP to a multiple of four reduces the numbers of cycles required to execute interrupt sequences and instructions.

2. **Interrupt table register:** The interrupt table register (INTB) points to an address where the relocatable vector table starts and is configured with 32 bits. After reset, value of the register is Undefined.

3. **Program counter:** Value after reset: Contents of addresses FFFFFFFCh to FFFFFFFFh. The program counter (PC) points to the address of the instruction that will be executed next. As soon as that instruction's execution starts, PC value is incremented and it points to the next instruction. The PC is configured with 32 bits.

4. **Processor Status Word (PSW):**

b31	b30	b29	b28	b27	b26	b25	b24	b23	b22	b21	b20	b19	b18	b17	b16
—	—	—	—	IPL[2:0]	IPL[2:0]	IPL[2:0]	IPL[2:0]	—	—	—	PM	—	—	U	I

b15	b14	b13	b12	b11	b10	b9	b8	b7	b6	b5	b4	b3	b2	b1	b0
—	—	—	—	—	—	—	—	—	—	—	—	O	S	Z	C

Figure 3.7   PSW. Source: *Hardware Manual*, page 2–5.

After reset, all the bits of the register hold the value zero.

- C Flag (Carry Flag): Whenever an operation results in a carry, borrow, or shift-out, this flag is set. The bit position of the carry flag is b0 and when it is set as 1, it means a carry has occurred. When it is 0, it means no carry has occurred. The symbol of the flag is C and it can be read and written by the CPU.
- Z Flag (Zero Flag): Whenever an operation results in a zero, this flag is set. The bit position of the zero flag is b1 and when it is set as 1, it means the result of an operation is zero. When it is 0, it means the result is non-zero. The symbol of this flag is Z and it can be read and written by the CPU.
- S Flag (Sign Flag): This flag indicates that the result of an operation was negative. The bit position of the sign flag is b2 and when it is set as 1, it means the result of an operation is negative. When it is 0, it means the result is non-negative. The symbol of this flag is S and it can be read and written by the CPU.
- O Flag (Overflow Flag): This flag indicates that an overflow occurred during an operation. Whenever an operation results in an overflow, this flag is set. The bit position of the overflow flag is b3 and when it is set as 1, it means the result of an operation resulted in an overflow. When it is 0, it means there was no overflow. The symbol of this flag is O and it can be read and written by the CPU.
- I Bit (Interrupt Enable): Whenever this bit is set, an interrupt can occur. If this bit is disabled, then even if an interrupt occurs an exception will not be accepted. The bit position of interrupt enable is b16 and when it is set as 1, it means interrupt is enabled which means interrupt requests will be accepted. When it is 0, then interrupt requests will not be accepted. The symbol of this flag is I and it can be read and written by the CPU.
- U Bit (Stack Pointer Select): This bit specifies the stack pointer as either the ISP or USP. When an interrupt occurs and the interrupt enable bit is set to 1, an exception request is accepted. When this happens this bit is set to 0 and then this register acts as an interrupt stack pointer. When the processor mode is switched from supervisor mode to user mode, this bit is set to 1. Now the register acts as a user stack pointer. The bit position of the stack pointer select is b17. The symbol of this flag is U and it can be read and written by the CPU.
- PM Bit (Processor Mode Select): This bit specifies the processor mode. When an interrupt occurs and the interrupt enable bit is set to 1, an exception request is accepted. When an exception is accepted, supervisor mode is selected and the bit is set as 0. When user mode is selected then this bit is selected as 1. The bit position of the processor mode select is b20. The symbol of this flag is PM and it can be read and written by the CPU.
- IPL [3:0] Bits (Processor Interrupt Priority Level): The IPL [3:0] bits specify the processor interrupt priority level. There are in total sixteen levels from

zero to fifteen, wherein priority level fifteen is the highest. When the priority level of a requested interrupt is higher than the processor interrupt priority level, the interrupt is enabled; and when the priority level of a requested interrupt is lower than the processor interrupt priority level then the interrupt request is not accepted. So if the IPL [3:0] bits is set to a level fifteen (Fh) then it will disable all interrupt requests. The only case where IPL [3:0] bits are set to level fifteen (Fh) is when a non-maskable interrupt is generated. When interrupts in general are generated, the bits are set to the priority levels of accepted interrupts. The bit positions of the processor interrupt priority level are from b27 to b24. The symbol of this flag is IPL [3:0] and it can be read and written by the CPU.

The following list shows sixteen priority levels.

b27	b26	b25	b24
0	0	0	0: Priority level 0 (lowest)
0	0	0	1: Priority level 1
0	0	1	0: Priority level 2
0	0	1	1: Priority level 3
0	1	0	0: Priority level 4
0	1	0	1: Priority level 5
0	1	1	0: Priority level 6
0	1	1	1: Priority level 7
1	0	0	0: Priority level 8
1	0	0	1: Priority level 9
1	0	1	0: Priority level 10
1	0	1	1: Priority level 11
1	1	0	0: Priority level 12
1	1	0	1: Priority level 13
1	1	1	0: Priority level 14
1	1	1	1: Priority level 15 (highest)

Reserved Bits:

The following bits are reserved in the PSW register. These bits are always read as 0. The write value should be 0.

b15 to b4; b19, b18; b23 to b21; b31 to b28

5. **Backup PC (BPC):** After reset, the value of the register is Undefined. The register is configured with 32 bits. The Backup PC (BPC) register assists in speeding up the response to interrupts. After a fast interrupt has been generated, the contents of the program counter (PC) are saved in the Backup PC register.

6. **Backup PSW (BPSW):** After reset, the value of the register is Undefined. The register is configured with 32 bits. After a fast interrupt has been generated, the contents of the processor status word (PSW) are saved in the Backup Processor status word (BPSW) register. The allocation of bits in the BPSW register corresponds to that in the PSW register.

7. **Fast Interrupt Vector Register (FINTV):** After reset, the value of the register is Undefined. The register is configured with 32 bits. As the name suggests, this register assists in speeding up the response to interrupts. As soon as a fast interrupt is generated, the FINTV register specifies a branch destination address.

8. **Floating-Point Status Word (FPSW):**

b31	b30	b29	b28	b27	b26	b25	b24	b23	b22	b21	b20	b19	b18	b17	b16
FS	FX	FU	FZ	FO	FV	—	—	—	—	—	—	—	—	—	—

b15	b14	b13	b12	b11	b10	b9	b8	b7	b6	b5	b4	b3	b2	b1	b0
—	EX	EU	EZ	EO	EV	—	DN	CE	CX	CU	CZ	CO	CV	RM[1:0]	RM[1:0]

Figure 3.8   FPSW. Source: *Hardware Manual,* page 2–9.

After reset, all the bits of the register hold the value zero.

The floating-point status word (FPSW) indicates the results of floating-point operations. The register can be broadly classified into three types of bit configuration. One type is enable bits, another type is flag bits, and the third type is cause bits. So for every exception that occurs, there exists an enable bit (Ej), a flag status bit (Fj), and an exception cause bit (Cj). When an exception handling enable bit (Ej) is enabled, which means when $Ej = 1$, corresponding Cj flag indicates the cause. If the exception handling is masked ($Ej = 0$), then the state of the Fj flag at the end of a series of instructions indicates whether an exception occurred. The Fj flag is the accumulation type flag where j represents X, U, Z, O, or V.

TABLE 3.2   Description of FPSW

BIT	SYMBOL	BIT NAME	DESCRIPTION	R/W
b1, b0	RM [1:0]	Floating-Point Rounding-Mode Setting	b1 b0 0 0 : Rounding to the nearest value. 0 1 : Rounding to 0. 1 0 : Rounding to $+\infty$. 1 1 : Rounding to $-\infty$.	R/W
b2	CV	Invalid Operation Cause Flag	0 : No invalid operation has been encountered. 1: Invalid operation has been encountered.	R/W*[1]
b3	CO	Overflow Cause Flag	0 : No overflow has occurred. 1: Overflow has occurred.	R/W*[1]
b4	CZ	Division-by-Zero Cause Flag	0 : No division-by-zero has occurred. 1: Division-by-zero Overflow has occurred.	R/W*[1]
b5	CU	Underflow Cause Flag	0 : No underflow has occurred. 1: Underflow has occurred.	R/W*[1]
b6	CX	Inexact Cause Flag	0 : No inexact exception has been generated. 1: Inexact exception has been generated.	R/W*[1]
b7	CE	Un-Implemented Processing Cause Flag	0 : No un-implemented processing has been encountered. 1: Un-implemented processing has been encountered.	R/W*[1]

Source: *Hardware Manual*, page 2–9.

Notes:
1. Writing 0 to the bit clears it. Writing 1 to the bit does not affect its value.
2. Positive denormalized numbers are treated as +0, negative denormalized numbers as −0.
3. When the EV bit is set to 0, the FV flag is enabled.
4. When the EO bit is set to 0, the FO flag is enabled.
5. When the EZ bit is set to 0, the FZ flag is enabled.
6. When the EU bit is set to 0, the FU flag is enabled.
7. When the EX bit is set to 0, the FX flag is enabled.
8. Once the bit has been set to 1, this value is retained until it is cleared to 0 by software.

(Continued)

TABLE 3.2 Description of FPSW—*Continued*

BIT	SYMBOL	BIT NAME	DESCRIPTION	R/W
b8	DN	0 Flush Bit of Denormalized Number	0: A denormalized number is handled as a denormalized number.	R/W
			1: A denormalized number is handled as 0.[*2]	
b9	—	(Reserved)	This bit is always read as 0. The write value should be 0.	R/W
b10	EV	Invalid Operation Exception Enable	0: Invalid operation exception is masked.	R/W
			1: Invalid operation exception is enabled.	
b11	EO	Overflow Exception Enable	0: Overflow exception is masked.	R/W
			1: Overflow exception is enabled.	
b12	EZ	Division-by-Zero Exception Enable	0: Division-by-zero exception is masked.	R/W
			1: Division-by-zero exception is enabled.	
b13	EU	Underflow Exception Enable	0: Underflow exception is masked.	R/W
			1: Underflow exception is enabled.	
b14	EX	Inexact Exception Enable	0: Inexact exception is masked.	R/W
			1: Inexact exception is enabled.	
b25 to b15	—	(Reserved)	These bits are always read as 0. The write value should be 0.	R/W
b26	FV[*3]	Invalid Operation Flag	0: No invalid operation has been encountered.	R/W
			1: Invalid operation has been encountered.[*8]	
b27	FO[*4]	Overflow Flag	0: No overflow has occurred.	R/W
			1: Overflow has occurred.[*8]	
b28	FZ[*5]	Division-by-Zero Flag	0: No division-by-zero has occurred.	R/W
			1: Division-by-zero has occurred.[*8]	
b29	FU[*6]	Underflow Flag	0: No underflow has occurred.	R/W
			1: Underflow has occurred.[*8]	

TABLE 3.2   Description of FPSW—*Continued*

BIT	SYMBOL	BIT NAME	DESCRIPTION	R/W
b30	FX*[7]	Inexact Flag 0: No	0: No inexact exception has been generated.	R/W
			1: Inexact exception has been generated.*[8]	
b31	FS	Floating-Point Flag Summary	This bit reflects the logical OR of the FU, FZ, FO, and FV flags.	R/W

■ RM [1:0] bits:
These bits specify the floating-point rounding-mode.
Explanation of Floating-Point Rounding Modes
  □ Rounding to the nearest value (the default behavior):
An inaccurate result is rounded to the available value that is closest to the result which would be obtained with an infinite number of digits. If two available values are equally close, rounding is done to the even alternative.
  □ Rounding towards 0:
An inaccurate result is rounded to the smallest available absolute value.
  □ Rounding towards $+\infty$:
An inaccurate result is rounded to the nearest available value in the direction of positive infinity.
  □ Rounding towards $-\infty$:
An inaccurate result is rounded to the nearest available value in the direction of negative infinity.

The default mode is to round off to the nearest value in order to return the most accurate value. The other modes, such as rounding towards 0, rounding towards $+\infty$, and rounding towards $-\infty$, are used to ensure precision.

■ Cj (Cause flag): The five floating-point exceptions based on IEEE 754 standard are overflow, underflow, inexact, division-by-zero, and invalid operation. The bit is set to 1 until and unless FPU instruction is executed. After that the bit is set to 0. When instructions like MVTC and POPC instructions write 0 to the bit, the bit is set to 0; and when they write 1, the bit retains the previous value.
■ DN Flag: When this bit is set to 0, a denormalized number is handled as a denormalized number; and when this bit is set to 1, a denormalized number is handled as 0.
■ Ej (Exception handle bit): When any of the five floating-point exceptions is generated by the FPU instruction, this bit then decides whether the CPU will handle the exception or not. When the bit is set to 0, the exception handling is masked and the

CPU will not handle the exception; when the bit is set to 1, the exception handling is enabled and CPU will handle the exception.

- Fj: While the exception handling enable bit (Ej) is 0 (exception handling is masked), if any of the five floating-point exceptions specified in the IEEE 754 standard is generated, the corresponding bit is set to 1. When Ej is 1 (exception handling is enabled), the flag retains its value. When the corresponding flag is set to 1, it remains 1 until it is cleared to 0 by software. (Accumulation flag)

- FS bit (Floating-point flag summary bit): This bit reflects the logical OR of the FU, FZ, FO, and FV flags.

Accumulator (ACC):

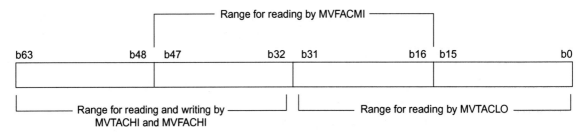

Figure 3.9 ACC. Source: *Hardware Manual,* page 2–12.

This register is configured with 64 bits and is mainly used for DSP instructions. It is also used for the multiply and multiply-and-accumulate instructions, where the prior value in the accumulator is modified by the execution of instruction. The examples of such instructions are EMUL, EMULU, FMUL, MUL, and RMPA. To write to the accumulator, MVTACHI and MVTACLO instructions are used. These instructions write data to the higher-order 32 bits (bits 63 to 32) and the lower-order 32 bits (bits 31 to 0). To read from the accumulator, MVFACHI and MVFACMI instructions are used. The MVFACHI and MVFACMI instructions read data from the higher-order 32 bits (bits 63 to 32) and the middle-order 32 bits (bits 47 to 16), of the accumulator.

3.2.3 Data Types

The RX CPU supports four types of data: integer, floating-point, bit, and string.

1. Integer:

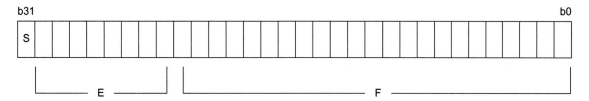

	b7 b0
Signed byte (8-bit) Integer	

Signed byte (8-bit) Integer

Unsigned byte (8-bit) Integer

Signed word (16-bit) Integer

Unsigned word (16-bit) Integer

Signed longword (32-bit) Integer

Unsigned longword (32-bit) Integer

Figure 3.10   Integer. Source: *Hardware Manual,* Figure 2.2, page 2–14.

2. Floating-Point:

The IEEE standard defines four different types of precision for floating point operations. They are single precision, double precision, single-extended precision, and double-extended precision. Most of the floating-point hardware follows IEEE 754 standard's single and double precision for floating point computations. RX family supports single precision floating-point computation. There are in total eight operations that can be done with such floating-point operands: FADD, FCMP, FDIV, FMUL, FSUB, FTOI, ITOF, and ROUND.

b31   b0

| S | | | | | | | | | | | | | | | | | | | | | | | | | | | | | | | |

E   F

Figure 3.11   Floating point. Source: *Hardware Manual,* Figure 2.3, page 2–14.

Single-precision floating-point
S: Sign (1 bit)
E: Exponent (8 bits)
F: Mantissa (23 bits)

$$\text{Value} = (-1)^{S} \times (1 + F \times 2^{-23}) \times 2^{(E-127)}$$

The floating-point format supports different values for exponent and mantissa. When the value of E is between 0 and 255 (i.e., $0 < E < 255$), then the number is considered as a normal number. For a signed zero number, the value of E and F should be 0. For denormalized numbers, the value of E is 0 and the value of F is greater than 0. When the value of E is 255 and the value of F is 0, then the number is considered as infinity. When the value of E is 255 and the value of F is greater than 0, then the number is not a number.

NOTE:

The number is treated as 0 when the DN bit in FPSW is 1. When the DN bit is 0, an unimplemented processing exception is generated.

3. **Bitwise Operations:**
   There are five different types of bit-manipulation instructions for bitwise operations: BCLR, BM*Cnd,* BNOT, BSET, and BTST. The register is a 32-bit register so the bits range from 0 to 31. In the Figure 3.12, notation looks like "#bit, R_n"; which means 'corresponding bit in register n.' Here the value of 'n' ranges from 0 to 15. So notation "#30, R1" suggests 30th bit in R1 register. For bitwise operation in memory, the notation is "#bit, mem." For instance, #2, [R2] means address [R2] and bit 2. The bit value ranges from 0 to 7. The addressing modes available to specify addresses are register indirect and register relative.

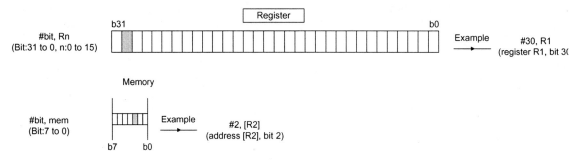

Figure 3.12   Bitwise Operation. Source: *Hardware Manual,* Figure 2.4, page 2–15.

4. **Strings:**
   The string data type consists of an arbitrary number of consecutive byte (8-bit), word (16-bit), or longword (32-bit) units. To work with strings there are seven string manipulation instructions: SCMPU, SMOVB, SMOVF, SMOVU, SSTR, SUNTIL, and SWHILE.

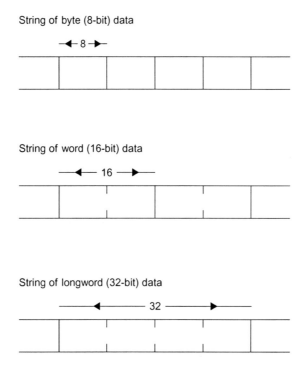

Figure 3.13   Strings. Source: *Hardware Manual,* Figure 2.5, page 2–15.

3.2.4   Endianness

Endianness refers to the arrangement of sub-units such as bytes within a longer data word, while storing it in memory. Basically there are two types of endianness: big endianness and little endianness.

■   Big endian: The most significant byte (MSB) is stored at the lowest byte address of the memory.

■   Little endian: The least significant byte (LSB) is stored at the lowest address of the memory.

As arrangements of bytes, the RX62N/RX621 Group supports both big endian, where the most significant byte (MSB) is stored at the lowest byte address of the memory; and little endian, where the least significant byte (LSB) is stored at the lowest address of the memory. For the RX CPU, instructions are always little endian, but the way the user wants to handle data decides endianness. Therefore, if a programmer wants to change the endianness, it can be changed.

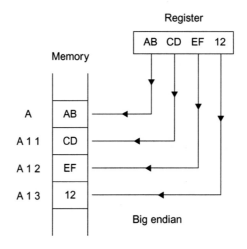

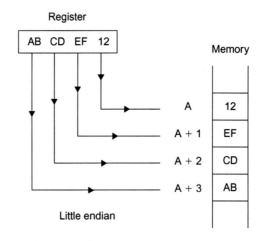

Figure 3.14   Endianness: Arrangement in memory.

3.2.5   Data Arrangement

1. **Data Arrangement in Registers:**
   Figure 3.15 shows the relation between the sizes of registers and bit numbers.
2. **Data Arrangement in Memory:**
   Data in memory have three sizes: byte (8-bit), word (16-bit), and longword (32-bit). According to the requirement, the data arrangement can be selected as little or big endian.
   Figure 3.16 shows the arrangement of data in memory.

Figure 3.15   Data arrangement in registers. Source: *Hardware Manual,* Figure 2.6, page 2–21.

Data type	Address	Little endian								Big endian							
		b7							b0	b7							b0
1-bit data	Address L	7	6	5	4	3	2	1	0	7	6	5	4	3	2	1	0
Byte data	Address L	MSB							LSB	MSB							LSB
Word data	Address M								LSB	MSB							
	Address M + 1	MSB															LSB
Longword data	Address N								LSB	MSB							
	Address N + 1																
	Address N + 2																
	Address N + 3	MSB															LSB

Figure 3.16   Data arrangement in memory. Source: *Hardware Manual,* Figure 2.7, page 2–21.

3.2.6   Bus Specification

In total, there are five different types of buses in RX62N microcontroller board. The following section lists various bus specifications. It describes whether the bus operates in synchronization with a clock or not.

1. **CPU bus:**
   - Instruction bus:
     It is connected to the CPU and to the on-chip memory such as on-chip RAM and on-chip ROM. It operates in synchronization with the system clock (ICLK).

> ▪ Operand bus:
> It is connected to the CPU and to the on-chip memory such as on-chip RAM and on-chip ROM. It operates in synchronization with the system clock (ICLK).

2. **Memory bus:**
   - ▪ Memory bus 1: It is connected to on-chip RAM.
   - ▪ Memory bus 2: It is connected to on-chip RAM.

3. **Internal main bus:**
   - ▪ Internal main bus 1: It is connected to the CPU and operates in synchronization with the system clock (ICLK).
   - ▪ Internal main bus 2: It is connected to the DMACA, DTC, and EDMAC. Also, it is connected to on-chip memory, namely on-chip RAM and on-chip ROM. It operates in synchronization with the system clock (ICLK).

4. **Internal peripheral bus:**
   - ▪ Internal peripheral bus 1: It is connected to peripheral modules and operates in synchronization with the system clock (ICLK).
   - ▪ Internal peripheral bus 2: It is connected to peripheral modules, on-chip ROM (for programming and erasure), and data-flash memory. It operates in synchronization with the peripheral-module clock (PCLK).
   - ▪ Internal peripheral bus 3: It is connected to peripheral modules (USB) and it operates in synchronization with the peripheral-module clock (PCLK).
   - ▪ Internal peripheral bus 4: It is connected to peripheral modules (EDMAC and ETHERC) and it operates in synchronization with the system clock (ICLK).
   - ▪ Internal peripheral bus 5: It is connected to peripheral modules and it operates in synchronization with the system clock (ICLK).
   - ▪ Internal peripheral bus 6: It is connected to on-chip ROM (for programming and erasure) and data-flash memory. It operates in synchronization with the peripheral-module clock (PCLK).

5. **External bus:**
   - ▪ CS area: It is connected to the external devices and it operates in synchronization with the external-bus clock (BCLK).
   - ▪ External bus SDRAM area: It is connected to the SDRAM and it operates in synchronization with the SDRAM clock (SDCLK).

Description of Buses

1. **CPU Buses:**
   The CPU buses consists of instruction and operand buses, which are connected to internal main bus 1 as shown in Figure 3.17. The instruction bus is used to fetch instructions for the CPU, while the operand bus is used for operand access. These buses are connected to on-chip RAM and on-chip ROM and therefore the CPU can directly access these areas. Direct access refers to that access which is not by way of internal main bus 1. In contrast to access through internal main bus 1, direct ac-

cess allows only reading the on-chip ROM by the CPU. Programming and erasure are handled by way of an internal peripheral bus. Internal main bus 1 handles bus requests for instruction fetching and operand access. The operand access has a higher priority than instruction fetching. The bus-access operations can proceed simultaneously, irrespective of whether the instruction fetching and operand access need different buses or not. For example, parallel access to an on-chip ROM and on-chip RAM or to an on-chip ROM and external space is possible.

2. **Memory bus:**

   There are two memory buses; namely memory bus 1 and memory bus 2. On-chip RAM is connected to memory bus 1 and on-chip ROM is connected to memory bus 2. Bus requests from the CPU buses and internal main bus 2 are handled through memory buses 1 and 2. Internal memory bus 2 has a higher priority than the CPU bus.

3. **Internal main bus:**

   The internal main bus consists of two buses; one is internal main bus 1, which is used by the CPU; and internal main bus 2, which is used by the other bus-master modules such as the DTC, DMACA, and EDMAC. Bus requests for instruction fetching and operand access are handled through internal main bus 1. Operand access has higher priority than instruction fetching. Bus requests from the DTC, DMACA, and EDMAC are handled by internal main bus 2. The order of priority is EDMAC, DMACA, and then DTC, as shown in Table 3.3. The bus access operations can proceed simultaneously. For instance, if the CPU and another bus master are requesting access to different buses; in this case, the respective bus-access operations will take place simultaneously. Internal main bus 2 has a higher priority than internal main bus 1. However, when the CPU executes the XCHG instruction, the only request that can access bus is the request from CPU, until and unless data transfer for the XCHG instruction is completed. If data transfer for the XCHG is completed, requests for bus access from other masters will be accepted. Furthermore, during reading and writing back of control information, the only bus master which has access is DTC. Bus requests from other masters are not accepted.

TABLE 3.3   Priority of Bus Masters.

PRIORITY	BUS MASTER
High ↑ | Low	EDMAC DMACA DTC CPU

Source: *Hardware Manual*, Table 12.3, page 12–5.

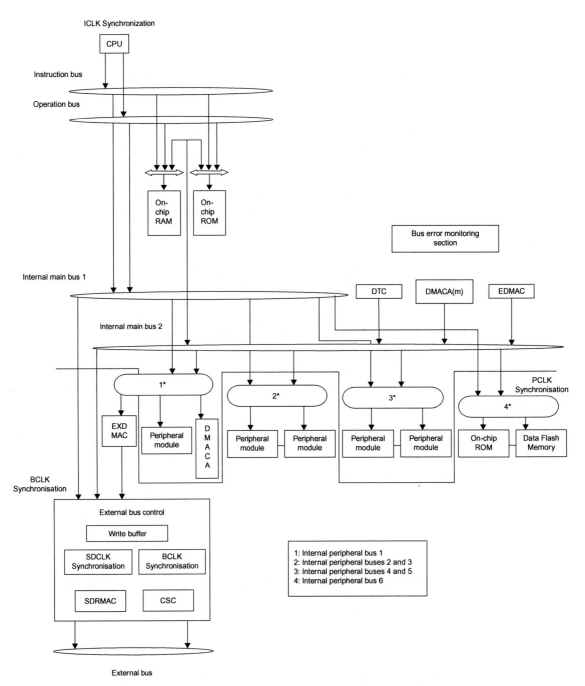

Figure 3.17 Bus Configuration. Source: *Hardware Manual,* Figure 12.1, page 12–2.

> **NOTES:**
>
> **BCLK (external-bus clock):** The maximum frequency of the clock is 100 MHz. The CSC (CS area controller) and the EXDMAC operate in synchronization with the BCLK.
> **SDCLK (SDRAM clock):** The maximum frequency of the clock is 50 MHz. The SDRAMC (SDRAM area controller) operates in synchronization with the SDCLK.
> **BCLK:** The frequency is the same as the BCLK as default. 1/2 BCLK can be supplied by setting the BCLK pin output select bit (BCLKDIV) in the system clock control register (SCKCR).
> The BCLK and the SDCLK should be operated with the same frequency (50 MHz as a maximum) when the SDRAM is in use.

4. **Internal peripheral buses:**
   The following table lists various peripheral buses and the peripheral modules to which they are connected:

TABLE 3.4   Connection of Peripheral Modules.

TYPES OF BUS	PERIPHERAL MODULES
Internal peripheral bus 1	DMACA
	EXDMAC
	Interrupt controller
	Bus error monitoring section
Internal peripheral bus 2	Peripheral modules other than those connected to internal peripheral buses 1, 3, 4, and 5
Internal peripheral bus 3	USB
Internal peripheral bus 4	EDMAC and ETHERC
Internal peripheral bus 5	Reserved area
Internal peripheral bus 6	Data flash memory

Source: *Hardware Manual*, Table 12.4, page 12–5.

Bus mastership requests from the CPU (internal main bus 1) and other bus masters (internal main bus 2) are handled through internal peripheral buses 1 to 6. Internal main bus 2 has higher priority than internal main bus 1.

5. **External Bus:**

This section lists various specifications of the external bus. Bus masters such as internal main bus 1, internal main bus 2, and EXDMAC keep requesting bus mastership. In such a scenario, the external bus controller arbitrates various requests and decides the master. The order of priority determines which bus master will handle mastership first, if all of them request at the same time. The order of priority is EXDMAC, internal main bus 2, and then internal main bus 1. The various areas of external bus and their specifications are as follows:

▨ External address space:

An external address space is divided into two specific areas. One area is further divided into eight areas (CS0 to CS7) and the other area is the SDRAM area (SDCS). This is how external address space is organized for better management. For each area the chip select signals can be output, an 8/16/32-bit bus space can be selected, and an endian mode can be specified.

▨ CS area controller:

The CS area controller deals with the read and write controls associated with CS areas (CS0 to CS7). In the controller, recovery cycles can be inserted. In read recovery up to fifteen cycles, and in the write recovery up to fifteen cycles can be inserted. The cycle wait function can wait up to thirty-one cycles. In the page access, wait function takes up to seven cycles. The controller uses wait control to set up timing of assertion and negation for chip-select signals (CS0# to CS7#) and for read signal (RD#) and write signals (WR0# to WR3#). It also sets up the timing with which data output starts and ends. It has two write access modes; one is single write strobe mode and other is byte strobe mode.

▨ SDRAM area controller:

The SDRAM Controller is a part of external bus. Several features are available in the SDRAM area controller. The SDRAM controller is capable of self-refresh and auto-refresh. It supports multiplexing output of row address/column address (8, 9, 10, or 11 bits). The CAS latency can be specified from one to three cycles.

▨ Write buffer function:

Write buffer function is used when there is data to be written to a buffer. When write data from the bus master has been written to the write buffer, the write access by the bus master is completed.

▨ Frequency:

As mentioned earlier, the CS area controller (CSC) operates in synchronization with the external-bus clock (BCLK), while the SDRAM area controller (SDRAMC) operates in synchronization with the SDRAM clock (SDCLK).

NOTE:

When different bus-master modules request access to different slave modules, then all of the different masters can be given access to different peripheral modules. This is known as parallel operation as all of the accesses are taking place at the same time. Consider the case where the CPU is fetching an instruction from on-chip ROM and at the same time an operand is needed from on-chip RAM. What will happen in such a scenario? Here the master module CPU wants to gain access to on-chip ROM as well as on-chip RAM. The DMACA simultaneously handles transfer between a peripheral bus and the external bus. In this example, the CPU uses instruction and operand buses for simultaneous access to on-chip ROM and RAM, respectively. So, with the help of instruction bus and operand bus, the CPU is able to fetch instructions and access an operand, both at the same time. Moreover, the DMACA simultaneously uses internal main bus 2 or the external bus to achieve parallel operation.

Bus Error Monitoring Section

Whenever an error occurs in a bus, the bus-error monitoring system comes into play. It monitors each individual area and whenever it detects an error, it generates an interrupt. Usually, two types of error occur in a bus, illegal address access error and timeout error. Whenever the bus-error monitoring system detects illegal access to an area, an illegal address access error is said to have occurred. Similarly, when the bus-error monitoring system detects any bus-access operation that is not being completed within 768 cycles, then a time out error is said to have occurred.

Types of Bus Error

As said earlier, there are mainly two types of error that can occur in a bus. The following section explains them briefly.

1. **Illegal Address Access:**
   To detect illegal access to an area, first of all a bit in a register has to be set up. The bit is called an illegal address access detection enable bit (IGAEN) and is usually set to 1 in the bus error monitoring enable register (BEREN). If that happens, accesses of the following types lead to illegal address access errors:
   - Access to those external areas for which operation has been disabled. The space area is disabled by setting up the value of registers CSnCNT.EXENB and SDCCR.EXENB as '0.'
   - With respect to areas other than those described above, access to illegal address ranges.
2. **Time out:**
   To detect time out error, first of all a bit in a register has to be set up. The bit is called a timeout detection enable bit (TOEN) and is usually set to 1 in the bus error monitoring enable register (BEREN). After setting up that bit, if any bus access is not completed within 768 cycles, then it leads to a timeout error. In the RX62N/RX621, a timeout error occurs only for access to CS areas. During access to any of the CS areas from CS0 to CS7, it might lead to timeout error if bus access is not completed (the WAIT# signal is not negated) within 768 external bus clock

(BCLK) cycles from the start of the access. When timeout error occurs, accesses to bus are prohibited. In fact, accesses from the bus master are rejected for 256 BCLK cycles. If a single bus request from bus master also contains generated multiple external bus accesses, then the bus access cannot be stopped by the timeout. At this time, timeout errors may occur repeatedly. The CPU is aware of the errors that are occurring in the bus section and whenever an error occurs the CPU is informed. The CPU does not poll for errors on the bus. Whenever there is an error, an interrupt is generated. The interrupt generated gives an indication to CPU that there is an error in the bus section. The IEN register in the ICU decides whether to generate an interrupt in the case of a bus error or not.

3.3   BASIC EXAMPLES

EXAMPLE 1

What is the difference between computer organization and architecture?

A computer's architecture is its abstract model and is the programmer's view in terms of instructions, addressing modes, and registers. A computer's organization expresses the realization of the architecture. Architecture describes what the computer does and organization describes how it does it. The architecture is like a blue print which mentions all the components and how they are connected, while the organization is an implementation of that blue print. Each vendor will have their own version of organization, and their own way of implementing the blue print.

Computer architecture = computer organization (what the machine looks like) + instruction set architecture (how you talk to the machine).

EXAMPLE 2

What is the difference between a microcontroller and a microprocessor?

The main difference is that a microcontroller incorporates features of a microprocessor (CPU, ALU, Registers) along with the presence of added features like RAM, ROM, I/O ports, counter, etc. In addition, microcontrollers are usually designed to perform a small set of specific functions; for example, the case of a Digital Signal Processor which performs a small set of signal processing functions, whereas microprocessors tend to be designed to perform a wider set of general purpose functions.

EXAMPLE 3

1. Can you, the user, store a value at memory location 0008 C067h? Why or why not?
   No, because address 0008 C067h corresponds to the memory area that stores special function registers. In the RAM, the memory addresses from 0000 0000h to 0001 8000h are reserved for special function registers and cannot be used by the user to save his data.
2. What area of Flash is available for the user program on the RX62N board? List the range of addresses and the exact size in bytes (not Kbytes).
   In RX62N, the memory addresses of the on-chip ROM or data flash ranges from 0010 0000h to 0010 8000h. The total number of bytes available for user program is 32768 bytes.

3.4   ADVANCED CONCEPTS

3.4.1   Pipelining

Pipelining is an important technique used to make fast CPUs. It is implemented to increase the instruction throughput (i.e., the number of instructions that can be executed in a unit of time) but it does not reduce the time taken to execute an individual instruction. The execution time of an individual instruction actually increases due to overhead caused by implementing the pipeline. The overhead in the pipeline is from register delay (setup time) and clock skew. Improvement in instruction throughput means programs run faster and have lower execution time, though no single instruction runs faster. The performance will be reduced if there is an imbalance between the stages. For instance, if execution stage takes more time than memory access stage or, in other words, an instruction stays in execution stage longer than memory access stage, then the performance degrades because the clock cannot be faster than the slowest stage. Pipelining would provide optimal CPU performance CPU if every instruction was independent of every other instruction but, unfortunately, most of the instructions are dependent on each other.

The RX CPU is based on the classical five-stage pipeline. During the execution of an instruction, it is converted into various micro-operations. The five stages of the pipeline are described below. Only the Instruction Fetch (IF) stage is executed in the terms of instructions while others are executed in terms of micro-operations.

The operation of pipeline and respective stages is described as follows:

1. **Instruction Fetch Stage (IF Stage):**
   In the IF stage, the CPU fetches 32/64 bit instructions from the memory. The Program counter (PC) fetches the instruction and then the PC is incremented by

4 or 8 since the instructions are 4 or 8 bytes long. The RX CPU has four 8-byte instruction queues. The RX CPU keep fetching instructions until the queues are filled.

2. **Instruction Decode Stage (ID Stage):**

   The main function of this stage is decoding. Instructions are decoded in the ID stage and are converted into micro-operations. In addition to the decoding of the instructions, the values of registers (operands) are also read from the register file. If the value of a register needed is the result of the preceding instruction, then the CPU executes a bypass process (BYP). This process is also called forwarding.

3. **Execution Stage (E Stage):**

   Two main types of calculation take place in this stage. One is normal ALU operations and the other is memory address calculations for memory access stage. Normal ALU operations are register to register operations which includes add, subtract, compare, and logical operations. The other calculations are memory reference operations which includes all load operations from the memory. During the execute stage, the ALU adds the two arguments; i.e., a register and a constant offset given in the instruction to produce an address by the end of this stage.

4. **Memory Access (M Stage):**

   Memory is accessed either for fetching an operand from the memory or storing an operand in the memory. The address of an operand is calculated in the precious execution stage. This stage (M Stage) is divided into two sub-stages, M1 and M2. The RX CPU enables respective memory accesses for M1 and M2.

   ▪ M1 stage (memory-access stage 1):

   In this sub-stage, operand memory accesses OA1 and OA2 are processed. A store operation is processed when a write request is received via the bus. During the Load operation, the operation proceeds to the M2 stage only when a read request is received via the bus. In addition to the request, if the load data is received at the same timing (i.e., no-wait memory access), then the operation proceeds to the WB stage.

   ▪ M2 stage (memory-access stage 2):

   In this sub-stage operand memory access OA2 is processed. In this sub-stage the CPU waits for the load data, and once received the operation proceeds to the WB stage.

5. **Write-back stage (WB stage):**

   The last stage of the pipeline writes data into the register file. In this stage, the operation result calculated in the execution stage and the data read from memory in the memory access stage are written to the register (RW). The data read from memory and the other type of data, such as the operation result, can be written to the register in the same clock cycles.

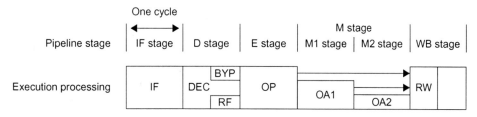

Figure 3.18 Pipeline Configuration and its Operation. Source: *Hardware Manual,* Figure 2.10, page 2–26.

Pipeline Basic Operation

Ideally, each pipeline stage should take the same amount of time to process the instruction. Unfortunately, ideal conditions are hard to achieve and hence stalls are created in the pipeline and performance is degraded. The slowest stage which takes the maximum amount of time becomes the bottleneck. Once the pipeline is filled, each instruction will come out of the pipeline after one clock cycle. In a non-pipelined processor, if there are n tasks to handle and each task takes m clock period , then total time taken to process n tasks is $n*m$ clock periods. In a pipelined processor, when it has m stages, ideally n tasks will take $(m + (n - 1))$ clock periods. So, if we calculate the speed-up gained in this scenario, it will be $n * m/\{m + (n - 1)\}$.

Hazards prevent the next instruction from executing at the next cycle. They reduce the performance and speed-up gained by pipelining. There are three types of hazards:

1. **Structural hazard:**

    It arises from resource conflicts when the hardware is not capable of supporting multiple instructions simultaneously in an overlapped manner.

2. **Data hazard:**

    It arises when an instruction depends on the result of previous instruction. For instance, in the pipeline, an instruction I + 1 depending on the result of instruction I will cause a data hazard because one of the operands of the instruction I +1 is the result of instruction I. In such a case, instruction I + 1 cannot execute, as the data is not available.

3. **Control hazard:**

    It arises from pipelining of branches and other instructions that change the program counter; i.e., when a set of instructions are control dependent on the branch condition, and what value the PC will take is not known until the execution stage or decode stage.

Hazards in the pipeline cause stalls in the pipeline which simply means stalling the pipeline. Allowing some instructions to proceed and delaying other instructions helps in avoiding the stall. When an instruction is stalled, the instructions issued (from the instruction stream) later than the stalled one are also stalled. And the ones which were issued earlier than the stalled instruction are allowed to proceed, so that the hazard goes away with time.

The following figures show typical cases that can occur in the pipeline. (In the following section, the abbreviation "mop" stands for micro-operations.)

1. **Pipeline flow with stalls:**
   In Figure 3.19 the first instruction is a division operation and its execution stage takes more than one cycle to complete. The other instructions, such as the 'ADD' instruction, if allowed to execute will complete execution before the division operation. Since out of order completion might create a problem, the pipeline has to be stalled.

Figure 3.19   Stalls created due to an Instruction that requires multiple cycles to execute in the E Stage. Source: *Hardware Manual*, Figure 2.20, page 2–32.

In Figure 3.20, the first instruction is a load instruction which takes more than one cycle to complete its operand access from memory. Again since in-order completion is important, therefore the later instructions have to be stalled and no more fetching of instructions takes place. As soon as the memory access completes, the pipeline is no longer stalled and instructions are passed to their next stage.

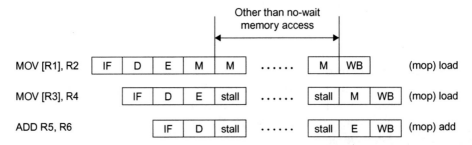

Figure 3.20   Stalls created due to an Instruction that requires more than one cycle for its operand access to execute in the E stage. Source: *Hardware Manual*, Figure 2.21, page 2–32.

Figure 3.21 shows how control dependencies in the code cause stalls in the pipeline. For instance, consider a simple "if statement."

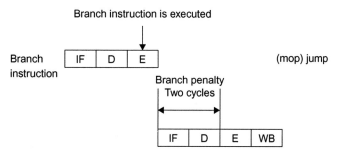

Figure 3.21   Stalls created due to control dependency on a Branch Instruction. Source: *Hardware Manual,* Figure 2.22, page 2–33.

```
Code0
.......
.......
if(Cond1){
    Code1
}
Code2
.........
.........
```

Code1 is control dependent on cond1. Code1 will only execute if Cond1 becomes true or is satisfied. Code2 is also control dependent on Cond1. When this code is converted into assembly code, a branch instruction such as jump executes. As the branch instruction goes into the instruction decode stage, it's time to fetch the next instruction. But which instruction should be fetched, Code1 or Code2? Since the decision is dependent on cond1 (branch instruction), and the result of the branch instruction will be available after execute stage (E stage), therefore the pipeline has to be stalled for two cycles. By the end of two cycles the address of next instruction is available in the program counter (PC), and then the next instruction will be fetched.

2. **Pipeline flow with no stall:**
   ▪ Forwarding/Bypass Process:
   Forwarding is a simple hardware technique used to minimize data hazard stalls. It is also called a bypass process. The result of an 'ADD' instruction is not needed until decode stage, or in extreme cases until execution stage. When the D stage of 'SUB' instruction needs the operand, it is not available since the result of 'ADD' instruction is not yet written into register, so a stall is created. If the result can be moved from the execution stage of 'ADD' instruction to the start of the execution stage of the 'SUB' instruction, then the need for a stall can be avoided. To achieve this, 'ALU result' from both the E stage and M stage is fed back to the ALU inputs. If the forwarding hardware detects that the previous ALU operation generated a result which is going to be one of the inputs of a current ALU operation, then the control logic selects the forwarded result as the ALU input instead of reading from the register file.

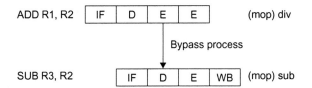

Figure 3.22   Forwarding done to reduce the number of stalls. Source: *Hardware Manual*, Figure 2.24, page 2–33.

   ▪ When WB stages of two instructions are overlapped:
   In this example, the first instruction is a 'MOV' instruction and the other instruction is an 'ADD' instruction. In Figure 3.23, the ADD instruction is more likely to create a structural hazard in the WB stage. But this does not happen; instead, both cause a write operation in the same cycle. In the first half of the cycle 'MOV' instruction writes and in the second half of the cycle 'ADD' instruction writes into the register.

Figure 3.23   When WB Stages of two instructions are overlapped. Source: *Hardware Manual*, Figure 2.25, page 2–33.

▓ When subsequent instructions write to the same register before the end of
memory load:
In the following example, even when the subsequent instruction writes to the
same register before the end of memory load the operation processing is
pipelined, because the WB stage for the memory load is canceled.

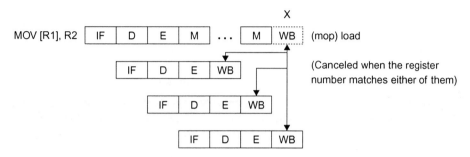

Figure 3.24 When subsequent Instruction writes to the same register before the end of
Memory Load. Source: *Hardware Manual,* Figure 2.26, page 2–34.

▓ When the load data is not used by the subsequent instruction: Out of order completion is allowed in pipelining if the correctness of the program is maintained. As
in the following situation, when the load data is not used by the subsequent instruction, the subsequent operations are not stalled and in fact are allowed to execute. So, subsequent instructions are executed earlier and instructions are
processed out-of-order.

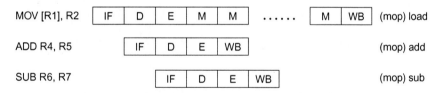

Figure 3.25 When Load Instruction data is not used by the subsequent Instruction. Source:
Hardware Manual, Figure 2.27, page 2–34.

3.4.2 Operating Modes

Operating Mode Types and Selection: There are five types of operating modes in the
RX62N/RX621 Group of MCUs. To specify the type of operating mode, the system control register 0 (SYSCR0) has to be set first. The bits that are set in the system control register are MD1, MD0, ROME, and EXBE. The MDE pin specifies the endianness.

TABLE 3.5   Selection of Operating Modes by the Mode Pins.

MD1	MD0	ROME	EXBE	OPERATING MODE	ON-CHIP ROM	EXTERNAL BUS
0	1	1	0	Boot mode	Enabled	Disabled
1	0	1	0	USB Boot mode	Enabled	Disabled
1	1	1	0	Single chip mode	Enabled	Disabled

Source: *Hardware Manual,* Table 3.1, page 3–1.

TABLE 3.6   Selection of Operating Modes by Register Setting.

ROME	EXBE	OPERATING MODE	ON-CHIP ROM	EXTERNAL BUS
0	0	Single chip mode	Disabled	Disabled
1	0	Single chip mode	Enabled	Disabled
0	1	On-chip ROM enabled extended mode	Disabled	Enabled
1	1	On-chip ROM enabled extended mode	Enabled	Enabled

Source: *Hardware Manual,* Table 3.2, page 3–1.

TABLE 3.7   Selection of Endianness.

MDE	ENDIAN
0	Little endian
1	Big endian

Source: *Hardware Manual,* Table 3.3, page 3–1.

TABLE 3.8   Registers Related to Operating Modes.

REGISTER NAME	SYMBOL	ACCESS SIZE
Mode monitor register	MDMONR	16
Mode status register	MDSR	16
System control register 0	SYSCR0	16
System control register 1	SYSCR1	16

Source: *Hardware Manual,* Table 3.4, page 3–2.

1. **Description of operating modes:**
   - Single-Chip Mode: In this mode, on-chip ROM can be either disabled or enabled, but external bus is always disabled and all I/O ports are accessible. The on-chip ROM is enabled when the microcontroller is started. When ROME bit is set to 1 in SYSCR0, then on-chip ROM is enabled and it is again disabled when ROME bit is set to 0. The same is not true in reverse operation. While the on-chip ROM is disabled (i.e., ROME bit is set to 0 in SYSCR0), it cannot be enabled by setting the ROME bit in SYSCR0 to 1.
   - On-chip ROM Enabled Extended Mode: In this mode, on-chip ROM is enabled and the external bus is always enabled. The on-chip ROM is enabled when the ROME bit is set to 1 in SYSCR0. The external bus is available as external extended mode when EXBE bit is set to 1 in SYSCR0. This mode allows some I/O ports to be used as data bus input/output, address bus output, or bus control signal input/output. The transition from this mode to single-chip mode (on-chip ROM enabled) is possible if 0 is written to EXBE, and a transition to on-chip ROM disabled extended mode is possible if 0 is written to ROME bit.
   - On-chip ROM Disabled Extended Mode: In this mode, on-chip ROM is disabled and external bus is always enabled. The on-chip ROM is disabled when ROME bit is set to 0 in SYSCR0. The external bus is available as external extended mode when EXBE bit is set to 1 in SYSCR0. This mode allows some I/O ports to be used as data bus input/output, address bus output, or bus control signal input/output. It allows transition from this mode to single-chip mode (on-chip ROM enabled) which is possible if 0 is written to EXBE. The transition to on-chip ROM enabled extended mode is not possible.
   - Boot Mode: Boot mode is provided for the flash memory. This mode functions in the same manner as single-chip mode except for data write/erase function to the flash memory.
   - USB Boot Mode: USB boot mode is provided for the flash memory. This mode functions in the same manner as single-chip mode except for data write/erase function to the flash memory.
2. **Transitions of Operating Modes:**
   - Operating Mode transitions according to Mode Pin Setting: Figure 3.26 shows operating mode transitions according to the setting of pins MD1 and MD0. Operating modes can shift in the direction of arrows.
   - Operating Mode Transitions according to Register Setting: Figure 3.27 shows operating mode transitions according to the setting of the ROME and EXBE bits in SYSCR0. Operating modes can shift in the direction of arrows.

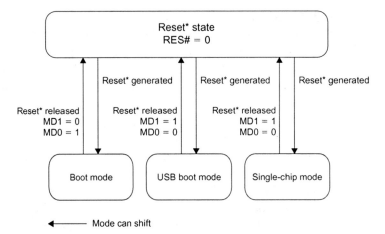

Figure 3.26 Operating mode transitions according to Mode Pin Setting. Source: *Hardware Manual*, Figure 3.1, page 3–8.

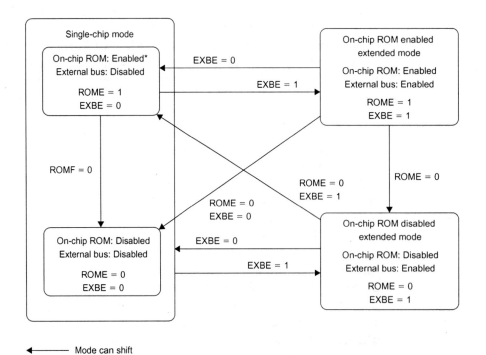

Figure 3.27 Operating mode transitions according to Mode Pin Setting. Source: *Hardware Manual*, Figure 3.1, page 3–8.

3.4.3　Memory Organization

This section discusses some of the basic concepts of memory organization. The basic memory unit is organized into an array of addressable units. In a byte-addressable memory, each memory location contains one byte (8-bits) of data. Another way of addressing the memory is by grouping the bytes into a larger block called words or longwords and addressing that block. Consider a memory unit having k locations (bytes). If, for addressing every location (byte) a unique n-bit identifier is used, then the number of locations that can be addressed would be 2^n. So, k is equal to 2^n which is equal to the size of the memory. If each location stores m-bit value then the memory is said to be organized into an array of $k \times m$ stored bits. The address of each memory location will be a unique n-bit identifier and the content at each location will be an m-bit value. Figure 3.28 shows the basic arrangement of memory unit. In this figure the memory unit is a byte-addressable memory and, as can be seen, each location is addressed by 4-bits; therefore the size of memory is 2^4 or 16 bytes.

Byte Addressing vs. Word Addressing

By using N address lines we can address 2^N distinct addresses, numbered 0 through $2^N - 1$. Most of the modern computers use byte addressing but there are other cases possible, such as word addressing. Consider the computer having 16-bit address space; if the addressing scheme is byte-addressing, then the addressable entities would be 2^{16} bytes with byte addresses from $0, 1, 2 \ldots .2^{16} - 1$. If the addressing scheme is word-addressing then the addressable entities would be 2^{15} words with byte addresses from $0, 2, 4 \ldots .2^{16} - 2$.

$$2^{16} \text{ bytes with byte addresses from } 0, 1, 2, \text{ to } 2^{16} - 1$$
$$2^{15} \text{ words with byte addresses } 0, 2, 4, \text{ to } 2^{16} - 2$$

0000	
0001	
0010	
0011	00101101
0100	
0101	
0110	
⋮	⋮
1101	10100010
1110	
1111	

Figure 3.28　Logical layout of a block of memory.

0	8 bits of data
1	8 bits of data
2	8 bits of data
3	8 bits of data
4	8 bits of data
5	8 bits of data
6	8 bits of data

Figure 3.29 Byte addressing.

0	16 bits of data
2	16 bits of data
4	16 bits of data
6	16 bits of data

Figure 3.30 Word addressing.

3.4.4 Memory Map

The following figure shows a memory map in various operating modes. The accessible areas will differ according to the operating mode and the states of control bits. This microcontroller has a 4-Gbyte address space, which ranges from 0000 0000h to FFFF FFFFh. The reserved areas shown in all three operating modes are not accessible by users/programmers.

In Figure 3.32, External Address Space is shown. It consists of CS areas (CS0 to CS7) and SDRAM area (SDCS). The CS area is further divided into eight areas (CS0 to CS7), each corresponding to the CSi signal output from a CSi ($i = 0$ to 7) pin.

3.4.5 I/O Registers

This section focuses on preventive measures that should be taken while using I/O registers. In some cases, after writing into I/O registers, you must check whether the write operation is completed. In some cases, a CPU behaves differently and could lead to unpredictable results. In such cases, the CPU starts executing subsequent instructions before the write operation is over. If the next instruction deals with the same I/O register, and it tries to read from the same register, then the subsequent instruction reads the value of an I/O register that is not yet updated. So, in such scenarios where the updated value of an I/O register is required in the future, or where a subsequent instruction must execute after the value in the I/O register is changed, special care must be taken. Examples of such situations could be where the subsequent instruction must be executed while an interrupt request is disabled, or where a WAIT instruction is executed immediately after the preprocessing for causing a

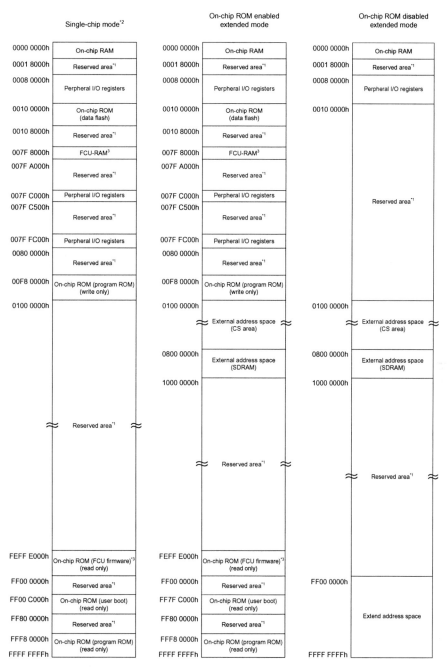

Note:
1. Reserved areas should not be accessed, since the correct operation of LSI is not guaranteed if they are accessed.
2. The address space in boot mode and user boot mode is the same as the address space in single-chip mode.
3. For details on the FCU, see section 37, ROM (Flash Memory for Code Storage) and section 38, Data Flash (Flash Memory for Data Storage) in the Hardware Manual.

Figure 3.31   Memory map in each operating mode. Source: *Hardware Manual,* Figure 4.1, page 4–1.

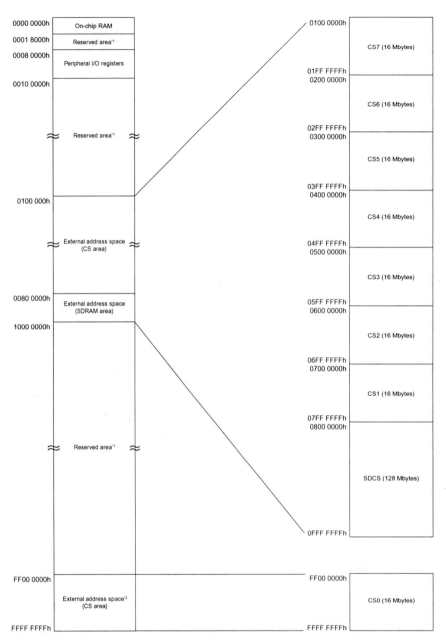

Note:
1.   Reserved areas should not be accessed, since the correct operation of LSI is not guaranteed if they are accessed.
2.   The CS0 are is disabled in on-chip ROM enabled extended mode.
     In this node, the address spare for addresses above 1000 0000h is as shown in Figure 3.1.

Figure 3.32   Correspondence between External Address Spaces, CS Areas (CS0 to CS7), and SDRAM area (SDCS) (In On-chip ROM Disabled Extended Mode). Source: *Hardware Manual,* Figure 4.2, page 4–2.

transition to the low power consumption state. The correct way to handle such situations is by waiting until the write operation is completed and following a debugging procedure. Follow these steps:

1. Write to an I/O register.
2. Read the value from the I/O register to a general register.
3. Execute the operation using the value read.
4. Execute the subsequent instruction.

Consider a situation where multiple registers need to be written first before subsequent in-struction can execute. In other words, subsequent instructions should be executed after the write operations are completed. In such a case only read the I/O register that was last writ-ten to, and execute the operation using that value. Do not read or execute operation for all the registers that were written to.

3.5   ADVANCED EXAMPLES

EXAMPLE 1

Show how the C arrays are laid out in memory for the Renesas board and compiler. Remember to pay attention to endianness, indicating which byte is located where. Assume the space for "*a*" starts in the first available space of user RAM (lowest address), and "*b*" starts 100 bytes (decimal) after where a starts.

a) int *a* [5]

ADDRESS	ARRAY ELEMENT	WHICH BYTE?
400	a[0]	Lower
401	a[0]	Upper
402	a[1]	Lower
403	a[1]	Upper
404	a[2]	Lower
405	a[2]	Upper
406	a[3]	Lower
407	a[3]	Upper
408	a[4]	Lower
409	a[4]	Upper

b) unsigned char b [4] [2]

ADDRESS	ARRAY ELEMENT	WHICH BYTE?
464	b[0][0]	
465	b[0][1]	
466	b[1][0]	
467	b[1][1]	
468	b[2][0]	
469	b[2][1]	
46A	b[3][0]	
46B	b[3][1]	

EXAMPLE 2

What is the speedup gained by implementing pipeline stages on a normal process?

Consider a normal process with n number of tasks, taking k number of clock periods to execute one task.

Then, the time taken by the process to complete n tasks $= n * k$ clock periods.

If k pipeline stages are implemented for the above scenario, then the time taken $= (k + (n - 1))$ clock periods.

Therefore,

$$\text{speedup} = d\,\frac{nk}{(k + (n - 1))}.$$

EXAMPLE 3

What are the various technologies used to implement embedded systems? Compare them on the basis of various parameters such as design cost, unit cost, upgrades and bug fixes, size, weight, power consumption, and system speed.

IMPLEMEN-TATION	DESIGN COST	UNIT COST	UPGRADES AND BUG FIXES	SIZE	WEIGHT	POWER	SYSTEM SPEED
Discrete logic	Low	Mid	Hard	Large	High	?	Very fast
ASIC	High ($500K/ mask set)	Very low	Hard	Tiny	Very low	Low	Obscenely fast
Programmable logic-FPGA,PLD	Low	Mid	Easy	Small	Low	Medium to high	Very fast
Microprocessor + memory + peripherals	Low to mid	Mid	Easy	Small to medium	Low to moderate	Medium	Moderate
Microcontrollers (including memory and peripherals)	Low	Mid to low	Easy	Small	Low	Medium	Slow to moderate
Embedded PC	Low	High	Easy	Medium	Moderate to high	Medium to high	Moderate

3.6   REFERENCES

Hardware Manual, Renesas 32-Bit Microcomputer, RX Family/RX600 Series. Renesas Electronics America, Inc., 2010. Print.

Hennesy, J. L. and Patterson, D. A. *Computer Architecture: A Quantitative Approach.* San Francisco, CA: Morgan Kaufmann Publishers, c2003. Print.

Parhami, B. *Computer Architecture: From Microprocessors to Supercomputers.* Oxford, New York: Oxford University Press, 2005. Print.

Stallings, W. *Computer Organization & Architecture: Designing for Performance.* Upper Saddle River, NJ: Pearson/Prentice Hall, c2006. Print.

Tomek, I. *Introduction to Computer Architecture.* Rockville, MD: Computer Science Press, c1981. Print.

3.7   EXERCISES

1. What are the benefits of a microprocessor/microcontroller-based embedded system over an ASIC-based embedded system?
2. Consider a college food court which involves five steps before you select and eat your food. Look at the following figure for solving the problem.

Suppose that in the food court pipeline the latency varies at each window. It varies from one to two minutes. When a student is done at each window he or she waits until the next window is available. Assume that there is no overhead involved while a student passes from one window to another window.
   a. How should this pipeline be used to maximize its throughput?
   b. Is the method of part 'a' applicable to a processor's data path?
   c. What would be the throughput of the scheme in part 'a' if the latency of each window were uniformly distributed?
   d. Discuss a method other than 'c' for improving throughput?
3. Which memory is the fastest?
   a. Level 2 cache
   b. Registers
   c. RAM
   d. Disk storage
   e. Level 1 cache
4. Consider 4 Kbyte SRAM chips having a data width of 4 bits. How many chips will be required to build a 32 MB memory unit with the word width of 8-bits?
5. The double word 0x AC35 FA34 is stored in memory addresses N through $N + 3$. Which of the following represents storage using little endianness?

a.

N	43
$N + 1$	AF
$N + 2$	53
$N + 3$	CA

b.

N	AC
$N + 1$	35
$N + 2$	FA
$N + 3$	34

c.

N	34
N + 1	FA
N + 2	35
N + 3	AC

d.

N	FA
N + 1	34
N + 2	AC
N + 3	35

6. How many bits wide is the program counter register?
   a. 32 bits
   b. 16 bits
   c. 8 bits
   d. 10 bits
   e. 12 bits

7. What will happen if you try to write to an array element larger than your array?
   a. An error will be reported.
   b. The program won't compile.
   c. Nothing.
   d. You don't know, but it will most likely be bad.
   e. The array will redefine itself bigger.

8. What is the total address space for our RX62N microcontroller?
   a. 31 Kbytes
   b. 384 Mbytes
   c. 4 Kbytes
   d. 4 Gbytes
   e. 1024 Kbytes

9. What are the benefits of a microprocessor/microcontroller-based embedded system over an FPGA-based embedded system?

10. What is the number of address bits required to address any byte in a memory that contains 4096 address spaces?
    a. 2
    b. 8
    c. 12
    d. 16
    e. 32

11. MCU can run in three modes: single chip, memory expansion, microprocessor modes. If used in single-chip mode, what areas in memory could be addressed?
    a. Only internal areas (SFR, internal RAM, internal ROM)
    b. Internal areas (SFR, internal RAM, internal ROM) and external memory areas
    c. SFR, internal RAM, and external memory
    d. SFR, external memory
    e. Only external memory

12. What is the number of address bits required to address any byte in a memory that contains 65536 address spaces?
    a. 2
    b. 8
    c. 12
    d. 16
    e. 20

13. Which of the following buses is not a valid bus?
    a. Instruction bus
    b. Internal main bus 1
    c. Internal peripheral bus 1
    d. External bus
    e. External operand bus

14. Out of the following which bus request has the highest priority?
    a. DMACA
    b. DTC
    c. CPU
    d. EDMAC

Chapter Four

Software Development Tools

4.1 LEARNING OBJECTIVES _____

In this chapter the reader will learn about:

- Process of compilation
- Features of the RX family compiler
- Debugging tools
- Features of the High-performance Embedded Workshop
- Various header files associated with C/C++ Compiler and the RX family

4.2 BASIC CONCEPTS _____

4.2.1 Compilation Mechanism

There are several steps involved from the stage of writing a C program to the stage of execution. Figure 4.1 shows these different steps.

In this process, a program written in C language gets translated into an assembly level program which the computer can understand. It can be seen from Figure 4.1 that the program passes through several processors before it is ready to be executed. The functions of each of these processors are:

- The **preprocessor** performs text replacement according to preprocessor directives. There are two main preprocessor directives—macro expansion (e.g. #define SIZE 30) and file inclusion (e.g. #include "config.h").
- The **compiler** transforms source code, written in a programming language such as C, or C++ *(source language)* into another target language *(object code)* which is of binary form.
- The **linker** is a program that takes one or more objects generated by a compiler and combines them into a single executable program.

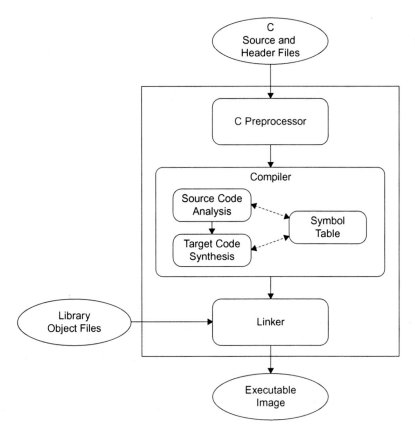

Figure 4.1   Compilation process for a C program.

The input and output to each of these processing stages is shown in Table 4.1.

TABLE 4.1   Input and Output to each Processor.

PROCESSOR	INPUT	OUTPUT
Preprocessor	C source code file	Source code file with processed preprocessor commands
Compiler	Source code file with processed preprocessor commands	Re-locatable object code
Linker	Re-locatable object code and the standard C library functions	Executable code in machine language

4.2.2   Compilers for Embedded Systems

Compilers for embedded systems differ from compilers for general-purpose processors (GPPs). Minimizing code and data size is often critical for embedded systems since memory sizes are limited due by price pressures. This makes compiler code and data size optimizations extremely important. The tongue-in-cheek "Software Gas Law" states that a program will eventually grow to fill all available resources. Embedded system software evolves as features are added and defects are fixed, while the hardware changes much more slowly. It is much easier to reprogram an MCU than redesign the hardware. As a result there is great value in compiler optimizations which can squeeze more code and data into the available resources.

Speed optimization is also often critical. However, it is done differently for embedded systems and GPPs. First, GPP instruction sets have evolved over time to enable extremely high clock rates (> 2 GHz) and deep instruction processing pipelines. Embedded processors with their lower clock rates do not need such deep pipelines, which leads to different code optimization trade-offs. Second, a lower clock rate means that embedded systems have a smaller performance penalty than GPPs for accessing memory instead of registers. This has two interesting effects. First, the compiler makes different optimization trade-offs with data allocation. Second, instruction sets for embedded systems can support memory-memory and bit-level operations rather than being forced into a load/store model.

4.2.3   RX Compiler Package

The RX compiler package includes the following embedded system development tools.

- **C/C++ Compiler**
  The compiler translates source code into assembly code, and typically also invokes the assembler and linker to create an executable file. The Compiler is ANSI-compliant and supports exception processing and template functions. It supports C or C++ and generates compact and high-speed object code. It offers general optimization techniques such as deletion of common expression and register allocation. There are additional non-ANSI features which are helpful or necessary for embedded systems.

- **Assembler**
  The Assembler translates assembly code into object (machine) code. It also provides pre-processor functions such as the file inclusion, conditional assembly, and macros, in order to simplify programming.

- **Optimizing Linkage Editor**
  The Linkage Editor processes object files generated by the compiler and assembler to create load modules and library files.

- **Standard Library Generator**
  The Standard Library Generator creates customized versions of the standard library files based on the user-specified options.

- **Simulator/Debugger**
  This Simulator/Debugger provides the capability for debugging in targetless system. It is also a highly accurate simulator, supporting program performance evaluation .
- **Utilities**
  The RX package contains various utility tools. Call Walker shows stack use corresponding to the C/C++ function call tree. Moreover, function allocation editing by drag & drop is available. Map Viewer provides a GUI display of the various sections in a map file (output by the Optimizing Linkage Editor).
- **IDE (Integrated Development Environment): HEW (High-performance Embedded Workshop)**
  High-Performance Embedded Workshop provides a GUI-based integrated development environment on Windows operating systems for the development and debugging of embedded applications for the Renesas microcontrollers. It supports seamless integration and easy access to all tools for coding, compiling, linking, and debugging. All the tools in the package together offer a variety of functions and increase productivity greatly.

Features of RX Family C/C++ Compiler

1. **Easy optimization setting and the optimization features**
    - Compiler Optimization: It provides an easy selection of optimization as in the selection of size, speed, priority, and also in the selection of the optimization level (optimize level: 0, 1, 2, or max).
    - Supports wide-ranging optimization when compiling; function's inline-expansion between files and symbol access optimization which uses external symbol allocation information from the optimization linker.
    - Has a detailed setting of optimization that is useful in loop expansions, instructions order, optimization range specification, register allocation, etc.
2. **Linker optimization**
    - Handles inter-module optimization such as the removal of an unreferenced symbol, optimization for branch order, and provides a detailed setting of partially disabled optimization.
3. **Optimization of standard library**
    - Application of compiler optimization: A standard library is targeted on optimization and a compact code is generated with the entire program.
4. **Easy translation environment from the existing product**
    - Supports the option of controlling different language specifications.
    - Language specification of another compiler is checked by the RX compiler.
    - RX supports Bi-endian operation. The compiler can select between big endian and little endian.

4.2.4   Debugging Tools

There are two primary tools for debugging embedded real-time systems:

a. **Debugger:** The debugger allows a developer to observe and control a program's execution and data. The execution can be started, paused and stopped, or advanced by a single instruction or program statement. Breakpoints can typically be inserted. Data stored in variables as well as raw memory and register values can be examined and modified.

b. **Monitor:** The monitor allows a developer to examine the program's temporal behavior. The most common monitors are oscilloscopes and logic analyzers connected to the embedded system. For instance, , while implementing interrupts in serial communication, one can measure useful information such as the duration of the transmit ISR and the receive ISR, or the delay between sending a character and receiving a reply. This information can be used to find maximum latency, and maximum frequency. Hence the monitor tool is helpful in giving you insights about the timing of various operations happening inside the system.

4.2.5   Introduction to HEW

This section deals with the concepts and functionalities associated with the High-performance Embedded Workshop V.4.08 (HEW).

Overview: HEW organizes your work with the concepts of workspaces and projects.

■ Workspace: This is the largest unit which contains programs written in the HEW workshop. It can have several projects. A project is automatically created when we create the workspace.

■ Project: The project is where you write your program. In fact, creating a new project is making a new program. You can also make hierarchical levels between several modules. It, along with other projects, will be included in the workspace.

A simple diagram below shows the relationship between a project and the workspace.

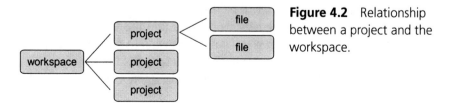

Figure 4.2   Relationship between a project and the workspace.

Creating or Opening a Project in HEW-IDE

To launch HEW, open the start menu, select **program,** select **Renesas,** select **HEW,** and then select the shortcut of the **High-performance Embedded Workshop.**

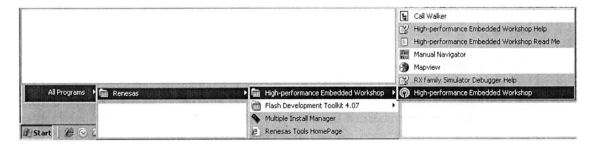

Figure 4.3   Launching of HEW. Source: *RX62N RDK Renesas toolchain quick start guide.*

Look for the dialog box just like this:

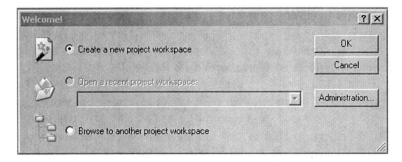

Figure 4.4   Welcome dialog box in HEW. Source: *HEW User Manual V.4.08,* page 15.

To create a new workspace:

- Select the **Create a new project workspace** option from the **Welcome!** dialog box, and click the **OK** button or select **[File → New Workspace].** The New Project Workspace dialog box will be displayed.
- Enter the name of the new workspace into the **Workspace Name** field. To select the directory in which you would like to create the workspace, use the Browse button or type the directory into the **Directory** field manually.
- Select the CPU family and Tool chain upon which you would like to base the workspace.

- When a new workspace is created, the HEW will also automatically create a project and place it inside the new workspace. From the project types list, select the type of project that you want to create from this list. The project types are of mainly three types: tool chain-only, debug-only, and a full project generator that contains both the debugger and tool chain aspect of the HEW.
- Click the **OK** button to create. This then launches the HEW window.

To open a new workspace:

- Select **Browse to another project workspace** option from the dialog box shown in Figure 4.4 and then click the **OK** button or **select [File → Open Workspace].** The Open Workspace dialog box will be displayed. Select the workspace file (".HWS" file) that you want to open.
- Click the **Select** button to open the Properties dialog box to open the workspace. Click the **Cancel** button to stop opening the workspace.

To open a recently used workspace:

- Select **Open a recent project workspace** in the dialog box: select the name of the workspace from the dropdown list, and then click the **OK** button.

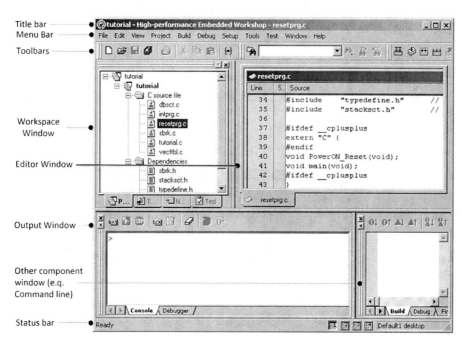

Figure 4.5   HEW workspace showing various windows. Source: *HEW User Manual V.4.08,* page 2.

Windows in HEW

There are three main windows in HEW:

Workspace Window: Shows the projects and files that are currently in the workspace. It has four tabs: Projects, Templates, Navigation, and Test.

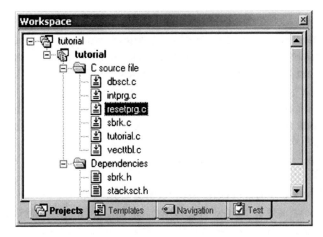

Figure 4.6   Workspace window in HEW. Source: *HEW User Manual V.4.08*, page 6.

Output Window: Shows the results of a various processes (e.g., build). By default, it has seven tabs (Build, Debug, Find in Files 1, Find in Files 2, Macro, Test, and Version Control) on display.

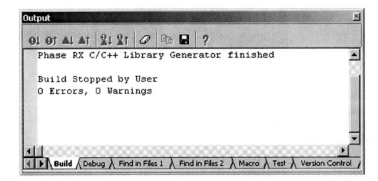

Figure 4.7   Output window in HEW. Source: *HEW User Manual V.4.08*, page 9.

Editor Window: Provides file viewing and editing facilities. It is in this window where you will edit files of your project. It allows you to have many files open at one time, so you can switch between them. You can edit them in whichever order you want. Each file has a separate tab associated with it, and you can navigate easily to any tab you want.

```
Line  S.  Source
76       //#endif
77
78       #pragma section ResetPRG          // output PowerON_Reset to PResetPRG section
79
80       #pragma entry PowerON_Reset
81
82       void PowerON_Reset(void)
83       {
84           set_intb(__sectop("C$VECT"));
85
86           _INITSCT();                    // Initialize Sections
87
88       //  _INIT_IOLIB();                 // Use SIM I/O
89
90       //  errno=0;                       // Remove the comment when you use errno
91       //  srand((_UINT)1);               // Remove the comment when you use rand()
92       //  _s1ptr=NULL;                   // Remove the comment when you use strtok()
93
94       //  HardwareSetup();               // Use Hardware Setup
95           nop();
96
97       //  _CALL_INIT();                  // Remove the comment when you use global class object
98
99           set_psw(PSW_init);             // Set Ubit & Ibit for PSW
100      //  chg_pmusr();                   // Remove the comment when you need to change PSW PMbit (
```

Figure 4.8   Editor window in HEW. Source: *HEW User Manual V.4.08,* page 9.

Concept of Configuration and Session

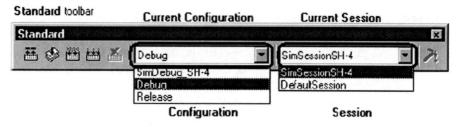

Figure 4.9   Configuration and session selection in HEW. Source: *HEW User Manual V.4.08,* page 20.

By looking at the Standard toolbar you will know your current configuration and session. You can also select your session and configuration by looking into the drop-down list box. For instance, Figure 4.9 shows that the selected debugger is "SH-4 Simulator" which works along with Renesas SuperH Standard toolchain.

Before going any further, let me clarify the concept of configuration and session.

Configuration

After selecting a toolchain, you will create a project. Once the project is created, the HEW will automatically create configurations **"Debug"** and **"Release."** As shown in Figure 4.9, configurations **"SimDebug_SH-4,"** "Debug," and "Release" are available. At the time of the creation of the project, if you have selected a target debugger HEW will automatically create a configuration best suited for that debugger. For instance, if you have selected **"SH-4 Simulator"** in the **Target** tab while creating a project, configuration **"SimDebug_SH-4"** is created. Configurations are the settings that have to be set before the building process starts. It can also be referred to as "build configuration."

Session

Sessions are the units basically used to manage various settings. For instance, they may refer to the settings associated with debugging options of a specific debugger and data values on the memory and register windows. The term "session" is also referred as "debugger session." If you look at the figure of the Standard toolbar (Figure 4.9), sessions "SimSessionSH-4" and "Default Session" are available. Information on each session is saved in an individual file in the HEW project. Just like a configuration is created as you create a project after selection of the toolchain, a session called "Default Session" is also created. Also, if you select a target debugger at the creation of project, a session is created for connecting the debugger. For example, if you have selected "SH-4 Simulator" in "Target" at the creation of a project, session "SimSessionSH-4" is automatically created.

4.2.6   Concepts of Header Files

Most of the programming languages (for instance C and C++) use header files. These files hold certain elements (program's source code) which are reusable. Header files contain common repeatable elements such as forward declarations of classes, subroutines, structure, unions, variables, and other identifiers. Declaring the same standardized identifiers in more than one source file can be a cumbersome task for a programmer.

The solution to this is declaring that identifier in a single header file and when there is a need for that identifier in some other source file, a programmer can just include that header file in order to include all declarations. The C standard library and C++ standard library traditionally declare their standard functions in header files that implement standard processing operations such as input/output and string handling. They can be used by including the standard include files which contain declarations for the corresponding libraries and definitions of the macro names necessary to use them.

Header Files Used in RX Family C/C++ Compiler

C and C++ are the most famous programming languages that implement the concept of header files.

Table 4.2 lists the various library types, and their corresponding standard include files. Some include files consist only of macros, as seen in Table 4.3, to improve the program efficiency.

Header Files Associated with RX62N

Some of the header files used in the demo program can be seen in Table 4.4.

TABLE 4.2   Library Types and Their Corresponding Header Files.

LIBRARY TYPES	DESCRIPTION	STANDARD INCLUDE FILES
Program diagnostics	Outputs program diagnostic information.	\<assert.h>
Character handling	Handles and checks characters.	\<ctype.h>
Mathematics	Performs numerical calculations such as trignometric functions.	\<math.h> \<mathf.h>
Non-local jumps	Supports transfer of control between functions.	\<setjmp.h>
Variable arguments	Supports access to variable arguments for functions with such arguments.	\<stdarg.h>
Input/output	Performs input/output handling.	\<stdio.h>
General utilities	Performs C program standard processing such as storage area management.	\<stdlib.h>
String handling	Performs string comparison, copying, etc.	\<string.h>
Complex arithmetic	Performs complex numeric operations.	\<complex.h>
Floating-point environment	Supports access to floating-point environment.	\<fenv.h>
Integer type format conversion	Manipulates greatest-width integers and converts integer format.	\<inttypes.h>
Multibyte and wide characters	Manipulates multibyte characters.	\<wchar.h> \<wctype.h>

Source: *Compiler Package User Manual, Renesas 32-Bit Microcomputer, RX Family/RX600 Series.* Renesas Electronics America, Inc., 2010. Table 9.26, page 328.

TABLE 4.3   Header Files that Contain Macros.

STANDARD INCLUDE FILE	DESCRIPTION
<stddef.h>	Defines macro names used in common by the standard include files.
<limits.h>	Defines various limit values relating to the compiler internal processing.
<errno.h>	Defines the value to be set in **errno** when an error is generated in a library function.
<float.h>	Defines various limit values relating to the limits of floating-point numbers.
<iso646.h>	Defines alternative spellings of macro names.
<stdbool.h>	Defines macros relating to logical types and values.
<stdint.h>	Declares integer types with specified width and defines macros.
<tgmath.h>	Defines type-generic macros.

Source: *Compiler Package User Manual,* Table 9.27, pg. 329.

TABLE 4.4   Header Files Used in Demo Program of RX62N Microcontroller Board.

STANDARD INCLUDE FILE	DESCRIPTION
<config.h>	Defines macros relating to the font size.
<glyph.h>	Defines external constants, typedef enumerations and structures, prototype for minimum, and full access for glyph API library.
<preamble.h>	Defines basic definitions of all simple constants and types.
<st7579_lcd.h>	Defines prototypes that are required by the LCD driver in the glyph API.
<yrdkrx62n_rspio.h>	Defines prototypes for the glyph communication API.
<typedefine.h>	Defines aliases of Integer Type.
<sbrk.h>	Defines macro relating to size of area managed by sbrk.
<vect.h>	Defines vector table.
<stacksct.h>	Defines macros that refer to setting of stack area.
<iodefine.h>	Define various input and output registers.

4.3   BASIC EXAMPLES

(Source: *High-performance Embedded Workshop V.4.08, User's Manual.* Renesas Electronics America, Inc., 2010.)

EXAMPLE 1

This is an example demonstrating how to Build, Debug, and Run a Project on the HEW-IDE.

If you are testing your board for the first time, you will test it with the demo code that comes with the package. After launching the main window, you probably want to download and run it on the board. Follow these steps to acquaint yourself with the whole process:

Step 1: Ensure that **'SessionRX600_E1_E20_SYSTEM'** session in the right-hand drop-down list on the tool bar is selected.

Step 2: Click the **<Connect>** button on the 'debug' toolbar.

When you click on the **connect** button, an initial settings window will appear. Ensure that you select the right MCU group and device. Select the debugging mode as shown in Figure 4.10.

Figure 4.10   Initial setting window while connecting the board.

After clicking **OK,** a window will pop up which will show the status as **connecting.** This window indicates whether an initial configuration has been done or not. See Figure 4.11 to get an idea.

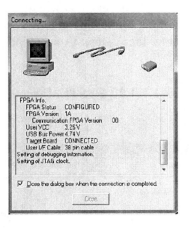

Figure 4.11 Window showing the status as connecting.

This window will show up for just a few seconds, and after that a configuration properties window will appear. You can see various configuration properties associated with **MCU, system, Internal flash memory overwrite,** and **external flash memory.** You can select any of them and edit the properties as your application demands. If you go to the **MCU** tab on the same window, you need to select one of three operating modes; i.e., **on chip ROM enabled extended mode, on chip ROM disabled extended mode,** or **single chip mode.** For the demo application, you can go on with the settings shown in the Figure 4.12.

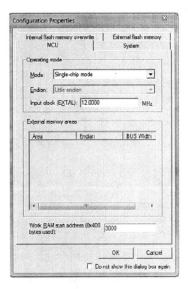

Figure 4.12 Window showing configuration properties.

Once connected, you can see the status in the output window (Figure 4.13) as **'connected.'** Also, you can see the status of the platform tab of other component windows. Here is the snapshot:

Figure 4.13   Window showing the status after the board has connected.

Step 3: The next step is building the program to check for any compiling error. Typically, in build process, each phase of the build takes a set of project files and builds them. If every file builds successfully, then the next phase is executed. Let me shed some light on the build process. The building process takes place in three phases: the Compiler is the first phase, the Assembler is the second phase, and the Linker is the third and final phase. During the Compiler phase, the C/C++ source files from the various projects are compiled in turns. During the Assembler phase, the assembler source files are assembled. During the Linker phase, all library files and output files from the Compiler and Assembler phases are linked together to produce the load module. Depending on your requirement, you can choose from the various build options available to you. If you want to build an individual file, first select it from project tab of the workspace window, and then you can select any one of these options:

- Click the **Build File** toolbar button (Figure 4.14)
- Select **Build <file>** from the pop-up menu
- Select the **[Build → Build File]** menu option
- Press CTRL + F7

If you want to build a project, you can select any one of these:

- Click the **Build** toolbar button (Figure 4.14)
- Press F7
- Select **[Build → Build]**
- Right-click on a project in the **Project** tab of the **Workspace** window and select **[Build → Build]** from the pop-up menu

Typically, the build operation compiles or assembles those files that are changed since the last build command. The **Build all** operation builds all files irrespective of whether the file has been modified or not.

For performing a **build all** operation, you may select any of these options:

- Click the **Build All** toolbar button (Figure 4.14)
- Select [**Build** → **Build All**]
- Right-click on a project in the **Projects** tab of the **Workspace** window and select [**Build** → **Build All**] from the pop-up menu

In each of the cases discussed, you can see the status of the build process in the **build** tab of the output window. An example that shows the status in the output window after the build process is next.

EXAMPLE

Build Finished
'x' Errors, 'x' Warnings

Here 'x' could be 0 or a larger number depending on your coding skills.

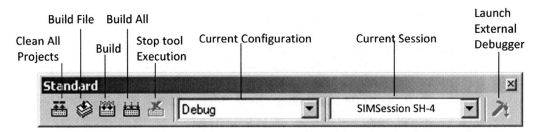

Figure 4.14   Explanation of icons on the toolbar. Source: *HEW User Manual V.4.08.*

Step 4: After the build process, you should download the code onto your board. For that, first go to the **debug** tab on the menu bar. Click on it and select **'download modules'** in the drop-down menu list. Click on **'all modules'** and wait for the HEW to download all modules onto the board. When downloaded, a status will appear on the memory tab of the other component window, indicating the memory area where the program has been downloaded. A snapshot of the same is shown in Figure 4.15.

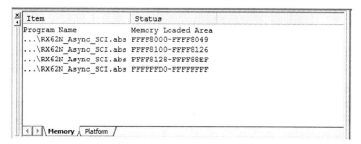

Figure 4.15   Memory tab of other component window showing status of download.

Step 5: After downloading the program onto the board, you need to make it run to see the response. Click on **'reset go'** from various other go options as shown in Figure 4.16.

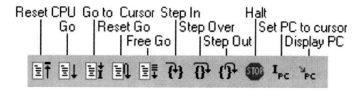

Figure 4.16   Explanation of icons on the toolbar. Source: *HEW User Manual V.4.08.*

You can easily see the response on the output window as well as on the MCU board. The status on the output window will look like: Reset CPU.

Step 6: If you need to halt the program for debugging or editing the code, you can just click on the red **stop** button, as seen in Figure 4.17.

Figure 4.17   Snapshot of toolbar before halting the program.

EXAMPLE 2

This is an example demonstrating how to create and save a header file in the workspace. This example also demonstrates how to add that header file to the current project, and how to edit it.

A programmer can create a 'Header file' when there is a need for some subroutines, structure, variables, unions, enumerations, and other definitions to be commonly repeated. Declaring the same identifiers again and again can be a tedious task, so the solution is creating a header file that contains all the elements that are being repeated in more than one source file. In a header file, a programmer just declares common declarations, and when there is need for any identifier the programmer can just include that header file in the main source file, and the purpose will be fulfilled in an easier way. Follow these steps to add a header file to your current project.

Step 1: Creating a header file

To create a new header file, you need to create a new editing window first. For this, you can apply one of the following:

- Click the **file** tab on the menu bar, and then click the **new file** option in the drop-down menu
- Press CTRL + N
- Click the new file toolbar icon ▢

By default, a new file will be given an arbitrary name which you can change when you save the file. To make a header file you just need to save that file as "**.h**" extension file. It is always good to name the file according to its functionality because other programmers who might want to edit the project later must also know the types of declarations the header file contains. This is the reason the header file that defines input and output registers is named **<iodefines.h>**. After you have created a file, the next step is to edit the file.

Step 2: Editing a header file

In the editor window, you can declare the basic definitions that are being repeated in more than one source file. Before writing the definitions and declarations, do yourself a favor by writing the description of the current header file, to give other programmers an idea as to what this header file contains in general. Then, you can proceed with writing your content as your application demands. After you have written those basic definitions, you can edit it by using the basic tools available to you such as the menu, toolbar, and keyboard shortcuts. In addition, HEW provides you the functionality of editing through a pop-up menu that is local to the editor window. That menu will appear when you right click in an editor window.

Table 4.5 outlines the basic operations.

TABLE 4.5   Basic Operations for Editing a Header File.

OPERATION	EFFECT	ACTION
Undo	Reverses the last editing operation.	Select [Edit → Undo]
		Press CTRL + Z
Redo	Repeats the last undone editing operation.	Select [Edit → Undo]
		Press CTRL + Z
Cut	Removes highlighted text and places it on the Windows clipboard.	Click the Cut toolbar button ( )
		Press CTRL + X
		Select [Edit → Cut]
		Select Cut from the pop-up menu
Copy	Places a copy of the highlighted text into the Windows clipboard.	Click the Copy toolbar button ( )
		Press CTRL + C
		Select [Edit → Copy]
		Select Copy from the pop-up menu
Paste	Copies the contents of the Windows® clipboard into the active window at the position of the insertion cursor.	Click the Paste toolbar button ( )
		Press CTRL + V
		Select [Edit → Paste]
		Select Paste from the pop-up menu
Clear	Removes highlighted text (it is not copied to the Windows clipboard).	Select [Edit → Clear]
		Press Delete
Select All	Selects (i.e. highlights) the entire contents of the active window.	Select [Edit → Select All]
		Press CTRL + A

Source: *HEW User Manual V.4.08,* page 120.

While you are editing your file, the title bar will show an asterisk (*). For instance global.h*

Step 3: Saving a header file

This step discusses how to save a file as a header file and how to save the contents of the editor window in general. To save the contents of a newly created file as a header file, make sure that it is an active window; i.e., open in an editor window, and then select one of the following:

- Click the **file** button on menu bar, then click the **new save** button in the drop-down menu
- Press CTRL + S
- Click the Save File toolbar icon (🖫)

Since the file has not been saved before, the save operation will provide a file save dialog box. Enter a filename, and ensure that you put "**.h**" as the extension of the file. After making it a (.h) header file, specify a directory and then click the **OK** button to create the file with the name given in the directory specified. If you edit and make changes to an already saved file, then you just need to click on the save icon. No dialog box will appear in this case. If you want to save the contents of the file under a new name, you must click the **file** button on the menu bar, then click the **save as** instead of the **new save** button in the drop-down menu. Again a file save dialog box will be displayed. Enter a filename, specify a directory, and then click the **OK** button to create the file with the name given in the directory specified. In order to save the contents of every open window, either click on the **save all** toolbar button (🖬) or Click the **file** button on the menu bar and then click the **save all** button in the drop-down menu.

NOTE:

Saving the file as a "**.h**" extension file is the key in making a newly created file a header file.

Step 4: Opening a header file

To open a file you can do one of the following operations:

- Click the **file open** toolbar button (📂)
- Press CTRL + O
- Click the **file** button on menu bar, and then click the **open** button in the drop-down menu

This operation will lead to the directory browser. You can then navigate to the desired directory to open the file. Once located, you can open that file.

NOTE:

You can use the **Files of Type** combo box to select the type of file you want to open. For instance, if you select '.h' extension in the combo box then you will be able to see only files that are of the '.h' extension. Surely this will narrow down your search.

Step 5: Adding a header file to the current project

For adding a header file to the current project click on the **projects** tab in the menu bar, and in the drop-down menu click on the **"add files"** button. This operation will lead to the directory browser. You can then navigate to the desired directory to find the header file. Once located, you can add that file by clicking the **"add"** button on the directory browser window. If you want to add that file to one of the folders in the workspace window, such as the C header file or C source file, then just go to that folder and right click. Select **add files** from the pop-up menu. Again the directory browser will pop-up and you can navigate to your desired file. Once added, you do not need to open that file in a conventional way as discussed in Step 4. Follow these steps to open that header file:

- Spot your file in workspace window and double-click the file to open it
- Select the file and click the right-hand mouse button; select **Open <file name>** from the pop-up menu
- If it is already selected, press enter

NOTE:

To remove a header file:

For removing a header file from the current project, click on the projects tab in the menu bar and in a drop-down menu, click on the **"remove files"** button. A window, as seen in Figure 4.18, will appear.

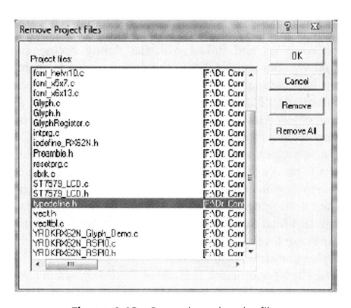

Figure 4.18 Removing a header file.

Select the header file you want to remove from your project. If you want to remove a header file from one of the folders in the workspace window, such as the C header file or C source file, then just go to that folder and right click. Select **remove files** from the pop-up menu. Again, the window shown in Figure 4.18 will appear and you can select the file you want to remove.

4.4   ADVANCED CONCEPTS

4.4.1   Advanced Debugging Concepts

(Source: *HEW User Manual V.4.08.*)

This section describes in detail the various debugging tools and operations present in high performance embedded workshop. As discussed in Section 4.2.4 there are two primary tools for debugging embedded real-time systems: the debugger and the monitor. This section discusses the first tool, the debugger, in detail. Details regarding the functionality and operations of the debugger and its related windows and dialog boxes are discussed. The debugger used in the RX family is the J-Link Debugger.

- **Debugger options in HEW**
  The debugger can debug at assembly language level, as well as at the C/C++ source level. It depends on which setting the user chooses. If users make the **debug** option enabled, the debugger debugs the code at C/C++ source language level; and if that setting is not enabled then the debugger by default debugs the code at assembly language level. More precisely, your C/C++ program must be compiled and linked with the **debug** option enabled for debugging at C/C++ source level. When the **debug** option is enabled, the compiler puts all the information necessary for debugging the C/C++ code into the management information file, which is usually called the 'debug object files.' Thus, the debug object files are those absolute files that contain only the specific information essential for debugging, instead of the whole C/C++ code. While creating a new project, an initial debug session will be automatically configured. A user has to ensure that the **debug** option is enabled on the compiler and linker while generating an object file for debugging. When the **debug** option is not enabled, then debugging information will not be present in your debug object file. You can still load that file into the debugger, but it will only debug at the assembly language level.
- **Debugger sessions in HEW**
  The High-performance Embedded Workshop offers you the functionality of storing all of your builder options into a configuration. This means you can put all of your building information into one place and refer to it with a name. Similarly, you

can store all the debugger options in a session. Later on, you can get back to the same session when required, and all of the debugger options will be restored. These sessions allow the user to specify target, download modules, and debug—which basically means you can have different sessions each targeted at different debugger options. For instance, you can easily have different sessions using the same target but with minor variations in session options. As an advantage, you can easily switch sessions as and when required. You can even modify certain things such as register values, or target settings such as clock speed. Look at Figure 4.19. The five sessions shown share the same target, but the sessions are slightly different with regard to the options defined.

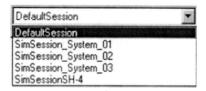

Figure 4.19   Sessions in HEW. Source: *HEW User Manual V.4.08,* page 356.

In this particular case, there is no need to rebuild because the sessions share the same download module and they are never directly related to the build configuration data. In addition, each session's information is stored in a separate file in the High-performance Embedded Workshop project so that you can later manipulate the data according to your application.

■ **Selecting a session:**
Click on the **debug** tab on the menu bar. In the drop-down menu, click on the **debug sessions** and the debug sessions dialog box will open. After that, select the session that you want to use from the **current session** drop-down list box, and then click the ok button.

Figure 4.20   Selecting a session. Source: *HEW User Manual V.4.08,* page 356.

■ **Adding a session:**
HEW provides you the functionality of creating and naming a new session with an attached target and setup. You can create a new session by clicking on the **file** tab on the menu bar. In the drop-down menu, click on **new session** and the new session dialog box will open.

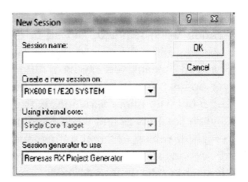

Figure 4.21 Creating and naming a new session.

You need to fill out the required fields one by one. You can start with the name of the new session, and then select the target you wish to use, followed by selecting the core from the internal core list. This item is only available when you use the synchronized debugging facility. Select the generator in the **session generator** to use the list. It is possible that there may be multiple generators that support the same target. The last step is to click the **OK** button to launch the generation process. At this point, an additional dialog box may be displayed for target setup options. When finished, a new session is added to the current project. It should be available in the session's drop-down list box on the main toolbar.

- **Removing a session:**
  Click on the **debug** tab on the menu bar. In the drop-down menu, click on the **debug sessions** option, and the debug sessions dialog box will open. After that, select the session that you want to remove and then click the **remove** button. Click the **OK** button to close the debug sessions dialog box.

NOTE:

It is not possible to remove the current session.

- **Saving session information:**
  You can save the new session by clicking on the **file** tab on the menu bar, and then in the drop down menu click on the **save session** button. If you have checked the **"prompt before saving session"** checkbox, a dialog box is displayed which asks you whether you wish to save the information. To see whether it is checked or not, click on the **settings** tab on the menu bar, then click on the **options** in the drop-down menu (a dialog box will appear), and then click on the **workspace** tab to look for the checked boxes.
- **Operating memory**
  This section describes one of the ways to debug your code. A user must know how to look at the memory in the CPU's address space. It would be very useful if a user

knows how to look at the memory area in different formats. This section also discusses ways to fill and move a memory block.

■ **Opening the memory window:**

A memory window is a window that shows the contents of contiguous memory areas. To open the window, click on the **view** tab on the menu bar. In the drop-down menu, click on the **CPU,** then on the **memory;** or click the Memory toolbar icon (🖅). A box, as shown in Figure 4.22, will pop up. It is known as the Display address box. In that box, you can specify the **display address, scroll start address,** and **scroll end address.**

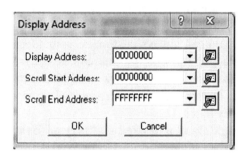

Figure 4.22   Display address box.

Click the **OK** button to launch the memory window. The display can be scrolled up and down. The range can be selected by entering the values of the scroll start and scroll end address fields in the display address box.

■ **Window configuration:**

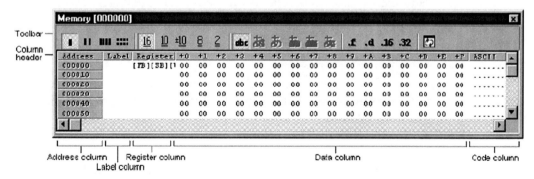

Figure 4.23   Memory window. Source: *HEW User Manual V.4.08,* page 381.

The **label** and **register** columns are hidden by default. You can make it visible by customizing the toolbar. The **label column** shows the name of the label allocated to the data on the first memory address displayed on the row. Similarly, the **register column** shows the name of the register allocated to data on the first memory address, displayed on the row. The '**+*n***' in the column header of the **data column** defines the offset value from the first address of the row. The header of the **code column** shows the code name. In order to change the first address being displayed, double-click the **address** or **label** column. In order to change the memory data at the selected address, double-click the **data** or **code** column. Changing the values can be recorded in a macro (Macro Recording) to help you remember previous settings. In case the new setting does not go your way, you can then always get back to your initial settings since you have the previous data saved somewhere. Moreover, values in the address, data, and code columns can be changed by in-place editing. You can always customize your toolbar by right-clicking, and when it displays a pop up window you can select from the various options available. For instance, one of the options would be '**move**' which moves a specified memory block. In this feature, macro recording is also available to retain your previous memory block.

■ **Setting data at a desired memory address:**
To set data at a memory address, you can do an in-place editing of the code as well as the data column.

 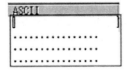

Figure 4.24 Data and Code column. Source: *HEW User Manual V.4.08*, page 383.

The first figure in Figure 4.24 shows the **data column** and second figure shows the **code column.** To change the contents of the memory, open a **set** dialog box. This is done as follows:

a. Double-click the Data column
b. Double-click the Code column
c. Select the data you want to change and choose **set** from the pop-up menu

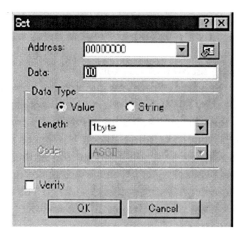

Figure 4.25   Set dialog box. Source: *HEW User Manual V.4.08,* page 384.

Fill in the required fields, such as **address** and **data type. Value** can be either a numeric value or a character. If you are setting a numeric value, then set **value** as the **data type.** If you are setting a character value, then select **string** as the **data type.** Make sure to select the **verify** check box.

▪ **Filling an area of memory with constant data:**
HEW provides you with the feature of setting the range of memory addresses with the constant value. For this, you need to select an address range to fill in the memory window. Select **fill** from the pop-up menu of the **memory** window, and then edit the **fill** dialog box.

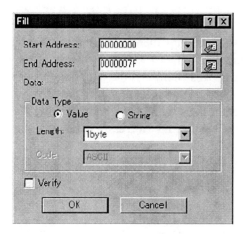

Figure 4.26   Fill dialog box. Source: *HEW User Manual V.4.08,* page 385.

You must enter the **start address** and **end address.** The **end address** can also be prefixed by a plus (+): the **end address** will become **(start address)** + (the entered value).

- **Copying an area of memory:**

  To copy an area of memory into another area, you can use the memory copy feature provided by HEW. First, select a copy-source address range in the memory window using the mouse. Right click on the memory window and choose **'move'** from the pop-up menu. The **move** dialog box opens as shown in Figure 4.27. Click on **the move address** field pop-up menu and choose the **copy destination address.** Check the **verify** check box. If you choose not to drag the copy-source address range, you have to enter the start and end address. The **end address** can also be prefixed by a plus (+): the **end address** will become the **(start address)** + (the entered value).

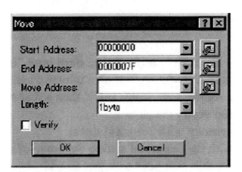

Figure 4.27   Move dialog box. Source: *HEW User Manual V.4.08*, page 386.

- **Comparing the memory contents:**

  To compare the contents of two memory blocks, you can use the memory compare feature provided by HEW. First, select a source address range in the memory window using the mouse. Right click on the memory window and choose **'compare'** from the pop-up menu. The **compare memory** dialog box opens as shown in Figure 4.28. Enter the **start address** of the destination memory area in the **compare address** field and the data length in the **data length** field. Check the **verify** check box. If you miss dragging the copy-source address range by any chance, you can enter the start and end address now. The **end address** can also be prefixed by a plus (+): the **end address** will become the **(start address)** + (the entered value).

Figure 4.28   Compare memory dialog box. Source: *HEW User Manual V.4.08*, page 386.

There exists only two cases, either mismatch or match. In the former case, the address where the mismatch was found is displayed in a message box. In the latter case, the message **"comparison successful"** appears.

■ **Saving memory contents in a text file:**

What if you want to edit the contents of some of the memory addresses, and before doing that you want to save those readings? HEW provides you the functionality of saving the memory contents in a text file using the **save memory contents** feature. First, select a source address range in the memory window by dragging the mouse. Right click on the memory window and choose **'save memory contents'** from the pop-up menu. The **save memory contents** dialog box opens as shown in Figure 4.29. Select the output range in the **memory save area field,** length of the data in the **data length** field, number of digits in the **column** field and the radix in the **radix** field. You can also select displaying/hiding the **Label column** and **Register column** by checking the **output the label column** and the **output the register column** fields, respectively. If you did not drag the address range to be saved, you must enter the output range.

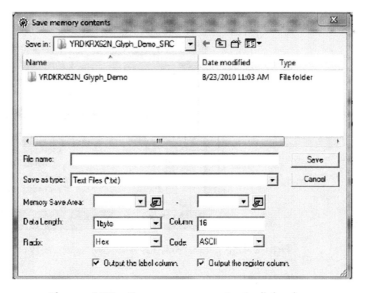

Figure 4.29   Save memory contents dialog box.

■ **Looking at I/O memory:**

A microcontroller contains various on-chip peripheral modules. The modules vary according to devices, but some of the common modules are DMA controllers, serial communications interfaces, A/D converters, integrated timer units, a bus state controller, and a watchdog timer. Accessing registers play a very important role in programming on-chip peripherals. Since the setting up of such on-chip peripheral registers is usually very important in an embedded microcontroller application, it would be very useful if we can look into the values of the registers. As discussed in the previous section, the memory view allows you to look at the data in the memory only as a byte, word, longword, single-precision floating-point, double-precision floating-point, or ASCII values. So the High-performance Embedded Workshop also provides an I/O window to analyze the values inside the registers.

■ **Opening the I/O window:**
To open the **I/O** window, click on the **view** tab on the menu bar. Select **CPU** from the drop down menu. Choose **I/O** to open the window or click the view I/O toolbar button ( ). Modules that match the on-chip peripheral modules organize the I/O register information. The I/O window has two tabs: **All Register** and **Selected Register.** When the **I/O** window is first opened, only a list of module names are shown on the **All Register** tabbed pane.

■ **Window configuration:**

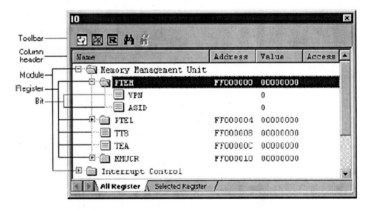

Figure 4.30   Input-output window. Source: *HEW User Manual V.4.08*, page 411.

The **All register tab** displays all I/O registers and the selected register tab displays selected I/O registers. By default, this page is blank. I/O registers can be used as and when required. While running the code, if the value of an I/O register is changed, the value is displayed in red. If you need to change the value of a register, then double click on the line of an I/O register. You can even record the value in a macro. In addition, the value can be changed in the **value** column by in-place editing. HEW provides various options which can be expanded by right-clicking on the I/O window. It will display a pop-up menu containing options such as **refresh, load I/O file, print, toolbar display, customize toolbar,** etc. For displaying the names, addresses and values of the I/O registers you can either double-click on the module name or select the module name. To select the module name, click on it or use the cursor keys, and press the right cursor key. The module display will expand to show the individual registers names, addresses, and their values. To close the I/O register display, once again double-click on the module name (or press the left cursor key).

▨ **Modifying the values of I/O registers:**
To modify the value of an I/O register, select either of the following:
In-place edit in the value column.

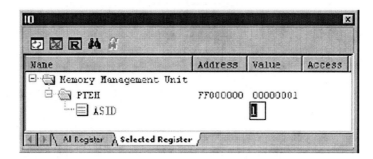

Figure 4.31   Selected register tab of Input-output window. Source: *HEW User Manual V.4.08,* page 413.

Double-click on the line of the I/O register or bit to open a dialog box.

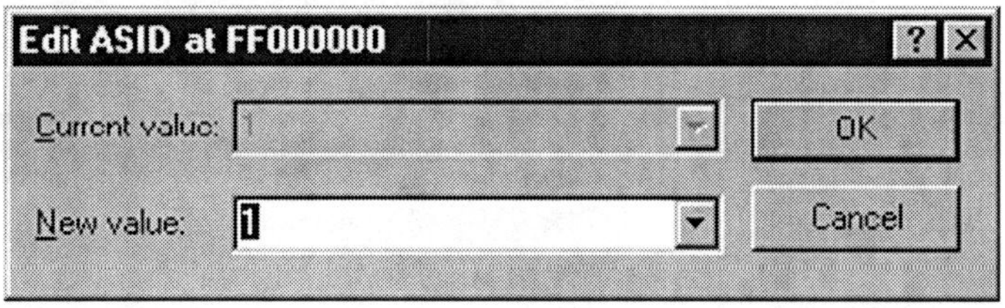

Figure 4.32   Edit dialog box. Source: *HEW User Manual V.4.08,* page 413.

▪ **Selecting the I/O register(s) for viewing:**
First, click on the **select register** tabbed pane of the I/O window. To view the value of the registers, open a pop-up menu by right-clicking within the window. Then select **I/O register,** and a dialog box will open as shown in Figure 4.33.

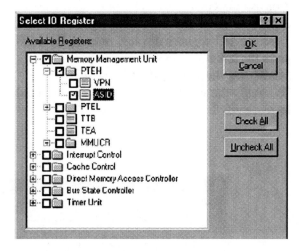

Figure 4.33 Selecting I/O register. Source: *HEW User Manual V.4.08,* page 414.

As you can see, there is a checkbox in front of every item; clicking on it selects the specific item. Clicking the '+' sign expands the collapsed item while clicking on '−' collapses the expanded item. If you select the checkbox for an item with '+' or '−' the checkboxes for all of its elements are also selected. Similarly, if you deselect the checkbox for an item, all of its elements are also deselected. You should select the checkboxes for the I/O register(s) you wish to view. After checking the item, click **OK** to close the dialog box. The selected I/O registers are shown on the **select I/O register** tabbed pane of the I/O window.

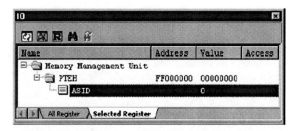

Figure 4.34 Selected register tab of Input-output window. Source: *HEW User Manual V.4.08,* page 415.

■ **Finding an I/O register:**
Many times you might want to know the value stored in a particular register. In such a case, instead of selecting an I/O register to view, you can try a faster way of directly accessing your desired register. In order to achieve this, right click within the window to open up a pop-up menu. After that select **find** and a dialog box will open as shown in Figure 4.35.

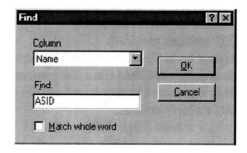

Figure 4.35   Find dialog box. Source: *HEW User Manual V.4.08,* page 416.

Fill in the fields one by one in any order you want. Select the **column** of an I/O register: you can select either the address or name of an I/O register. Then in the **find** field, select the string to be found in the selected column. The characters are case-insensitive. You can use the **'match whole word'** feature to completely match the string entered. If you type a more general word and want to see all registers that partially match with the entered string, then do not check the **'match whole word'** box. Finally, click **OK** to start the search from the first line.

4.4.2   The J-Link Debugger

(Source: http://www.segger.com/cms/jlink.html.J-Link Debugger)
The debugger used for the RX family is the J-Link Debugger. J-Link RX supports all RX-CPUs with RX600 core and JTAG interface. The RX610 Group, RX62N Group, and RX621 Group are compatible with this debugger. The J-Link RX is compatible to the Renesas E1 emulator and works with the Renesas HEW and the IAR Embedded Workbench for RX (EWRX).

Features

- Flash breakpoints are much faster on J-Link than on E1 or E20. J-Link uses different techniques like: Instruction set simulation, use of hardware breakpoints where possible, dynamic conversion of breakpoint types, flash caching, CRC, and others to minimize the amount of times a flash breakpoint is set or removed.
- It supports direct download into flash memory.
- It also supports software breakpoints in flash memory (Flash breakpoints).
- Seamless integration into the Renesas HEW & IAR Embedded Workbench IDE.
- Virtual UART support (C2E support) provided.
- All kinds of events are supported (execution break, data access, trace break, combination/sequence of events).
- USB 2.0 interface provided.
- JTAG speed up to 12 MHz or 25 MHz (depending on the J-Link model).
- No power supply required since it is powered through the USB.
- All JTAG signals can be monitored and the target voltage can be measured.
- Supports multiple devices.
- Wide target voltage range: 1.2V—3.3V, 5V tolerant.
- Target power supply: J-Link can supply up to 300 mA to target with overload protection.

4.4.3   Description of the Header Files Used in the RX Family

1. **<config.h>**
   This is a configuration file for the generic API for graphics LCD glyph; i.e., **"glyph.c"**. It defines macro names used in common in the **"glyph.h"** include file. The macros defined here can be used to select the font size. It includes a header file **"preamble.h"** which defines simple types and constants.

2. **<glyph.h>**
   This is the main header file for glyph API library. The Generic API for Graphics LCD (nicknamed "Glyph") is a reusable software design to support multiple projects where the LCD size and resolution may change, but the basic feature set will stay consistent. Glyph is a standard library interface for use with any graphic LCD. It uses macros already defined in the header file **"config.h"**. It defines external constants, typedef enumerations, typedef structures, prototype for minimum access, and prototype for full access.

   a. Type: External constant
      This declares constant values for various font sizes that will be available to all users of glyph API.

```
Example:
extern const uint8_t * FontHelvr10_table[256];
```

FontHelvr10_table is a macro defined in **"config.h"** that signifies the default font size.

b. Type: Typedef definition

The **typedef** keyword defines new types or provides an alternative name to the already existing types.

1) The **typedef** allows you to use **t_glyphhandle** as a type rather than using void*. Now, **t_glyphhandle** can be used to declare a pointer to the type void.

```
Example:
typedef void *T_glyphHandle.
```

2) The **enum** keyword is used to create an enumerated type that consists of constants that represent error identifiers of the glyph API. Since each subsequent value is incremented by one over the previous constant, the value of GLYPH_ERROR_ILLEGAL_OPERATION is 1.

```
Example:
typedef enum {
   GLYPH_ERROR_NONE = 0,
   GLYPH_ERROR_ILLEGAL_OPERATION
} T_glyphError;
```

3) The **enum** keyword is used to create enumerated type that consists of constants that represent status values of the glyph API. By default, the first constant in an enumeration is assigned value zero, and each subsequent value is incremented by one over the previous constant. In this particular case, since each constant is given a specific value, each subsequent value is not incremented. Instead, it retains the value that is set in the declaration.

```
Example:
typedef enum {
   GLYPH_STATUS_READY = 0,
   GLYPH_STATUS_BUSY = 2,
   GLYPH_STATUS_FULL = 4
} T_glyphStatusBits;
```

4) The **enum** keyword is used to create enumerated type that consists of constants that represent font values of the glyph API. By default, the first

constant in an enumeration is assigned value zero, and each subsequent value is incremented by one over the previous constant.

```
Example:
typedef enum {
    GLYPH_FONT_8_BY_8,
    GLYPH_FONT_8_BY_16,
    GLYPH_FONT_5_BY_7,
    . . . . . . . . . . . . . . . .
} T_glyphFont;
```

5) The **enum** keyword is used to create an enumerated type that consists of constants which define drawing modes of the glyph API. Since each subsequent value is incremented by one over the previous constant, the value of GLYPH_CMD_ERASE_BLOCK is 8.

```
Example:
typedef enum {
    GLYPH_CMD_NOP = 0,
    GLYPH_CMD_SCREEN_CLEAR,
    GLYPH_CMD_SCREEN_INVERT,
    GLYPH_CMD_SCREEN_REGULAR,
    . . . . . . . . . . . . . . . . . . . . . . . . . . . . . .
} T_glyphDrawMode;
```

6) Description: The **enum** keyword is used to create enumerated type that consists of constants that represent the glyph API registers. These are used by **Glyph Read** and **Glyph Write** to specify a function of the glyph API to run.

```
Example:
typedef enum {
    GLYPH_STATUS = 0,
    GLYPH_CHAR_X,
    GLYPH_CHAR_Y,
    . . . . .
    . . . . .
    . . . . .
    GLYPH_CONTRAST,
    GLYPH_CONTRAST_BOOST
} T_glyphRegisters;
```

7) A **struct** in C programming language is a collection of elements, in which each element belongs to a different type. The total storage required for a struct object is the sum of the storage requirements of all the elements. This typedef allows you to use **T_glyphVersionInfo** as a type rather than using a struct. Now, **T_glyphVersionInfo** can be used instead of **struct T_glyphVersionInfo** whenever you want to declare a new instance of the structure_glyph_version_info named T_glyphVersionInfo. The structure below contains elements that depict various versions of glyph API structure.

```
Example:
typedef struct_glyph_version_info
{
    uint8_t strVersionAPI[50];
    uint8_t strVersionIMPL[50];
    int32_t nVersionAPIMajor;
    int32_t nVersionAPIMinor;
    int32_t nVersionIMPLMajor;
    int32_t nVersionIMPLMinor;
    int32_t nImplementationID;
} T_glyphVersionInfo;
```

8) In future statements, you can use the specifier **T_LCD_API** (instead of the expanded struct T_LCD_API) to refer to the structure and create an instance. The structure below contains elements that are used in applications where LCD is required. This is a glyph API LCD structure which is frequently used by the LCD drivers.

```
Example:
typedef struct {
    /* Adding Font-Decal Section */
    const uint8_t ** iFont;
    /* Define Global Variables */
    uint32_t iCharX_Position;
    uint32_t iCharY_Position;
    uint32_t iCharX2_Position;
    uint32_t iCharY2_Position;
    uint32_t iCharFont;
    . . . . . .
    . . . . . .
    . . . . . .
```

```
        T_glyphError (*iWrite)(T_glyphHandle aHandle, uint32_t
        aRegister, uint32_t Value);
    } T_LCD_API;
```

9) In future statements, you can use the specifier T_Comm_API (instead of the expanded struct T_Comm_API) to refer to the structure and create an instance. The following structure contains elements that are used in applications where communication needs to be set up. This is a glyph API communication structure which is frequently used by the Communication drivers.

```
Example:
typedef struct {
    T_glyphError (*iOpen)(T_glyphHandle aHandle);
    void (*iCommandSend)(int8_t cCommand);
    void (*iDataSend)(int8_t cData);
} T_Comm_API;
```

10) In future statements, you can use the specifier T_glyphworkspace (instead of the expanded struct T_glyphworkspace) to refer to the structure and create an instance. The following structure contains elements that are used in applications where LCD is required and communication needs to be set up. This is a glyph API workspace structure which is frequently used by Communication and LCD drivers.

```
Example:
typedef struct {
    T_LCD_API *iLCDAPI;
    T_Comm_API *iCommAPI;
} T_glyphWorkspace;
```

c. Type: Function

Glyph API provides you the capability to interact with the graphical LCD. The prototypes defined in the following example are used to access the glyph API library definitions. Its implementation totally depends on the type of application. These prototypes define the functions for minimum and full access of the members of the glyph libraray.

```
Examples:
Prototypes for minimum access:
T_glyphError GlyphOpen(T_glyphHandle *aHandle, int32_t
    aAddress);
```

```
T_glyphError GlyphClose(T_glyphHandle *aHandle);
T_glyphError GlyphWrite(T_glyphHandle aHandle,
    uint32_t aRegister, uint32_t * aValue);
T_glyphError GlyphRead(T_glyphHandle aHandle,
    uint32_t aRegister, uint32_t *aValue);
Prototypes for full access:
T_glyphError GlyphGetStatus(T_glyphHandle aHandle,
    T_glyphStatusBits *aStatus);
T_glyphError GlyphSetX(T_glyphHandle aHandle, uint32_t aX);
T_glyphError GlyphSetY(T_glyphHandle aHandle, uint32_t aY);
. . . . . . . .
. . . . . . . .
T_glyphError GlyphSetContrastBoost(T_glyphHandle aHandle,
    uint8_t cContrastBoost);
```

3. **<preamble.h>**

    Description: This header file contains basic definitions of all simple constants
    and types. The purpose of this file is to maintain compatibility between the com-
    pilers and hardware. It defines macros which can be used in other header files or
    in source code of any application.

    a. Type: Constant.

    ```
    Example:
    #define ON 1
    #define OFF 0
    #define ENABLE 1
    #define DISABLE 0
    ```

    b. Type: Typedef definitions.

    In future statements, any variable can be used as a type instead of its pre-
    existing type. For instance, Int8_t can be used as a type instead of a signed
    char.

    ```
    Example:
    typedef signed char int8_t;
    typedef unsigned char uint8_t;
    typedef signed short int16_t;
    ```

c. Type: Bit definitions.
A bit from b0 to b7 signifies some hexadecimal value as defined in the following example.

```
Example:
#define b0 0x01
#define b4 0x10
#define b7 0x80
```

4. **<st7579_lcd.h>**
Description: It defines prototypes that are required by the LCD driver in the glyph API. It includes all the definitions of "glyph.h".
Note: The name of the header file comes from st7579 which is a driver and controller LSI for the graphic dot-matrix liquid crystal display systems. This chip is connected directly to a microprocessor, accepts 3-line serial peripheral interface (SPI) with a four wire independent transmit only, displays data, and can store an on-chip display data RAM of 68×102 bits.

a. Type: Macros
These macros signify function sets, which are used to define the function set call for every command that is sent to the ST7579 Display controller. When setting the display controller to the four different function sets of commands to be sent to the controller, setting the function set also sets the following:

```
MX direction: normal or reverse i[0:1]
MY direction: normal or reverse [0:1]
PD controller active or power down [0:1]
```

If the preprocessor directive #if, is set to 1, then every Function Set call will produce MY set to the reverse direction. This is required for Glyph to work. Otherwise, MY will be set to the normal direction and Glyph will not work. These function sets do not take any arguments and do not return any value.

```
Example:
#if 1
//MY reverse direction
#define LCD_FUNCTION_ZERO 0X28
#define LCD_FUNCTION_ONE 0X29
#define LCD_FUNCTION_TWO 0X2A
#define LCD_FUNCTION_THREE 0X2B
//command sets
#define LCD_DISPLAY_REVERSE 0x280D
```

```
#define LCD_DISPLAY_NORMAL 0x280C
#else
//MY normal direction
#define LCD_FUNCTION_ZERO 0X20
#define LCD_FUNCTION_ONE 0X21
#define LCD_FUNCTION_TWO 0X22
#define LCD_FUNCTION_THREE 0X23
//command sets
#define LCD_DISPLAY_REVERSE 0x200D
#define LCD_DISPLAY_NORMAL 0x200C
#endif
```

b. Type: Functions

   1) The prototypes defined in the following example are used to access "glyph LCD API" library definitions.

```
Example:
T_glyphError ST7579_Open(T_glyphHandle aHandle,
  uint32_t aAddress);
T_glyphError ST7579_Close(T_glyphHandle aHandle);
T_glyphError ST7579_Write(T_glyphHandle aHandle,
  uint32_t aRegister, uint32_t aValue);
T_glyphError ST7579_Read(T_glyphHandle aHandle,
  uint32_t aRegister, uint32_t *aValue);
```

   2) The prototypes defined in following example are used to access "LCD API" library definitions.

```
Example:
void ST7579_Config(T_glyphHandle aHandle);
void ST7579_SetSystemBiasBooster(T_glyphHandle aHandle,
  int8_t c Value 0 To 17);
void ST7579_SetVO_Range(T_glyphHandle aHandle,
  int32_t n Value 0 to 254);
```

5. <YRDKRX62N_RSPI0.h>

Description: This header file defines prototypes for the glyph communication API.

NOTE:

The name of the header file indicates the hardware it is associated with. It is Y Renesas Development Kit (RDK) for Renesas RX62N Group CPU. The transmitter number is 0 and the operational channel is 3.

The Chip Select for the flash device (LCD) is set to PC_2. This is the RSPI channel used to communicate with the ST7579 Graphics Display. The RSPI configuration has the baud rate generator set for maximum speed, which is PLCK/2 or 25 MHz. The communications protocol followed is SPI 3-Wire Transmit only MASTER SPI. Its Slave Device is OKAYA LCD with a ST2579 microprocessor.

```
Example:
void YRDKRX62N_CommandSend(int8_t cCommand);
void YRDKRX62N_DataSend(int8_t cData);
T_glyphError YRDKRX62N_RSPIOpen(T_glyphHandle aHandle);
```

6. **<typedefine.h>**
   Description: In further statements, any variable can be used as a type instead of its pre-existing type. For instance, _SBYTE can be used as a type instead of signed char. Here, an underscore before the variable name SBYTE signifies that it is a global variable.

```
Example:

typedef signed char _SBYTE;
typedef unsigned char _UBYTE;
typedef signed short _SWORD;
```

7. **<sbrk.h>**
   Description: This is a header file for sbrk.c. It defines a macro that signifies the size of the area managed by sbrk.

```
Example:
#define HEAPSIZE 0x400
```

8. **<vect.h>**
   Description: This header file defines various vectors. The vector list is basically a list which indicates where the ISRs (interrupt subroutines) are located in memory. Each entry in the list is called a vector. Vector signifies the four bytes address of each ISR. Some of the vectors are reserved—like vector 16 is reserved by an interrupt Excep_BUSERR; i.e., the ISR to be called when exception happens during a bus error; and the rest of them are free to be occupied. Vector table starts with the vectors that refer to the fixed interrupts. These vectors cannot be changed since they point to ISRs at hardware-defined addresses such as undefined instruction, supervisor instruction, floating point, NMI, Dummy, or BRK. Then comes the variable vectors that point to ISRs at user-definable vectors.

```
Example:
Fixed interrupts:
//Exception(Supervisor Instruction)
#pragma interrupt (Excep_SuperVisorInst)
void Excep_SuperVisorInst(void);
//Exception(Undefined Instruction)
#pragma interrupt (Excep_UndefinedInst)
Variable Interrupts:
#pragma interrupt (Excep_BUSERR(vect = 16))
void Excep_BUSERR(void);
//vector 17 reserved
//vector 18 reserved
//vector 19 reserved
//vector 20 reserved
//FCU_FCUERR
#pragma interrupt (Excep_FCU_FCUERR(vect = 21))
void Excep_FCU_FCUERR(void);
//vector 22 reserved
```

9. **<stacksct.h>**
    Description: This header file defines macros that refer to the setting of the stack area.

    ```
    Example:
    #pragma stacksize su = 0x300
    #pragma stacksize si = 0x100
    ```

10. **<iodefine_RX62N.h>**
    Description: This header file uses numerous macros, about sixty-eight structures, one union, and four enumerations to define the various input and output registers.

    Example:
    a. Macros:

    ```
    #pragma bit_order left
    #pragma unpack
    #define SYSTEM (* (volatile struct st_system
        __evenaccess *)0x80000)
    #define BSC (* (volatile struct st_bsc __evenaccess *)0x81300)
    #define IEN__IRQ1 IEN1
    #define IEN__IRQ2 IEN2
    ```

b. Structure:

The structure below defines various input and output registers that are used in analog to digital conversion. Within the structure, a union is being used to declare variables of different types. It is the same as structure, except that instead of struct you write union. Also, in union you can only store information in one field at any one time. Technically, it can be seen as a chunk of memory that is used to store variables of different types. Once a new value is assigned to a field, the existing data is wiped over and rewritten with the new data.

```
Example:
struct st_da {
    unsigned short DADR0;
    unsigned short DADR1;
    union {
        unsigned char BYTE;
        struct {
            unsigned char DAOE1:1;
            unsigned char DAOE0:1;
            unsigned char DAE:1;
            unsigned char:5;
        } BIT;
    } DACR;
    union {
        unsigned char BYTE;
        struct {
            unsigned char DPSEL:1;
            unsigned char:7;
        } BIT;
    } DADPR;
};
```

In this example, the structure **st_da** contains four members; namely DADR0, DADR1, union DACR, and a union DADPR. This is an example of nested unions. Union DACR has two members. BYTE and structure BIT. The BIT member is a structure with four bit-field members, DAOE1, DAOE0, DAE and one nameless field member, all of them are of type unsigned char. Member BYTE is of type unsigned char. Union DADPR has two members, BYTE and structure BIT. The BIT member is a structure with two bit-field members, DPSEL and one nameless field member, both of which are of type unsigned char. Member BYTE is of type unsigned char. At any given time, each union element holds either the unsigned char represented by BYTE or the structure represented by BIT. The other two variables of st_da are of type unsigned char. Table 4.6 provides an explanation of the terms that were used in the previous example.

TABLE 4.6   Register Description.

ADDRESS	NUMBER OF BITS	MODULE-ABBREVIATION	REGISTER NAME	REGISTER ABBREVIATION
0008 80C0h	16	D/A	D/A data register 0	DADR0
0008 80C2h	16	D/A	D/A data register 1	DADR1
0008 80C4h	8	D/A	D/A control register	DACR
0008 80C5h	8	D/A	D/A data placement register	DADPR

c. Enumerations:

These are used to define various ICU registers.

1) Usage of some specific registers such as IR (interrupt register), DTCER (DTC activation enable register), IER (interrupt request enable register), and IPR (Interrupt source priority register) follows. The bit access operation is "bit name (interrupt source, name)". A part of the interrupt source can be omitted.

```
Example:
IR(TPU0,TGI0A) = 0;
DTCER( ,IRQ0) = 1;
IEN(CMT0,CMI0) = 1;
IPR(MTU0,TGIA0) = 3;
IPR(MTU0,TGI ) = 3;   //TGIA0,TGIB0,TGIC0,TGID0 is same
level.
IPR(CMT0, CMI0) = 1;
IPR(CMT0, ) = 1;   //CMT0 interrupt is only one factor.
```

2) Usage of the interrupts listed in vector table:

#pragma interrupt Function_Identifier (vect = **).The number of vector is "(interrupt source, name)".

```
Example:
#pragma interrupt INT_MTU0_TGIA0(vect = VECT(MTU0,TGIA0))
#pragma interrupt INT_IRQ0 (vect = VECT( ,IRQ0))
#pragma interrupt INT_CMT0_CMI0 (vect = VECT(CMT0,CMI0))
```

3) Usage of some specific system registers such as MSTPCRA (Module stop control register A), MSTPCRB (Module stop control register B), MSTPCRC (Module stop control register C), and MSTPCRD (Module stop control register D) is given as follows: The bit access operation is "MSTP (name)". The name that can be used is a macro name defined with "iodefine.h".

```
Example:
MSTP (TMR2) = 0;    //TMR Unit 1 (TMR3/TMR2)
MSTP (PPG1) = 0;    //PPG1
MSTP (MTU6) = 0;    //MTU Unit 1 (TPU6 to TPU11)
MSTP (CMT3) = 0;    //CMT Unit 1 (CMT2/CMT3)
```

4.5   ADVANCED EXAMPLES

(Source: *HEW User Manual V.4.08.*)

EXAMPLE 1

This example demonstrates how to look at the contents of the CPU's general registers.

To view the contents, first open the register window. For this, click on the **view** tab on the menu bar, and in the popup menu select **CPU** from the drop down menu. Choose **register** to open the window or click on the registers toolbar button (▣).The Register window gives the status of current register and flag data. You can even modify the register/flag value from the window.

Window Configuration

Double-clicking the register display line opens a dialog box, which allows you to change a register value. Everything can be recorded by macro recording. This is helpful in a case where you want to get back to older values. The easy way to change the register's contents is by using in-place editing. Also, you can change a flag value by clicking the button corresponding to the flag. If you right click on the window, you can change the display radix point and the register bank.

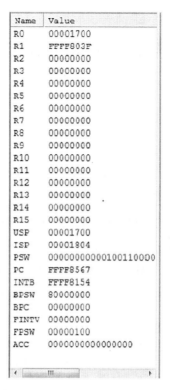

Name	Value
R0	00001700
R1	FFFF803F
R2	00000000
R3	00000000
R4	00000000
R5	00000000
R6	00000000
R7	00000000
R8	00000000
R9	00000000
R10	00000000
R11	00000000
R12	00000000
R13	00000000
R14	00000000
R15	00000000
USP	00001700
ISP	00001804
PSW	00000000000100110000
PC	FFFF8567
INTB	FFFF8154
BPSW	80000000
BPC	00000000
FINTV	00000000
FPSW	00000100
ACC	0000000000000000

Figure 4.36   Register window.

Popup menu:

Changing the Register Display Radix

To change the display radix, right click the mouse on the register to be changed and select **display radix** from the pop-up menu. You can select one of the four radix options shown in Table 4.7.

Setting the Layout

To change the layout of the register window, choose **layout** from the pop-up menu. The following settings are displayed:

Radix: It Switches display or non-display of the radix.

TABLE 4.7 Display Radix Point and the Register Bank Options.

MENU OPTION	FUNCTION
Radix: Hex	Displays in hexadecimal
Dec	Displays in Decimal
Oct	Displays in Octal
Bin	Displays in Binary
Layout: Radix	Switches display or non-display of radix
FLAGs	Switches display or non-display of flags display area
Settings	Chooses a register to be displayed
Edit	Changes a register's contents
Refresh	Refreshes the Register window
Lock Refresh	Disables refresh of the Register window
Split	Splits up the window display
Save To File	Saves register contents in a text file
Source: *HEW User Manual V.4.08,* page 418.	

Flags: It Switches display or non-display of the flags display area.

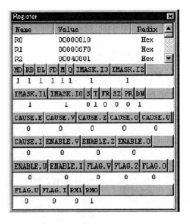

Figure 4.37 Displays the radix and flags. Source: *HEW User Manual V.4.08,* page 420.

Choosing a Register to be Displayed

Figure 4.38 shows the dialog box which is displayed when you choose the **settings** tab from the **register** pop-up menu. In this way you can choose a register to be displayed in the Register window.

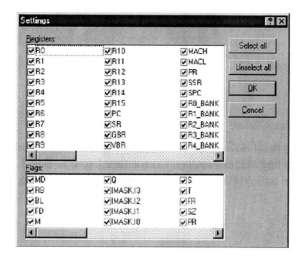

Figure 4.38   Settings dialog box to select register to be displayed. Source: *HEW User Manual V.4.08,* page 420.

Modifying the Register Contents

To change the register contents, enter a value in the **value** field of the register as shown in Figure 4.39.

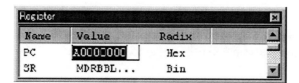

Figure 4.39   In place modification of register value. Source: *HEW User Manual V.4.08,* page 421.

To change a register's contents, open the **Set Value** dialog box as described in the following and select one of the operations:

1. Double-click the register to be changed.
2. Select the register and choose the Edit option from the pop-up menu.

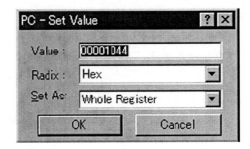

Figure 4.40 Set value dialog box. Source: *HEW User Manual V.4.08,* page 421.

Setting the Flag Value

When the flag itself is displayed, click the flag which you want to change. Every time a flag is clicked, the flag status switches from either 1 to 0 or 0 to 1. If a flag is composed of multiple bits, then a dialog box will open, where you can enter a value.

Screenshot:

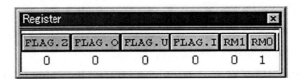

Figure 4.41 Flag status. Source: *HEW User Manual V.4.08,* page 422.

When the flag is displayed in the register, double-click the FLG line. A dialog box will open and then you can enter the value to be changed.

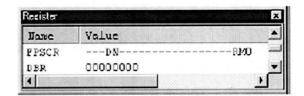

Figure 4.42 Debugger (FLG line (FPSCR)). Source: *HEW User Manual V.4.08,* page 422.

Saving Register Contents

To save the register contents in a text file, choose **Save to file** from the register pop-up menu. The **Save As** dialog box will open, which allows you to specify the file name.

EXAMPLE 2

Displaying memory contents as waveforms.

NOTE:

Support for this function depends on the debugger.

To analyze the data that has just been saved into the memory, creating a waveform could be a very good option. It gives insight into how your code is responding to the application that you are making. For creating a waveform, first you need to open the **waveform properties** dialog box. Click on the **view** tab on the menu bar, select **graphics,** and then **waveform** to get the **waveform** window. The other way is to just click on the waveform toolbar button (⊟).

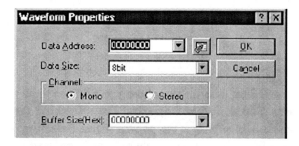

Figure 4.43   Waveform properties dialog box. Source: *HEW User Manual V.4.08,* page 407.

You need to fill in the properties before going any further. For **data address** property, you need to specify the start address of the data in memory. It should be displayed in hexadecimal. **Data size** property signifies the size of the data, which can be either 8 bit or 16 bit. Two types of channels are supported: **mono** and **stereo.** Select **buffer size** to specify the buffer size of the data in hexadecimals. Now click the **OK** button to open the **waveform** window. You can change the display contents later by right clicking the window and choosing **'properties'** from the pop-up menu. In the pop-up menu, some of the other fields are zoom in, zoom out, zoom magnification, scaling, refresh now, etc.

Figure 4.44 shows the display of the memory contents as a waveform. The *X*-coordinate refers to the number of sampling data and the *Y*-coordinate refers to the sampling value.

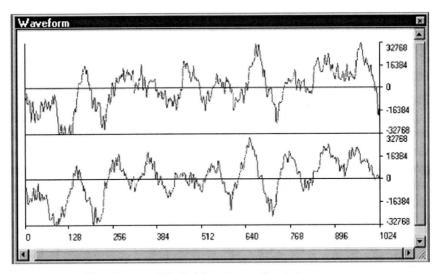

Figure 4.44   Memory contents as waveform. Source: *HEW User Manual V.4.08*, page 407.

If you double-click the coordinate where you wish to view the sampling information, the **sample information** dialog box appears. For refreshing the window, there is a function called **auto refresh,** available in the pop-up menu. Selecting **auto refresh** and then **non refresh** will not refresh the window. Selecting **auto refresh** and then **stop** from the pop-up menu will allow the window contents to be automatically refreshed. Selecting **auto refresh** and then **real time** from the pop-up menu will allow the window contents to be refreshed while the user program is running. To specify the refresh interval, select **update interval** from the pop-up menu. This item can be selected only when it is supported by the debugger.

4.6   REFERENCES

RX Compiler Package, http://america.renesas.com/products/tools/coding_tools/c_compilers_assemblers/rx_compiler/rx_c_tools_product_landing.jsp

Hardware Manual, Renesas 32-Bit Microcomputer, RX Family/RX600 Series. Renesas Electronics America, Inc., 2010. Print.

Compiler Package User Manual, Renesas 32-Bit Microcomputer, RX Family/RX600 Series. Renesas Electronics America, Inc., 2010. Print.

High-performance Embedded Workshop V.4.08, User's Manual. Renesas Electronics America, Inc., 2010. Print.

4.7 EXERCISES

1. What is the difference between compilers used for embedded systems and compilers used for desktops PCs?
2. How does the linker differ from the compiler?
3. Other than macro definition, for what purpose can the "#define" identifier can be used?
4. What are the various phases of the building process in HEW?
5. Where in HEW debugger options are saved and why?
6. Can all debuggers display the contents of the memory as a waveform?
7. For what purpose is synchronized debugging used?
8. We have an integer array called x. All the numbers from 1 to 100 appear exactly once in x but the numbers are not sorted (e.g., the order can be $x[100] = \{2; 10; 3; 8; 9; 4; 97; 94; \ldots\ldots\ldots .37; 99\}$). Due to alpha particles destroying a particular entry in x, a number is missing and is read as 0 when accessed. Use less than ten lines of C code (one statement per line) to find the missing number (not the index) and put it in an integer variable called missing. Don't forget to include proper documentation suggested in coding guidelines (comments, header, etc.).

   (Hint: consider the current $\sum_{i=0}^{99} x[i]$ and what the uncorrupted value of $\sum_{i=0}^{99} x[i]$ would be).

9. What is the one thing that all of our code should have?
   a. Your name and file name in comments at the top of every file.
   b. Twelve subroutines.
   c. A while(1) loop in every subroutine.
   d. A function call to the ST7579_LCD.c file.
   e. None of the above.
10. Which header file defines prototypes for the glyph communication API?
    a. yrdkrx62n_rspio.h
    b. config.h
    c. ST7579_lcd.h
    d. glyph.h
    e. sbrk.h

11. Which header file is mandatory to include in source code if your code uses an Interrupt Subroutine?
    a. <stacksct.h>
    b. <vect.h>
    c. ST7579_lcd.h
    d. glyph.h
    e. sbrk.h

12. Which of the following fully describes the outcome of the code below?

```
int i, sum;
sum = 0;
i = 0;
for(i = N; i < 100; i++)
{
    if((i % 2))
    sum += i;
}
```

    a. Add all the numbers from 0 to 100 and put the result in sum.
    b. Add all the odd numbers from 0 to 100 and put the result in sum.
    c. Add all the even numbers from 0 to 100 and put the result in sum.
    d. Add all the odd numbers from N to 100 and put the result in sum.
    e. Add all the even numbers from N to 100 and put the result in sum.

13. Which of the following is not a part of the compiler?
    a. Linker
    b. Pre-processor
    c. Code generator
    d. Garbage collector
    e. Parser

14. Consider the code below. The first printf statement below prints "1C3F". What is printed by the second printf?

```
union {
    int w;
    char b[2];
} x;
x.w = 0x1C3F;
printf("%X \ n", x.w);
x.b[1] = 0xA6;
printf("%X \ n", x.w);
```

a. 1C3F
b. A63F
c. 1CA6
d. 1A6F
e. None of the above.

15. In C, the term *volatile* is applied to a variable in order to:
    a. Tell the compiler that a variable's value may change due to forces other than the program in which the variable appears.
    b. Tell the compiler that a variable's value is not constant.
    c. Mark that a variable may be optimized out of the code when unused.
    d. Tell the compiler to store the variable's value in "volatile" ram instead of "non-volatile" ram, such as an EEPROM.
    e. None of the above.

16. For our processor and compiler, does the stack grow toward larger or smaller addresses?
    a. Larger
    b. Neither
    c. Smaller
    d. Both
    e. None of the above

17. For our processor and compiler,
    a. How many bytes are required to represent the data type: char?
       1) 1   **2)** 2   **3)** 3   **4)** 4   **5)** 8
    b. How many bytes are required to represent the data type: int?
       1) 1   **2)** 2   **3)** 3   **4)** 4   **5)** 8
    c. How many bytes are required to represent the data type: short?
       1) 1   **2)** 2   **3)** 3   **4)** 4   **5)** 8
    d. How many bytes are required to represent the data type: long?
       1) 1   **2)** 2   **3)** 3   **4)** 4   **5)** 8
    e. How many bytes are required to represent the data type: float?
       1) 1   **2)** 2   **3)** 3   **4)** 4   **5)** 8

18. A C source program is converted into an executable file with the help of:
    a. An interpreter
    b. A compiler
    c. An operating system
    d. None of the above

19. Which among the following best describes a header file?
   a. A file that consists of functions
   b. A file that consists of definitions and macros
   c. A file that is a main source file
   d. A file that consists of standard library functions

20. State the difference between the following two #include directives:

```
#include <"Config.h">
#include <Config.h>
```

Chapter Five

Software Engineering for Embedded Systems

5.1 LEARNING OBJECTIVES

We have tremendous flexibility when creating software; we make many decisions going from an idea to a final working system. There are **technical decisions,** such as which components we use to build a system, their internal structure, and how we interconnect them. Some of the technical decisions will lead to a product that works, but not all will. There are also **process decisions,** such as how we plan to build the system and how to select those components. Similarly, some process decisions can lead to an easier or more predictable development effort, while others will lead to project delays or cancellation, or can even bankrupt the company. A good software process will evolve over time, incorporating lessons learned from each project's successes and failures. Hence a good process will make it easier to do the technical work. The goal of this chapter is to show how both **process** and **technical** issues need to be considered to successfully create a product on time and on budget.

In this chapter we try to present just the most critical concepts to help the reader understand that "does the code work?" is **one question,** but **not the only question** to answer. There are many excellent books and articles which go into great depth on software engineering for embedded and general purpose software; a few are listed in the references section. For example, Jack Ganssle has a "top ten list" of why embedded systems projects get into trouble (Ganssle, J.). In this chapter we discuss how a good software engineering process addresses eight of them. Phil Koopman presents a detailed and practical book on embedded software development processes and issues (Koopman, P.). We will refer the reader to specific chapters in the latter text periodically in order to keep this chapter short and readable.

5.2 INTRODUCTION

5.2.1 Risk Reduction

Reducing risks is a driving force behind software engineering and project management. A software development organization can benefit by constantly refining its processes as it learns both what it does well, and how to improve what it does poorly.

Developing embedded software is usually **unpredictable.** For example:

- What if there is a bug in our code? What if the compiler sometimes seems to generate buggy code?
- What if the code we need to write actually turns out to be a lot more complex than we thought?
- What if we don't have enough memory for our program or its data? What if the processor can't run our code fast enough?
- What if activating a motor resets the processor due to a weak power supply?
- What if that external A/D converter peripheral doesn't seem to work the way the datasheet said it would?
- What if the lead developer wins the lottery and quits a month before the product deadline?
- What if the new developer we hired turns out to be incompetent, lazy, or both?
- What if half of our development team gets sick, is laid off, or is reassigned?
- What if the customer adds new requirements every week, or wants the product done two months early?

If any of these risks actually occur they will increase the amount of development work needed. Whether it affects the product development deadlines depends on how much overtime the development team is willing to put in, whether other developers can help out, whether anything in the development process turns out to be faster than expected, and so forth. Missing deadlines will have negative financial impacts: project costs will increase and income from product sales will be delayed. Some of these risks also have other impacts: higher power consumption, fewer features, board redesign, and so forth.

Ganssle identifies "Unrealistic Schedules" as the number one reason for embedded system project problems. Successful software organizations create a **development plan** for the project to show development tasks and output products, as well as risk management approaches. Koopman discusses development plans in detail in Chapters 2 through 4 of his book *Better Embedded System Software* (Koopman).

5.3 SOFTWARE DEVELOPMENT STAGES

5.3.1 Development Lifecycle Overview

The embedded product lifecycle has multiple steps, as shown in Figure 5.1.

The software process consists of multiple steps within the embedded product lifecycle. One example process model is the V model, shown in Figure 5.2. It consists of:

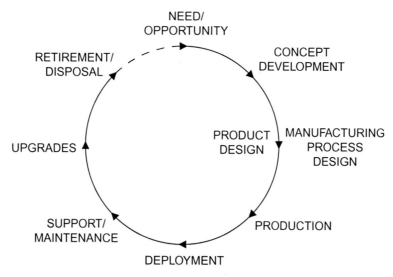

Figure 5.1   The embedded product lifecycle. Courtesy P. Koopman.

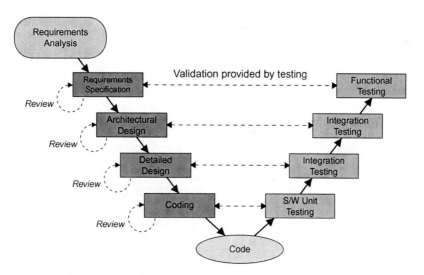

Figure 5.2   The "V" model of software development emphasizes testing at each level of design detail.

▪ Defining system requirements.
▪ Creating an architectural or high-level design, deciding on the general approach to build the system, and then creating appropriate hardware and software architectures.

- Creating detailed designs.
- Implementing code and performing unit testing.
- Integrating the code components and performing integration testing.
- Changing the code after "completion" to fit custom deployment requirements, fix bugs, add features, etc.

The process breaks a problem into smaller easier problems through the process of **top-down design** or **decomposition.** Each small problem is solved and the solutions are combined into a software solution. There are many approaches possible:

- Do we design everything up front, and then code it? This is called a **big up-front design.**
- Do we have a prototype or a previous version which we can build upon?
- Do we design and build a little at a time?
- What do we work on first, the easy or the hard parts?

Which model we should use depends on the types and severity of risks. Some industries may be required to follow a specific development process in order for the product to receive certification. Ganssle identifies "Poorly Defined Process" as reason number six for embedded system project troubles.

In this chapter we will use an example embedded system to illustrate the issues involved. Our target system is an electronic chartplotter for boats. The chartplotter can display a depth chart on a graphical LCD with an icon superimposed to show the boat's current position and direction, as shown in Figure 5.3. This helps the user steer the boat to avoid shallow water. Alternatively, we may choose to have a numerical display and omit the chart, as shown

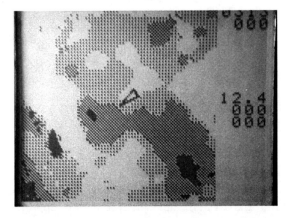

Figure 5.3   Chartplotter screen with boat icon overlaid on depth chart.

Figure 5.4   Chartplotter screen with numerical depth and speed information.

in Figure 5.4. The chartplotter receives position, direction, and speed information from a GPS receiver, and depth and battery voltage information from a depth sounder.

Later in this chapter we discuss various development models. At this point, it is sufficient to understand that there are different ways to "slice and dice" the work to be done, keeping in mind that we should develop each sub-system in the order: **architect-design-implement.** For example, don't start writing code if you haven't designed the algorithm yet. This sequencing is quite important, so we discuss it further.

5.3.2   Requirements

A system design begins with functional requirements. Ganssle identifies "Vague Requirements" as reason number five for projects getting into trouble. Koopman presents an excellent discussion of software requirements (Chapters 5 through 9) so we will just present a high-level view here.

- Requirements should be **written down.** This helps everyone have the same picture of what needs to be accomplished, and makes omissions easier to spot.
- There are three types of requirements. **Functional** requirements define what the system needs to do. **Nonfunctional** requirements describe emergent system behaviors such as response time, reliability, and energy efficiency. **Constraints** define the limits on the system design, such as cost and implementation choices.
- There are multiple ways to **express requirements,** both in text and graphically. The most appropriate and convenient method should be used. Graphical methods

such as state charts, flow charts, and message sequence charts should be used whenever possible because (1) they concisely convey the necessary information and (2) they often can be used as design documents.

■ Requirements should be **traceable to tests.** How will the system be tested to ensure that a requirement is met? Requirements should be quantified and measurable.

■ The requirements should be **stable.** Frequent changes to requirements ("churn") often have side effects and disrupt the ideal prioritization of work tasks. It is easy for the latest changed requirement to be interpreted as the most important requirement, when in fact this is rarely the case.

5.3.3   Design Before Coding

One of the most effective ways to reduce risks in developing software is to **design before writing code**[1]. Ganssle identifies "Starting Coding Too Soon" as reason number nine for projects getting into trouble. We refer to high-level design as the architecture, and the low-level design as the detailed design.

■ **Writing code locks you in to specific implementations** of an algorithm, data structure, object, interface method, and so forth. If this happens before you understand the rest of the system, then you probably haven't made the best possible choice, and may end up having to make major changes to the code you've written, or maybe even throw it away.

■ Designing the system before coding also gives you an **early insight** into what parts are needed, and which ones are likely to be complex. This helps prevent the surprises which slow down development. One of the best ways of reducing schedule risk is to understand the system in depth before creating a schedule, and then add in extra time buffers for dealing with the risky parts. **Estimation** is the process of predicting how long it will take to create the system.

■ Designs should include graphical documents such as flowcharts and state machines when possible. The goal is to have a **small and concise set of documents** which define how the system should do its work. Graphical representations are easier to understand than code because they abstract away many implementation details, leaving just the relevant items[2]. This makes it easy for others to understand your design and identify risks. It also helps bring new hires up to speed on the project and reduces the chances they'll break something when they start maintaining or enhancing the code.

---

[1] There is related prior work in carpentry: Think thrice, measure twice, cut once.

[2] Different businesses may have differing levels of formality (e.g., UML), but do not underestimate the benefit of a simple diagram (whether hand-written or created in Visio).

5.3.4   Peer Reviews of Design Artifacts

It is very helpful to have other team members review artifacts before proceeding to the next phase of development. First, having another perspective on an issue brings in greater experience and helps detect oversights. Ganssle identifies "Bad Science" as reason number seven for projects getting into trouble. Second, if you know that someone else will be reviewing what you are creating, you are likely to be more careful and professional. Peer reviews should be applied to all development artifacts: **requirements, test plans, architecture, detailed designs,** and **code.** We refer the reader elsewhere for more details on peer reviews (Koopman).

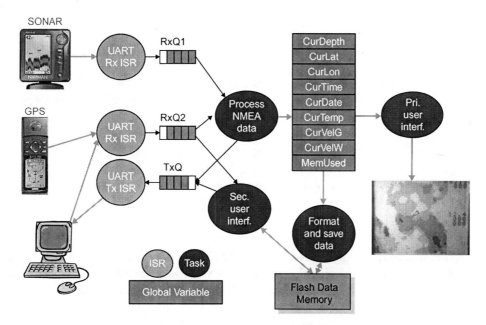

Figure 5.5   System architecture for chartplotter.

5.3.5   System Architecture and Design Approach

The system architecture defines your approach to building the system. What pieces are there, and how are they connected? What type of microcontroller and peripherals will be used? What major pieces of software will there be? How do they communicate? What will make them run at the right time? We present a summary of architectural concepts here, and encourage the reader to dig deeper in the referenced text (see Chapter 10 and Chapter 11 in Koopman).

In Figure 5.5 we see the system architecture for the chartplotter. Sonar and GPS information is delivered through two serial ports to the system. We will use interrupt service routines and queues to buffer the data between the serial ports and the main application task code. There are four separate tasks in the system:

- The Process NMEA Data task will receive the data from the sonar and GPS, decode it, and update the relevant variables which indicate current depth, position, and so forth.
- The Primary User Interface task will update the display.
- The Format and Save Data task will convert the depth and other variables into a human-readable text format and write them to flash memory.
- The Secondary User Interface task will provide a serial console interface so we can read the logged data from flash memory, erase it, and perform other system maintenance functions.

We also see how information is shared between tasks in the system:

- Queues buffer the incoming and outgoing serial data.
- A table of global variables is written by Process NMEA Data and read by two other tasks.

How does this architecture meet the most critical aspects of the requirements? These may be related to time, safety, robustness, or something else which is application-specific. In any case it is important to convey these concepts.

Time-Critical Processing

It is quite helpful to have a section in the architecture document which describes **which processing is time-critical,** and **how the system is architected** to ensure the timing requirements are met. For example, consider a light dimmer controller:

The system must switch power outputs within 50 microseconds of a zero-crossing of the AC power line. Failure to switching within this time will lead to electrical noise and interference with other devices. The system is designed so that a hardware analog window comparator detects zero crossings and triggers a non-maskable interrupt. All power output switching is performed by the ISR, which controls its outputs based on flags set by the main code which indicates which outputs to enable. Hence interrupts must not be disabled for longer than x microseconds.

The system must shut down within 10 ms of an overcurrent or overvoltage condition occurring. Failure to shut down within this time can lead to equipment damage and failure. We plan to use a periodic interrupt running at 1 kHz in order to sample dedicated analog hardware comparators which detect these conditions. Because of the 1 kHz interrupt rate, interrupts must not be disabled for longer than 8 ms, in order to allow a 1 ms safety margin.

Further information on real-time system design is available in Chapter 14 of the referenced text (Koopman).

Safety-Critical Processing

It is quite helpful to have a section in the architecture document which describes **which processing is safety-critical** and **how the system is architected,** to ensure the safety requirements are met. For example:

The software tasks X, Y, and Z are safety-critical. They cannot be modified without triggering recertification. In order to ensure real-time performance, we use a preemptive scheduler and assign X, Y, and Z priorities higher than all other tasks. In order to minimize the chances of data corruption, all critical variables used by X, Y and Z are protected by storing them with complements or with a block CRC.

Again, there is further detailed information in the referenced text (Chapters 26–30 in Koopman cover critical system properties).

5.3.6   Detailed Design

After we have decided upon an architecture for the system, we can work on designing the subsystems within it. Again, graphical representations can be quite useful; especially if the corresponding requirements are graphical, as in this and similar cases they can be reused.

For example, state-based system behavior is best presented graphically. Figure 5.6 shows a finite state machine design for a UART Receive data ISR (the two circles labeled "UART Rx ISR" in Figure 5.5) which recognizes certain valid NMEA-0183 messages and enqueues them for later decoding. Corrupted or unneeded messages are discarded, saving buffer space in RAM and processor time. These messages have a specific format which includes the talker type (GPS, depth sounder, etc.), the message type, multiple data fields (often with each followed by engineering units), and a checksum for error detection.

We use an FSM-plus-ISR combination for two reasons. First, we want to minimize the amount of time spent in the ISR. Structuring the problem as an FSM allows us to write code which doesn't waste any time waiting for things to happen. The ISR is only executed when the UART has received a byte of data. Second, parsing data such as text is a good match for FSMs as it allows us to define rules to step through the different fields in a message and validate them.

Figure 5.7 shows a flowchart design for the task "Process NMEA Data" which decodes these enqueued messages and acts on the data. This code is much less time-critical, so it is implemented in a task which the scheduler runs after being notified that the RxQ holds at least one valid message. The flowchart emphasizes the consecutive and conditional processing nature of the activity: decode the message, check to see if it is valid or not, update variables, and so on.

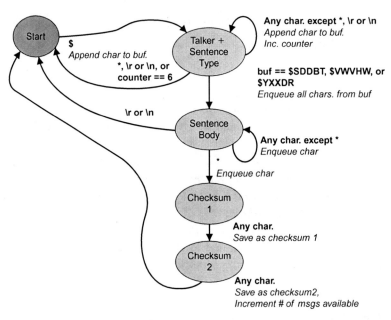

Figure 5.6 Finite state machine design for recognizing NMEA-0183 depth below transducer, heading and speed through water, and battery voltage messages.

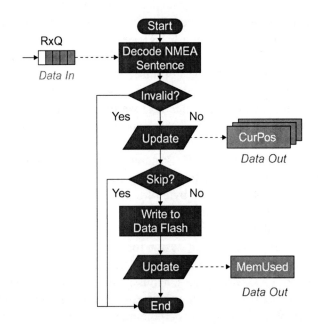

Figure 5.7 Flowchart for decoding NMEA sentence and saving data to flash memory.

There are various other representations available beyond these two workhorses, so we direct the reader other texts (see Chapter 12 and Chapter 13 of Koopman).

5.3.7 Implementation

Now that we have a detailed design it should be straightforward to proceed to the actual implementation of the code. C is the dominant programming language for embedded systems, followed by C++ and assembly language. C is good enough for the job, even though there are some languages which are much safer. The risk with C is that it allows the creation of all sorts of potentially unsafe code. Ganssle identifies "The Use of C" (or "The Misuse of C") as reason eight for projects getting into trouble. There are a few points to keep in mind as you develop the code:

- Three fundamental principles should guide your decisions when implementing code: simplicity, generality, and clarity (Kernighan and Pike).
  - Simplicity is keeping the programs and functions short and manageable.
  - Generality is designing functions that can work, in a broad sense, for a variety of situations and that require minimum alterations to suit a task.
  - Clarity is the concept of keeping the program easy to understand, while remaining technically precise.
- Code should conform to your company's **coding standards** to ensure that it is easy to read and understand. See Koopman's Chapter 17 for more information on why coding style matters. There are many coding standards examples available (Ganssle, J.). The rules we have seen broken most often, and which have the biggest payoff, are these:
  - Limit function length to what fits onto one screen or page.
  - Use meaningful and consistent function and variable naming conventions.
  - Avoid using global variables.
  - If you find yourself writing the same code with minor variations, it may be worth parameterizing the code so only one version is needed.
- Data sharing in systems with preemption (including ISRs) must be done very carefully to avoid data race vulnerabilities. See Chapter 12 of this text and Koopman's Chapters 19 and 20 for more details.
- **Static analysis** should be used to ensure that your code is not asking for trouble. Most (if not all) compiler warnings should be turned on to identify potential bugs lurking in your source code. Tools such as LINT are also helpful and worth considering.
- **Magic numbers** are hard-coded numeric literals used as constants, array sizes, character positions, conversion factors, and other numeric values that appear directly in programs. They complicate code maintenances because if a magic number is used in multiple places, and if a change is needed, then **each location** must

be revised and it is easy to forget about one. Similarly, some magic numbers may depend on others (e.g., a time delay may depend on the MCU's clock rate). It is much better to use a **const variable** or a **preprocessor #define** to give the value a meaningful name which can be used where needed.

- It is important to **track available design margin** as you build the system up. How much RAM, ROM, and nonvolatile memory are used? How busy is the CPU on average? How close is the system to missing deadlines? The Software Gas Law states that software will expand to fill all available resources. Tracking the resource use helps give an early warning. For more details, see Koopman's discussion on the cost of nearly full resources.

- **Software configuration management** should be used as the code is developed and maintained to support evolving code and different configurations as well.

5.3.8   Software Testing

Testing is an important part of software development. It is essentially impossible to develop error-free non-trivial software in a single try. It is especially difficult to design up-front a system which will handle all possible input conditions (including failures) correctly. Ganssle identifies "Inadequate Testing" and "Writing Optimistic Code" as reasons number three and two for projects getting in trouble. Koopman covers verification and validation of systems in detail.

Testing the developed software ensures that the product meets the requirements defined. That is, **testing proves that the software does what it is supposed to do.** A corollary is that **testing identifies the software's weaknesses.** These defects are typically prioritized based on their criticality.

Although one can never completely test a program, some tests are more useful and important than others. Hence, it makes sense to think while planning the tests in order to get the biggest return. Testing should be a logical, disciplined, and systematic process, rather than a rote and mechanical process. As with other subjects covered here, there are many excellent texts on software testing for further information (Phillips).

There are several independent dimensions of testing to consider:

- Software tests may or may not depend on the internal details of how the module is built. **Black box testing** assumes no knowledge about the internal structure, and focuses instead on functionality. **White box (or clear box)** testing takes advantage of such knowledge, so it can be more efficient in finding faults.

- Software testing should be done at **various phases** of the development process. **Unit tests** are performed during coding on a per-module basis. **Integration tests** are performed as the system is assembled (integrated) from modules.

- **Regression testing** ensures that past bugs which were fixed have not been re-introduced.

Do We Know How the System is Built?

Black Box Testing tests the functionality of the software by treating it like a black box with unknown contents. **How** the software performs a task **is unknown and unimportant** to the test. The only needed thing to pass the test is for the software to do what it should. There are many types of black box testing. Among them are tests for readiness, finite state machine, cause-effect graphing, boundary value testing, and user profile:

- Readiness: This test checks if a function is present and functional, and ready for testing. Black box testing should always begin with this form of testing.
- Finite state machine: Much software can be considered as finite state machines that transit between different states based on different events. This form of testing tests the transitioning between states and for errors that may occur with them.
- Cause effect graphing: This form of testing helps to organize the concepts in other black box techniques. For this test, the tester organizes all possible inputs and outputs of a program. This results in a form of a complete software test and helps to systematically organize test cases.
- Boundary value testing: In this form of testing the inputs to the test system are divided into meaningful sets and then tested in groups. One value from each set is then input to the system rather than the whole set. This helps save time.
- User profile: This form of testing focuses on how the user intends to use the software and which errors are important to their proper functioning while using the software. This minimizes the amount of time needed to be put into testing. However, learning what part of the program is used often is the difficult part of the test.

White Box Testing relies on knowledge of the structure of the software. It is also known as clear box testing. **How** the software performs a task **is known** to the testers, enabling them to identify probable errors. Important elements of white box testing are coverage and branch and conditioning testing.

- Coverage: The aim of white box testing is to cover every statement, state, and path in a program within the constraints of time and money. This can be a daunting task, especially if the program has many conditional statements.
- Branch and condition testing: The goal of branch testing is to traverse every path through the program. One way to do this is to use a flow chart of the program. The first test goes through one part of the program. The next one differs from the one before. In this manner, all paths are traversed, even those that share a common part.

How Many Modules Do We Test at a Time?

Individual **unit testing** of modules is typically done by the software developer as the code is created. As the developer has intimate knowledge of the implementation of the module, this testing is typically white-box testing to maximize the effectiveness. The developer writes test harness code to run the unit under specific conditions and verify the correct responses. Unit testing is quite effective because if there is a bug, it is in that module's code, design, or requirements.

With **integration testing** each module is merged into the main program and is tested to check if it works individually as well as with the rest of the program without causing any errors. There are often scenarios where a subroutine works perfectly on its own, but fails when integrated into the overall system due to unexpected dependencies, requirements, or interactions.

There are various types of integration testing: Bottom up, top down, sandwich, and build. Selecting the type of integration testing depends upon the people and product involved in development.

- Bottom up: This is one of the classic approaches for design and testing. Each problem is broken down into smaller parts and solutions are written for them, also called modules. Each module is tested individually and combined into subsystems which in turn are also tested and then combined into a larger system. This goes on till the complete solution is acquired and tested.
- Top down: The top down form of integration testing is similar to the bottom up form, but starts with a fully tested main routine. Modules are added to the main routine one after the other and tested as a combination. The process thus continues until all the modules have been added to the main program and tested.
- Sandwich: The sandwich testing form combines the bottom up and the top down forms of testing. The top down part tests the main controlling subsystems whereas the bottom up part integrates and tests the individual modules into subsystems.
- Build: The build form of integration testing starts with a core system to which functionally related module sets are added consecutively.

There is also a "worst-practice" integration testing method known as **Big Bang** testing. With this form of testing, all modules are combined and tested as a whole. Big bang testing is not advisable with untested modules as diagnosing the error can be very difficult—which of the many modules is really causing the problem? Or is an interaction between two or more modules the cause?

How Do We Keep from Breaking Old Bug Fixes?

The goal of **regression testing** is to ensure that bugs which were found in past testing were fixed and are still fixed. Sometimes an effort to fix a bug introduces other bugs. Regression testing uses a suite of tests which triggered bugs in the past. Automated regression testing allows developers to verify quickly and easily that their bug fix really is a fix. Regression testing may be applied to both unit and integration testing.

5.4   SOFTWARE DEVELOPMENT LIFECYCLE MODELS

We now discuss software development lifecycle models in more detail. We can divide them into two categories: waterfall (big up front design) and everything else (build a piece at a time). The advantage of the latter approaches is that they deliver portions of the implementation to the customer and other stakeholders earlier. This allows problems and misconceptions to be found earlier, and therefore fixed without disrupting the schedule as much. Projects with greater risks will benefit more from more iterative approaches, while less risky projects may be implemented more efficiently with a less iterative approach.

This chapter only provides a general description of these software processes. Further details can be found in the references of this chapter.

5.4.1   Waterfall Process

The waterfall model of software development is an idealized process which assumes that we know everything up front. The process gets its name because the processes flows down the steps like falling water. This process is most appropriate when the problem is very well understood so there is little risk. The following are the steps for the waterfall process:

1. Determine user needs
2. Gather requirements
3. Design
4. Build
5. Test
6. Demonstrate user product

Figure 5.8 illustrates the waterfall process. In practice, there are often arrows jumping back up the waterfall[3] which makes this model an idealization.

```
    User Needs
   Requirements
     Design              Waterfall Process
      Build
       Test
     User Product
```

Figure 5.8   The waterfall process expressed as a V-chart.

---

[3] Imagine salmon leaping upstream over the rapids.

5.4.2   Iterative Process

The iterative process is used to deliver a product in increments. The customers define the goals of the product at the beginning of development and are always anxious to have something quickly working. The iterative process provides the product to the customer in parts and provides developers an opportunity to learn about the product and the customer while building the product. This type of process is typically used when there is enough time for developing a project in parts and the customer is eager to provide feedback on the how the product functions while it is being developed. Figure 5.9 illustrates the iterative process.

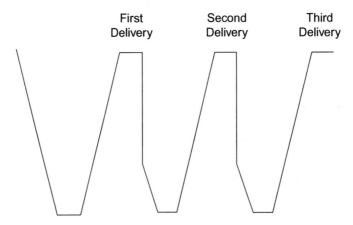

Figure 5.9   Example of an iterative process with one development team, expressed as a V-chart.

5.4.3   Spiral Process

The spiral process combines many fundamental contents of different process models into a single process. This process works best for projects that have a high risk of failure, such as research projects dealing with developing a new technology. Figure 5.10 illustrates the spiral process. Each cycle starts with the steps shown in the upper left quadrant, which are objectives (goals to achieve), constraints (limitations on resources), and alternatives (different approaches to achieve the objectives). The second quadrant (clockwise direction) shows the next steps in the process, which are risk analysis and prototyping. It begins with alternatives produced in the first quadrant. The developers then use the prototypes to analyze each alternative's risks and gain more insight. The third quadrant consists of the evaluation and decision making processes, followed by building the solution. The final quadrant consists of understanding what to do for the next cycle, which is repeated in the first quadrant. The developers revise the previous phases and create a plan for the next quadrant, review the same, and then decide whether to go ahead with the plan or stop building the project.

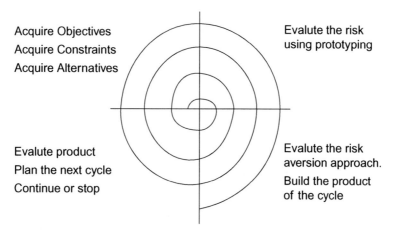

Figure 5.10   The general spiral process.

5.4.4   Agile Development Methods

The most common agile development methods are scrum, extreme programming, and lean development. These methods seek to deliver the product to the customer in satisfactory condition as early as possible in a continuous manner.

Let's examine scrum. With scrum, development activity is divided into a series of sprints lasting two to four weeks. At the end of the sprint the team will have a working, deliverable software product. There are three main types of participants:

- The product owner speaks for the customer.
- The team delivers the product.
- The Scrum Master is responsible for eliminating obstacles from the team's path.

Each sprint begins with the team members and product owner discussing features from a prioritized feature list (the product backlog). The product owner identifies the desired features, and the team estimates which can be delivered within the sprint, adding them to a task list called the sprint backlog. The sprint backlog is frozen for the sprint, so that the team members have clear goals during that development period. Each day during the sprint there is a brief (fifteen minute) status meeting in which each team member answers three specific questions:

- What have you done since yesterday's meeting?
- What are you going to do today?
- Are there any issues keeping you from meeting your goals?

The Scrum Master then seeks to address the issues. Finally, each sprint is time-boxed. If a feature is not completed by the end of the sprint, it goes back into the product backlog. One of scrum's main strengths is the short development cycle, which improves the speed of feedback. There are other aspects to scrum which we do not cover here, but further details are available in numerous texts on the subject.

5.4.5   Prototyping

Prototyping is a popular and useful software process, especially when determining the look and feel of the software has a higher priority than its basic functions. One of the drawbacks of the prototyped process is that when the waterfall model of development is used the developer may create something completely different from what the customer expected, since the requirements are gathered only at the beginning of the development process. Thus, prototyping is better when it is performed as either an iterative or evolutionary process.

Two basic types of prototypes used are the throw away and evolutionary prototype. In the throw away prototype, developers use a demonstration tool or language. Once the customer is satisfied with the prototype, the developers throw away the prototype and build the actual product with real programming languages. In the evolutionary prototype, the developers use code from the prototype in the actual system.

5.5   RECAP

- A major risk of software development is starting coding too early. Designing the system and its components before coding reduces development risks significantly, and also provides other benefits.
- Industry follows many (and sometimes differing) processes when developing software. A process gives a directional path to developing software in an organized manner, and allows the people developing the software and using the software to maintain expectations from the development process at regular intervals.
- Pseudo code and graphical methods to design solutions to a software programming problem allows understanding, resolving, and maintaining logical flow of a program. They can also be directly included in the documentation for the program.
- Testing is an integral part of software testing and software not subjected to testing is bound to fail. There are different techniques available for testing which should be applied as appropriate.

5.6   REFERENCES

Ganssle, Jack. "Breakpoints: Jack's Top Ten." *Embedded Systems Design,* December (2006): 61–63. Print.

Ganssle, Jack. *The Art of Designing Embedded Systems.* 2nd ed. Lawrence, KS: Newnes, 2008. Print.

Kernighan, Brian W., and Rob Pike. *The Practice of Programming.* Indianapolis: Addison-Wesley, 1999. Print.

Koopman, Philip J. *Better Embedded System Software.* New Castle, PA., Drumnadrochit Education, 2010. Print.

Phillips, Dwayne. *The Software Project Manager's Handbook: Principles That Work at Work.* Los Alamitos, CA: John Wiley & Sons, 2004. Print.

5.7   EXERCISES

1. Create a set of requirements for a vending machine which accepts coins and one-dollar bills, and provides change. Assume that each type of item has its own button.
2. Create a set of requirements for a controller for an elevator in a ten-story building.
3. Create a state machine for use in a cellphone to identify local phone numbers, long-distance phone numbers, and invalid phone numbers.
4. Estimate how long it will take you to create a working program to flash the LEDs on your favorite microcontroller board at a frequency proportional to the ambient Celsius temperature. Then go ahead and create the program. Log the time spent for each development activity. Analyze the time required for each activity, the accuracy of your estimations, and finally suggest improvements.

Chapter Six

Converting Between the Analog and Digital Domains

6.1 LEARNING OBJECTIVES

Embedded systems often measure physical parameters such as light intensity and temperature. These parameters are analog but the embedded system's microcontroller requires digital values to work on. An Analog to Digital Converter (ADC) is used to convert those parameters into a digital form.

In some cases, the microcontroller may need to provide analog signals to another system. For this, the digital output produced by the microcontroller has to be converted to analog an analog before being fed to the interfaced system. A Digital to Analog Converter (DAC) is used for this purpose.

In this chapter we will learn about:

- Converting an analog value to digital, mathematically
- ADCs in the RX62N
- Setting up registers and using the 12-bit and 10-bit ADC
- Using a DAC

6.2 BASIC CONCEPTS

A microcontroller represents information digitally: a voltage less than $V_{cc}/2$ represents a logical 0, while a voltage above $V_{cc}/2$ represents a logical 1. An analog signal can represent an infinite number of possible values. For example, consider an electronic thermometer with an output voltage which is proportional to the temperature in Celsius: V_{out} = Temperature*0.05 V/°C. At 5° C, V_{out} = 0.25 V. At 40° C, V_{out} = 2.0 V. At 40.1° C, V_{out} = 2.005 V. If we connect this thermometer directly to a microcontroller's digital input we will not be able to measure temperatures very accurately. In fact, we can only determine if the voltage is above or below $V_{cc}/2$. Assuming a supply voltage of 3.3 V, we can only determine if the temperature is above or below (3.3 V/2)/(0.05 V/°C) = 33° C, throwing away all other temperature information. In order to preserve this information we need a more sophisticated conversion approach.

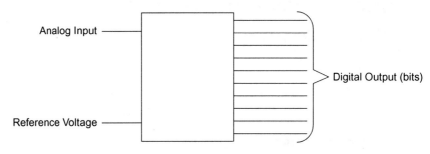

Figure 6.1 Simple ADC.

An ADC measures an analog input voltage and determines a digital (binary) value which represents it best. This measurement process is called *quantization*. The conversion is based on reference voltages which define the high (V_{+Ref}) and low (V_{-Ref}) ends of the input voltage range. Often microcontrollers have V_{-Ref} connected to ground (0 V). An input voltage of V_{+Ref} will result in an output code which is all ones, while an input voltage of V_{-Ref} will result in an output code of all zeroes. An intermediate input voltage will result in the proportional binary code value. This is discussed in more detail in Section 6.2.3.

A block diagram for a simple ADC is shown in Figure 6.1. The number of bits in the digital output is called the *resolution* of the ADC. A 10-bit ADC produces an output with 10 bits, with 1024 (2^{10}) different binary outputs. Thus, in a 10-bit ADC, a range of input voltages (analog) will map/translate to a unique binary output (0000000000 to 1111111111). A 12-bit ADC will have 4096 (2^{12}) unique binary outputs to represent 0 to 100% of an analog input.

Quantization usually introduces some error. A specific code (e.g. 0000101010) corresponds to a *range* of analog input voltages. The term *quantization error* describes how large the error can be. An ADC with higher resolution has more binary codes possible, which reduces the range of voltages corresponding to each code. This reduces the quantization error.

$$Quantization\ error = \frac{1}{(2*2^N)}, \text{ where } N = \text{number of quantization levels.}$$

The rate at which new outputs are calculated in an ADC is called the *conversion rate* or *sampling frequency*. Sampling theory states that an input signal with no frequency components greater than or equal to one half of the sampling frequency (called the *Nyquist frequency*) will be completely and accurately represented by the samples. If the input signal has any frequency components above the Nyquist frequency, these will be *aliased* by the sampling and appear as noise in the signals (as lower frequency components).

Hence input signals may be bandwidth-limited with a low-pass filter before sampling and quantization. In addition, the system is typically designed so that the Nyquist frequency is well above the filter's corner frequency, allowing the use of less expensive, lower-order filters.

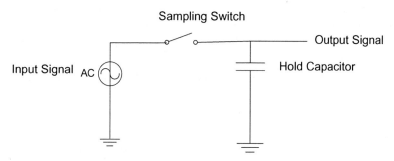

Figure 6.2   Sample and hold circuit.

Some types of ADC will generate incorrect results if the analog input signal changes too much during the conversion time. To avoid this problem, a *sample and hold* circuit (shown in Figure 6.2) can be used to sample the input voltage and save it in a capacitor. The capacitor is then disconnected from the input voltage by opening the sampling switch. The output signal can then be sampled by the ADC without interference from the changing input.

6.2.1   Analog to Digital Conversion by Successive Approximation

Analog to Digital conversion can be performed using many methods, such as Flash Conversion, Dual Slope Integrating, and Successive Approximation. The ADC method used in the RX62N board is Successive Approximation. Conversion using this method gives good resolution and has a wide range.

In the Successive Approximation method, the input voltage is repeatedly compared with the output of a DAC, until the best approximation is achieved. The DAC is fed by the current value of the approximation. The binary value of the approximate is found in every step of this method and is stored in the SAR. The SAR then compares the binary value and the reference voltage. Successive Approximation requires the same number of clock cycles as the output bits of the ADC; i.e., 12-bit ADC requires 12 clock cycles and 10-bit ADC requires 10 clock cycles (ADC clock cycles, not CPU clock cycles) to perform A/D conversion.

This process can be better understood with an example. The reference voltage for the RX62N board is 3.3 V. Let us assume that an input voltage of 2.5 has to be converted to digital form and the ADC used is 10-bit.

In the first clock cycle, 2.5 V is compared with 1.65 V (voltage is generated by the DAC and is half the reference voltage of 3.3 V). The 2.5 V is greater than 1.65 V and hence a '1' is set at the MSB of the binary value of the approximate, making the value 1xxxxxxxxx. This value is stored in the SAR.

In the second clock cycle, the input (2.5 V) is compared with 2.47 V (halfway between 1.65 V and 3.3 V). Since the input (2.5 V) is greater than the output from DAC (2.47 V), the next bit of the binary value is set to '1.' The binary value of the approximate is now 11xxxxxxxx.

In the third clock cycle, the input (2.5 V) is compared with 2.89 V, (halfway between 2.47 V and 3.3 V). The input (2.5 V) is less than the output from DAC (2.89 V), so the next bit of the binary value is set to '0.' The binary value of the approximate is now 110xxxxxxx.

In the next cycle, the input (2.5 V) is compared with 2.68 V, (halfway between 2.47 V and 2.89 V). The input (2.5 V) is less than the output from DAC (2.68 V), so the next bit of the binary value is set to '0.' The binary value of the approximate is now 1100xxxxxx.

The same process takes place until all the bits of the binary value are found. The final result of this conversion is 1100000111.

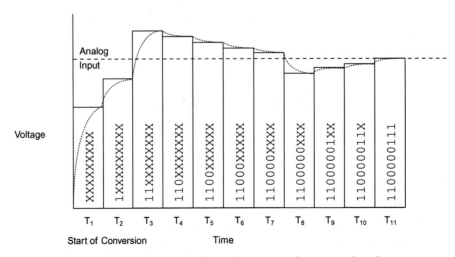

Figure 6.3 A/D conversion using successive approximation.

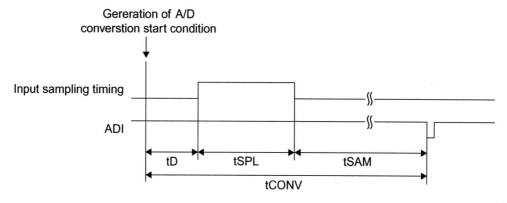

Figure 6.4 ADC conversion timing. Source: *Hardware Manual, Renesas 32-Bit Microcomputer, RX Family/ RX600 Series.* Renesas Electronics America, Inc., 2010, page 1748.

6.2.2 Conversion Speed

The analog input is sampled after A/D conversion start delay time (tD). Input sample time (tSPL) is the time that the capacitor in the sample and hold circuit takes to charge. Successive conversion time (tSAM) is the time after which the next conversion can start. It is fixed at 25 ADC clock cycles.

Conversion time (tCONV), or sampling time, is the inverse of conversion speed or sampling frequency. Conversion time is the sum of tD, tSPL, and tSAM only during the first conversion. The following conversions always have a conversion time of tSPL and tSAM.

A/D Sampling State Register (ADSSTR) gives the flexibility of altering the sampling time. One may want to alter this if the analog input signal has high impedance or if the analog input is a fast changing signal and the original sampling time is insufficient, or when the Peripheral module clock (PCLK) is slow.

6.2.3 Transfer Function Calculation

The digital value for a particular analog value can be found mathematically. This can be useful as a guide to see if the ADC output obtained is correct.

EXAMPLE OF SETTING	SETTING RANGE	SAMPLE TIME*
Standard (initial value)	19h	0.5 μs (When PCLK = ADCLK = 50 MHz)
Analog input signal impendance is high and the sampling time may be insufficient	1Ah to FFh	Example: FFh 5.1 μs (When PCLK = ADCLK = 50 MHz)
Input sampling time is less than the initial value when ADCLK is below 50 MHz.	02h to 18h	Example: 14h 0.5 μs (When PCLK = ADCLK = 40 MHz)

Figure 6.5   ADSSR settings. Source: *Hardware Manual*, page 1748.

ITEM	SYMBOL	FORMULA MIN	FORMULA MAX
A/D conversion start delay time (1)	ID	$\dfrac{3}{\text{PCLK (MHz)}}$	$\dfrac{1}{\text{ADCLK (MHz)}} + \dfrac{4}{\text{PCLK (MHz)}}$
Input sampling time (2)	ISPL	$\dfrac{\text{Setting value of ADSSTR}}{\text{ADCLK (MHz)}}$	
Successive conversion time (3)	ISAM	$\dfrac{25}{\text{ADCLK (MHz)}}$	
A/D conversion time[*1]	ICONV	(1) + (2) + (3)	
A/D conversion time[*2]	ICONV	(2) + (3)	

Notes: 1. A/D conversion time in single mode and scan mode (first round)
2. A/D conversion time in scan mode (after the second round)

Figure 6.6   ADC conversion time. Source: *Hardware Manual*, page 1749.

If V_{in} is the sampled input voltage, $V_{+\text{ref}}$ is the upper end of the input voltage range, $V_{-\text{ref}}$ is the lower end of the input voltage range, and n is the number of bits of resolution in ADC, then the digital output *(n)* can be found using the following formula:

$$n = \left[\frac{(V_{\text{in}} - V_{-\text{ref}})(2^N - 1)}{V_{+\text{ref}} - V_{-\text{ref}}} + \frac{1}{2} \right] \text{int}$$

$$n = \left[\frac{(V_{in})(2^N - 1)}{V_{+ref}} + \frac{1}{2}\right] int \quad (if \ V_{-ref} = 0)$$

6.3   BASIC EXAMPLES

6.3.1   Conversion Speed

Let us calculate the conversion time for the first conversion. Let PCLK = ADCLK = 50 Mhz, and ADSSR is the standard value of 19h.

From Figure 6.6, it can be seen that for the first conversion:

$$tCONV = (tD + tSPL + tSAM)$$
$$tCONV = (3 \, / \, PCLK + ADSSR \, / \, ADCLK + 25 \, / \, ADCLK)$$

ADSSR value is 19h or 25_{10}. Decimal value has to be used for calculation.

$$tCONV = (3 \, / \, 50 \, MHz + 25 \, / \, 50 \, MHz + 25 \, / \, 50 \, MHz)$$
$$tCONV = (0.06 \, \mu s + 0.5 \, \mu s + 0.5 \, \mu s)$$
$$tCONV = 1.06 \, \mu s$$

While calculating conversion time for the second and subsequent conversions,

$$tCONV = (tSPL + tSAM).$$

6.3.2   Digital Value for a Given Analog Value

Let us assume that the analog voltage to be calculated is 2.7 V and the 12-bit ADC has to be used. The digital value will be:

$$n = \left[\frac{(V_{in})(2^N - 1)}{V_{+ref}} + \frac{1}{2}\right] int \quad (Since \ V_{-ref} = 0)$$

$$= \left[\frac{(2.7)(2^{12} - 1)}{3.3} + \frac{1}{2}\right]$$

$$= \left[\frac{(2.7)(4095)}{3.3} + \frac{1}{2}\right]$$

$$n = 3352_{10}$$

6.3.3 Step Size

While reference voltage is the maximum analog value that can be converted to digital form, step size is the smallest change in voltage that can be converted. Step size is also known as the resolution of the ADC.

$$\text{Step Size} = \frac{(V_{\text{ref}})}{2^N} \ (\text{Since } V_{-\text{ref}} = 0)$$

The step size for 10-bit ADC $= \dfrac{(3.3)}{2^{10}} = 3.2 \text{ mV}$

The step size for 12-bit ADC $= \dfrac{(3.3)}{2^{12}} = 0.8 \text{ mV}$

The resolution (step size) of the 12-bit ADC is much better than that of the 10-bit ADC. Hence, for applications, which need to detect very small changes in voltage, 12-bit ADC should be used.

6.4 ADVANCED CONCEPTS

The RX62N has a 12-bit and a 10-bit A/D converter. Depending on the resolution the application needs, either the 12-bit or 10-bit ADC should be selected. By default peripherals are in the stop state. They can be enabled by using the Module Stop Register A or B (MSTPRA or MSTPRB). To use the 12-bit ADC, SYSTEM.MSTPCRA.BIT.MSTPA17 must be set to 0; and to use the 10-bit ADC, SYSTEM.MSTPCRA.BIT.MSTPA22 and SYSTEM.MSTPCRA.BIT.MSTPA23 must be set to 0.

The ADC has eight channels (AN0 to AN7). They are at Port 4 pin 0 to 7. To use a particular channel, the respective port has to be set up as input. For example, to use AN0, port 4 pin 0 use `PORT4.DDR.BIT.B0 = 0`. For inputs, the Input Buffer Control Register (ICR) also has to set up. This can be done using `PORT4.ICR.BIT.B0 = 1`.

Next, the ADC registers have to be set up. The 12-bit ADC and the 10-bit ADC have different registers. In this section we shall see how to set the registers and use the use the different operating modes of the ADCs.

6.4.1 12-Bit A/D Converter

The ADC usually consists of a sample and hold circuit and a comparator. The sample and hold circuit gets a one-time snap shot of the analog input (voltage) and this is compared against a reference voltage using the comparator.

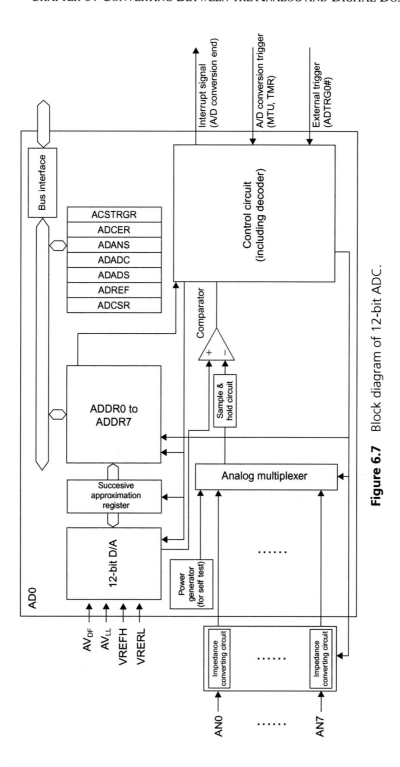

Figure 6.7   Block diagram of 12-bit ADC.

Registers

The 12-bit ADC registers are presented as structures and unions for easy manipulation, just like the ports, in the 'iodefine_RX62N.h' file. The registers can be accessed using the syntax S12AD.REGISTER.WORD to set up an entire register or S12AD.REGISTER.BIT.BIT_NAME to set up a particular bit of a register.

A/D Data Registers n (ADDRn) (n = A to H)

The 12-bit ADC has eight Data Registers each corresponding to the input channels of the ADC. A/D data registers ADDRA to ADDRH are 16-bit read-only registers. They store the A/D conversion results of channels AN0 to AN7. The width of the ADDRn (16-bit) is greater than the width of the ADC output (12-bit). To avoid reading wrong data, the output has to be aligned either to the right or left of ADDRn. This can be done using the A/D Control Extended Register (ADCER). This is explained a little later.

A/D Control Register (ADCSR)

The ADCSR is used to select different settings of the ADC.

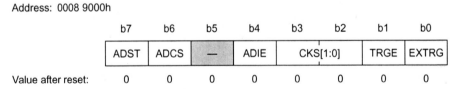

Address: 0008 9000h

	b7	b6	b5	b4	b3	b2	b1	b0
	ADST	ADCS	—	ADIE	CKS[1:0]		TRGE	EXTRG
Value after reset:	0	0	0	0	0	0	0	0

Figure 6.8 A/D control register. Source: *Hardware Manual,* page 1717.

The b0 bit is used to specify if an external trigger, ADTRG0# (port 0 pin 7), should start A/D conversion. If 1 is set, the microcontroller starts A/D conversion when a trigger is received. The value 0 is set when A/D conversion is to be started by other means.

To receive the external trigger (if b0 = 0), the external trigger has to be enabled. This is done by setting b1 bit to 1. The value 0 disables external trigger.

The frequency of the ADC clock can be selected using the following table. PCLK is the peripheral clock.

TABLE 6.1 Clock Selection.

b3	b2	FUNCTION
0	0	PCLK/8
0	1	PCLK/4
1	0	PCLK/2
1	1	PCLK

The A/D Scan Conversion End Interrupt Enable (ADIE) bit is used to enable or disable A/D interrupt after A/D conversion has been performed. Setting this bit to 0 disables the interrupt, and setting it to 1 enables this interrupt.

The A/D Scan Conversion Mode Select (ADCS) is used to select mode of operation of the ADC. Setting this bit to 0 selects Single Cycle Scan Mode, and setting it to 1 selects continuous mode.

The A/D Conversion Start (ADST) is used to stop/start the A/D conversion. Setting this bit to 1 starts the ADC and setting it to 0 stops the ADC. If ADC is to be started using software trigger, ADST must be set to 1 only after all the ADC registers have been set up. Hence set ADST $= 0$ when setting up this register initially.

A/D Channel Select Register (ADANS)

This register is 16 bits wide and is used to select the channel(s) on which A/D conversion should be performed. The top 8 bits (b15 to b8) are reserved and the bottom 8 bits (b7 to b0) are used to select channels. To select a channel, set the corresponding bit to 1. For example, to select channel 0, set S12AD.ADANS.WORD = 0x0001; and to select all eight channels set S12AD.ADANS.WORD = 0x00FF.

A/D-Converted Value Addition Mode Select Register (ADADS)

The 12-bit ADC has a special setting which is called the Converted Value Addition Mode. This setting is used to successively convert and sum two to four times the channels that have been selected using the ADANS register. To perform value addition on a particular channel, set S12AD.ADADS.BIT.ADS $[n] = 1$ ($n = 0$ to 7).

Address: 0008 9008h

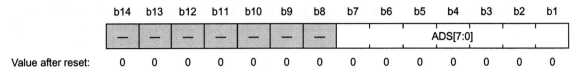

Value after reset: 0   0   0   0   0   0   0   0   0   0   0   0   0   0

Figure 6.9 A/D converted value addition mode select register. Source: *Hardware Manual,* page 1720.

To understand value addition better, let us consider an example in which all eight channels have been selected (S12AD.ADANS.WORD = 0x00FF) and value addition is to be performed on channels 2 and 6.

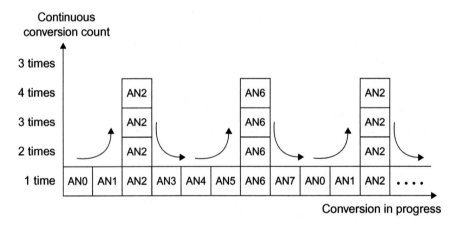

Figure 6.10 A/D converted value addition mode. Source: *Hardware Manual,* page 1720.

According to our example, analog inputs at channels 0, 1, 3, 4, 5, and 7 are A/D converted once, but inputs at channels 2 and 6 are successively converted four times (the number of times can be changed) and added. This added value is stored in the A/D data register. Finding the average of this value can improve A/D conversion accuracy.

A/D-Converted Value Addition Count Select Register (ADADC)

The ADADC is the register that is used to select the number of times the value adding has to be performed. This register is an 8-bit register. The top 6 bits are reserved and the lower

2 bits (b1, b0) are used to select the value addition count. Value addition can be performed two to four times. The setting for the value addition count can be seen from the following table.

TABLE 6.2 A/D Converted Value Addition Count Setting.

b1	b0	FUNCTION
0	0	1-time conversion (no addition)
0	1	2-time conversion (addition once)
1	0	3-time conversion (addition twice)
1	1	4-time conversion (addition three times)

A/D Control Extended Register (ADCER)

The ADCER is a 16-bit register. All bits except bit 5 and bit 15 of this register are reserved. Bit 5 is for Automatic Clearing Enable (ACE). Thus, setting bit 5 to 1 enables automatic clearing of the Data Register once the A/D value has been read by the microcontroller. This setting makes sure that older A/D values are not read by mistake.

Bit 15 (ADRFMT) of the ADCER is used to select the format of the Data Register. Setting bit 15 to 0 sets the format of the Data Register to right alignment. Setting this bit to 1 selects left alignment of Data Register. However, if the A/D converted value addition mode is selected, this formatting becomes void. Selection of the value addition mode automatically sets left alignment format for the Data Register. Note that the number of bits output after value addition is fourteen and not twelve.

A/D Start Trigger Select Register (ADSTRGR)

The ADSTRGR is an 8-bit register. The top four bits (b7 to b4) of this register are reserved and the lower four bits (b3 to b0) are used to select the type of trigger that will start the Analog to Digital Conversion process.

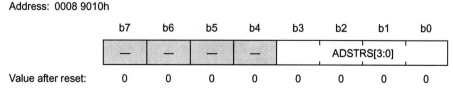

Figure 6.11 A/D start trigger select register. Source: *Hardware Manual,* page 1723.

A/D conversion can be started by one of three sources. They are a) Multi-function Timer pulse Unit (MTU) and Timer (TMR), b) external trigger (ADTRG0#), and c) Software Trigger. To choose a type of trigger, use the following table.

TABLE 6.3   Trigger Selection.

MODULE	SOURCE	REMARKS	ADSTRS[3]	ADSTRS[2]	ADSTRS[1]	ADSTRS[0]
ADC	ADST	Software trigger	—	—	—	—
External input	ADTRG0#	A/D conversion startup trigger pin	0	0	0	0
MTU	TRG1N	Input capture/compare match A from MTU0	0	0	0	1
	TRG2N	Input capture/compare match B from MTU0	0	0	1	0
	TRG3N	Input capture/compare match from MTU0 to MTU4	0	0	1	1
	TRG4N	Input capture/compare match from MTU6 to MTU10	0	1	0	0
	TRG5N	Compare match E from MTU0	0	1	0	1
	TRG6N	Compare match F from MTU0	0	1	1	0
	TRG7N	Compare match from MTU4	0	1	1	1
	TRG8N	Compare match from MTU10	1	0	0	0
TMR	TRG9N	Compare match from TMR0	1	0	0	1
	TRG10N	Compare match from TMR2	1	0	1	0

Source: *Hardware Manual*, page 1723.

When the MTU and TMR are to be used as the trigger, the TRGE bit in ADCSR has to be set to 1 and the EXTRG bit in ADCSR has to be set to 0.

When an external input is to be used as the trigger (ADTRG0#), the TRGE bit in ADCSR has to be set to 1 and the EXTRG bit in ADCSR has to be set to 1. ADTRG0# has to be set up as an input pin and ICR has to be enabled.

Software trigger is enabled at all times irrespective of the values set using TRGE, EXTRG, and ADSTRGR bits in ADCSR.

Let us now look at an example of setting up the registers of the 12-bit ADC. It is always better to write register set up as a function.

```
1. void ADC_Init(){
2.     SYSTEM.MSTPCRA.BIT.MSTPA17 = 0;
3.     S12AD.ADCSR.BYTE = 0x0C;
4.     S12AD.ADANS.WORD = 0x01;
5.     S12AD.ADCER.BIT.ACE = 1;
6.     S12AD.ADCER.BIT.ADRFMT = 0;
7. }
```

The setting up of registers has been written as a function named ADC_Init() in line 1. In line 2, the 12-bit ADC has been selected using the Module Stop Control Register A. In line 3, the Control Register is set up—the Software trigger has been enabled (b1 = 0, b0 = 0), the clock PCLK (b3 = 1, b2 = 1) has been selected, A/D Interrupt Enable has not been enabled (b4 = 0) and Single-Cycle Scan mode has been selected (b6 = 0). In line 4, channel 0 (AN0) has been selected. Next, automatic clearing of ADDRn (line 5) and right alignment of ADDRn (line 6) is done.

Operation

The 12-bit ADC is capable of operating in two modes: single-cycle scan mode and continuous scan mode.

Single-Cycle Scan Mode

In this mode, one to eight channels (number of channels selected using ADANS register) are scanned/converted to digital once in ascending order and then the ADC is stopped. This can be better understood with the following figure in which conversion is performed on three channels (AN4, AN5, and AN6).

The ADC in Single-Cycle Scan Mode is started (represented by (1) in Figure 6.12) when the ADST bit (ADCSR) is set to 1. The channels are A/D converted in ascending order (AN4, AN5, AN6) and the converted value is stored in the respective Data Register (represented by (2) in the figure). An ADI interrupt request is raised is ADIE bit (ADCSR) is enabled (represented by (3) in the figure). Finally, the ADST bit gets cleared to 0 when inputs of all the channels have been converted (represented by (4) in the figure).

The ADC operates similarly when ADC is started using MTU, TMR, or an external trigger input.

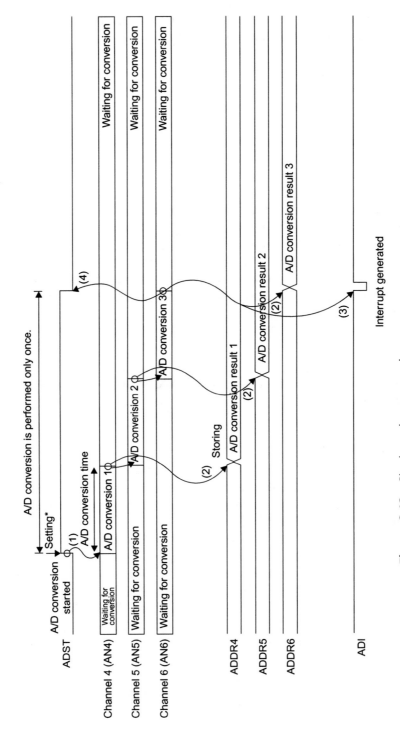

Figure 6.12 Single-cycle scan mode. Source: *Hardware Manual*, page 1724.

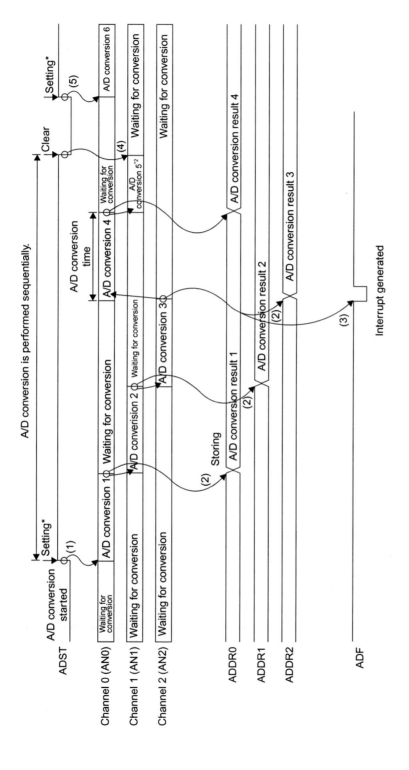

Figure 6.13 Continuous scan mode. Source: *Hardware Manual*, page 1725.

Notes: 1. ↓ indicates the point when the instruction is executed by software.
2. Converted data are ignored.

Continuous Scan Mode

In this mode, one to eight channels (number of channels selected using ADANS register) are scanned/converted to digital continuously in ascending order until the ADC is stopped manually. This can be better understood with the following figure in which conversion is performed on three channels (AN0, AN1, and AN2).

The ADC in Continuous Scan Mode is started (represented by (1) in Figure 6.13) when the ADST bit (ADCSR) is set to 1.

The channels are A/D converted in ascending order (AN0, AN1, AN2) and the converted value is stored in the respective Data Register (represented by (2) in the figure). An ADI interrupt request is raised is ADIE bit (ADCSR) is enabled (represented by (3) in the figure).

Unlike Single-Cycle Scan Mode, the above two processes ((1) and (2)) are repeated until the ADST is set to 0 manually. When ADST is set to 1, the ADC stops and enters a wait state. When ADSR is set to 1 later, A/D conversion starts again.

The ADC operates similarly when ADC is started using MTU, TMR, or an external trigger input.

6.4.2 10-Bit A/D Converter

The RX62N has two 10-bit A/D converters (Units 0 and 1). Each unit can convert up to four analog input channels. Channels AN0 to AN3 are considered as unit 0 and channels AN4 to AN7 are considered as unit 1.

Like the 12-bit ADC, 10-bit ADC registers are also presented as structures and unions for easy manipulation, just like the ports, in the 'iodefine_RX62N.h'file. The registers can be accessed using the syntax AD.REGISTER.WORD to set up an entire register or AD.REGISTER.BIT.BIT_NAME to set up a particular bit of a register.

Registers

A/D Data Register (ADDRn) (n = A to D)

The 10-bit ADC has four Data Registers, each corresponding to the input channels of the ADC. A/D data registers ADDRA to ADDRD are 16-bit read-only registers. They store the A/D conversion results of channels AN0 to AN3, or AN4 to AN7. The width of the ADDRn (16-bit) is greater than the width of the ADC output (10-bit). To avoid reading wrong data, the output has to be aligned either to the right or left of ADDRn. This can be done using the DPSEL bit in the A/D Placement Register (ADDPR). This will be explained a little later.

A/D Control/Status Register (ADCSR)

The Control/Status Register is used to select the input channels, start or stop A/D conversion, and enable or disable ADI interrupt.

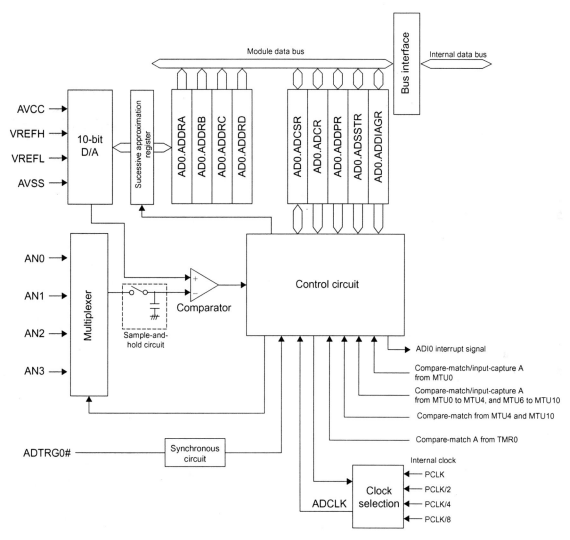

Figure 6.14 Block Diagram of 10-bit ADC (Unit 0).

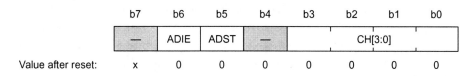

Figure 6.15 A/D control/status register. Source: *Hardware Manual*, page 1737.

The CH [3:0] is used to select the analog channels which have to be A/D converted. The channels can be selected using the following table.

TABLE 6.4 Channel Selection.

b3	b2	b1	b0	CHANNEL
0	0	0	0	AN0 or AN4
0	0	0	1	AN0 and AN1 or AN4 and AN51
0	0	1	0	AN0 to AN2 or AN4 to AN6
0	0	1	1	AN0 to AN3 or AN4 to AN7

The A/D Start bit (ADST) is used to start or stop the ADC. Setting this bit to 1 starts the ADC, and setting it to 0 stops the ADC. The A/D Scan Conversion End Interrupt Enable (ADIE) is used to enable or disable the A/D scan conversion end interrupt (ADI). When A/D conversion is complete, an interrupt is generated. Setting the ADIE bit to 1 enables the interrupt and setting it to 0 disables the interrupt.

A/D Control Register (ADCR)

The Control register is used to select the type of A/D conversion mode, clock, and trigger.

Figure 6.16 A/D control register. Source: *Hardware Manual*, page 1739.

Like the 12-bit ADC, the 10-bit ADC also has different modes of operation. They are Single mode, Continuous Scan mode, and One-cycle scan mode. Setting MODE [1:0] to 00 is used to select Single mode, 10 to select Continuous Scan mode, and 11 to select One-cycle mode. Setting MODE [1:0] to 01 is prohibited. Details of these modes are explained later.

The ADC clock can be set using the CSK [1:0] bits. Setting CKS [1:0] to 00 is used to select PCLK/8, 01 to select PCLK/4, 10 to select PCLK/2, and 11 to select PCLK. PCLK is the peripheral clock.

The TRGS bits are used to select the type of trigger that will start the A/D conversion process.

TABLE 6.5 Trigger Select for 10-bit ADC Unit 0.

b7	b6	b5	TRIGGER
0	0	0	Software Trigger
0	0	1	Compare-match/input-capture A from MTU0 to MTU4
0	1	0	Compare-match from TMR0
0	1	1	Trigger from ADTRG0#
1	0	0	Compare-match/input-capture A from MTU0
1	0	1	Compare-match/input-capture A from MTU06 to MTU10
1	1	0	Compare-match/input-capture A from MTU04
1	1	1	Compare-match/input-capture A from MTU10

The trigger select for Unit 1 is similar to the above table but 011 selects trigger from ADTRG1# and 100 selects compare-match/input-capture B from MTU0.

A/D Data Placement Register (ADDPR)

The A/D output registers (ADDRn) are 16-bits wide, but the output of the ADC is 10-bits wide. Hence the data in the Data Register has to be aligned. The A/D Data Placement Register (ADDPR) is used to align data. This register is 8 bits wide. All bits except the eighth bit are reserved. The DPSEL bit is the eighth bit. Setting this bit to 0 aligns data to the right (LSB), and setting it to 1 aligns data to the left (MSB).

A/D Self-Diagnostic Register (ADDIAGR)

This register is used to check if the 10-bit ADC has any defects. This register is an 8-bit register and the lower two bits (b1 and b0) are used to set up the test voltage for fault detection. To perform fault detection, do the following:

- Set up the ADC in Single mode (AD.ADCR.BIT.MODE = 00)
- Enable analog input AN0 (AD.ADCSR.BIT.CH = 0000)
- Set up software trigger for the ADC (AD.ADCR.TRGS = 000)
- Set the test voltage by setting (AD.ADDIAGR.DIAG) using Table 6.7
- Start conversion (AD.ADCSR.BIT.ADST = 1)

TABLE 6.6 Test Voltage Setting.

b1	b0	FUNCTION
0	0	Self-diagnostic function is off
0	1	A/D conversion of $V_{ref} \times 0$ voltage value is enabled
1	0	A/D conversion of $V_{ref} \times \frac{1}{2}$ voltage value is enabled
1	1	A/D conversion of $V_{ref} \times 1$ voltage value is enabled

The test voltage (0V or $V_{ref}/2$ or $2V_{ref}$) is A/D converted and the result is stored in ADDRA. The result should approximately be 0_{10} if 0V was chosen as test voltage, 1023_{10} if V_{ref} was chosen, and 2046_{10} if $2V_{ref}$ was chosen. If the result does not correspond to these values then the ADC is at fault.

Self-diagnosis takes the same time as A/D conversion for one channel.

Let us now look at an example of setting up the registers of the 10-bit ADC. It is always better to write register set up as a function.

```
1. void ADC_Init(){
2.     SYSTEM.MSTPCRA.BIT.MSTPA23 = 0;
3.     SYSTEM.MSTPCRA.BIT.MSTPA22 = 0;
4.     AD.ADCSR.BYTE = 0x03;
5.     AD.ADCR.BYTE = 0x0F;
6.     AD.ADDPR.BYTE = 0x00;
7.     AD.ADDIAGR.BYTE = 0x0;
8. }
```

The setting up of registers has been written as a function named ADC_Init() in line 1. The 10-bit ADC has been selected using the Module Stop Control Register A (lines 2 and 3). In line 4, the Control/Status Register is set up—four channels (AN0 to AN3) have been selected and A/D Interrupt Enable has not been enabled (b6 = 0). Next, One-Cycle Scan mode, PCLK, and software trigger have been selected using the A/D Control Register in line 5. The format of the Data Register has been set to right alignment using line 6. In line 7 the A/D Self-diagnostic function has been turned off as we are not trying to detect any faults.

Operation

The 10-bit A/D converter has two operating modes: Single Mode and Scan Mode. In the Single Mode, A/D conversion is performed on the specified single channel only once. In the Scan mode, A/D conversion is performed sequentially on the specified channel(s) (up to four). The Scan Mode can be further classified as the One-Cycle Scan mode and the Continuous Scan mode. The operation of the One-Cycle scan mode is the same as the

Single-Cycle Scan mode of the 12-bit ADC and the operation of the Continuous Scan mode is the same as the continuous Scan mode of the 12-bit ADC.

6.4.3   D/A Converter

The Digital to Analog converter, as the name suggests, is used to convert Digital Signals to Analog values. A DAC can convert bits to signals only if the Nyquist condition is met. The output of the DAC is in the form of pulses and this could cause harmonics above the Nyquist frequency. This could be avoided by using a low-pass filter. DACs face the issue of high output impedance and slow settling time.

DACs are used in digital devices such as iPods to play back stored music. The RX62N has a 10-bit Digital to Analog converter. This DAC has two channels.

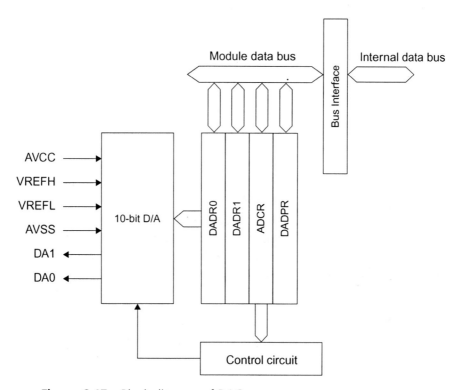

Figure 6.17   Block diagram of DAC. Source: *Hardware Manual,* page 1762.

D/A Registers

The DAC has three registers that have to be set in order to perform D/A conversion. They are D/A Data Register, D/A Control Register, and D/A Data Placement Register.

D/A Data Register (DADRm) (m = 0, 1)

DADR0 and DADR1 are 16-bit registers which store the digital value that has to be converted to analog. The format of the 10-bit data register can be changed by setting the DPSEL bit (D/A Data Placement Register).

D/A Control Register (DACR)

The D/A Control register is an 8-bit register used to enable or disable D/A conversion. It is also used to select the channel for the D/A operation.

Address: 0008 80C4h

b7	b6	b5	b4	b3	b2	b1	b0
DAOE1	DAOE0	DAE	—	—	—	—	—

Value after reset: 0 0 0 0 0 0 0 0

Figure 6.18 D/A control register. Source: *Hardware Manual*, page 1764.

The lower five bits (b0 to b4) are reserved. The b5, b6, and b7 bits can be set Table 6.7.

D/A Data Placement Register (DADPR)

The format of the D/A Data Register can be set using this register. This is an 8-bit register. All bits except the eighth bit are reserved. The eighth bit is the Data Placement Selection bit (DPSEL). Setting DPSEL to 0 aligns the D/A Data Register to the right (LSB), and setting it to 1 aligns the D/A Data Register to the left (MSB).

Operation

The RX62N has two circuits for D/A conversion and they can operate independently. To perform D/A conversion:

- Port 0 pin 5 or Port 0 pin 3 has to be set up as the output port (PORT0.DDR.BIT. B3 = 1) and disable ICR (PORT0.ICR.BIT.B3 = 0) for channel 0 (DA0) and PORT0.DDR.BIT.B5 = 1 and PORT0.ICR.BIT.B5 = 0 for channel 1 (DA1).
- The value to be converted has to be written into the D/A Data Register.
- DAOEn bit (n = 0 or 1) in DACR has to be set to 1.

TABLE 6.7 Setting of DACR.

BIT	SYMBOL	BIT NAME	DESCRIPTION
b4 to b0	—	(Reserved)	These bits are read as 1. The write value should always be 1.
b5	DAE*[1]	D/A Enable	0: D/A conversion is independently controlled on channels 0 and 1.
			1: D/A conversion on channels 0 and 1 is controlled as a single whole.
b6	DAOE0	D/A Output Enable 0	0: Analog output of channel 0 (DA0) is disabled.
			1: D/A conversion of channel 0 is enabled. Analog output of channel 0 (DA0) is enabled.*[2]
b7	DAOE1	D/A Output Enable 1	0: Analog output of channel 1 (DA1) is disabled.
			1: D/A conversion of channel 1 is enabled. Analog output of channel 1 (DA1) is enabled.*[2]

Source: *Hardware Manual,* page 1764.

If a new value is written to DADRn ($n = 0$ or 1), conversion takes place again. Conversion takes place until DAOEn bit ($n = 0$ or 1) is cleared.

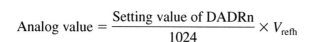

$$\text{Analog value} = \frac{\text{Setting value of DADRn}}{1024} \times V_{\text{refh}}$$

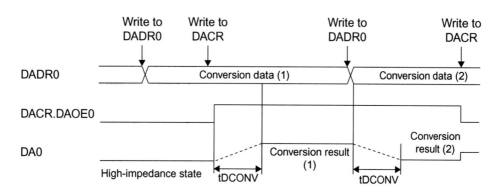

[Legend]
tDCONV: D/A conversion time

Figure 6.19 Operation of DAC. Source: *Hardware Manual,* page 1766.

6.5   ADVANCED EXAMPLES

6.5.1   12-Bit ADC

Let us consider the example of a simple 12-bit ADC. A DC voltage supply of 3 V is converted to its corresponding digital code and displayed on the LCD. To perform this Single-Cycle Scan mode an AN0 will be used. Software trigger will be used to start the ADC.

```
1.  #include "iodefine_RX62N.h"
2.  #include <stdlib.h>
3.  #include <stdio.h>
4.  #include "src\Glyph\Glyph.h"
5.  #define LCD_LINE1 0
6.  #define LCD_LINE2 1
7.  #define LCD_LINE3 2
8.  #define LCD_LINE4 3
9.  void ADC_Init(void);
10. void BSP_Display_String(int8_t, char *);
11. T_glyphHandle G_lcd;
12. void main(void){
13.     unsigned short ADC_out;
14.     int i = 0;
15.     char ADC_OUT[13];
16.     PORT4.DDR.BIT.B0 = 0;
17.     PORT4.ICR.BIT.B0 = 1;
18.     if(GlyphOpen(&G_lcd, 0) == GLYPH_ERROR_NONE){
19.         GlyphNormalScreen(G_lcd);
20.         GlyphSetFont(G_lcd, GLYPH_FONT_6_BY_13);
21.         GlyphClearScreen(G_lcd);
22.         BSP_Display_String(LCD_LINE1,"12-bit ADC");
23.         ADC_Init();
24.         while(1){
25.             if(S12AD.ADCSR.BIT.ADST == 0 && i == 0){
26.                 ADC_out = S12AD.ADDRA & 0X0FFF;
27.                 sprintf(ADC_OUT,"%d",ADC_out);
28.                 BSP_Display_String(LCD_LINE2,ADC_OUT);
29.                 i++;
30.             }
31.         }
32.     }
33.     GlyphClose(&G_lcd);
34. }
```

```
35. void ADC_Init(){
36.     SYSTEM.MSTPCRA.BIT.MSTPA17 = 0;
37.     S12AD.ADCSR.BYTE = 0x0C;
38.     S12AD.ADANS.WORD = 0x01;
39.     S12AD.ADCER.BIT.ACE = 1;
40.     S12AD.ADCER.BIT.ADRFMT = 0;
41.     S12AD.ADSTRGR.BIT.ADSTRS = 0x0;
42.     S12AD.ADCSR.BIT.ADST = 1;
43. }
44. void BSP_Display_String(int8_t aLine, char * aText){
45.     int8_t y = aLine * 16;
46.     GlyphEraseBlock(G_lcd, 0, y, 95, y + 15);
47.     GlyphSetXY(G_lcd, 0, y);
48.     GlyphString(G_lcd, (uint8_t *)aText, strlen(aText));
49. }
```

The iodefine_RX62N.h in line 1 defines the ports and the ADC registers which need to be set for the ADC operation. Hence it should be included in the program. Line 2 and line 3 are used to include standard C libraries. The src\Glyph\Glyph.h header file in line 4 is included to enable the LCD display. The start of the LCD lines has been set up as macros in lines 5 to 8. G_lcd is a variable of type T_glyphHandle (line 11) used to open the graphic LCD.

In lines 9 and 10, the functions ADC_Init and BSP_Display_String have been proto-typed. The ADC_Init() function (lines 35 to 43) is used to set up the registers for the Single-Cycle Scan mode on AN0 and use a software trigger to start the ADC. The Module Stop Control Register A (MSTPCRA) is set such that the 12-bit ADC is selected (line 36). The A/D Control register (ADCSR) is set for software trigger, PCLK, and Single-cycle scan mode (line 37). Channel AN0 is selected and the A/D Channel Select register (ADANS) is set accordingly (line 38). Automatic clearing of the data registers and right-alignment of the data register has been selected (lines 39 and 40). The A/D Start Trigger Select register (ADSTRGR) is set for the software trigger (line 41). The 12-bit ADC is then started (line 42). The BSP_Display_String() function is used to display strings on the specified line of the LCD.

In the main program, three variables have been used: ADC_out, ADC_OUT, and *i*. ADC_out declared in line 13 is used to get the ADC value from the data register. ADC_OUT declared in line 15, is a string which contains the ADC_out in string form so that it can be displayed on the LCD. The variable *i*, declared in line 14, is used to print the A/D value once on the LCD.

Next, the Port 4 pin 0 (AN0) is set up as an input pin (lines 16 and 17). The LCD is then set up and the string '12-bit ADC' is made to display on the LCD (lines 18 to 22). ADC_Init() function is called to initialize the ADC registers and start the conversion (line 23).

After conversion is complete, the ADST bit of the ADCSR gets cleared to 0. This condition is checked (line 25) and the next few lines are executed only once using the variable 'i.' If conversion is complete, the A/D converted value is written to the variable ADC_out (line 26). The Data Register was set to be right aligned. Hence to avoid reading wrong bits, the value 0X0FFF is used to mask the upper four bits (using zeros) and read the lower twelve bits (right bits). ADC_out is then converted into a string ADC_OUT (line 27) and displayed on the LCD (line 28).

Output

When a 3 V input was given to channel AN0, the A/D conversion result displayed was 3728. Using the formula, the A/D value is 3723.

6.5.2   10-Bit ADC

```
1.  #include "iodefine_RX62N.h"
2.  #include <stdlib.h>
3.  #include <stdio.h>
4.  #include "src\Glyph\Glyph.h"
5.  #define LCD_LINE1 0
6.  #define LCD_LINE2 1
7.  #define LCD_LINE3 2
8.  #define LCD_LINE4 3
9.  void ADC_Init(void);
10. void BSP_Display_String(int8_t, char * );
11. T_glyphHandle G_lcd;
12. void main(void){
13.     unsigned short ADC_value;
14.     int i = 0;
15.     char ADC_OUT[13];
16.     PORT4.DDR.BIT.B0 = 0;
17.     PORT4.ICR.BIT.B0 = 1;
18.     if(GlyphOpen(&G_lcd, 0) == GLYPH_ERROR_NONE){
19.         GlyphNormalScreen(G_lcd);
20.         GlyphSetFont(G_lcd, GLYPH_FONT_6_BY_13);
21.         GlyphClearScreen(G_lcd);
22.         BSP_Display_String(LCD_LINE1,"12-bit ADC");
23.         ADC_Init();
```

```
24.        while(1){
25.            if(AD0.ADCSR.BIT.ADST == 0 && i == 0){
26.                ADC_value = AD0.ADDRA & 0x0FFF;
27.                sprintf (ADC_OUT,"%d",ADC_value);
28.                BSP_Display_String(LCD_LINE2,ADC_OUT);
29.                i++;
30.            }
31.        }
32.    }
33.    GlyphClose(&G_lcd);
34. }
35. void ADC_Init(){
36.    SYSTEM.MSTPCRA.BIT.MSTPA23 = 0;
37.    AD0.ADCSR.BYTE = 0x00;
38.    AD0.ADCR.BYTE = 0x0C;
39.    AD0.ADDPR.BYTE = 0x00;
40.    AD0.ADDIAGR.BYTE = 0x0;
41.    AD0.ADCSR.BIT.ADST = 1;
42. }
43. void BSP_Display_String(int8_t aLine, char * aText){
44.    int8_t y = aLine * 16;
45.    GlyphEraseBlock(G_lcd, 0, y, 95, y + 15);
46.    GlyphSetXY(G_lcd, 0, y);
47.    GlyphString(G_lcd, (uint8_t *)aText, strlen(aText));
48. }
```

The iodefine_RX62N.h in line 1 defines the ports and the ADC registers which need to be set for the ADC operation. Hence it should be included in the program. Line 2 and line 3 are used to include standard C libraries. The src\Glyph\Glyph.h header file in (line 4) is included to enable the LCD display. The start of the LCD lines has been set up as macros in lines 5 to 8. G_lcd is variable of type T_glyphHandle (line 11) used to open the graphic LCD).

In lines 9 and 10, the functions ADC_Init and BSP_Display_String have been proto-typed. The ADC_Init() function (lines 35 to 42) is used to set up the registers for Single mode on AN0 (unit 0) and use a software trigger to start the ADC. The Module Stop Control Register A (MSTPCRA) is set such that Unit 0 of 10-bit ADC is selected (line 36). The A/D Control register (ADCSR) is used to select Channel 0 (AN0) and disable A/D end in-terrupt (line 37).The A/D Control Register (ADCR) is used to select Single mode, PCLK and software trigger (line 38). The Data Placement register (ADDPR) is used to select right alignment (line 39).The Self-Diagnostic function is set to off by default and it need not be set explicitly if the Self-Diagnostic function is not going to be used. The ADC is then started (line 42). The BSP_Display_String() function is used to display strings on the specified line of the LCD.

In the main program three variables have been used: ADC_value, ADC_OUT, and *i*. ADC_value declared in line 13 is used to get the ADC value from the data register. ADC_OUT declared in line 15, is a string which contains the ADC_value in string form so that it can be displayed on the LCD. The variable *i*, declared in line 14, is used to print the A/D value once on the LCD.

Next, the Port 4 pin 0 (AN0) is set up as an input pin (lines 16 and 17). The LCD is then set up and the string '10-bit ADC' is made to display on the LCD (lines 18 to 22). ADC_Init() function is called to initialize the ADC registers and start the conversion (line 23).

After conversion is complete, the ADST bit of the ADCSR gets cleared to 0. This condition is checked (line 25) and the next few lines are executed only once using the variable '*i*.' If conversion is complete, the A/D converted value is written to the variable ADC_value (line 26). The Data Register was set to be right aligned. Hence, to avoid reading wrong bits, the value 0X0FFF is used to mask the upper four bits (using zeros) and read the lower twelve bits (right bits). ADC_value is then converted into a string ADC_OUT (line 27) and displayed on the LCD (line 28).

Output

When a 3 V input was given to channel AN0, the A/D conversion result displayed was 1007. Using the formula, the A/D value is 930.

6.5.3   DAC

To understand how to program DACs let us look at an example in which DAC unit1 has been used.

```
1. #include "iodefine_RX62N.h"
2. #include <stdlib.h>
3. #include <stdio.h>
4. #include "src\Glyph\Glyph.h"
5. void DAC_Init(void);
6. T_glyphHandle G_lcd;
7. void main(void){
8.     PORT0.DDR.BIT.B5 = 1;
9.     PORT0.ICR.BIT.B5 = 0;
```

```
10.      if(GlyphOpen(&G_lcd, 0) == GLYPH_ERROR_NONE){
11.          GlyphNormalScreen(G_lcd);
12.          GlyphSetFont(G_lcd, GLYPH_FONT_6_BY_13);
13.          GlyphClearScreen(G_lcd);
14.          BSP_Display_String(LCD_LINE1,"DAC");
15.          DAC_Init();
16.          while(1){}
17.      }
18.      GlyphClose(&G_lcd);
19. }
20. void DAC_Init(){
21.      SYSTEM.MSTPCRA.BIT.MSTPA19 = 0;
22.      DA.DADR1 = 102;
23.      DA.DACR.BYTE = 0x9F;
24. }
25. void BSP_Display_String(int8_t aLine, char * aText){
26.      int8_t y = aLine * 16;
27.      GlyphEraseBlock(G_lcd, 0, y, 95, y + 15);
28.      GlyphSetXY(G_lcd, 0, y);
29.      GlyphString(G_lcd, (uint8_t *)aText, strlen(aText));
30. }
```

Programming the DAC also requires the same header files as the ADC example. The output of DAC1 can be observed on DA1, which is port 0 pin 5. This pin is set up as an output pin to observe the result (lines 8 and 9). The DAC has been set up using the DAC_Init() function (line 15). In the DAC_Init() function, the DAC unit is started up by setting SYSTEM.MSTPCRA.BIT.MSTPA19 to 0 (line 21). The digital value that has to be converted to analog value is set using DA.DADR1 (line 22), and DAC unit 1 has been selected by setting DA.DACR.BYTE = 0x9F.

Thus the DAC can be programmed and the analog value can be observed from port 0 pin 5 using a multimeter.

6.6   RECAP

Thus we have seen how the ADC and DAC of the RX62N board can be programmed. The methods discussed above have been using polling. Polling is not very efficient. An efficient method of using these features would be using interrupts. Interrupts are discussed in detail in Chapter 9.

6.7   REFERENCES

Hardware Manual, Renesas 32-Bit Microcomputer, RX Family/RX600 Series. Renesas Electronics America, Inc., 2010. Print.

RX62N Quick Start Guide. Renesas Electronics America, Inc., 2010. Computer Disc.

RX Family C/C++ Compiler, Assembler, Optimizing Linkage Editor; Compiler Package User's manual. Renesas Electronics America, Inc., 2010. Print.

6.8   EXERCISES

1. What is the output code (in decimal) of a 12-bit ADC with $V_{in} = 2.7$ V? $V_{+ref} = 5$ V? $V_{-ref} = -5$ V?

2. What is the output code (in decimal) of a 10-bit ADC with $V_{in} = 3$ V? $V_{+ref} = 5$ V? $V_{-ref} = 0$ V?

3. Given the following information of a particular analog to digital converter, determine the value of the digitally represented voltage and the step size of the converter:
   - The device is 10-bit ADC with a V_{+ref}—reference voltage of 3.3 volts and a V_{-ref} reference voltage of 0 volts.
   - The digital representation is: 0100110010.

4. What is the maximum quantization error for a 10-bit ADC with $V_{+ref} = 3.3$ V, $V_{-ref} = 0$ V?

5. Write a simple subroutine to set up the ADC registers for a 12-bit ADC operation of the following specifications: continuous scan mode, software triggered, PCLK/4, and Channel AN3.

6. Identify the modifications to be made if the above problem works on the value addition mode (3—time conversion).

7. Write a subroutine to set up the registers for a 10-bit ADC operation of the following specifications: continuous scan mode on channels AN1 and AN2, software triggered, PCLK/2, and data aligned to the LSB end.

8. Write a program to display the percentage of light intensity given a light sensor circuit. Record the 'darkness' (cover the sensor to make it dark) and 'brightness' (shine a bright LED or other light on the sensor) values. Identify the correct calibration such that the average room light lies between these values.

Chapter Seven

Serial Communications

7.1 LEARNING OBJECTIVES

Microcontrollers often need to communicate with other devices. Sending information serially (rather than in parallel) reduces the number of signal connections needed, saving space and cost. This chapter introduces how microcontrollers can exchange information serially using the UART, SPI, and I^2C communication controllers.

7.2 BASIC CONCEPTS OF SERIAL COMMUNICATIONS

Communication is the exchange of information between entities. In computers, information can be of any form which can be represented in a digital form. The medium of communication is electrical signals that vary continuously between high and low. The patterns in which they vary follow a set of rules that dictate the information the two entities want to exchange. Also these signals can be communicated one at a time, or as we are familiar with by now, bit by bit; or all at the same time on a single set of wires. The former is called serial communication wherein the information/data is sent one bit at a time, and the latter is called parallel communication where more than a single bit of data is shifted out at the same time from one side of the communication channel. Also there can be information channels where both ends can send as well as receive information at the same time. Such channels are called full duplex channels.

Parallel communication is primarily used when there is a need to transfer data at a very high speed over short distances, such as inside a computer from one peripheral to another. In such cases, the data and its delivery is of utmost importance. Parallel forms of communication are usually implemented using a bus. You may already be familiar with commonly used terms when talking about computer peripherals such as the IDE bus or the PCI bus. A fact to note is that these are low capacitance wires bundled together to form the bus and are usually not extremely long. Among other factors which affect the choice of parallel or serial communication are: the PCB board space, number of I/O pins, density, capacitance, signal integrity, and optical/electrical.

Serial communication, on the other hand, is a preferred medium when data is to be transferred over long distances. This may include a range of a couple hundred feet, from one building to another, or one computer to another. Serial communication is usually much slower than parallel. However, with the advent of time and technology, serial busses are becoming more and more high speed and are now also being used for short distances; i.e., internal communication mechanisms of computers.

In this chapter, we will primarily deal with serial communication only to establish data transfer between the Renesas microcontroller and a PC or other microcontroller boards or devices using various protocols such as USART, SPI, and I²C. It should be noted that there are other protocols beyond these that are also available with the RX62N; however, they require implementation using complex techniques. As you go through this chapter you will learn:

- The basics of each technique for serial communication, through polling; since polling is the best way to understand the exact details of the working of the peripheral device.
- The practical working of each technique through guided and intricately explained examples.
- How to distinguish between the implementation of each technique and the overheads of communication along with necessary precautions.

Before we jump into understanding the working of each serial communication interfacing technique, it is necessary to understanding the terminologies that are used while talking about serial communication, and also understand the need for communication. So why would we need communication between different peripherals? A few examples are mentioned below:

- Parallel Computation: In these cases, a complex problem is broken down into smaller, less complex parts and is distributed to other computers on a network, solved and then returned back to the source. The result is a reduction in the time taken to solve the problem, full use of available resources, etc.
- Data acquisition from remote locations: This is prominent in industrial applications where there are sensors deployed in the field or inside a factory. The sensors continuously gather data and send it to a central controller which monitors them and controls the overall system.
- Control of remote devices such as smart transducers.
- Developing fault tolerant systems.

Terminologies

Serial Port: A communication junction that provides for connecting a cable responsible for conducting electrical signals between the communicating entities, usually a 9 pin DBI male/female header.

Bus: One or more wires shared between devices in order to communicate electrical signals.

Baud Rate: Number of symbols transferred per second. A symbol may represent one or more bits of data through its encoding.

Bit Rate: Number of bits of information transferred per second.

Start Bit: Initial bit sent on the communication channel before communication begins.

Stop Bit: Final bit sent on the communication channel before communication terminates.

Parity Bit: A bit included in the communicated data whose status determines the parity (even/odd) of the information/data byte transferred.

Simplex Communication: A communication channel that can perform communication in only one direction, for example, family radios and walkie-talkies.

Full Duplex Communication: A communication channel is considered to be full duplex if both entities at the end of the channel can communicate in both directions simultaneously; i.e., transmit and receive data.

Half Duplex Communication: A communication channel/port is said to be half duplex if it can either transmit or receive data at an instant of time, but not simultaneously.

Synchronous: A clock signal accompanies the data being transmitted on a separate line thereby synchronizing the two end processors. Examples of such buses are HDMI and DVI for video signals.

Asynchronous: A clock signal does not accompany the data being transmitted. Instead an internal clock is maintained on both ends of the communicating modules to assist in synchronizing the data transfer. Typical PC serial port communications devices are an example of such transfers.

Now that we are familiar with some of the terms and needs of serial communication, we are ready to learn a few of the different interfaces available with the RX62N in detail. **Section 7.2** will introduce basic concepts applicable to each serial communication interface. **Section 7.3** will demonstrate the concepts of **Section 7.2** by providing an example for each interface. **Section 7.4** will describe advanced concepts of serial communication and **Section 7.5** will demonstrate them with more complex examples.

7.2.1   Introduction to the RX62N Serial Communication Interfacing

In order to fulfill the previously mentioned needs for communication between the processor and its desired peripherals or other devices, the RX62N has been provided with various mechanisms. These include the serial communication interface (SCI), Renesas serial peripheral interface (RSPI), and the Renesas Inter Integrated Chip (RIIC) bus interface. All three interfaces perform the same task of communicating data between various entities serially; i.e., one bit every cycle, however, the manner in which they do so is different for each interface. Depending upon the different requirements of communication, such as speed, number of devices needed to connect to, or topography of the communication, you may choose between the three different interfaces as desired. The three interfaces along with their features are described in the following:

Serial Communication Interface (SCI): This interface provides for one of the oldest and most fundamental methods in serial communication, the Universal Synchronous/Asynchronous Receiver/Transmitter (USART). The RX62N microcontroller has a total of six of these interfaces available which support USART communication as well as provide an interface to smart cards. The SCI has a variable transfer speed due to the availability of an on chip bit-rate generator and can transfer data with either the MSB or LSB leading the communication. It also provides for multi-processor communication functions. Other available functions include data length selection (i.e., 7 or 8 bits), number of stop bits, parity selection, clock source selection, receive error detection, and break detection. Details of the SCI are further discussed in **Section 7.2.2.**

Serial Peripheral Interface (RSPI): The Renesas SPI is a means for high-speed synchronous data transfer between the microcontroller and other connected serial peripherals, such as an SD card or other Renesas microcontrollers. The RSPI provides two channels for serial transfer. Each channel has either 3 or 4 pins; i.e., MISO, MOSI, SPCK, and SSL depending upon the mode of operation. The RSPI also has interchangeable data formats with which one can transmit either the LSB or MSB at the start of communication. The RSPI is also capable of handling data as either a master or slave. These shall be further discussed in **Section 7.2.3.** The number of bits transferred by the RSPI can be varied between eight to thirty-two bits. The RSPI operates through the means of a double buffer for both transmission and reception; each of which is 128-bits long, thereby permitting storage of four 32-bit long frames.

I^{2}C Bus Interface (RIIC): The RIIC is a simple, powerful, and flexible serial transmission method that generally operates using only two wires with a well-defined protocol. The RIIC provides for two channels with variable communication formats and transfer rates up to 1 Mbps. Also a total of 128 devices may be connected on a single RIIC bus may be connected at a time with only the requirement of a pull up resistor. Details of the RIIC bus are discussed in **Section 7.2.4.**

Table 7.1 provides for a comparison between the mentioned interfaces:

TABLE 7.1 Comparison Between Different Interfaces.

	SERIAL COMMUNICATION INTERFACE	RENESAS SERIAL PERIPHERAL INTERFACE	RENESAS INTER INTEGRATED CHIP BUS
Modes	USART/Smart Card interface	Four wire/Three wire mode	I^{2}C mode or SM bus mode
Max transfer speed	1.92 Mbps with PCLK @ 50 Mhz	Up to 25 Mbps	Up to 1Mbps
Max. number of devices/slaves connected per bus	1	8 SPI integrated channels for slave selection	127
Number of wires required for communication (not including ground)	2 to 3	3 to 4	2
Max. length of wires[1]	500 ft @ 9600 bps	10 feet with clock speed of few kHz	10 meters @ 100 kbps
Number of bits per unit transfer (excluding start and stop)	7 or 8	Up to 32 bits	8
Slave selection method	Addressed during communication when in multiprocessor communication mode, or else not available.	Using slave select line	Through addressing

[1]Becke et al., *Comparing Bus Solutions; High-Performance Linear/Interface: An Application Report,* Texas Instruments, revised 2004. http://www.lammertbies.nl/download/ti-appl-slla067a.pdf

Now that we have an idea of some of the different available techniques of serial communication available on the Renesas board and the differences between each of them, we can proceed to the details of operation for each interface available.

7.2.2 Universal Asynchronous Receiver and Transmitter

The UART/USART is one of the oldest mechanisms available for the serial transmission of data. The idea of a UART was developed in order to convert parallel data into serial data to be transmitted over large distances. This is usually done by means of a shift register which shifts out a one bit per clock cycle. Given the premise that the shift register clocks out a one bit per clock cycle, it requires one clock cycle to fill the shift register in parallel; and where the clock provided to both the CPU and the shift register is the same, one can easily determine that serial transmission is at least N times slower than parallel transmission, where N is the number of bits available in the serial register; i.e., if the size of the shift register is eight bits, serial communication is at least eight times slower than parallel communication. Before we jump into detailed concepts of the Renesas UART, let us look at the mechanism of a shift register.

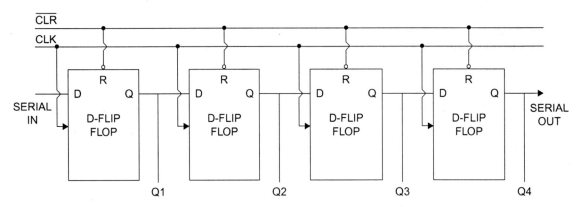

Figure 7.1 Serial Input Parallel Output (SIPO) shift register.

If one is familiar with digital circuits, one may easily note from Figure 7.1 that a shift register is nothing but a series of cascaded flip-flops that share the same clock. The most commonly used flip-flop for shift registers is the D flip-flop where the D stands for Delayed. More detailed information on the D flip-flop can be found in *Digital Logic and Microprocessor Design with VHDL* (Hwang), but in essence it is enough to know that the flip-flop outputs the state of the input (D), or data, for every rising edge of the clock, and maintains it until the next rising edge. Depending on the configuration, there can be two types of shift registers, Parallel In Serial Out (PISO) and Serial In Parallel Out (SIPO). A PISO type shift register usually shifts out data serially, that is, the data is input to the shift register through a parallel bus and gets shifted out onto the serial bus in parallel, and is therefore used on the transmitter side of the interface; whereas the SIPO type shift register takes data in serially and converts it to parallel form, and is thus used at the receiver side of the interface. The two types of shift registers are shown in Figure 7.1 and Figure 7.2 respectively. This is the basis of operation for the UART. More reading on the electronics part of the flip-flops can be found at http://faculty.lasierra.edu/~ehwang/digitaldesign (Hwang, *Digital Logic and Microprocessor Design with VHDL*).

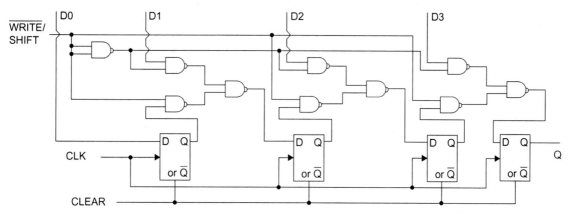

Figure 7.2   Parallel Input Serial Output (PISO) shift register.

Now that we are aware of the basic mechanism of UART serial communication, it is worthwhile to notice that there are various other overheads to communication that are required, such as ensuring that the data has been communicated properly and identified. These are usually done by addition of extra bits in the communication process. Additional bits are padded to the eight bits of data, and then the data is transmitted. The additional bits padded are the START and STOP bits. When not communicating, both the TX(transmit) and RX(receive) lines are held in the Hi-Z (high impedance) state. When transmission/reception of data is about to occur, the line is first pulled low. This period is called the START bit and is maintained for one clock cycle. After eight bits of data transmission, the line is pulled high again and maintained high. This is the STOP bit and is maintained for at least one clock cycle before the next byte of data can be communicated. In this manner data is recognized over the channel for reception. But this does not yet resolve the problem of incorrect data transmission. Over distances, electrical signals have a tendency to weaken, reduce in amplitude, and also pick up noise. This may result in data corruption. This is checked by the addition of an extra bit to the data, also called the parity. The parity bit is set to 1 or 0 in order to make the total number of 1 bits even (for even parity) or odd (for odd parity). One more note is that all the above mentioned transactions are performed at logic levels; i.e., voltages range from 0 to 3 V at most 5 V. These voltages are very much susceptible to noise and signal corruption over long distances. To prevent this, an amplifier circuit boosts and inverts the voltages so that they vary from −15 V (logic high) to +15 V (logic low). These are the voltage levels for the telecommunications Recommended Standard 232(RS-232). A level-shifting inverter circuit converts the RS232 voltages back to logic levels at each receiver. More information regarding the RS-232 standard can be found in "EIA Standard RS-232-C Interface between Data Terminal Equipment and Data Communication Equipment Employing Serial Data Interchange" (Electronic Industries Association). This concludes the basic working mechanism of the UART. Now we come to the control part of the UART, which is essentially done by means of a few special function registers (SFRs) that are linked to the serial communications interface available with the Renesas Microcontroller.

Registers Related to the SCI in UART Mode

The Serial Communications Interface provides for a Universal Synchronous Transmitter/Receiver, a Universal Asynchronous Transmitter/Receiver, and a Smart Card interface. The Renesas Microcontroller has six serial communication interfaces, which can provide for the previously mentioned three communication methods. However, before one can use the SCI it needs to be properly configured to work in one of the three modes. We shall be configuring the SCI to work as a UART, and therefore we would be talking about the special function registers and the values to be injected into them to make the UART work successfully. Finally, we will discuss how to test the configured UART and the physical variations possible to the communication signals.

The special function registers related to the UART are:

- Serial Mode Register (SMR)
- Bit Rate Register (BRR)
- Serial Control Register (SCR)
- Transmit Data Register (TDR)
- Serial Status Register (SSR)
- Receive Data Register (RDR)
- Smart Card Mode Register (SCMR)
- Serial Extended Mode Register (SEMR)

Smart Card Mode Register (SCIx.SCMR): This is the register that selects whether the SCI is going to be in either the Smart Card Interface mode or act as a UART or USART. It has four bits that need to be assigned values. However, since we are only concerned with setting up the SCI as a UART, the only bit we need to be concerned with is the SMIF bit. Setting this bit to 1 causes the particular SCI to enter smart card interface mode else the SCI can behave as either a Synchronous or Asynchronous transmitter/receiver. Hence we always set it to 0.

b7	b6	b5	b4	b3	b2	b1	b0
BCP2	—	—	—	SDIR	SINV	—	SMIF

Value after reset: 1   1   1   1   0   0   1   0

Figure 7.3 The SCI Smart card mode register. Source: *Hardware Manual, Renesas 32-Bit Microcomputer, RX Family/RX600 Series,* Renesas Electronics America, Inc., 2010, page 1418.

Serial Mode Register (SCIX.SMR)

This special function register is concerned with operational variations of the UART. The register details are as follows:

b7	b6	b5	b4	b3	b2	b1	b0
CM	CHR	PE	PM	STOP	MP	CKS[1:0]	

Value after reset: 0   0   0   0   0   0   0   0

Figure 7.4 The SCI Serial mode register. Source: *Hardware Manual,* page 1405.

- Clock speed applied to the shift register: The clock applied to the Shift Register which is related to the TDR is the PCLK. The frequency of this clock can be reduced by means of a frequency divider. This is selectable by the CKS1 and CKS0 bits which give combinations to divide the PCLK frequency by 1, 4, 16, or 64. Refer to Table 7.2 for details. These bits usually depend upon the acceptable baud rate error and the value of the BRR register.

- Whether the communication line is concerned with multiprocessor communication: Setting the Multiprocessor mode bit MP in the SMR causes the UART to become aware of multiprocessor communication taking place on the channel. If one is not using multiprocessor communication, this bit is set to 0.

  Multiprocessor mode (or 9 bit wake-up mode, or multidrop mode) was a very common way of placing more than one slave on an UART bus or giving it multidrop capability. In these systems when the ninth bit was set as a high this indicated that the remaining eight bits were the address of the device that the Master wanted to communicate with. All devices processed the address field. Only the device with the corresponding address continued to communicate, all other devices went back to "sleep" waiting for the next address command. In most devices that support MP the UART peripheral will create an interrupt when the ninth bit is high. This allows the devices that are not actively communicating with the Master to ignore all other traffic on the bus, reducing the overhead on those MCUs.

■ Stop bit length: STOP determines the length of the Stop bit, whether it is either one or two bits wide. Setting this bit to 0 selects length of stop bit as 1 whereas setting it to 1 causes the length of stop bit to be 2 bits wide.

■ Parity mode: Setting this bit to 1 causes the parity bit to be high when the parity of the data is odd; whereas, setting this bit to 0 causes the parity bit to be high if the parity of the data is even.

■ Parity enable: Setting the PE bit to 1 enables the transmission of the parity bit and disables otherwise.

■ Length of data being transmitted: Setting the CHR bit to 1 truncates the size of the data being transmitted to seven bits, or else 8-bit long data is transmitted.

■ Communications mode: The CM bit determines the operation of the SCI, whether it is operating in synchronous or asynchronous mode. If this bit is set to 1, the interfaces act in the Clock synchronous mode, or else it enters the Clock asynchronous mode. If operating in the Clock synchronous mode, a clock signal can be generated on the SCLK line by the transmitter which also acts as the clock input to the shift register on the receiver end of the module. Selection whether the clock is input or output is dependent on the state of the CKE bit in register SCIx.SCR.

Serial Control Register (SCIx.SCR)

This register is responsible for controlling the Serial Communications Interface; whether it is turned on or off, the choice of input clock to the shift register, and function of the SCK pin. The register details are as follows:

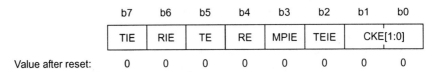

b7	b6	b5	b4	b3	b2	b1	b0
TIE	RIE	TE	RE	MPIE	TEIE	CKE[1:0]	

Value after reset: 0   0   0   0   0   0   0   0

Figure 7.5   The SCI serial control register. Source: *Hardware Manual*, page 1409.

■ Clock Enable bits (CKE 0, CKE 1): These bits determine which clock is to be used when transferring data, internal or external, and the function of the SCKn pin corresponding to the SCIn module. The Table 7.2 determines the functions depending on each of the four combinations of the 2 bits when the SCI is in Asynchronous mode.

■ Transmit end interrupt enable: Setting this bit to 1 and 0 enables and disables the transmit end interrupt that is generated every time a byte is transmitted from the SCI.

- Multiprocessor Interrupt Enable: This bit is related to Multiprocessor communication and is usually set to 0 when there is no multiprocessor communication occurring on the bus.
- Receive Enable: Setting this bit to 0 and 1 disables and enables reception of data on the Rxn pin, respectively.
- Transmit Enable: Setting this bit to 0 and 1 disables and enables transmission of data on the Txn pin, respectively.
- Receive Interrupt Enable: Setting this bit to 1 and 0 enables and disables the generation of a receive interrupt, respectively.
- Transmit Interrupt Enable: Setting this bit to 1 and 0 enables and disables the generation of a transmit interrupt, respectively.

Serial Status Register (SCIx.SSR)

This is a read only type of register (except for bit 0) which determines the condition of the currently received byte over the corresponding SCI by means of various flag bits.

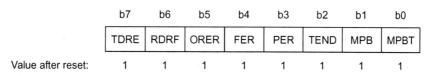

Figure 7.6 The SCI serial status register. Source: Hardware Manual, page 1411.

- Multiprocessor bit transfer: This bit sets the value of the multiprocessor bit for adding to the transmission frame
- Multiprocessor bit (received): This bit holds the value of the multiprocessor bit in the received frame. Note that the value of this bit does not change when RE bit in SCR is kept as 0. This is a read only type bit.
- Transmit End Flag: This flag is set at the end of transmission of a byte from the TDR or in case the serial transmission is disabled. Resetting this flag requires one to write data to the TDR.
- Parity Error Flag: This bit indicates a parity error has occurred during reception in asynchronous mode and reception ends abnormally. When a parity error occurs, data is maintained in the RDR and the parity error flag is set but subsequent reception in terminated until PER is reset
- Error signal status flag: This flag is set when a low error signal and reset after clearing to 0 manually
- Overrun Error Flag: This flag is set if data is received in RDR before the previous data has been read. The flag is cleared when 0 is written to it.

Bit Rate Register (SCIx.BRR)

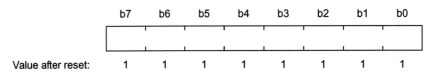

Value after reset: 1   1   1   1   1   1   1   1

Figure 7.7   The SCI bit rate register. Source: *Hardware Manual,* page 1419.

This is the register that controls the generation of the clock signal to be provided to the shift registers. Table 7.2 shows the relation between the value N input into the BRR and the bit rate B for normal asynchronous mode. In asynchronous mode, one should note that there is always a minor difference in timings between the two processors involved in communication, due to the minor differences in parts (oscillator circuits). The actual bit rate may not exactly meet the desired rate because only rates which can be generated by dividing PCLK by multiples of 16 are possible. Therefore, an error in communication, such as loss of reception of a bit, may occur if the bit rate mismatch (error) between the transmitter and receiver is too large. Table 7.2 defines a few standard values of BRR along with the generated bit rate's percentage error for each case.

TABLE 7.2   Bit Rates and Percent Errors
(N = BRR value, n = Clock source setting with CKS bits in SMR).

| BIT RATE (bit/s) | OPERATING FREQUENCY PCLK (MHZ) | | | | | | | | | | | |
| | 25 | | | 30 | | | 33 | | | 50 | | |
	n	N	ERROR (%)	n	N	ERROR (%)	n	N	ERROR (%)	n	N	ERROR (%)
110	3	110	−0.02	3	132	0.13	3	145	0.33	3	221	−0.02
150	3	80	0.47	3	97	−0.35	3	106	0.39	3	162	−0.15
300	2	162	−0.15	2	194	0.16	2	214	−0.07	3	80	0.47
600	2	80	0.47	2	97	−0.35	2	106	0.39	2	162	−0.15
1200	1	162	−0.15	1	194	0.16	1	214	−0.07	2	80	0.47
2400	1	80	0.47	1	97	−0.35	1	106	0.39	1	162	−0.15
4800	0	162	−0.15	0	194	0.16	0	214	−0.07	1	80	0.47
9600	0	80	0.47	0	97	−0.35	0	106	0.39	1	40	−0.77
19200	0	40	−0.76	0	48	−0.35	0	53	−0.54	0	80	0.47
31250	0	24	0.00	0	29	0.00	0	32	0	0	49	0.00
38400	0	19	1.73	0	23	1.73	0	26	−0.54	0	40	−0.77

Transmit Data Register (SCIx.TDR)

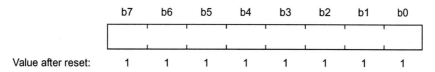

Figure 7.8   The SCI transmit data register. Source: *Hardware Manual,* page 1404.

This register contains the data to be transmitted over the communication channel. The data is usually eight bits long and is padded with the start, stop, and parity bits. The TDR acts as a buffer to the transmit shift register which is the actual register responsible for shifting out the data serially on to the transmit pin.

Receive Data Register (SCIx.RDR)

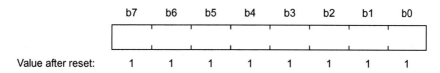

Figure 7.9   The SCI receive data register. Source: *Hardware Manual,* page 1404.

This register contains the data received over the communication channel. The data is usually eight bits long and is stripped off the start, stop, and parity bits.

Variations to the UART

Before we move on to other techniques of serial communication, it is worthwhile to mention that there are other UART-based communication standards which use different types of voltage signaling, such as the RS-422, RS-423, RS-449, and RS-485. More readings on these can be found at http://focus.ti.com/lit/an/slla070d/slla070d.pdf (Soltero et al.).

7.2.3   Renesas Serial Peripheral Interface

Serial Peripheral Interface (SPI) uses synchronous communication, so a dedicated clock signal must be transmitted in addition to the serial data. Providing this clock signal lets us simplify the hardware down to just the shift registers and some minor supporting logic. This is much simpler than the USART, as there is no need for a bit rate generator, start and stop bits, and other modules. The dedicated clock signal determines the bit rate. This interface is similar to the USART. SPI is a full duplex mode of communication in which data can be transmitted and received simultaneously. The SPI was designed by Motorola to achieve high speed data transfer between peripherals of a microcontroller, and generally requires three wires for communication. In case multiple slave devices (devices to communicate with) are attached on the SPI bus, additional lines for selecting the device are required. However if not more than one slave device is connected on the bus, communication may be performed with only three wires. A typical SPI set up between a microcontroller and a peripheral is shown in Figure 7.10. As seen in the figure, the devices connected on the SPI bus usually have one master and one or more slave peripherals. However a multi-master mode may also be used. Master devices are usually microcontrollers or processors that control the flow of data to and from the slave peripheral device. The four required lines for communication are Serial Clock (SCLK), Master In Slave Out (MISO), Master Out Slave In (MOSI), and Slave Select (SSL).

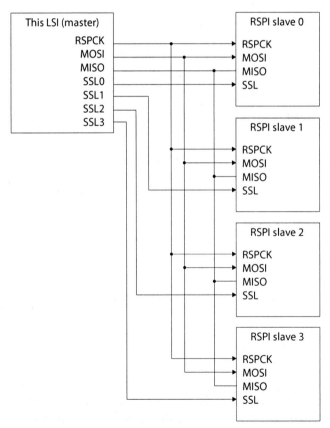

Figure 7.10 Serial Peripheral Interface bus; Single master with multiple slaves connected. Source: *Hardware Manual,* page 1664.

Serial Clock: Accompanying each data transfer is a clock signal that synchronizes the Master and Slave device. The length of the clock signal also determines the amount of data transferred on the MISO and MOSI pins. The serial clock is always generated by the master device and the slave synchronizes itself and the data transfer using the same clock.

Master Out Slave In: This line is similar to the transmit line of the USART, provided the Master device remains the same.

Master In Slave Out: This line is similar to the receive line of the USART, provided the Master device remains the same.

Slave Select: This pin, when acting as an output pin, provides for an active low signal that activates or de-activates the slave. The slave is usually in sleep mode until this line is toggled to the desired state (low or high) for activating the device. When in multi master mode, this pin acts as an input, and when pulled low indicates that another master is trying to communicate on the SPI bus.

Now that we have an introduction to the physical part of the SPI interface, it is time to understand the working. But before we move on, it is worthwhile to note some of the features of the Renesas SPI that are different from most other microcontrollers. The Renesas Microcontroller has two independent SPI modules with multiple (four) slave select lines for each channel. The important features of the Renesas Serial Peripheral Interface are:

- Transmit only operation available.
- Switching of phase and polarity of the serial clock.
- LSB/MSB first option.
- 128-bit transmit/receive buffers.
- Transfer bit length is selectable as 8, 9, 10, 11, 12, 13, 14, 15, 16, 20, 24, or 32 bits.
- Up to four frames can be transferred in one round of transmission/reception (each frame consisting of up to 32 bits).
- Mode fault error, overrun error, and parity error detection.
- A transfer of up to eight commands can be executed sequentially in looped execution with SSL signal value, bit rate, RSPCK polarity/phase, transfer data length, LSB/MSB-first, burst, RSPCK delay, SSL negation delay, and next-access delay which can be changed for each command.
- A transfer can be initiated by simply writing to the transmit buffer.

General Working of SPI Modules

During every SPI transfer, there always exists a Master device and a slave device. The master device is the one responsible for performing the transfer of data and generating the clock signal for performing the synchronous transfer of data. The slave device, while receiving data also sends out data of its own to the master over the MISO line. Thus full duplex communication occurs. The slave is active only when the master pulls the corresponding Slave Select Line low. This results in a "chip select" and activates the slave device.

Events take place in this sequence:

- Master selects slave by pulling SSL low, thereby activating the slave device for communicating data.
- Master starts synchronous transfer of data by sending out a clock signal over the SCLK pin and the data over the MOSI line. The master waits until the data transfer completes.
- On reception of the serial clock signal from the master, the slave device starts outputting data that it might want to transfer to the master.
- Data transfer halts as soon as the clock signal stops.
- Master deselects the slave by pulling the SSL line high.

Configurations of the Renesas SPI

The Renesas microcontroller SPI bus can be configured to have:

- Single Master Single Slave
- Single Master Multiple Slaves
- Multiple Masters Multiple Slaves

For the sake of simplicity, and understanding the basics of SPI, we shall consider only the Single Master Single Slave configuration. These configurations are shown in Figures 7.11 to 7.13.

Registers Related to the Renesas Serial Peripheral Interface

The following describes the registers that are responsible for control of the RSPI with a short explanation, and the values to be assigned to each bit for setting up the SPI in the single master single slave configuration with the RX62N functioning as the master device.

Serial Peripheral Control Register (SPCR): This register controls the operating mode of the RSPI. The functions of the bits are as follows:

- SPMS: This is the RSPI mode select bit which determines whether the SPI will act as a three wire (SCLK, MOSI, MISO) or a four wire interface (SCLK, MOSI, MISO, and SSLn). Setting this bit to 0 makes the RSPI operate in four wire mode whereas setting it to 1 makes the RSPI function in three wire clock synchronous mode. When operating in four wire mode, the pins SSL0 to SSL3 become available for chip selection; the default chip (slave) select pin being SSL0. When

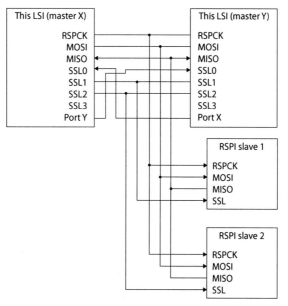

Figure 7.11   Multiple Masters Multiple Slaves. Source: *Hardware Manual*, page 1666.

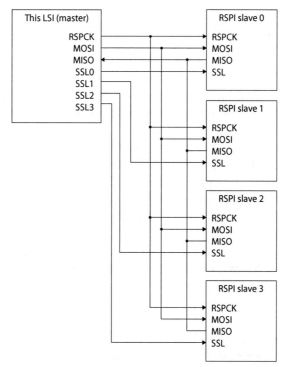

Figure 7.12   Single Master Multiple Slaves. Source: *Hardware Manual*, page 1664.

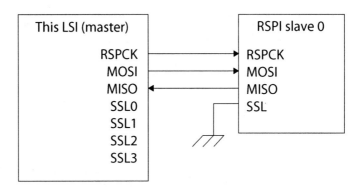

Figure 7.13   Single Master Single Slave (also shows clock synchronous configuration). Source: *Hardware Manual,* page 1663.

	b7	b6	b5	b4	b3	b2	b1	b0
	SPRIE	SPE	SPTIE	SPEIE	MSTR	MODFEN	TXMD	SPMS
Value after reset:	0	0	0	0	0	0	0	0

Figure 7.14   The SPI serial peripheral control register. Source: *Hardware Manual,* page 1635.

operating in three wire mode, it is assumed that either the desired chip is selected manually or there is only one active SPI slave on the device.

- TXMD: This is the Communications Operating Mode Select bit that determines whether the SPI will be acting in full duplex mode or perform transmit operations only.
- MODFEN: This bit enables or disables mode fault error detection. Mode fault error occurs when the SPI is in master mode and an external device drives a slave select pin low.
- MSTR: This bit determines whether the microcontroller acts as a master or a slave.
- SPEIE: Setting this bit to 1 enables the generation SPI error interrupt. This interrupt occurs when the RSPI module detects a mode fault or an overrun error, and sets the corresponding bits in the status register SPSR to 1.
- SPTIE: Setting this bit to 1 enables SPI transmit interrupt to indicate that the transmit buffer is empty.
- SPE: Setting this bit to 1 enables the SPI module.
- SPRIE: Setting this bit to 1 enables SPI receive interrupt. The interrupt occurs whenever the receive buffer is successfully written without errors.

Serial Peripheral Control Register (SPCR2):   This register adds to the controllability of the operating mode of the Renesas SPI. The functions of the bits are as follows:

b7	b6	b5	b4	b3	b2	b1	b0
—	—	—	—	PTE	SPIIE	SPOE	SPPE

Value after reset: 0   0   0   0   0   0   0   0

Figure 7.15 The SPI serial peripheral control register 2. Source: *Hardware Manual*, page 1653.

- ▨ SPPE: The SPPE bit enables or disables the parity function. The parity bit is added to transmit data, and parity checking is performed for receive data when the communications operating mode select bit (TXMD) in the RSPI control register (SPCR) is 0 and the SPPE bit in SPCR2 is 1. The parity bit is added to transmit data but parity checking is not performed for receive data when the SPCR.TXMD bit is 1 and the SPPE bit in SPCR2 is 1.
- ▨ SPOE: When even parity is set, parity bit addition is performed so that the total number of 1-bits in the transmit/receive character plus the parity bit is even. Similarly, when odd parity is set, parity bit addition is performed so that the total number of 1-bits in the transmit/receive character plus the parity bit is odd. The SPOE bit is valid only when the SPPE bit is 1.
- ▨ SPIIE: The SPIIE bit enables or disables the generation of RSPI idle interrupt requests when the RSPI being in the idle state is detected and the IDLNF flag in the RSPI status register (SPSR) is cleared to 0.
- ▨ PTE: The PTE bit enables the self-diagnosis function of the parity circuit in order to check whether the parity function is operating correctly.

Slave Select Polarity (SSLP): This register sets the polarity of the slave select lines SSL0 to SSL3 of the Renesas SPI module. SSLP has four usable bits that select the polarity (active low/active high) for the corresponding slave select lines.

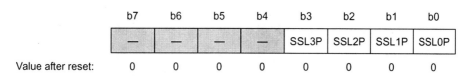

b7	b6	b5	b4	b3	b2	b1	b0
—	—	—	—	SSL3P	SSL2P	SSL1P	SSL0P

Value after reset: 0   0   0   0   0   0   0   0

Figure 7.16 The SPI slave select polarity register. Source: *Hardware Manual*, page 1637.

Setting the SSLxP bits to 0 sets the SSLx pin to active low, while setting SSLxP bit to 1 sets the SSLx pin to active high ($x = 0$ or 1 or 2 or 3).

Serial Peripheral Pin Control Register (SPPCR): This register sets the modes of the RSPI pins.

	b7	b6	b5	b4	b3	b2	b1	b0
	—	—	MOIFE	MOIFV	—	SPOM	SPLP2	SPLP
Value after reset:	0	0	0	0	0	0	0	0

Figure 7.17 The SPI pin control register. Source: *Hardware Manual,* page 1638.

- SPLP: When the SPLP (SPI Loopback) bit is set to 1, the RSPI shuts off the path between the MISOn pin and the shift register, and between the MOSIn pin and the shift register, and connects (reverses) the input path and output path for the shift register (loopback mode).
- SPLP2: The function of this bit is the same as the SPLP. When the SPLP2 bit is set to 1, the RSPI shuts off the path between the MISOn pin and the shift register, and between the MOSIn pin and the shift register, and connects (reverses) the input path and output path for the shift register (loopback mode).
- SPOM: The SPI Output Mode bit when set to 0 sets the RSPI output pins to function as CMOS output pins, or open drain output pins when set to 0.
- MOVIFV: If the MOSI Idle Fixed Value bit is 1 in master mode, the MOIFV bit determines the MOSIn pin output value during the SSL negation period (including the SSL retention period during a burst transfer).
- MOVIFE: The MOSI Idle Value Fixing Enable bit fixes the MOSI output value when the RSPI in master mode is in an SSL negation period (including the SSL retention period during a burst transfer). When the MOIFE bit is 0, the RSPI outputs the last data from the previous serial transfer during the SSL negation period. When the MOIFE bit is 1, the RSPI outputs the fixed value set in the MOIFV bit to the MOSI bit.

Serial Peripheral Status (SPSR): This register is an indicator of the current operating status of the RSPI.

	b7	b6	b5	b4	b3	b2	b1	b0
	—	—	—	—	PERF	MODF	IDLNF	OVRF
Value after reset:	x	0	x	0	0	0	0	0

Figure 7.18 The SPI serial peripheral status register. Source: *Hardware Manual,* page 1640.

■ OVRF: This Overrun error flag is set when a serial transfer ends while the SPCR.TXMD bit is 0 and the receive buffer holds data that has not yet been read out, thereby indicating an overrun error. It is cleared when the CPU writes the value 0 to the OVRF bit.

■ IDLNF: The RSPI Idle Flag indicates the transfer status of the RSPI. The IDLNF, when in master mode, is cleared when all of the following conditions are satisfied:

  ☐ The SPCR.SPE bit is 0 (RSPI is initialized).
  ☐ The transmit buffer (SPTX) is empty (data for the next transfer is not set).
  ☐ The SPSSR.SPCP[2:0] bits are 000 (beginning of sequence control).
  ☐ The RSPI internal sequencer has entered the idle state (status in which operations up to the next-access delay have finished).

  The IDLNF bit, when in master mode, is set when any of the above conditions are not satisfied, thereby indicating a non-idle state.

  When acting as a slave, this bit is set when the SPCR.SPE bit is 1 (RSPI function is enabled) and cleared when SPCR.SPE bit is 0 (RSPI is initialized).

■ MODF: A SPI Mode Fault is detected in a multi master mode when the input level of the SSLn pin changes to the active level while the SPCR.MSTR bit is 1 (master mode) and the SPCR.MODFEN bit is 1 (mode fault error detection is enabled). When in slave mode, a mode fault is detected when the SSLn pin is negated before the RSPCK cycle necessary for data transfer ends while the SPCR.MSTR bit is 0 (slave mode) and the SPCR.MODFEN bit is 1 (mode fault error detection is enabled), the RSPI detects a mode fault error. The MODF flag is cleared by writing 0 to the MODF bit.

■ PERF: The Parity Error Flag is set when a serial transfer ends while the SPCR.TXMD bit is 0 and the SPCR2.SPPE bit is 1. This bit is cleared when CPU reads SPSR when the PERF bit is 1, and then writes the value 0 to the PERF bit.

Serial Peripheral Data Register (SPDR): This register contains data to be transmitted and data received over the SPI channel. Data written to this register is transmitted over the SPI channel. When this register is read from it returns the data received over the transmission channel.

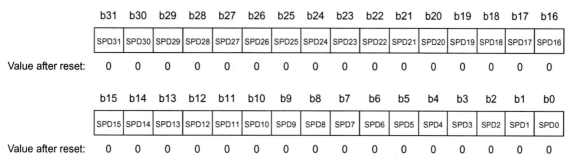

Figure 7.19 The SPI serial peripheral data register. Source: *Hardware Manual,* page 1643.

The frame length and the number of bits transferred from this register depends upon the setting of the SPFC[1:0] and SPB[3:0] bits.

Serial Peripheral Sequence Control (SPSCR): This register sets the sequence method when the RSPI operates in master mode.

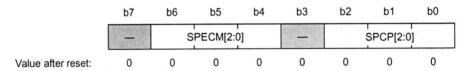

Figure 7.20 The SPI serial peripheral sequence control register. *Source: Hardware Manual,* page 1644.

- SPSLN[2:0]: The SPI Sequence Length Specification bits specify a sequence length when the RSPI performs sequential operations in master mode. When in slave mode, the RSPI always refers to SPCMD0.

Serial Peripheral Sequence Status (SPSSR): This register indicates the sequence control status when the RSPI operates in master mode.

b7	b6	b5	b4	b3	b2	b1	b0
—	SPECM[2:0]			—	SPCP[2:0]		

Value after reset: 0 0 0 0 0 0 0 0

Figure 7.21 The SPI serial peripheral sequence status register. *Source: Hardware Manual,* page 1645.

- SPCP[2:0]: The RSPI command pointer bits point to the SPCMDn currently being executed.
- SPEM[2:0]: The RSPI Error command in conjunction with the SPSR register points to the command SPCMDn which caused an error.

Serial Peripheral Bit Rate Register (SPBR): The value of this register determines the rate of data transfer.

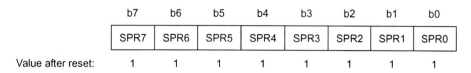

b7	b6	b5	b4	b3	b2	b1	b0
SPR7	SPR6	SPR5	SPR4	SPR3	SPR2	SPR1	SPR0

Value after reset: 1   1   1   1   1   1   1   1

Figure 7.22 The SPI bit rate register. Source: *Hardware Manual,* page 1646.

The SPBR register can have any value from 0 to 255. The following table shows a few example bit rate settings.

TABLE 7.3 Example Bit Rate Settings (n = SPDR value, N = BRDV[1:0]); value in SPCMDx.

SPBR (n)	BRDV[1:0] Bits (N)	DIVISION RATIO	BIT RATE PCLK = 32 MHz	PCLK = 36 MHz	PCLK = 40 MHz	PCLK = 50 MHz
0	0	2	16.0 Mbps*	18.0 Mbps*	20.0 Mbps*	25.0 Mbps*
1	0	4	8.00 Mbps	9.00 Mbps	10.0 Mbps	12.5 Mbps
2	0	6	5.33 Mbps	6.00 Mbps	6.67 Mbps	8.33 Mbps
3	0	8	4.00 Mbps	4.50 Mbps	5.00 Mbps	6.25 Mbps
4	0	10	3.20 Mbps	3.60 Mbps	4.00 Mbps	5.00 Mbps
5	0	12	2.67 Mbps	3.00 Mbps	3.33 Mbps	4.16 Mbps
5	1	24	1.33 Mbps	1.50 Mbps	1.67 Mbps	2.08 Mbps
5	2	48	667 kbps	750 kbps	833 kbps	1.04 Mbps
5	3	96	333 kbps	375 kbps	417 kbps	521 kbps
255	3	4096	7.81 kbps	8.80 kbps	9.78 kbps	12.2 kbps

Serial Peripheral Data Control Register (SPDCR): This register determines the number of frames that can be stored in SPDR, controls the SSLn pin output reading from SPDR, and selects width access to SPDR.

b7	b6	b5	b4	b3	b2	b1	b0
—	—	SPLW	SPRDTD	SLSEL[1:0]		SPLF[1:0]	

Value after reset: 0   0   0   0   0   0   0   0

Figure 7.23 The SPI serial peripheral data control register. Source: *Hardware Manual,* page 1647.

■ SPFC[1:0]: These bits specify the number of frames that can be stored in SPDR. Up to four frames can be transmitted or received in one round of transmission or reception, and the amount of data is determined by the combination of the RSPI data length specification bits (SPB[3:0]) in the RSPI command register (SPCMD), the RSPI sequence length specification bits (SPSLN[2:0]) in the RSPI sequence control register (SPSCR), and the number of frames specification bits (SPFC[1:0]) in the RSPI data control register (SPDCR). Also, the SPFC[1:0] bits specify the number of received data at which the RSPI receive buffer full interrupt is requested. The following table shows the frame configurations that can be stored in SPDR and examples of combinations of settings for transmission and reception.

TABLE 7.4   Setting the Number of Frames Transmitted from SPDR.

SETTING	SPB[3:0]	SPSLN[2:0]	SPFC[1:0]	NUMBER OF FRAMES FOR TRANSFER	NUMBER OF FRAMES AT WHICH RECEIVE BUFFER FULL INTERRUPT OCCURS OR TRANSMIT BUFFER HOLDING DATA IS RECOGNIZED
1–1	N	000	00	1	1
1–2	N	000	01	2	2
1–3	N	000	10	3	3
1–4	N	000	11	4	4
2–1	N, M	001	01	2	2
2–2	N, M	001	11	4	4
3	N, M, O	010	10	3	3
4	N, M, O, P	011	11	4	4
5	N, M, O, P, Q	100	00	5	1
6	N, M, O, P, Q, R	101	00	6	1
7	N, M, O, P, Q, R, S	110	00	7	1
8	N, M, O, P, Q, R, S, T	111	00	8	1

■ SLSEL[1:0]: SSL Pin Output Selection bits control the SSLn pin output in master mode for the corresponding RSPI.

TABLE 7.5   SSL Pin Output Selection Configuration/Function.

	SLSEL [1:0] = 00	SLSEL [1:0] = 01	SLSEL [1:0] = 10	SLSEL [1:0] = 11
SSL3	Output	I/O	I/O	Setting prohibited
SSL2	Output	I/O	I/O	
SSL1	Output	I/O	Output	
SSL0	Output	Output	Output	

Serial Peripheral Clock Delay Register (SPCKD): The value of this register sets a pe-riod from the beginning of SSL signal assertion to the clock oscillations on the RSPK line.

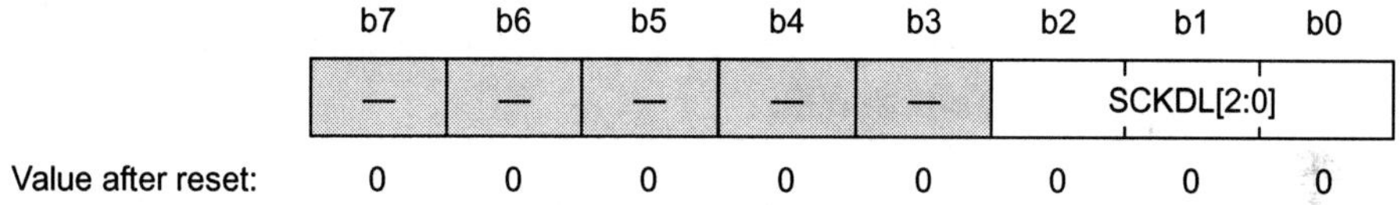

b7	b6	b5	b4	b3	b2	b1	b0
—	—	—	—	—	SCKDL[2:0]		

Value after reset: 0   0   0   0   0   0   0   0

Figure 7.24   The SPI serial peripheral clock delay register. Source: *Hardware Manual,* page 1650.

- SCKDL [2:0]: The RSPCK Delay Setting bits set an RSPCK delay value when the SPCMD.SCKDEN bit is 1. When using the RSPI in slave mode, set the SCKDL[2:0] bits to 000.

Slave Select Line Negation Delay (SSLND): This register sets a period/delay from the transmission of final RSPCK edge to the negation of the SSL signal during a serial transfer by the RSPI in master mode.

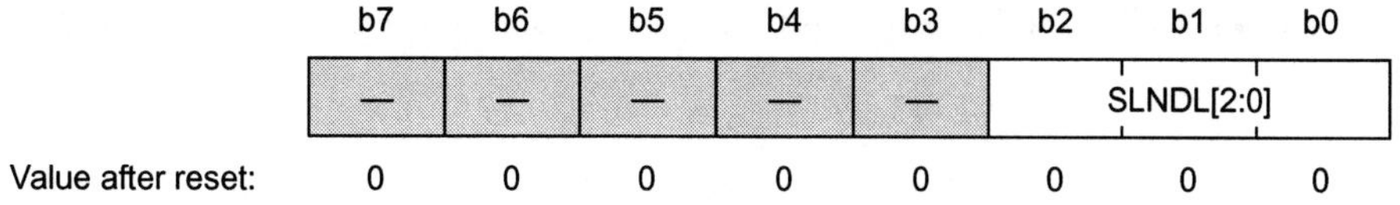

b7	b6	b5	b4	b3	b2	b1	b0
—	—	—	—	—	SLNDL[2:0]		

Value after reset: 0   0   0   0   0   0   0   0

Figure 7.25   The SPI serial peripheral slave select negation delay register. Source: *Hardware Man-ual,* page 1651.

- SLNDL [2:0]: The SSL Negation Delay Setting bits set an SSL negation delay value when the RSPI is in master mode. When using the RSPI in slave mode, set the SLNDL [2:0] bits to 000.

Serial Peripheral Next Access Delay Register (SPND): This register sets a non-active period after termination of a serial transfer.

	b7	b6	b5	b4	b3	b2	b1	b0
	—	—	—	—	—	SPNDL[2:0]		
Value after reset:	0	0	0	0	0	0	0	0

Figure 7.26 The SPI serial peripheral next access delay register. Source: *Hardware Manual*, page 1652.

- SPNDL [2:0]: The RSPI Next-Access Delay Setting bits set a next-access delay when the SPCMD.SPNDEN bit is 1. When using the RSPI in slave mode, set the SPNDL[2:0] bits to 000.

Serial Peripheral Command Register (SPCMDx): SPCMD0 to SPCMD7 are used to set a transfer format/method for the RSPI in master mode. The SPCMDx register has various fields that can be set to control the corresponding feature of the RSPI.

	b15	b14	b13	b12	b11	b10	b9	b8
	SCKDEN	SLNDEN	SPNDEN	LSBF	SPB[3:0]			
Value after reset:	0	0	0	0	0	1	1	1

	b7	b6	b5	b4	b3	b2	b1	b0
	SSLKP	SSLA[2:0]			BRDV[1:0]		CPOL	CPHA
Value after reset:	0	0	0	0	1	1	0	1

Figure 7.27 The SPI serial peripheral command register. Source: *Hardware Manual*, page 1655.

- CPHA: The RSPCK Phase Setting bit sets an RSPCK phase of the RSPI in master mode or slave mode. Data communications between RSPI modules require the same RSPCK phase setting between the modules.

- BRDV[1:0]: Bit Rate Division Setting bits are used to determine the bit rate. A bit rate is determined by combinations of the settings in the BRDV[1:0] bits and SPBR (See **Section** 32.2.8, RSPI Bit Rate Register (SPBR) in the hardware manual). The settings in SPBR determine the base bit rate. The settings in the BRDV[1:0] bits are used to select a bit rate, which is obtained by dividing the base bit rate by 1, 2, 4, or 8. In SPCMD0 to SPCMD7, different BRDV[1:0] bit settings can be specified. This permits the execution of serial transfers at a different bit rate for each command.
- SSLA[2:0]: The SSL Signal Assertion Setting bits control the SSL signal assertion when the RSPI performs serial transfers in master mode. Setting the SSLA[2:0] bits controls the assertion for the SSL0 to SSL3 signals. When an SSL signal is asserted, its polarity is determined by the set value in the corresponding SSLP. When the SSLA[2:0] bits are set to 000 in multi-master mode, serial transfers are performed with all the SSL signals in the negated state (as the SSLn0 pin acts as input). When using the RSPI in slave mode, set the SSLA[2:0] bits to 000.
- SSLKP: SSL Signal Level Keeping bit RSPI in master mode performs a serial transfer, the SSLKP bit specifies whether the SSL signal level for the current command is to be kept or negated between the SSL negation timing associated with the current command and the SSL assertion timing associated with the next command. When using the RSPI in slave mode, the SSLKP bit should be set to 0.
- SPB[3:0]: RSPI Data Length Setting bits set a transfer data length for the RSPI in master mode or slave mode.
- LSBF: RSPI LSB First bit sets the data format of the RSPI in master mode or slave mode to MSB first or LSB first.
- SPNDEN: RSPI Next-Access Delay Enable
- The SPNDEN bit sets the period from the time the RSPI in master mode terminates a serial transfer and sets the SSL signal inactive until the RSPI enables the SSL signal assertion for the next access (next-access delay). If the SPNDEN bit is 0, the RSPI sets the next-access delay to 1 RSPCK + 2 PCLK. If the SPNDEN bit is 1, the RSPI inserts a next-access delay in compliance with the SPND setting. When using the RSPI in slave mode, the SPNDEN bit should be set to 0.

Port Function Control Register G (PFGSPI): The PFGSPI special function register is used to select I/O pins for RSPI channel 0.

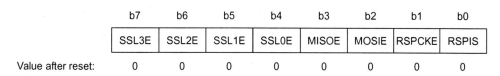

	b7	b6	b5	b4	b3	b2	b1	b0
	SSL3E	SSL2E	SSL1E	SSL0E	MISOE	MOSIE	RSPCKE	RSPIS
Value after reset:	0	0	0	0	0	0	0	0

Figure 7.28 The port function control register. Source: *Hardware Manual,* page 1665.

■ RSPIS Bit (RSPI Pin Select): This bit selects a pin for an RSPI input/output. As an enable bit is provided for each RISPI input/output pin, the input/output pin is selectable while the corresponding enable bit is 1. Otherwise, the pin cannot be selected.

■ RSPCKE Bit (RSPCK Enable): This bit enables or disables the output of the RSPCK pin. Set this bit to 1 to use the RSPCK pin.

■ MOSIE Bit (MOSI Enable): This bit enables or disables the output of the MOSI pin. Set this bit to 1 to use the MOSI pin.

■ MISOE Bit (MISO Enable): This bit enables or disables the output of the MISO pin. Set this bit to 1 to use the MISO pin.

■ SSL0E Bit (SSL0 Enable): This bit enables or disables the output of the SSL0 pin. Set this bit to 1 to use the SSL0 pin.

■ SSL1E Bit (SSL1 Enable): This bit enables or disables the output of the SSL1 pin. Set this bit to 1 to use the SSL1 pin.

■ SSL2E Bit (SSL2 Enable): This bit enables or disables the output of the SSL2 pin. Set this bit to 1 to use the SSL2 pin.

■ SSL3E Bit (SSL3 Enable): This bit enables or disables the output of the SSL3 pin. Set this bit to 1 to use the SSL3 pin.

Configuring the RSPI to Function in Single Master Single Slave Mode

This is the simplest configuration possible in which we have 1 slave device connected to the Renesas Serial Peripheral Interface. **Section 7.3.2** describes the setup of the aforementioned RSPI registers for the Single Master Single Slave configuration as shown in Figure 7.29.

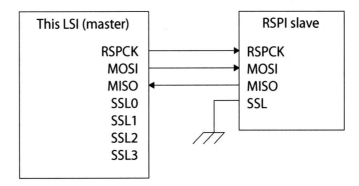

Figure 7.29 Single Master Single Slave Configuration. Source: *Hardware Manual*, page 1662.

7.2.4   Renesas Inter Integrated Circuit Bus

The Inter Integrated Circuit (I^2C) bus was invented by Philips Electronics for serial communications between low speed peripherals in an embedded system. The bus allows multiple peripheral devices to be connected on the same set of wires to communicate with each other with only two devices, one master device and one slave device, communicating with each other at a given time. The bus mainly consists of two wires Serial Clock (SCL) and Serial Data (SDA) that are responsible for transferring the data from one end to the other. These lines are constantly held high by pull up resistors when the bus is inactive. All devices connected on these lines need to communicate with the I^2C protocol. Figure 7.30 illustrates devices connected on an I^2C bus.

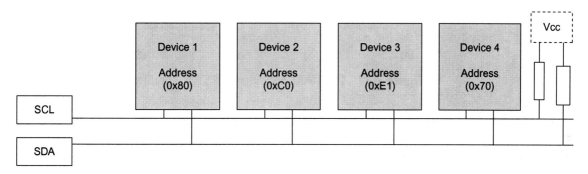

Figure 7.30 Four Devices Connected on the I^2C Bus with pull up resistors. 128 such devices can be connected on a single bus.

I^2C Bus Protocol

Each device connected on the bus is assigned a 7-bit address. Data is usually transferred as a byte plus an additional bit and is accompanied by a clock signal that synchronizes the data transfer between the communicating devices. The device that takes control of the bus at the beginning of communication is usually the master device, and is responsible for addressing the slave device and generating a clock signal during data transmission.

Before any form of data transfer takes place, a device wanting to transfer data must take control of the bus. This is done by monitoring the bus. If the bus is currently held high (both SDA and SCL are at a high voltage), it implies that the bus is currently free. Otherwise the bus is assumed to be busy and the device must wait for the bus to be free in order to transmit data. When the bus becomes free, the master acquires the control of the bus by sending a START condition in which the device pulls the SDA line low while keeping the SCL line high and thus becomes the current master of the bus. Figure 7.31 (A) illustrates a START condition. The generation of the START condition also informs the other devices that the bus is currently busy, and the other devices start listening to the next byte to be transferred on the bus.

When the current master of the bus is ready to release the bus from its control, it transmits a STOP condition in which the SDA line gets pulled high while the SCL line is high. During the entire period in which the master is in control of the bus, the SDA line is constantly held low, except that when there is data being transmitted there is toggling of both lines. Figure 7.31 (B) shows a STOP condition.

Figure 7.31   (A) START condition; (B) STOP condition.

Once control of the bus is obtained, the next priority for the master is to address the slave device by transmitting one byte which consists of a seven bit address and one bit that specifies if the master device wants to read from or write to the slave device. This bit is called the Read/Write bit (R/W). If this bit is low, it indicates that the master wants to write to the slave device; if high, the master device wishes to read from the slave. The status of the R/W bit determines whether the next transactions are going to be read from or written to the slave devices. After transfer of these eight bits, the master clocks out an additional pulse while keeping the SDA high. If a device with the transmitted seven bit address is presently listening on the bus, it responds immediately on the ninth clock pulse by pulling the SDA line low. This is an ACK bit signaling an acknowledgement, and the slave device becomes an active listener on the bus while other devices stop listening to the bus. Thus the master is now ready to transfer more data to the slave. If the SDA line remains low during the ninth clock pulse, the master gets a "no acknowledgement" (NACK) indication and stops transfer of data by sending a STOP bit.

I^2C Communication Modes

Depending upon the initial transactions mentioned above, a device can be set up in any of the four following modes:

- Master Transmitter: In this mode, the device functions as a master and transmits data to a slave after acquiring the control of the bus. This device usually transmits the seven bit address with the R/W bit set to write. It may also transmit additional bytes if an ACK is received for every byte it transfers.

- Master Receiver: In this mode, the device functions as a master and clocks out data from the slave. In this case, the master generates the clock pulses to which the slave toggles data on the SDA pin. Before any reception can take place, the master must output the slave device address with the R/W bit set to R and then output the desired number of clock cycles with pseudo data (usually 0xFF). On every ninth clock pulse, the master receiver is required to send an ACK pulse to the slave device acknowledging the reception of data. Slave device stops transmitting the data to the master receiver as soon as the master clocks a NACK as the ninth bit on the most recent 8 byte data.

- Slave Transmitter: A device enters this mode when another device gains control of the bus and addresses the device with the address assigned to it with the R/W bit set to R. Such a device works in conjunction with a master receiver and responds to commands sent to it by the master receiver. The slave device stops transmitting the data to the master receiver as soon as the master clocks a NACK as the ninth bit on the most recent 8 byte data.

- Slave Receiver: A device enters this mode as soon as it is successfully addressed by a master transmitter with the R/W bit transmitted as W. The slave device is required to clock out an ACK bit for every relevant byte it successfully received.

Now that we understand some of the basics of the I²C protocol, we can move on to understand the detailed working of the I²C interface provided by Renesas; i.e., the Renesas Inter Integrated Circuit bus interface and the registers related to it. Figure 7.32 shows the typical transfers supported by the RIIC interface.

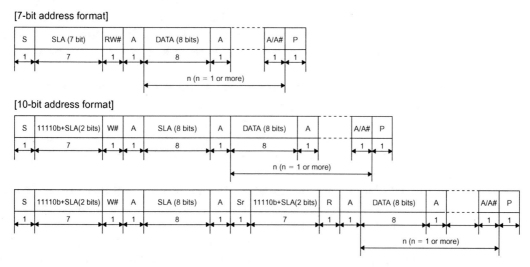

Figure 7.32 Typical data transfers supported by the Renesas I²C Interface. Source: *Hardware Manual,* page 1662.

Registers related to the RIIC interface:

I²C Bus Control Register 1 (ICCR1): ICCR1 enables or disables the RIIC, resets the internal state of the RIIC, outputs an extra SCL clock cycle, and manipulates and monitors the SCLn pin and SDAn pin.

Bits in this register are:

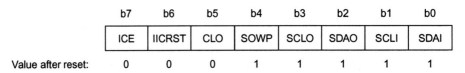

b7	b6	b5	b4	b3	b2	b1	b0
ICE	IICRST	CLO	SOWP	SCLO	SDAO	SCLI	SDAI

Value after reset:

0	0	0	1	1	1	1	1

Figure 7.33 The ICCR1 register. Source: *Hardware Manual,* page 1483.

- I²C Bus Interface Enable (ICE): Setting this pin to 1 enables the RIIC transfer function (the SCLn pin and SDAn pin drive the bus) and vice versa.
- I²C Interface Internal Reset (IICRST): Setting this bit to 1 initiates the RIIC reset resulting in all control, mode, and status registers resetting to default values. This bit needs to be manually cleared to finish the reset. The bit should usually be set when the ICE bit is set to 0. If this bit is set when ICE is 1, it resets the BC[2:0] bits in ICMR1; the ICSR1, ICSR2, ICDRS registers; and the internal states of the RIIC.
- (CLO): Setting this bit to 1 causes the RIIC interface to output an extra SCL clock cycle (the CLO bit is cleared automatically after one clock cycle is output).
- (SOWP): This bit controls the modification of the SCLO and SDAO bits. Setting this bit to 0 allows the SCLO and SDAO bits to be rewritten. This bit is always written as 1.
- (SCLO): This bit controls the output level of the SCLn pin. This bit also monitors the output state of the SCLn pin. Setting this bit to 0 sets the SCLn pin to low level, and vice versa.
- (SDAO): This bit controls the output level of the SDAn pin. This bit also monitors the output state of the SDAn pin. Setting this bit to 0 sets the SDAn pin to low level, and vice versa.
- (SCLI): This bit monitors the input level of the SCLn pin. If this bit is high, it implies that the SCL pin is acting as input and is high. If this bit is low, it implies that the SCL pin is acting as input and is low.
- (SDAI): This bit monitors the input level of the SDAn pin. If this bit is high, it implies that the SDA pin is acting as input and is high. If this bit is low, it implies that the SDA pin is acting as input and is low.

I²C Bus Control Register 2 (ICCR2): ICCR2 has a flag function that indicates whether or not the I²C bus is occupied and whether the RIIC is in transmit/receive or master/slave mode, as well as a function to issue a start or stop condition. Bits in this register are:

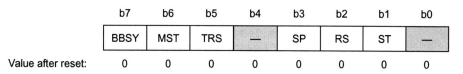

Figure 7.34   The ICCR2 register. Source: *Hardware Manual*, page 1486.

- ▓ (BBSY): The BBSY flag indicates whether the I²C bus is occupied (bus busy) or released (bus free). This bit is set to 1 when the SDAn line changes from high to low under the condition of SCLn = high, assuming that a start condition has been issued. When the SDAn line changes from low to high under the condition of SCLn = high, this bit is cleared to 0 after the bus free time (specified in ICBRL) start condition is not detected, assuming that a stop condition has been issued or if an Internal Interface Reset occurs.
- ▓ (MST): This bit indicates whether the RIIC interface is acting as a master or slave mode. This bit is set when:
  - ▢ A start condition is issued normally according to the start condition issuance request (when a start condition is detected with the ST bit set to 1).
  - ▢ A 1 is written to the MST bit with the MTWP bit in ICMR1 set to 1.

  It is reset when:
  - ▢ A stop condition is detected.
  - ▢ The AL (arbitration lost) flag in ICSR2 is set to 1.
  - ▢ A 0 is written to the MST bit with the MTWP bit in ICMR1 set to 1.
  - ▢ A 1 is written to the IICRST bit in ICCR1 to apply an RIIC reset or an internal reset.

  Manual setting of this is permitted only when MTWP in ICMR1 is 1.
- ▓ (TRS): This bit indicates transmit or receive mode. This bit is set when:
  - ▢ A start condition is issued normally according to the start condition issuance request (when a start condition is detected with the ST bit set to 1).
  - ▢ The R/W# bit added to the slave address is set to 0 in master mode.
  - ▢ The address received in slave mode matches the address enabled in ICSER, with the R/W# bit set to 1.
  - ▢ A 1 is written to the TRS bit with the MTWP bit in ICMR1 set to 1.

This bit is cleared when:

- ☐ A stop condition is detected.
- ☐ The AL (arbitration lost) flag in ICSR2 being set to 1.
- ☐ In master mode, reception of a slave address to which an R/W# bit with the value 1 is appended.
- ☐ In slave mode, a match between the received address and the address enabled in ICSER, when the value of the received R/W# bit is 0 (including cases where the received address is the general call address).
- ☐ In slave mode, a restart condition is detected (a start condition is detected with ICCR2.BBSY = 1 and ICCR2.MST = 0).
- ☐ When 0 is written to the TRS bit with the MTWP bit in ICMR1 set to 1.
- ☐ When 1 is written to the IICRST bit in ICCR1 to apply an RIIC reset or an internal reset.

A combination of this bit and the MST bit indicates the operating mode of the RIIC. Also, writing to this bit is not necessary during normal usage.

- ▨ (SP): This bit is used to request that a stop condition be issued in master mode. This bit is manually set to 1 to request to issue a stop condition, a stop condition is issued only when the BBSY flag is set to 1 (bus busy) and the MST bit is set to 1 (master mode). This bit is set when a 1 is written to it and cleared when any of the following conditions occur:
  - ☐ A 0 is written to the SP bit after reading SP = 1.
  - ☐ A stop condition has been issued or a stop condition is detected.
  - ☐ The AL (arbitration lost) flag in ICSR2 is set to 1.
  - ☐ A start condition and a restart condition are detected.
  - ☐ A 1 is written to the IICRST bit in ICCR1 to apply an RIIC reset or an internal reset.
- ▨ (RS): This bit is used to request that a restart condition be issued in master mode. When this bit is set to 1 to request to issue a restart condition, a restart condition is issued when the BBSY flag is set to 1 (bus busy) and the MST bit is set to 1 (master mode). This bit is set when a 1 is written to it and cleared when any of the following conditions occur:
  - ☐ A 0 is written to the RS bit.
  - ☐ A restart condition has been issued or a start condition is detected.
  - ☐ The AL (arbitration lost) flag in ICSR2 is set to 1.
  - ☐ A 1 is written to the IICRST bit in ICCR1 to apply an RIIC reset or an internal reset.
- ▨ (ST): This bit is used to request transition to master mode and issuance of a start condition. When this bit is set to 1 to request to issue a start condition, a start condition is issued when the BBSY flag is set to 0 indicating that the bus is free. This bit is set when a 1 is written to it and cleared when any of the following conditions occur:
  - ☐ A 0 is written to the ST bit.

   □   A start condition has been issued.

   □   The AL (arbitration lost) flag in ICSR2 is set to 1.

   □   A 1 is written to the IICRST bit in ICCR1 to apply an RIIC reset or an internal reset.

I²C Mode Register 1 (ICMR1): ICMR1 specifies the internal reference clock source within the RIIC, indicates the number of bits to be transferred, and protects the MST and TRS bits in ICCR2 from being written. Bits in this register are:

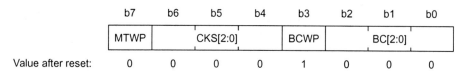

Figure 7.35 The ICMR1 register. Source: *Hardware Manual*, page 1490.

   ■   (MTWP): This bit controls the modification of the MST and TRS bits in ICCR2. Setting this bit enables writing to the MST and TRS bits in ICCR2.

   ■   (CKS[2:0]): These bits select a reference clock source (IICϕ) inside the RIIC. Table 7.6 shows the selections possible:

TABLE 7.6 Clock Source Selection for the RIIC Interface.

CKS2	CKS1	CKS0	CLOCK SOURCE TO RIIC
0	0	0	PCLK/1 clock
0	0	1	PCLK/2 clock
0	1	0	PCLK/4 clock
0	1	1	PCLK/8 clock
1	0	0	PCLK/16 clock
1	0	1	PCLK/32 clock
1	1	0	PCLK/64 clock
1	1	1	PCLK/128 clock

- (BCWP): Clearing this bit to 0 enables a value to be written in the BC[2:0] bits.
- (BC[2:0]): These bits function as a counter that indicates the number of bits remaining to be transferred at the detection of a rising edge on the SCLn line. Although these bits are writable and readable, it is not necessary to access these bits under normal conditions. To write to these bits, specify the number of bits to be transferred plus one (data is transferred with an additional acknowledge bit) between transferred frames when the SCLn line is at a low level. Table 7.7 shows how the Bit counter indicates the number of bits remaining:

TABLE 7.7   Bit Counter Indications.

BC2	BC1	BC0	NUMBER OF BITS REMAINING
0	0	0	9
0	0	1	2
0	1	0	3
0	1	1	4
1	0	0	5
1	0	1	6
1	1	0	7
1	1	1	8

I²C Mode Register 2 (ICMR2):   ICMR2 has a timeout function and an SDA output delay function. Bits in this register are:

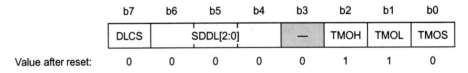

Value after reset:

b7	b6	b5	b4	b3	b2	b1	b0
DLCS	SDDL[2:0]			—	TMOH	TMOL	TMOS
0	0	0	0	0	1	1	0

Figure 7.36   The ICMR2 register. Source: *Hardware Manual*, page 1492.

- (DCLS): This bit is used to select the internal reference clock (IICφ) if set to 0, or the internal reference clock divided by 2 (IICφ/2) if set to 1, as the clock source of the SDA output delay time.
- (SDDL[2:0]): The SDA output can be delayed by the SDDL[2:0] setting. This counter works with the clock source selected by the DLCS bit. The setting of this function can be used for all types of SDA output, including the transmission of the acknowledge bit.

TABLE 7.8

SDDL2	SDDL1	SDDL0	DELAY TIME WHEN DCLS = 0	DELAY TIME WHEN DCLS = 1
0	0	0	No Delay in output	No Delay in output
0	0	1	1 IICφ cycle	1 or 2 IICφ cycles
0	1	0	2 IICφ cycle	3 or 2 IICφ cycles
0	1	1	3IICφ cycle	5 or 2 IICφ cycles
1	0	0	4 IICφ cycle	7 or 2 IICφ cycles
1	0	1	5 IICφ cycle	9 or 2 IICφ cycles
1	1	0	6 IICφ cycle	11 or 2 IICφ cycles
1	1	1	7 IICφ cycle	13 or 2 IICφ cycles

- ▪ (TMOH): This bit is used to enable (when set to 1) or disable (when set to 0) the internal counter of the timeout function to count up while the SCLn line is held high when the timeout function is enabled (TMOE bit = 1 in ICFER).
- ▪ (TMOL): This bit is used to enable (when set to 1) or disable (when set to 0) the internal counter of the timeout function to count up while the SCLn line is held low when the timeout function is enabled (TMOE bit = 1 in ICFER).
- ▪ (TMOS): This bit is used to select long mode or short mode for the timeout detection time when the timeout function is enabled (TMOE bit = 1 in ICFER). When this bit is set to 0, long mode is selected. When this bit is set to 1, short mode is selected. In long mode, the timeout detection internal counter functions as a 16 bit-counter. In short mode, the counter functions as a 14 bit-counter. While the SCLn line is in the state that enables this counter as specified by bits TMOH and TMOL, the counter counts up in synchronization with the internal reference clock (IICφ) as a count source.

I^{2}C Mode Register 3 (ICMR3): ICMR3 has functions to send/receive acknowledge and to select the RDRF set timing in RIIC receive operation, WAIT operation, and the SCLn pin and SDAn pin input level of the RIIC. Bits in this register are:

	b7	b6	b5	b4	b3	b2	b1	b0
	SMBS	WAIT	RDRFS	ACKWP	ACKBT	ACKBR	NF[1:0]	
Value after reset:	0	0	0	0	0	0	0	0

Figure 7.37 The ICMR3 register. Source: *Hardware Manual*, page 1494.

- ▦ (SMBS): Setting this bit to 1 selects the SMBus and enables the HOAE bit in ICSER. Otherwise the interface acts as the standard I^{2}C interface.
- ▦ (WAIT): This bit is valid only in receive mode and is used to control whether to hold the period between the ninth SCL clock cycle and the first SCL clock cycle low until the receive data buffer (ICDRR) is completely read each time single-byte data is received in receive mode.
- ▦ (RDRFS): This bit is used to select the RDRF flag set timing in receive mode and also to select whether to hold the SCLn line low at the falling edge of the eighth SCL clock cycle. When the RDRFS bit is 0, the SCLn line is not held low at the falling edge of the eighth SCL clock cycle, and the RDRF flag is set to 1 at the rising edge of the ninth SCL clock cycle. When the RDRFS bit is 1, the RDRF flag is set to 1 at the rising edge of the eighth SCL clock cycle and the SCLn line is held low at the falling edge of the eighth SCL clock cycle. The low-hold of the SCLn line is released by writing a value to the ACKBT bit. After data is received with this setting, the SCLn line is automatically held low before the acknowledge bit is sent. This enables processing to send ACK (ACKBT = 0) or NACK (ACKBT = 1) according to receive data.
- ▦ (ACKWP): This bit is used to control the modification of the ACKBT bit.
- ▦ (ACKBT): This bit holds the acknowledgement to be sent in receive mode. When set to 0, ACK is transmitted as 0, and vice versa.
- ▦ (ACKBR): This bit is used to store the acknowledge bit information received from the receive device in transmit mode. This bit is set to 1 when a 1 is received as the acknowledge bit with the TRS bit in ICCR2 set to 1. This bit is set to 0 when a 0 is received as the acknowledge bit with the TRS bit in ICCR2 set to 1, or an interface internal reset occurs.
- ▦ (NF [1:0]): These bits are used to select the number of stages (1, 2, 3, or 4) of the digital noise filter.

I^{2}C Bus Function Enable Register (ICFER): ICFER enables or disables the timeout function, the arbitration lost detection function, and the receive operation suspension function during NACK reception, and selects the use of a digital noise filter circuit and SCL synchronous circuit. Bits in this register are:

	b7	b6	b5	b4	b3	b2	b1	b0
	FMPE	SCLE	NFE	NACKE	SALE	NALE	MALE	TMOE
Value after reset:	0	1	1	1	0	0	1	0

Figure 7.38 The ICFER register. Source: *Hardware Manual,* page 1497.

- ▦ (FMPE): This bit is used to specify whether to use a slope control circuit for Fast-mode Plus[fm+].

- (SCLE): This bit is used to specify whether to synchronize the SCL clock with the SCL input clock. Normally, set this bit to 1.
- (NFE): This bit is used to specify whether to use a digital noise filter circuit.
- (NACKE): This bit is used to specify whether to continue or discontinue the transfer operation when NACK is received from the slave device in transmit mode. Normally, set this bit to 1.
- (SALE): This bit is used to specify whether to cause arbitration to be lost when a value different from the value being transmitted is detected on the bus in slave transmit mode (such as when slaves with the same address exist on the bus, or when a mismatch with the transmit data occurs due to noise).
- (NALE): This bit is used to specify whether to cause arbitration to be lost when ACK is detected during transmission of NACK in receive mode (such as when slaves with the same address exist on the bus, or when two or more masters select the same slave device simultaneously with a different number of receive bytes).
- (MALE): This bit is used to specify whether to use the arbitration lost detection function in master mode. Normally, set this bit to 1.
- (TMOE): This bit is used to enable or disable the timeout function.

I²C Bus Status Enable Register (ICSER):   ICSER enables or disables comparison of slave addresses, general call address detection, device-ID command detection, and host address detection. Bits in this register are:

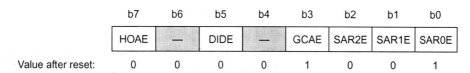

b7	b6	b5	b4	b3	b2	b1	b0
HOAE	—	DIDE	—	GCAE	SAR2E	SAR1E	SAR0E

Value after reset: 0   0   0   0   1   0   0   1

Figure 7.39   The ICSER register. Source: *Hardware Manual,* page 1499.

- (HOAE): This bit is used to specify whether to ignore a received host address (0001 000b) when the SMBS bit in ICMR3 is 1.
- (DIDE): This bit is used to specify whether to recognize and execute the Device-ID address when a device ID (1111 100b) is received in the first frame after a start condition or restart condition is detected. Setting this bit to 1 enables Device ID detection.
- (GCAE): This bit is used to specify whether to ignore the general call address (0000 000b + 0 [W]: All 0) when it is received. When this bit is set to 1, if the received slave address matches the general call address as the first frame received after the START condition, the GCA bit is set in the I²C status register 1.
- (SAR2E): This bit is used to enable or disable the received slave address and the slave address set in SARL2 and SARU2.

- (SAR1E): This bit is used to enable or disable the received slave address and the slave address set in SARL1 and SARU1.
- (SAR0E): This bit is used to enable or disable the received slave address and the slave address set in SARL0 and SARU0.

I²C Bus Interrupt Enable Register (ICIER): ICIER enables or disables various interrupt sources. Bits in this register are:

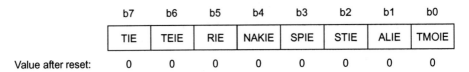

	b7	b6	b5	b4	b3	b2	b1	b0
	TIE	TEIE	RIE	NAKIE	SPIE	STIE	ALIE	TMOIE
Value after reset:	0	0	0	0	0	0	0	0

Figure 7.40 The ICIER register. Source: *Hardware Manual,* page 1501.

- (TIE): This bit is used to enable or disable transmit data empty interrupts (ICTXI) when the TDRE flag in ICSR2 is set to 1.
- (TEIE): This bit is used to enable or disable transmit end interrupts (ICTEI) when the TDRE flag in ICSR2 is set to 1. An ICTEI interrupt request is canceled by clearing the TEND flag or the TEIE bit to 0.
- (RIE): This bit is used to enable or disable receive data full interrupt requests (ICRXI) when the RDRF flag in ICSR2 is set to 1.
- (NAKIE): This bit is used to enable or disable NACK reception interrupt requests (NAKI) when the NACKF flag in ICSR2 is set to 1. A NAKI interrupt request is canceled by clearing the NACKF flag or the NAKIE bit to 0.
- (SPIE): This bit is used to enable or disable stop condition detection interrupt requests (SPI) when the STOP flag in ICSR2 is set to 1. An SPI interrupt request is canceled by clearing the STOP flag or the SPIE bit to 0.
- (STIE): This bit is used to enable or disable start condition detection interrupt requests (STI) when the START flag in ICSR2 is set to 1. An STI interrupt request is canceled by clearing the START flag or the STIE bit to 0.
- (ALIE): This bit is used to enable or disable arbitration lost interrupt requests (ALI) when the AL flag in ICSR2 is set to 1. An ALI interrupt request is canceled by clearing the AL flag or the ALIE bit to 0.
- (TMOIE): This bit is used to enable or disable timeout interrupt requests (TMOI) when the TMOF flag in ICSR2 is set to 1. TMOI interrupt request is canceled by clearing the TMOF flag or the TMOIE bit to 0.

I²C Bus Status Register 1 (ICSR1): ICSR1 indicates various address detection status. Bits in this register are:

b7	b6	b5	b4	b3	b2	b1	b0
HOA	—	DID	—	GCA	AAS2	AAS1	AAS0

Value after reset:　0　　0　　0　　0　　0　　0　　0　　0

Figure 7.41　The ICSR1 register. Source: *Hardware Manual*, page 1503.

▪ (HOA): When the received slave address matches the host address (0001 000b) with the HOAE bit in ICSER set to 1 (host address detection enabled).

▪ (DID): This bit is set when the first frame received immediately after a start condition or restart condition is detected matches a value of (device ID (1111 100b) + 0 [W]) with the DIDE bit in ICSER set to 1 (Device-ID address detection enabled), and is cleared when 0 is written to the DID bit after reading DID = 1, when a stop condition is detected, or when the first frame received immediately after a start condition or restart condition is detected does not match a value of the device IDs assigned to the device.

▪ (GCA): When the received slave address matches the general call address with the GCAE bit in ICSER set to 1 (general call address detection enabled). This flag is set to 1 at the rising edge of the ninth SCL clock cycle in the frame. This bit is cleared when a stop condition is detected, an internal interface reset occurs, the address does not match the general call address (0b0000000 + [0]), or if 0 is written to the GCA bit after reading GCA = 1.

▪ (AAS2): This bit is set if either the 7-bit or 10-bit slave address is received/addressed by the master transmitter. This bit is cleared when a stop condition is detected, an internal interface reset occurs, an address mismatch has occurred, or if 0 is written to the AAS0 bit after reading it.

▪ (AAS1): This bit is set if either the 7-bit or 10-bit slave address is received/addressed by the master transmitter. This bit is cleared when a stop condition is detected, an internal interface reset occurs, an address mismatch has occurred, or if 0 is written to the AAS0 bit after reading it.

▪ (AAS0): This bit is set if either the 7-bit or 10-bit slave address is received/addressed by the master transmitter. This bit is cleared when a stop condition is detected, an internal interface reset occurs, an address mismatch has occurred, or if 0 is written to the AAS0 bit after reading it.

I²C Bus Status Register 2 (ICSR2):　ICSR2 indicates various interrupt request flags and statuses. Bits in this register are:

b7	b6	b5	b4	b3	b2	b1	b0
TDRE	TEND	RDRF	NACKF	STOP	START	AL	TMOF

Value after reset:　0　　0　　0　　0　　0　　0　　0　　0

Figure 7.42　The ICSR2 register. Source: *Hardware Manual*, page 1501.

- ■ (TDRE): This flag when set to 1 indicates that ICDRT contains no transmit data.
- ■ (TEND): This flag when set to 1 indicates that data has been transmitted.
- ■ (RDRF): This flag when set to 1 indicates that ICDRR contains receive data.
- ■ (NACKF): This flag when set to 1 indicates that NACK is detected.
- ■ (STOP): This flag when set to 1 indicates that stop condition is detected.
- ■ (START): This flag when set to 1 indicates that start condition is detected.
- ■ (AL): This flag when set to 1 indicates that arbitration is lost.
- ■ (TMOF): This flag when set to 1 indicates that timeout is detected.

Slave Address Register Upper (SARUm): SARUm selects 7-bit address format or 10-bit address format and sets the upper bits of a 10-bit slave address. Bits in this register are:

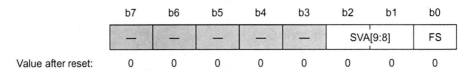

Figure 7.43 The SARUm register. Source: *Hardware Manual,* page 1512.

- ■ (SVA[9:8]): These two bits are the upper bits 10-bit address.
- ■ (FS): This bit, when set to 0 selects the seven bit address format and when set to 1 selects the ten bit addressing format for the device.

Slave Address Register Lower (SARLm): SARLm sets slave address m (7-bit address or lower eight bits of 10-bit address). Bits in this register are:

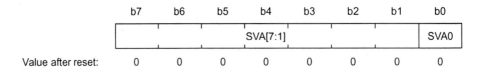

Figure 7.44 The SARLm register. Source: *Hardware Manual,* page 1511.

- ■ SVA[7:1]: When the 7-bit address format is selected (SARUm.FS = 0) these bits function as a 7-bit address. When the 10-bit address format is selected (SARUm.FS = 1) these bits function as the lower eight bits of a 10-bit address in combination with the SVA0 bit. While the SARmE bit in ICSER is 0, the setting of these bits is ignored.
- ■ SVA0: This bit forms the LSB of the 10-bit or 7-bit address assigned to the device.

I²C Bus Bit Rate Low Level Register (ICBRL): ICBRL is a 5-bit (BRL[4:0]) register used to set the low-level period of the SCL clock. It also works to generate the data setup time for automatic SCL low-hold operation. ICBRL counts the low-level period with the internal reference clock source (IICϕ) specified by the CKS[2:0] bits in ICMR1. When the RIIC is used only in slave mode, this register needs to be set to a value longer than the data setup time. Bits in this register are:

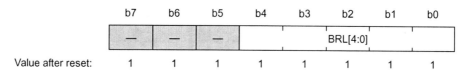

Figure 7.45   The ICBRL register. Source: *Hardware Manual,* page 1513.

I²C Bus Bit Rate High Level Register (ICBRH): ICBRH is a 5-bit (BRH[4:0]) register used to set the high-level period of SCL clock. ICBRH is valid in master mode. If the RIIC is used only in slave mode, this register need not be set. ICBRH counts the high-level period with the internal reference clock source (IICϕ) specified by the CKS[2:0] bits in ICMR1. Bits in this register are:

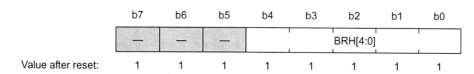

Figure 7.46   The ICBRH register. Source: *Hardware Manual,* page 1514.

I²C Bus Transmit Data Register (ICDRT): ICDRT is an 8-bit readable/writable register that stores transmit data. When ICDRT detects a space in the I²C bus shift register (ICDRS), it transfers the transmit data that has been written to ICDRT to ICDRS and starts transmitting data in transmit mode. ICDRT can always be read and written. Write transmit data to ICDRT once when a transmit data empty interrupt (ICTXI) request is generated. Bits in this register are:

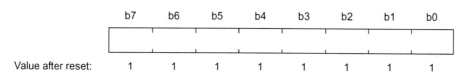

Figure 7.47   The ICDRT. Source: *Hardware Manual,* page 1516.

I²C Bus Receive Data Register (ICDRR): ICDRR is an 8-bit read-only register that stores received data. When one byte of data has been received, the received data is transferred from the I²C bus shift register (ICDRS) to ICDRR to enable the next data to be received. ICDRR cannot be written. Read data from ICDRR once when a receive data full interrupt (ICRXI) request is generated. Bits in this register are:

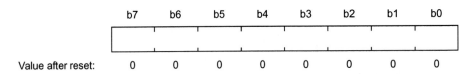

Figure 7.48 The ICDRR register. Source: *Hardware Manual,* page 1516.

I²C Bus Shift Register (ICDRS): ICDRS is an 8-bit shift register used to transmit and receive data as shown below. ICDRS cannot be accessed directly.

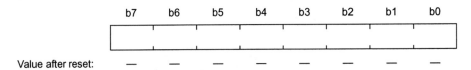

Figure 7.49 The ICDRS register. Source: *Hardware Manual,* page 1516.

7.3 BASIC EXAMPLES

In this section we shall put into implementation the theoretical concepts learned in **Section 7.1** and **Section 7.2,** the process of setting up the interfaces, and understand the practical working of each of the communication interfaces. Interfaces studied so far include the USART using the SCI, SPI using the RSPI, and the two wire serial interface using the RIIC interface. **Sections 7.3.1 to 7.3.3** demonstrate the procedures to setup communication using each of the aforementioned interfaces by means of simple examples.

7.3.1 Basic Transmission/Receiving of Serial Data via UART

Aim: Demonstration of only transmission and only reception using the UART interface of SCI.

Requirements: PC with High-performance Embedded Workshop 4.0 or 4.0+, RX62N Development kit, PC with RS-232 communication port.

Details: In this example, we will setup the RX62N processor to transmit a single byte of information and receive a single byte of information at 9600 baud, no parity, and 1 stop bit via polling.

Procedure: The process of transmitting and receiving a data byte from the SCI ports can be divided into three parts: Initialization, Transmitting/Receiving the actual data, Getting ready to transmit the next byte/saving the received data into the desired location.

As seen in Figure 7.50 the registers required to control the USART SCI are: Baud Rate Register (BRR), Serial Control Mode Register (SCMR), Serial Status Register (SSR), Serial Control Register (SCR), Serial Mode Register (SMR), and Serial Extended Mode Register (SEMR). Upon proper configuration of the values of each of these registers, the SCI can be set up in the desired USART mode with a given baud rate. The step of Initialization consists of setting up the initial values of these registers.

In the next step, for transmission, Transmit Data Register (TDR) is filled with the desired value of the data and on the few next clock cycles the data is output on the corresponding SCI port. This concludes the process of transmitting data. In the case of receiving data, a flag is raised whenever a data byte is received in the Receive Data Register (RDR). This may cause an interrupt to occur. When the receive flag is raised, we need to copy the contents of the RDR into the desired location and conclude the process of reception.

The following code snippets show the process for setting up the SCI 2 of RX62N for initialization, transmission, and reception:

```
1. void init_SCI2(void){
2.    MSTP(SCI2) = 0;
3.    IOPORT.PFFSCI.BIT.SCI2S = 1;
4.    PORT1.DDR.BIT.B2 = 0;
5.    PORT1.ICR.BIT.B2 = 1;
6.    PORT1.DDR.BIT.B3 = 1;
7.    SCI2.SCR.BYTE = 0;
8.    SCI2.SMR.BYTE = 0x00;
9.    SCI2.SCR.BIT.RIE = 1;
10.   SCI2.SCR.BIT.TIE = 1;
11.   IR(SCI2, RXI2) = 0;
12.   IR(SCI2, TXI2) = 0;
13.   IEN(SCI2, RXI2) = 0;
14.   IEN(SCI2, TXI2) = 0;
15.   SCI2.BRR = 12;
16.   SCI2.SCR.BYTE |= 0x30;
17. }
```

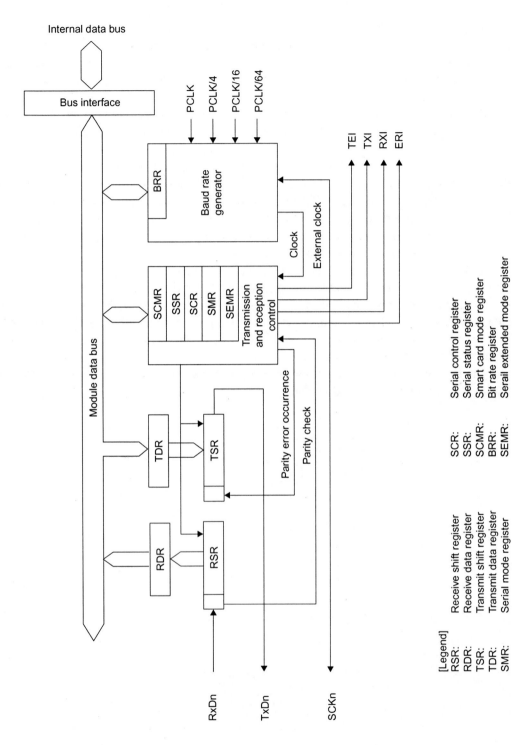

Figure 7.50 Serial Communications Architecture. *Source: Hardware Manual, page 1339.*

[Legend]
RSR: Receive shift register   SCR: Serial control register
RDR: Receive data register   SSR: Serial status register
TSR: Transmit shift register   SCMR: Smart card mode register
TDR: Transmit data register   BRR: Bit rate register
SMR: Serial mode register   SEMR: Serial extended mode register

Explanation of Initialization Code

Line 2:   `MSTP(SCI2) = 0;`
This line of code enables the SCI2 module on the Renesas Microcontroller.

Line 3:   `IOPORT.PFFSCI.BIT.SCI2S = 1;`
This line enables the use of TxD2-B and RxD2-B. This line of code is applicable to ports that support differential mode of communication.

Line 4:   `PORT1.DDR.BIT.B2 = 0;`
Here, the SCI 0 interface is setup such that the on-chip baud rate generation circuit is used and the SCK pin operates as a normal Digital I/O pin. The transmission end interrupt is disabled with normal reception, Serial transmission is enabled, reception is disabled, transmit interrupt and reception interrupt are disabled.

Line 5:   `PORT1.ICR.BIT.B2 = 1;`
Here the input buffer to RxD2-B is enabled.

Line 6:   `PORT1.DDR.BIT.B3 = 1;`
This line of code enables TxD2-B on port 1 pin 3 as output.

Line 7:   `SCI2.SCR.BYTE = 0;`
This line of code disables the transmission and reception.

Line 8:   `SCI2.SMR.BYTE = 0x00;`
This line of code sets the SCI in Asynchronous mode with 8 bits of data being transmitted with no parity, 1 stop bit, and no frequency division for PCLK.

Line 9:   `SCI2.SCR.BIT.RIE = 1;`
This line of code enables the receive interrupts of the SCI2. These need to be enabled in order to generate flags which we will poll to acquire data.

Line 10:   `SCI2.SCR.BIT.TIE = 1;`
This line of code enables the transmit interrupts of the SCI2. These need to be enabled in order to generate flags which we will poll to acquire data.

Line 11:   `IR(SCI2, RXI2) = 0;`
Clear the interrupt request bits for the receive.

Line 12:   `IR(SCI2, TXI2) = 0;`
Clear the interrupt request bits for the transmit.

Line 13:   `IEN(SCI2, RXI2) = 0;`
Disable interrupt request for receive from RXI 2.

Line 14:   `IEN(SCI2, TXI2) = 0;`
Disable interrupt request for receive from TXI 2.

Line 15:   `SCI2.BRR = 12;`
           Set the Baud rate register for communication to occur at 115200 baud.

Line 16:   `SCI2.SCR.BYTE |= 0x30;`
           Enable Transmission and reception. We are now ready to transmit and receive data.

The following code snippet shows the process for transmitting data from the SCI2 of RX62N:

```
1. int transmit_data(unsigned char data){
2.     while(IR(SCI2, TXI2) == 0)
3.        ;
4.     IR(SCI2, TXI2) = 0;
5.     SCI2.TDR = data;
6. }
```

Explanation of Transmission Code

Line 2:   `while(IR(SCI2, TXI2) == 0);`
          This line of code makes the microcontroller enter a wait state until the transmit buffer becomes empty and generates an interrupt request.

Line 3:   `;`

Line 4:   `IR(SCI2, TXI2) = 0;`
          This line of code clears the interrupt request generated when the transmit buffer becomes empty.

Line 5:   `SCI2.TDR = data;`
          This line of code copies the one byte data passed as an argument to the function in to the transmit data register.

The following code snippet shows the process for receiving data from the SCI2 of RX62N:

```
1. unsigned char receive_data(void){
2.     unsigned char rcvd_data = 0;
3.     while(IR(SCI2, RXI2) != 1)
4.        ;
5.     rcvd_data = SCI2.RDR;
6.     IR(SCI2, RXI2) = 0;
7.     return(rcvd_data);
8. }
```

Explanation of Reception Code

Line 2:   `unsigned char rcvd_data = 0;`
Here we initialize an unsigned character variable "rcvd_data" to hold the data received from the SCI2 RxD2-B pin.

Line 3:   `while(IR(SCI2, RXI2) != 1)`
This line of code makes the microcontroller enter a wait state until an interrupt request is generated after data is successfully received in the RDR.

Line 4:   `;`

Line 5:   `rcvd_data = SCI2.RDR;`
Here we copy the contents of the data received in the receive data register RDR into the variable rcvd_data.

Line 6:   `IR(SCI2, RXI2) = 0;`
We now clear the interrupt request flag generated due to reception of data, and make the SCI2 interface ready to receive data again.

Line 7:   `return(rcvd_data);`
Here we return the received data back to the main program/function.

Putting it together:

```
1. void main(void){
2.     init_sci2();
3.     transmit_data('A');
4.     unsigned char data = 0;
5.     data = receive_data();
6.     printf("\ndata = %c",data);
7.     return 0;
8. }
```

Explanation of Main Program

Line 2:   `init_sci2;`
We call and execute the initialization function so that the SCI 2 gets set up as a UART functioning at 115200 baud, no parity, 1 stop bit, and clocking with no frequency division of PCLK.

Line 3:   `transmit_data('A');`
We call and execute the transmit_data function to transmit a character "A" over the transmission line.

Line 4:   `unsigned char data = 0;`
Here a unsigned character variable "data" is declared and initialized to 0.

Line 5: `data = receive_data();`

Here we call the function receive_data to receive data from the SCI2. The function returns a character when data is received from SCI2 and is stored in the variable "data."

Line 6: `printf("\ndata = %c",data);`

Here we print the value of the variable data as a character over the standard output of the microcontroller.

Line 7: `return 0;`

This line of code terminates the program and the microcontroller comes to a halt.

7.3.2   Basic Transmission of Data Using Serial Peripheral Interface Bus

Aim: Demonstration of transmitting data with the serial peripheral interface bus.

Requirements: PC with High-performance Embedded Workshop 4.0 or 4.0+, RX62N Development kit, Digital Oscilloscope, Oscilloscope probes.

Details: In this example, we will set up the RX62N processor to transmit a single byte of information using the clock synchronous serial peripheral interface bus.

Procedure: The process of transmitting and receiving a data byte from the RSPI ports can be divided in to three parts; namely: initialization, selection of a slave device, and transmitting/receiving the actual data.

As seen in Figure 7.51 the registers required to control the RSPI are: SPCR, SPCR2, SSLP, SPPCR, SPSR, SPDR, SPSSR, SPDCR, SSLND, SPCKD, SPND, SPCMD, and SPBR. Upon proper configuration of the values of each of these registers, the RSPI can be set up in the desired clock synchronous mode with a given bit rate. The step of Initialization consists of setting up the initial values of these registers.

In the next step for slave selection, a chip select/active low signal is output from one of the SSL pins, or any other digital I/O pins, bringing the device out of the sleep state.

Next, the SPDR and SPCMDn registers are loaded with the proper values and the data is transmitted as soon as the RSPI becomes idle.

In order to view the transmission of data, it is recommended to connect an oscilloscope probe to the SCK, MOSI, MISO, and SSL-0 pins. If configuration of the RSPI is done as shown in initialization code, an output similar to that of Figure 7.52 would be observed on the oscilloscope. For our configuration D_1 was connected to serial clock, D_2 connected to Master Out Slave In, D_3 connected to Master In Slave Out and D_4 was connected Slave Select/Chip Select pins.

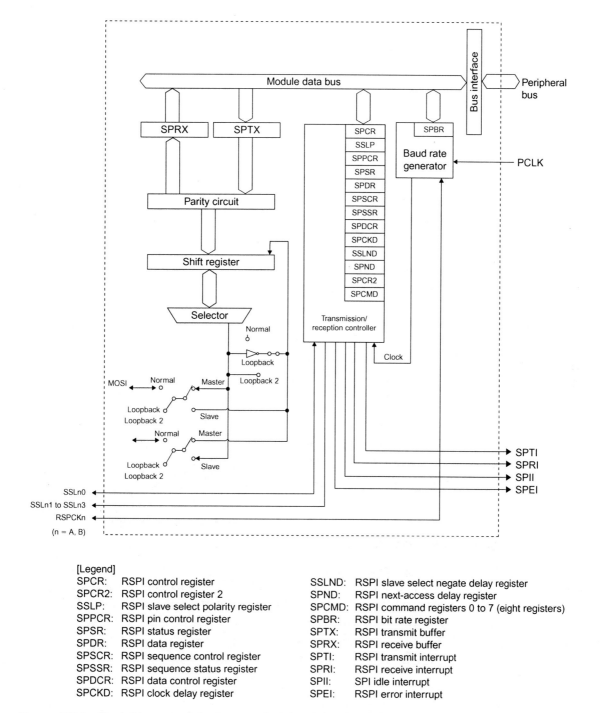

[Legend]
SPCR: RSPI control register
SPCR2:   RSPI control register 2
SSLP: RSPI slave select polarity register
SPPCR: RSPI pin control register
SPSR: RSPI status register
SPDR: RSPI data register
SPSCR: RSPI sequence control register
SPSSR: RSPI sequence status register
SPDCR: RSPI data control register
SPCKD: RSPI clock delay register

SSLND: RSPI slave select negate delay register
SPND: RSPI next-access delay register
SPCMD: RSPI command registers 0 to 7 (eight registers)
SPBR: RSPI bit rate register
SPTX: RSPI transmit buffer
SPRX: RSPI receive buffer
SPTI: RSPI transmit interrupt
SPRI: RSPI receive interrupt
SPII: SPI idle interrupt
SPEI: RSPI error interrupt

Figure 7.51   Block Diagram of the Renesas Serial Peripheral Interface. Source: *Hardware Manual,* page 1631.

The following are the codes for initialization, transmission, and the main program.

```
 1. void Init_RSPI(void){
 2.     MSTP(RSPI0) = 0;
 3.     IOPORT.PFGSPI.BIT.RSPIS = 0;
 4.     PORT.PFGSPI.BIT.RSPCKE = 1;
 5.     IOPORT.PFGSPI.BIT.SSL3E = 0;
 6.     IOPORT.PFGSPI.BIT.MOSIE = 1;
 7.     PORTC.DDR.BIT.B4 = 1;
 8.     PORTC.DR.BIT.B4 = 1;
 9.     PORTC.DDR.BIT.B7 = 1;
10.     PORTC.DR.BIT.B7 = 1;
11.     PORTC.DDR.BIT.B6 = 1;
12.     PORTC.DR.BIT.B6 = 1;
13.     PORTC.DDR.BIT.B5 = 1;
14.     PORTC.DR.BIT.B5 = 1;
15.     RSPI0.SPPCR.BYTE = 0x00;
16.     RSPI0.SPBR.BYTE = 0x00;
17.     RSPI0.SPDCR.BYTE = 0x00;
18.     RSPI0.SPCKD.BYTE = 0x00;
19.     RSPI0.SSLND.BYTE = 0x00;
20.     RSPI0.SPND.BYTE = 0x00;
21.     RSPI0.SPCR2.BYTE = 0x00;
22.     RSPI0.SPCMD0.WORD = 0x0700;
23.     RSPI0.SPCR.BYTE = 0x6B;
24.     RSPI0.SSLP.BYTE = 0x08;
25.     RSPI0.SPSCR.BYTE = 0x00;
26. }
```

Explanation of Initialization Code

Line 2:   `MSTP(RSPI0) = 0;`
This line of code enables the RSPI0(RSPI-A) module on the Renesas Microcontroller, since the SPI2 is the interface connected to the RS-232 convertor on board the development kit.

Line 3:   `IOPORT.PFGSPI.BIT.RSPIS = 0;`
This line of code Selects the proper bank of pins for SPI0.

Line 4:   `IOPORT.PFGSPI.BIT.RSPCKE = 1;`
SCK (PC.5) is active and acts as a serial clock output.

Line 5:   `IOPORT.PFGSPI.BIT.SSL3E = 0;`
SSL3 (PC.2) is inactive (toggled as GPIO instead).

Line 6:   `IOPORT.PFGSPI.BIT.MOSIE = 1;`
MOSI (PC.6) is active.

Line 7:   `PORTC.DDR.BIT.B4 = 1;`
Select Port C bit 4 as Chip select pin, set up chip select pin, make it an output.

Line 8:   `PORTC.DR.BIT.B4 = 1;`
Set level to high so as to not perform a chip select.

Line 9:   `PORTC.DDR.BIT.B7 = 0;`
Set MISO as an input.

Line 10:   `PORTC.DR.BIT.B7 = 1;`
Enable input buffer for peripheral.

Line 11:   `PORTC.DDR.BIT.B6 = 1;`
Set MOSI as an output.

Line 12:   `PORTC.DR.BIT.B6 = 1;`
Enable input buffer for peripheral.

Line 13:   `PORTC.DDR.BIT.B5 = 1;`
Set SCK as an output.

Line 14:   `PORTC.DR.BIT.B5 = 1;`
Set level to inactive.

Line 15:   `RSPI0.SPPCR.BYTE = 0x00;`
Initialize SPI (per flowchart in hardware manual), no loopback, CMOS Output.

Line 16:   `RSPI0.SPBR.BYTE = 0x00;`
Run the RSPI at Full Speed with PCLK frequency of 48 MHz.

Line 17:   `RSPI0.SPDCR.BYTE = 0x00;`
16-bit data 1 frame 1 chip select.

Line 18:   `RSPI0.SPCKD.BYTE = 0x00;`
This line of code sets up the RSPI to have two clock delays before next access to SPI device.

Line 19:   `RSPI0.SSLND.BYTE = 0x00;`
This line of code sets up the RSPI to have two clock delays after de-asserting SSL.

Line 20: `RSPI0.SPND.BYTE = 0x00;`
This line of code sets up the RSPI to have two clock delays before next access to SPI device.

Line 21: `RSPI0.SPCR2.BYTE = 0x00;`
Initialize the RSPI with no parity, no idle interrupts.

Line 22: `RSPI0.SPCMD0.WORD = 0x0700;`
MSB first 8-bit data, keep SSL low.

Line 23: `RSPI0.SPCR.BYTE = 0x6B;`
Enable RSPI 3-wire in master mode with RSPI Enable Transmit only and Interrupts.

Line 24: `RSPI0.SSLP.BYTE = 0x08;`
SSL3A Polarity is active high.

Line 25: `RSPI0.SPSCR.BYTE = 0x00;`
Transmit One frame of data.

Transmission Code

```
1. void RSPI_Transmit_LWord(int16_t sLowWord, int16_t sHighWord){
2.     PORTC.DR.BIT.B4 = 0;
3.     while(RSPI0.SPSR.BIT.IDLNF)
4.         ;
5.     RSPI0.SPDR.WORD.L = sLowWord;
6.     RSPI0.SPDR.WORD.H = sHighWord;
7.     while(RSPI0.SPSR.BIT.IDLNF)
8.         ;
9.     (void)RSPI0.SPDR.WORD.L;
10.    (void)RSPI0.SPDR.WORD.H;
11.    PORTC.DR.BIT.B4 = 1;    //CS OFF
12. }
```

Explanation of Transmission Code

Line 2: `PORTC.DR.BIT.B4 = 0;`
Here we set the bit to be pulled low so as to perform a chip select manually to begin transmission.

Line 3: `while(RSPI0.SPSR.BIT.IDLNF)`
Wait for the RSPI to become idle. Program proceeds as soon as the IDLNF flag becomes 0.

Line 4: `;`

Line 5: `RSPI0.SPDR.WORD.L = sLowWord;`
Set the lower word of the SPDR to the value passed through the argument.

Line 6: `RSPI0.SPDR.WORD.H = sHighWord;`
Set the higher word of the SPDR to the value passed through the argument.

Line 7: `while(RSPI0.SPSR.BIT.IDLNF);`
Wait for the RSPI to finish transmission.

Line 8: `;`

Line 9: `(void)RSPI0.SPDR.WORD.L;`
Read the lower word of the SPDR;

Line 10: `(void)RSPI0.SPDR.WORD.H;`
and read the higher word of the SPDR to clear interrupt flag.

Line 11: `PORTC.DR.BIT.B4 = 1 ;`
Set the Chip select pin to high to terminate transmission.

Main Code

```
1. void main(void) {
2.    Init_RSPI();
3.    while(1)
4.        RSPI_Send_LWord(0x0000, 0x0055);
5. }
```

Explanation of Main Code

Line 2: `Init_RSPI();`
We initialize the Renesas SPI by calling the Init_RSPI function.

Line 3: `while(1)`
Perform the next step forever.

Line 4: `RSPI_Send_LWord(0x0000, 0x0055);`
Transmit 0x00000055.

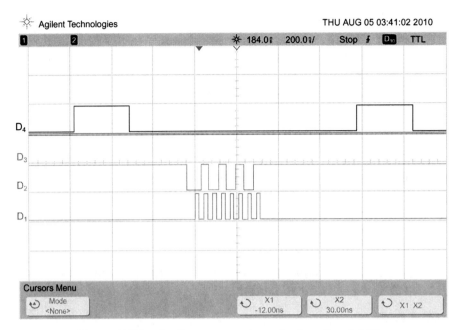

Figure 7.52   Oscilloscope capture of a functional RSPI.

7.3.3   Basic Transmission and Reception of Data Using the Renesas I²C Bus

Aim: To demonstrate the setting up of the RIIC module to transmit and receive data from a peripheral.

Details: In this example we will set up the RIIC peripheral module to transmit and receive 1 byte of data from an on board peripheral device.

Requirements: PC with High-performance Embedded Workshop 4.0 or 4.0+, RX62N Development kit, Digital Oscilloscope, Oscilloscope probes.

Procedure: The YRDKRX62N development kit has an on board accelerometer ADXL345. This is a three axis accelerometer capable of measuring accelerations in the X, Y, and Z axis directions. The ADXL345 can communicate the measured values through the SPI and I²C buses. Depending on the mode of communication selected using the CS pin, one can use either of the two communication methods to obtain details and data from the ADXL345. The ADXL345 is composed of several registers that it constantly updates when not in the SLEEP or STAND BY mode. One particular register of interest is the 0x00 register that contains the value 0xE5 that symbolically represents "345." Therefore when the 0x00 address location is read using the I²C mechanism, the value 0xe5 is acquired/read. The address that we are going to write to is the pointer address for the ADXL 345 which is the default register location select for the first byte of data transferred to the device after transmitting the device address 0x3A. The procedure for writing data to a peripheral device is:

1. Generate START condition.
2. Transmit address of device to communicate with and wait for the acknowledge bit to arrive.
3. Transmit the data to be communicated with the device and wait for the acknowledge bit to arrive for each byte transmitted.
4. If all bytes to be communicated have been transmitted, generate a STOP condition.

The procedure to read data from a peripheral device is in two parts that consist of writing to the register pointer and then reading the desired bytes from the peripherals. In the first half of the read cycle, the RX62N:

1. Generate a START condition.
2. Transmit address of device to communicate with and wait for acknowledge bit to arrive.
3. Transmit the value of the register pointer and wait for an acknowledge.
4. Generate a STOP condition.

Next comes the read cycle which begins with:

1. Generating a START condition.
2. Transmitting the address of the **device to communicate with +1** (note that this address is always odd) and wait for an acknowledge.
3. Generate clock cycles or generate pseudo transactions of 0xFF to which the slave device or peripheral clocks out the desired data. To each byte successfully received the RIIC has to output an ACK bit which is a 0 on the ninth bit. If the Master receiver RX62N wishes to terminate a transaction, it needs to generate a NACK, which is a 1 on the ninth bit of the last desired byte.
4. Generate a STOP condition.

To be able to do all of these activities, the microcontroller needs to be configured/initialized properly. The following code shows the procedure for initialization of the RIIC channel 0 aboard the RX62N. If RIIC channel 1 is available, then similar steps should be followed:

```
1. void RiicIni(unsigned char in_SelfAddr){
2.     SYSTEM.MSTPCRB.BIT.MSTPB21 = 0;
3.     RIIC0.ICCR1.BIT.ICE = 0;
4.     RIIC0.ICCR1.BIT.IICRST = 1;
5.     RIIC0.ICCR1.BIT.IICRST = 0;
6.     RIIC0.SARU0.BIT.FS = 0;
7.     RIIC0.SARL0.BYTE = in_SelfAddr;
```

```
 8.        RIIC0.ICMR1.BIT.CKS = 7;
 9.        RIIC0.ICBRH.BIT.BRH = 28;
10.        RIIC0.ICBRL.BIT.BRL = 29;
11.        RIIC0.ICMR3.BIT.ACKWP = 1;
12.        RIIC0.ICIER.BIT.RIE = 1;
13.        RIIC0.ICIER.BIT.TIE = 1;
14.        RIIC0.ICIER.BIT.TEIE = 0;
15.        RIIC0.ICIER.BIT.NAKIE = 1;
16.        RIIC0.ICIER.BIT.SPIE = 1;
17.        RIIC0.ICIER.BIT.STIE = 0;
18.        RIIC0.ICIER.BIT.ALIE = 0;
19.        RIIC0.ICIER.BIT.TMOIE = 0;
20.        PORT1.ICR.BIT.B3 = 1;
21.        PORT1.ICR.BIT.B2 = 1;
22.        RIIC0.ICCR1.BIT.ICE = 1;
23. }
```

The following is the explanation of the above code line by line:

Line 1:   `void RiicIni(unsigned char in_SelfAddr)`
Declaring the function and the arguments.

Line 2:   `SYSTEM.MSTPCRB.BIT.MSTPB21 = 0;`
Enable the RIIC channel zero.

Line 3:   `RIIC0.ICCR1.BIT.ICE = 0;`
Disable the RIIC channel 0 manually just to make sure.

Line 4:   `RIIC0.ICCR1.BIT.IICRST = 1;`
Reset the RIIC0 module.

Line 5:   `RIIC0.ICCR1.BIT.IICRST = 0;`
Release the reset.

Line 6:   `RIIC0.SARU0.BIT.FS = 0;`
Set the device address as a 7 bit address.

Line 7:   `RIIC0.SARL0.BYTE = in_SelfAddr;`
Set the device address from the argument of the function.

Line 8:   `RIIC0.ICMR1.BIT.CKS = 7;`
Select clock input to the RIIC0 module as PCLK/128.

Line 9:   `RIIC0.ICBRH.BIT.BRH = 28;`
Set the bit counter for the high level of the serial clock cycle.

Line 10:   `RIIC0.ICBRL.BIT.BRL = 29;`
Set the bit counter for the low level of the serial clock cycle.

Line 11:   `RIIC0.ICMR3.BIT.ACKWP = 1;`
Disable write protect for the ACK bit.

Line 12:   `RIIC0.ICIER.BIT.RIE = 1;`
Enable the Receive data full interrupt.

Line 13:   `RIIC0.ICIER.BIT.TIE = 1;`
Enable the Transmit data full interrupt.

Line 14:   `RIIC0.ICIER.BIT.TEIE = 0;`
Enable the Transmit End interrupt.

Line 15:   `RIIC0.ICIER.BIT.NAKIE = 1;`
Enable the NACK received interrupt.

Line 16:   `RIIC0.ICIER.BIT.SPIE = 1;`
Enable the Stop condition received interrupt.

Line 17:   `RIIC0.ICIER.BIT.STIE = 0;`
Disable the Start condition received interrupt.

Line 18:   `RIIC0.ICIER.BIT.ALIE = 0;`
Disable the Arbitration lost interrupt.

Line 19:   `RIIC0.ICIER.BIT.TMOIE = 0;`
Timeout interrupt request is disabled.

Line 20:   `PORT1.ICR.BIT.B3 = 1;`
Enable input buffer on PORT1 pin 3.

Line 21:   `PORT1.ICR.BIT.B2 = 1;`
Enable input buffer on PORT1 pin 2.

Line 22:   `RIIC0.ICCR1.BIT.ICE = 1;`
Enable the RIIC0 module.

Line 23:   `}`
End of function definition.

The process to uninitialized the RIIC0 is

```
1. void RiicUnIni(void){
2.    SYSTEM.MSTPCRB.BIT.MSTPB21 = 1;
3. }
```

The following is the explanation of the above code line by line:

Line 1:   `void RiicUnIni(void){`
Declare the function name to uninitialization

Line 2:   `SYSTEM.MSTPCRB.BIT.MSTPB21 = 1;`
Disable the RIIC0 module

Line 3:   `}`
End function definition

The following snippet of code demonstrates how data transfer takes place, using polling:
There are three essential parts to data transfer when using the I^2C protocol:

1. Generating the START condition.
2. Performing the transfer.
3. Sending the STOP condition.

The following is the code for generating the START condition:

```
 1. unsigned char RiicSendStart(void){
 2.     if(RIIC0.ICCR1.BIT.ICE){
 3.         while(RIIC0.ICCR2.BIT.BBSY)
 4.             ;
 5.         RIIC0.ICCR2.BIT.ST = 1;
 6.         while(!(RIIC0.ICCR2.BIT.BBSY && RIIC0.ICSR2.BIT.START))
 7.             ;
 8.         RIIC0.ICSR2.BIT.START = 0;
 9.         return 1;
10.     }
11.     else return 0;
12. }
```

The following is the explanation for the above code:

Line 1:   `unsigned char RiicSendStart(void){`
Declare the function name and arguments.

Line 2:   `if(RIIC0.ICCR1.BIT.ICE){`
Check if the RIIC0 module is enabled.

Line 3:   `while(RIIC0.ICCR2.BIT.BBSY)`
Wait here until the bus becomes free.

Line 4:   `;`

Line 5:   `RIIC0.ICCR2.BIT.ST = 1;`
When bus becomes free, request for transmitting a START condition.

Line 6:   `while(!(RIIC0.ICCR2.BIT.BBSY && RIIC0.ICSR2.BIT.START))`
Wait here until START condition is detected by the RIIC0 module.

Line 7:   `;`

Line 8:   `RIIC0.ICSR2.BIT.START = 0;`
After detecting the module, disable the interrupt bit in the status register.

Line 9:   `return 1;`
Report success.

Line 10:   `}`

Line 11:   `else return 0;`
Report failure if RIIC0 module is not enabled.

Line 12:   `}`

The following is the code for generating the STOP condition:

```
1. unsigned char RiicSendStop(void){
2.    if(RIIC0.ICCR1.BIT.ICE){
3.       while(RIIC0.ICCR2.BIT.BBSY){
4.          RIIC0.ICCR2.BIT.SP = 1;
5.       }
6.       return 1;
7.    }
8.    else return 0;
9. }
```

The following is the explanation for the code given above:

Line 1:   `unsigned char RiicSendStop(void){`
Declare the function name and arguments.

Line 2:   `if(RIIC0.ICCR1.BIT.ICE){`
If the RIIC0 module is enabled perform the following steps.

Line 3:   `while(RIIC0.ICCR2.BIT.BBSY){`

Line 4:   `RIIC0.ICCR2.BIT.SP = 1;`
While the bus is busy, request to generate a stop condition.

Line 5:   `}`

Line 6:   `return 1;`
Report Success.

Line 7:   `}`

Line 8:   `else return 0;`
If the RIIC0 module is disabled report failure.

Line 9:   `}`

The following is the code for writing a data byte to a peripheral device on the I^2C bus:

```
1. unsigned char RiicWriteByte(unsigned char slave_addr, unsigned
   char slave_register_num, unsigned char data_byte){
2.     RIIC0.ICDRT = slave_addr & (0xFE);
3.     while(!RIIC0.ICSR2.BIT.TDRE)
4.         ;
5.     RIIC0.ICDRT = slave_register_num;
6.     while(!RIIC0.ICSR2.BIT.TEND){
7.         if(RIIC0.ICSR2.BIT.NACKF){
8.             RIIC0.ICSR2.BIT.NACKF = 0;
9.             return 0;
10.        }
11.    }
12.    while(!RIIC0.ICSR2.BIT.TDRE)
13.        ;
14.    RIIC0.ICDRT = data_byte;
15.    while(!RIIC0.ICSR2.BIT.TEND){
16.        if(RIIC0.ICSR2.BIT.NACKF){
17.            RIIC0.ICSR2.BIT.NACKF = 0;
18.            return 0;
19.        }
20.    }
21.    while(!RIIC0.ICSR2.BIT.TDRE)
22.        ;
23.    while(!RIIC0.ICSR2.BIT.TEND){
24.        if(RIIC0.ICSR2.BIT.NACKF){
25.            RIIC0.ICSR2.BIT.NACKF = 0;
26.            return 0;
27.        }
28.    }
29.    return 1;
30. }
```

The following is the explanation for the above codes:

Line 1:   `unsigned char RiicWriteByte2(unsigned char slave_addr,`
           `unsigned char slave_register_num, unsigned char data_byte){`
           Declare and define the function and its arguments.

Line 2: `RIIC0.ICDRT = slave_addr & (0xFE);`
Fill the transmit buffer with the slave address input as an argument to the function.

Line 3: `while(!RIIC0.ICSR2.BIT.TDRE)`
Wait until the Transmit data empty flag becomes high.

Line 4: `;`

Line 5: `RIIC0.ICDRT = slave_register_num;`
Fill the transmit data buffer with the slave register number to be written to.

Line 6: `while(!RIIC0.ICSR2.BIT.TEND){`
Since the RIIC has a double buffer for transmission and reception, we need to wait until the previous transmission is finished.

Line 7: `if(RIIC0.ICSR2.BIT.NACKF){`
Check if a NACK is received in response to the transmit operation.

Line 8: `RIIC0.ICSR2.BIT.NACKF = 0;`
If a NACK is received, then Reset the NACKF flag.

Line 9: `return 0;`
And report failure.

Line 10: `}`

Line 11: `}`

Line 12: `while(!RIIC0.ICSR2.BIT.TDRE)`
Wait here until the transmit data register becomes empty again.

Line 13: `;`

Line 14: `RIIC0.ICDRT = data_byte;`
Fill the transmit data register with the actual data byte that needs to be transmitted.

Line 15: `while(!RIIC0.ICSR2.BIT.TEND){`
Since the RIIC has a double buffer for transmission and reception, we need to wait until the previous transmission is finished.

Line 16: `if(RIIC0.ICSR2.BIT.NACKF){`
Check if a NACK is received in response to the transmit operation.

Line 17: `RIIC0.ICSR2.BIT.NACKF = 0;`
If a NACK is received, then Reset the NACKF flag.

Line 18: `return 0;`
And report failure.

Line 19: `}`

Line 20: `}`

Line 21: `while(!RIIC0.ICSR2.BIT.TDRE)`
Wait here until the transmit data register becomes empty again.

Line 22: `;`

Line 23: `while(!RIIC0.ICSR2.BIT.TEND){`
Since the RIIC has a double buffer for transmission and reception, we need to wait until the previous transmission is finished.

Line 24: `if(RIIC0.ICSR2.BIT.NACKF){`
Check if a NACK is received in response to the transmit operation.

Line 25: `RIIC0.ICSR2.BIT.NACKF = 0;`
If a NACK is received, then Reset the NACKF flag.

Line 26: `return 0;`
And report failure.

Line 27: `}`

Line 28: `}`

Line 29: `return 1;`
If all goes well, report success.

Line 30: `}`

The following is a piece of code similar to the above code, however it writes only the slave address and the register number to the I^{2}C peripheral device. This is useful when reading data from the peripheral device in which one needs to write to the slave device the register from which the data is to be transferred and then data is read consecutively from the registers.

```
1. unsigned char RiicWriteByte(unsigned char slave_addr, unsigned
   char data_byte){
2.    RIIC0.ICDRT = slave_addr & (0xFE);
3.    while(!RIIC0.ICSR2.BIT.TDRE)
4.        ;
5.    RIIC0.ICDRT = data_byte;
6.    while(!RIIC0.ICSR2.BIT.TEND){
7.        if(RIIC0.ICSR2.BIT.NACKF){
8.            RIIC0.ICSR2.BIT.NACKF = 0;
9.            return 0;
10.       }
11.   }
12.   while(!RIIC0.ICSR2.BIT.TDRE)
13.       ;
```

```
14.     while(!RIIC0.ICSR2.BIT.TEND){
15.         if(RIIC0.ICSR2.BIT.NACKF){
16.             RIIC0.ICSR2.BIT.NACKF = 0;
17.             return 0;
18.         }
19.     }
20.     return 1;
21. }
```

The following is the code for reading a data byte from a peripheral device on the I^{2}C bus:

```
1. unsigned char RiicReadByte(unsigned char slave_addr, unsigned char
   slave_register_num){
2.     RiicWriteByte(slave_addr,slave_register_num);
3.     RiicSendStop();
4.     RIIC0.ICSR2.BIT.STOP = 0;
5.     RiicSendStart();
6.     while(!RIIC0.ICSR2.BIT.TDRE)
7.         ;
8.     RIIC0.ICDRT = slave_addr | (0x01);
9.     while(!RIIC0.ICSR2.BIT.RDRF)
10.         ;
11.     if(RIIC0.ICSR2.BIT.NACKF == 0){
12.         RIIC0.ICMR3.BIT.WAIT = 1;
13.         RIIC0.ICMR3.BIT.ACKBT = 1;
14.         read_byte = RIIC0.ICDRR;
15.         while(!RIIC0.ICSR2.BIT.RDRF)
16.             ;
17.         RIIC0.ICSR2.BIT.STOP = 0;
18.         RIIC0.ICCR2.BIT.SP = 1;
19.         read_byte = RIIC0.ICDRR;
20.         while(!RIIC0.ICSR2.BIT.STOP)
21.             ;
22.         return read_byte;
23.     }
24.     else return 0xFF;
25. }
```

The following explains the above given code :

Line 1:   `unsigned char RiicReadByte(unsigned char slave_addr, unsigned char slave_register_num){`

Line 2:   `RiicWriteByte(slave_addr,slave_register_num);`
Write the data register from which the data is to be read.

Line 3:   `RiicSendStop();`
Send a STOP condition.

Line 4:   `RIIC0.ICSR2.BIT.STOP = 0;`
Reset the STOP condition flag.

Line 5:   `RiicSendStart();`
Send a START condition over the I^{2}C Bus.

Line 6:   `while(!RIIC0.ICSR2.BIT.TDRE)`
Wait here until transmit buffer gets empty.

Line 7:   `;`

Line 8:   `RIIC0.ICDRT = slave_addr | (0x01);`
Request a read from the peripheral device by transmitting the read address as Slave device (write) address +1.

Line 9:   `while(!RIIC0.ICSR2.BIT.RDRF)`
Wait until the read buffer becomes full.

Line 10:   `;`

Line 11:   `if(RIIC0.ICSR2.BIT.NACKF == 0){`
If a ACK is received; i.e., the device is ready, do the following actions.

Line 12:   `RIIC0.ICMR3.BIT.WAIT = 1;`
Set the WAIT bit to 1, due to which the period between ninth clock cycle and first clock cycle is held low.

Line 13:   `RIIC0.ICMR3.BIT.ACKBT = 1;`
Set the ACK bit transmitted as 1, which corresponds to a NACK for the peripheral device.

Line 14:   `read_byte = RIIC0.ICDRR;`
Read dummy data from the I^{2}C receive data register.

Line 15:   `while(!RIIC0.ICSR2.BIT.RDRF);`
Wait here until the ICDRR becomes full again when the shift register transfers data from itself to the ICDRR. This is due to double buffering of data.

Line 16:   `;`

Line 17: `RIIC0.ICSR2.BIT.STOP = 0;`
Reset the status of the STOP bit in the ICSR2.

Line 18: `RIIC0.ICCR2.BIT.SP = 1;`
Request for generation of STOP signal.

Line 19: `read_byte = RIIC0.ICDRR;`
Read data from the ICDRR.

Line 20: `while(!RIIC0.ICSR2.BIT.STOP)`
Wait here until the STOP condition is generated.

Line 21: `;`

Line 22: `return read_byte;`
Return the Data received as the return value of the function.

Line 23: `}`

Line 24: `else return 0xFF;`
If a NACK was received return 0xFF (or any desired value) as a Failure value.

Line 25: `}`

The following code shows the entire process of reading one byte from a peripheral connected on the I^{2}C bus:

```
 1. void main(void){
 2.     RiicIni(0x10);
 3.     RiicSendStart();
 4.     RiicWriteByte2(0x3A, 0x2D, 0x00);
 5.     RiicSendStop();
 6.     RiicSendStart();
 7.     i = RiicReadByte(0x3A, 0x00);
 8.     RiicSendStop();
 9.     RiicUnIni();
10.     while(1)
11.         ;
12. }
```

The following is the explanation of the above code:

Line 1: `void main(void){`
Define the main function.

Line 2:   `RiicIni(0x10);`
Initialize the I²C module RIIC0 with self address as 0x10.

Line 3:   `RiicSendStart();`
Send a START condition.

Line 4:   `RiicWriteByte2(0x3A, 0x2D, 0x00);`
Write a byte 0x00 to the register 0x2D of the peripheral device with address 0x3A.

Line 5:   `RiicSendStop();`
Send a STOP condition.

Line 6:   `RiicSendStart();`
Send a START condition again.

Line 7:   `i = RiicReadByte(0x3A, 0x00);`
Read a byte from the register 0x00 of the peripheral with address 0x3A.

Line 8:   `RiicSendStop();`
Send a STOP condition.

Line 9:   `RiicUnIni();`
Disable the RIIC0 interface.

Line 10: `while(1)`
Wait here forever.

Line 11: `;`

Line 12: `}`

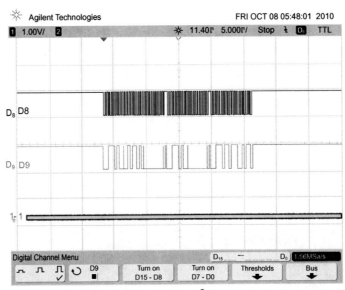

Figure 7.53   Oscilloscope Capture of the complete I²C communication for Basic Example 7.3.3.

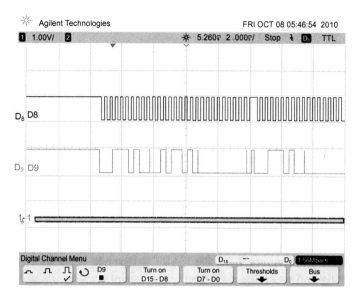

Figure 7.54 Oscilloscope Capture of the beginning of I²C communication for Basic Example 01 (scaled along x-axis). There are three data bytes transferred for the write cycle (first twenty-seven clock pulses).

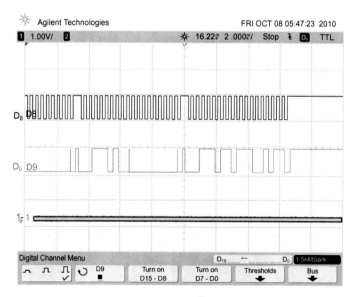

Figure 7.55 Oscilloscope Capture of the end of I²C communication for Basic Example 7.3.3 (scaled along the x-axis). There are two cycles here, each consisting of two data bytes. First is the 2 byte write cycle and the other is the 2 byte read cycle.

7.4   ADVANCED CONCEPTS

Now that we have learned the details of the working behind various communication techniques with polling; i.e., the UART, SPI, and I²C interfaces, in this section we will study some of the advanced features and implementations of the same. Concepts learned in these chapters will be implemented in **Section 7.5** by means of examples. Concepts learned in this section will require basic knowledge of interrupts and interrupt service routines, and additional hardware to be present. It is advisable for the reader to be aware of the additional peripherals being used while illustrating the advanced features of the communication techniques in this section.

7.4.1   Applying FIFO Data Structures for Transmission and Reception Using the UART Serial Communications Interface

As mentioned in **Section 7.2.1** the UART in essence contains a single byte buffer each for transmitting and receiving data from other peripherals connected via the UART interface. These buffers are occasionally filled with data and then the data is transmitted or received. But what if an application is required to transmit data continuously? Usually the peripherals of a Microcontroller operate slower than the actual processing unit. In short, the data output by the processing unit to be transmitted is more quickly generated than transmitted. In such a case, there are two options available: wait for the peripheral to finish transmitting the current data and then load the peripheral with new data, or maintain a First In First Out type of mechanism in which bulk data is stored in a given data structure and then transmitted as and when the peripheral becomes available. The advantage of the latter technique is that the processing unit is free to perform other tasks as data transmission is going on. Before we move on to understanding the design of a UART FIFO, let us take a quick look at a FIFO data structure.

A FIFO type data structure can be visualized as a queue of units standing in line for service. The unit that gets in line first gets service earlier than the unit that enters the queue at a later point of time. This is quite contrary to a LIFO type of data structure in which the last unit to enter the queue gets service prior to the one which entered the queue earlier. FIFOs are generally used wherever operations are to be done on all data in a sequential/consecutive manner. An example of a FIFO is shown in Figure 7.56.

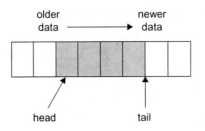

Figure 7.56   Example of a FIFO (queue).

As seen in Figure 7.56 the FIFO consists of a head and a tail where the head contains data that was added to the queue earlier, whereas the tail end contains relatively new data. The size of the queue is also maintained by monitoring variables. Essentials for regulating queues for the UART SCI are as follows:

- Need to maintain one queue for transmission and one queue for reception.
- The transmit ISR unloads data from the transmission queue.
- The receive ISR loads data to the reception queue.
- Pointers are used to maintain the head and tail of the queue.
- A variable "size" keeps track of the current size of the queue.
- Pointers are wrapped around the queue when queue is not empty but the queue reaches the end of the allotted area.
- The main program is responsible for loading the transmit queue and unloading the receive queue.

Queues are implemented with interrupt service routines and not polling, since polling requires the microcontroller to wait and do nothing until current operation is performed. Interrupt Service Routines, on the other hand, are performed intermittently when required and do not disturb the working of the main program. As we shall see in the Advanced Example 7.5.1, the queues will be loaded at a single occasion and then the main program proceeds without waiting for the transmission to complete. The ISRs continue to occur intermittently and finish the transfer of data. The following is the algorithm followed for the complex example in **Section 7.5.1.**

- Initialize the UART.
- Set up switches and define the size of the queue.
- Define a FIFO queue structure consisting of a data array, a pointer to the head of the array, a pointer to the tail of the array, and a variable for holding the current size of the queue.
- Allot memory for two queues, one for transmission and other for reception.
- Define function for checking if a queue is empty and another function to check if a queue is full.
- Initialize the queues by setting the data in the queue, head and tail to zero.
- Define a function for queuing data in a given queue. In order for the data to be queued, perform a check if the queue is full. If queue is not full, then queue data by adding to the tail of the array, update the tail and size values, and report success. Otherwise abort queuing and report failure.
- Define a function for dequeuing data. In order to dequeue data, check if the queue is empty. If the queue is not empty, copy a byte of data from the head of the queue, update the head and size of the queue, and return the copied variable. If the queue is empty, exit the function.

- Define the interrupt service routines that do the following:
  - □ Transmit routines: Check if the queue is empty. If the queue is not empty, dequeue a byte of data from the transmission queue and give it to the transmit buffer of the microcontroller.
  - □ Receive routine: Try to enqueue the data to the receive queue. If the queue is full, provide with an indication.

Setting up the interrupts: The following is the procedure for setting up the serial communication interface interrupts:

- In the vect.h file define the vector table locations of the interrupts and declare them as follows:
  - □ #pragma interrupt (Excep_SCI2_RXI2(vect = 223)) void Excep_SCI2_RXI2 (void);
  - □ #pragma interrupt (Excep_SCI2_TXI2(vect = 224)) void Excep_SCI2_TXI2 (void);
- In the file intprg.c write the detailed interrupt service routines for transmit and receive under the function names void Excep_SCI2_RXI2 (void) and void Excep_SCI2_TXI2 (void).

7.4.2 Multiprocessor Communication Using the Renesas Serial Peripheral Interface

One of the advantages of the serial peripheral interface is the high rate of data transfer. Data is usually transferred at a rate more than 1 MHz's. These speeds are much higher than most other communication protocols and makes SPI well suited for setting up communication amongst processors. As an example, we shall set up two microcontrollers, one as a master and the other as a slave, and demonstrate high speed data transfer between the two. This setup can be used for various applications such as rapid data accumulation or distributed problem solving; in which a problem is split up into various smaller sections and sent to different processors, solved simultaneously in parts, and then transferred back to the main processor. The following section will demonstrate how to set up two microcontrollers, one in master mode and the other in slave mode, such that data can be rapidly transferred between two or more processors. In essence the setup here is the Single Master Multiple Slave configuration, as shown in Figure 7.57.

Data transfer in the above mentioned configuration is done by means of interrupts and interrupt service routines. The two important interrupts for SPI transfer are the SPTIx and SPRIx interrupts, where $x = 0, 1$ and "x" is the module number of the RSPI, RSPI0/RSPIA, and RSPI1/RSPIB. Timing details of the interrupts and data transfer are described as follows.

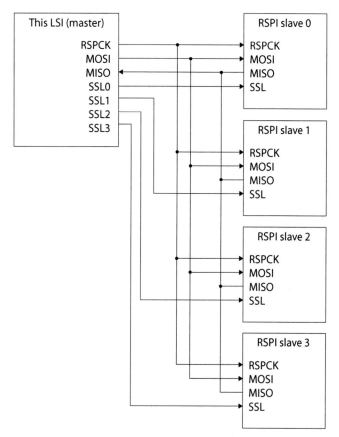

Figure 7.57   Single Master Multiple Slaves. Source: *Hardware Manual,* page 1664.

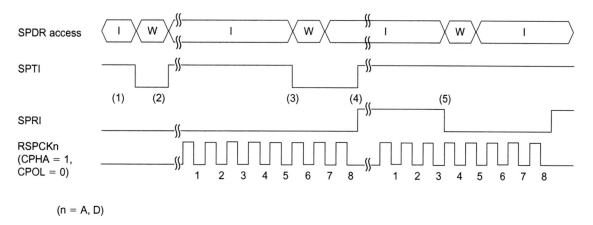

(n = A, D)

Figure 7.58   Operation and timing diagram of SPI interrupts. Source: *Hardware Manual,* page 1681.

Interrupts occur at times (1) to (5) and are as follows:

1. If the interrupts are enabled and currently no data is present in the transmit buffer, an interrupt, SPTI, is generated, which writes to SPDR. Since the transmit buffer is empty, data is copied into the transmit buffer.
2. When the shift register is/becomes empty, the RSPI copies the data from the transmit buffer to the shift register, starts shifting out the data, and generates a transmit buffer empty request (SPTI).
3. When transmit data is written to SPDR by the transmit buffer empty interrupt routine, the data is transferred to the transmit buffer. Because the data being transferred serially is stored in the shift register, the RSPI does not copy the data in the transmit buffer to the shift register.
4. The serial transfer ends. Since the receive buffer is empty, the RSPI copies the received data from the shift register into the receive buffer and generates a receive buffer full interrupt SPRI. As the transmit buffer is filled from step 3, the RSPI copies the data from the transmit buffer into the shift register and resumes transmission of data.
5. When SPDR is read by the receive buffer full interrupt routine, the RSPI sends the data in the receive buffer to the bus inside the chip.

In this manner, the data transfer keeps occurring continuously when the RSPI is enabled. Next we will proceed to the setting up of the microcontrollers in required modes and then proceed to use FIFO queues as explained and demonstrated in **Section 7.4.1.** Using FIFO queues for communication simplifies the transfer of data and enables fast and continuous communication. Rules for operating the queues remain the same as in **Section 7.4.1** however one must notice that now data transfer is taking place in both directions at the same time, with much higher speeds as compared to the SCI interface. For setting up multiprocessor communication, at least two microcontrollers are needed. One microcontroller will be set up in Master mode while the other will be set up in the Slave mode. The complex example in **Section 7.5.2** follows the algorithms for the two microcontrollers as mentioned in the following:

Master Algorithm

- Initialize one Renesas Microcontroller as the master device by assigning the correct values for the registers.
- Define a FIFO queue structure consisting of a data array, a pointer to the head of the array, a pointer to the tail of the array, and a variable for holding the current size of the queue.
- Allot memory for two queues, one for transmission and the other for reception.

- Define function for checking if the queue is empty, and another function to check if the queue is full.
- Initialize the queues by setting the data in the queue, head and tail to zero.
- Define a function for queuing data in a given queue. In order for the data to be queued, perform a check if the queue is full. If the queue is not full, then queue data by adding to the tail of the array, update the tail and size values, and report success. Otherwise, abort queuing and report failure.
- Define a function for dequeuing data. In order to dequeue data, check if the queue is empty. If the queue is not empty, copy a byte of data from the head of the queue, update the head and size of the queue, and return the copied variable. If the queue is empty, exit the function.
- Define the interrupt service routines that do the following:
  - Transmit routines: Check if the queue is empty. If the queue is not empty, dequeue a byte of data from the transmission queue and give it to the transmit buffer of the microcontroller.
  - Receive routine: Try to enqueue the data to the receive queue. If the queue is full, provide with an indication.

Setting up the interrupts: The following is the procedure for setting up the serial communication interface interrupts:

- In the vect.h file define the vector table locations of the interrupts and declare them as follows:
  - #pragma interrupt (Excep_RSPI0_SPRIO(vect = 45)) void Excep_RSPI0_SPRIO (void);
  - #pragma interrupt (Excep_RSPI0_SPTIO(vect = 46)) void Excep_RSPI0_SPTIO (void);
- In the file intprg.c write the detailed interrupt service routines for transmit and receive under the function names void Excep_RSPI0_SPRIO (void) and void Excep Excep_RSPI0_SPTIO (void).

Slave Algorithm

- Initialize another Renesas Microcontroller as the slave device by assigning the correct values for the registers.
- Define a FIFO queue structure consisting of a data array, a pointer to the head of the array, a pointer to the tail of the array, and a variable for holding the current size of the queue.
- Allot memory for two queues, one for transmission and the other for reception.
- Define function for checking if the queue is empty, and another function to check if the queue is full.

- Initialize the queues by setting the data in the queue, head and tail to zero.
- Define a function for queuing data in a given queue. In order for the data to be queued, perform a check if the queue is full. If the queue is not full, then queue data by adding to the tail of the array, update the tail and size values, and report success. Otherwise, abort queuing and report failure.
- Define a function for dequeuing data. In order to dequeue data, check if the queue is empty. If the queue is not empty, copy a byte of data from the head of the queue, update the head and size of the queue, and return the copied variable. If the queue is empty, exit the function.
- Define the interrupt service routines that do the following:
  - Transmit routines: Check if the queue is empty. If the queue is not empty, dequeue a byte of data from the transmission queue and give it to the transmit buffer of the microcontroller.
  - Receive routine: Try to enqueue the data to the receive queue. If the queue is full, provide with an indication.

Setting up the interrupts: The following is the procedure for setting up the serial communication interface interrupts:

- In the vect.h file define the vector table locations of the interrupts and declare them as follows:
  - #pragma interrupt (Excep_RSPI0_SPRIO(vect = 45)) void Excep_RSPI0_SPRIO (void);
  - #pragma interrupt (Excep_RSPI0_SPTIO(vect = 46)) void Excep_RSPI0_SPTIO (void);
- In the file intprg.c write the detailed interrupt service routines for transmit and receive under the function names void Excep_RSPI0_SPRIO (void) and void Excep_RSPI0_SPTIO (void).

7.4.3 Transfer of Data Between Peripherals Connected on the I^{2}C Bus Using FIFOs

In section 7.2.3 we explained the details of the Renesas I^{2}C interface module and the procedure for setting it up. In section 7.3.3 we demonstrated how to transfer a single byte of data to and from a peripheral. As observed, there is a lot of overhead to transfer a single byte to a peripheral. It thus makes sense to transfer more than one byte at a single time to the device.

Most devices that operate using the I^{2}C interface store and read out data bytes from registers; i.e., we read and write data from registers of the device. The devices usually have a register address pointer which points to the register to write to or read from. This register is usually auto incremented when the data is transferred. This allows us to transfer multiple bytes to and from the device. Thus we can use FIFOs to implement the transfer of data. The easiest method to operate the FIFOs is by using interrupts.

The following are the algorithms to read and write data to the device. Data provided to the transmit buffer is from the transmit FIFO and data received from the receive buffer is input into the receive FIFO:

Writing data to a peripheral device/Master transmitter operation using interrupts:

1. Set the IICRST bit in ICCR1 to 1 (internal reset) and then clear the IICRST bit to 0 (canceling reset) with the ICE bit in ICCR1 cleared to 0 (disabling the interface). This initializes the internal state and the various flags of ICSR1. After that, set registers SARLn, SARUn, ICSER, ICMR1, ICBRH, and ICBRL ($n = 0$ to 2), and set the other registers as necessary (for initial settings of the RIIC, see Figure 30.5 in the hardware manual). When the necessary register settings have been completed, set the ICE bit to 1 (to enable transfer). This step is not necessary if initialization of the RIIC has already been completed.

2. Read the BBSY flag in ICCR2 to check that the bus is open, and then set the ST bit in ICCR2 to 1 (start condition issuance request). Upon receiving the request, the RIIC issues a start condition. At the same time, the BBSY flag and the START flag in ICSR2 are automatically set to 1 and the ST bit is automatically cleared to 0. At this time, if the start condition is detected, and the internal levels for the SDA output state and the levels on the SDAn line have matched while the ST bit is 1, the RIIC recognizes that issuing of the start condition as requested by the ST bit has been successfully completed, and the MST and TRS bits in ICCR2 are automatically set to 1, placing the RIIC in master transmitter mode. The TDRE flag in ICSR2 is also automatically set to 1 in response to the setting of the TRS bit to 1.

3. Check that the TDRE flag in ICSR2 is 1, and then write the value for transmission (the slave address and the R/W# bit) to ICDRT. Once the data for transmission are written to ICDRT, the TDRE flag is automatically cleared to 0, the data are transferred from ICDRT to ICDRS, and the TDRE flag is again set to 1. After the byte containing the slave address and R/W# bit has been transmitted, the value of the TRS bit is automatically updated to select master transmitter or master receiver mode in accord with the value of the transmitted R/W# bit. If the value of the R/W# bit was 0, the RIIC continues in master transmitter mode. Since the ICSR2.NACKF flag being 1 at this time indicates that no slave device recognized the address or that there was an error in communications, write 1 to the ICCR2.SP bit to issue a stop condition. For data transmission with an address in the 10-bit format, start by writing 1111 0b, the two higher-order bits of the slave address, and W to ICDRT as the first address transmission. Then, as the second address transmission, write the eight lower-order bits of the slave address to ICDRT.

4. After confirming that the TDRE flag in ICSR2 is 1, write the data for transmission to the ICDRT register. The RIIC automatically holds the SCLn line low until the data for transmission are ready, or a stop condition is issued.

5. After all bytes of data for transmission have been written to the ICDRT register, wait until the value of the TEND flag in ICSR2 returns to 1, and then set the SP bit in ICCR2 to 1 (stop condition issuance request). Upon receiving a stop condition issuance request, the RIIC issues the stop condition.

6. Upon detecting the stop condition, the RIIC automatically clears the MST and TRS bits in ICCR2 to 00b and enters slave receiver mode. Furthermore, it automatically clears the TDRE and TEND flags to 0, and sets the STOP flag in ICSR2 to 1.

7. After checking that the ICSR2.STOP flag is 1, clear the ICSR2.NACKF and STOP flags to 0 for the next transfer operation.

The following two figures show the timings of the operations:

Reading data from a peripheral device/Master receiver operation:

1. Set the IICRST bit in ICCR1 to 1 (internal reset) and then clear the IICRST bit to 0 (canceling reset) with the ICE bit in ICCR1 cleared to 0 (disabling the interface). This initializes the internal state and the various flags of ICSR1. After that, set registers SARLn, SARUn, ICSER, ICMR1, ICBRH, and ICBRL ($n = 0$ to 2), and set the other registers as necessary (for initial settings of the RIIC, see Figure 30.5 in the hardware manual). When the necessary register settings have been completed, set the ICE bit to 1 (to enable transfer). This step is not necessary if initialization of the RIIC has already been completed.

2. Read the BBSY flag in ICCR2 to check that the bus is open, and then set the ST bit in ICCR2 to 1 (start condition issuance request). Upon receiving the request, the RIIC issues a start condition. When the RIIC detects the start condition, the BBSY flag and the START flag in ICSR2 are automatically set to 1 and the ST bit is automatically cleared to 0. At this time, if the start condition is detected and the levels for the SDA output and the levels on the SDAn line have matched while the ST bit is 1, the RIIC recognizes that issuing of the start condition as requested by the ST bit has been successfully completed. As a result the MST and TRS bits in ICCR2 are automatically set to 1, placing the RIIC in master transmitter mode. The TDRE flag in ICSR2 is also automatically set to 1 in response to setting of the TRS bit to 1.

3. Check that the TDRE flag in ICSR2 is 1, and then write the value for transmission (the first byte indicates the slave address and value of the R/W# bit) to ICDRT. Once the data for transmission are written to ICDRT, the TDRE flag is automatically cleared to 0, the data are transferred from ICDRT to ICDRS, and the TDRE flag is again set to 1. Once the byte containing the slave address and R/W# bit has been transmitted, the value of the ICCR2.TRS bit is automatically updated to

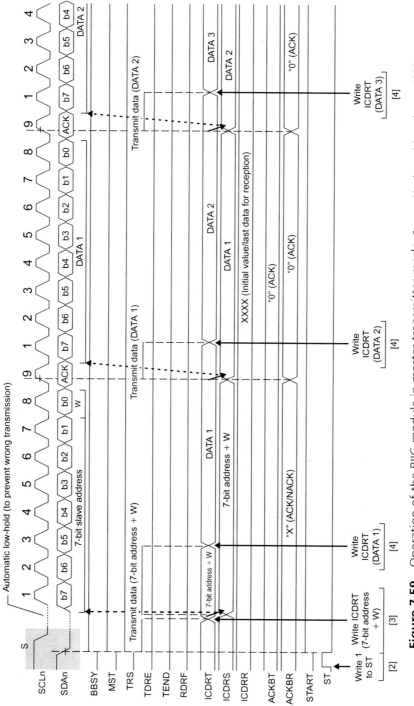

Figure 7.59 Operation of the RIIC module in master transmitter mode. Source: *Hardware Manual*, page 1522.

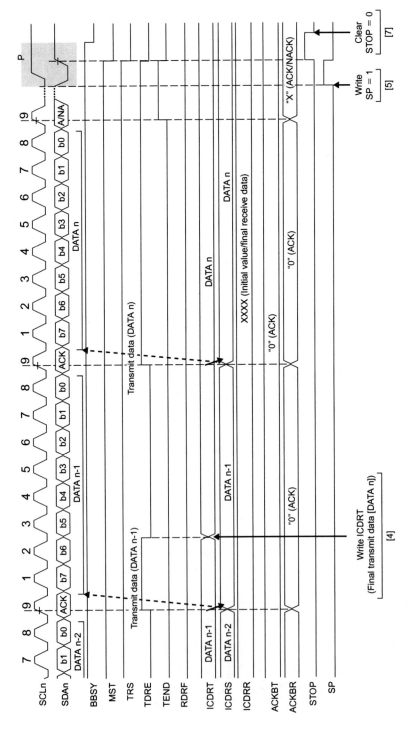

Figure 7.60   RIIC module in master transmitter mode. *Source: Hardware Manual,* page 1522.

select master transmitter or master receiver mode in accord with the value of the transmitted R/W# bit. If the value of the R/W# bit was 1, the TRS bit is cleared to 0 on the rising edge of the ninth cycle of SCLn (the clock signal), placing the RIIC in master receiver mode. At this time, the TDRE flag is automatically cleared to 0 and the ICSR2.RDRF flag is automatically set to 1.

Since the ICSR2.NACKF flag being 1 at this time indicates that no slave device recognized the address or there was an error in communications, write 1 to the ICCR2.SP bit to issue a stop condition. For master reception from a device with a 10-bit address, start by using the master transmission to issue the 10-bit address, and then issue a restart condition. After that, transmitting 1111 0b, the two higher-order bits of the slave address, and the R bit places the RIIC in master receiver mode.

4. Dummy read ICDRR after confirming that the RDRF flag in ICSR2 is 1. This makes the RIIC start output of the SCL (clock) signal and start data reception.

5. After one byte of data has been received, the RDRF flag in ICSR2 is set to 1 on the rising edge of the eighth or ninth cycle of SCL clock (the clock signal) as selected by the RDRFS bit in ICMR3. Reading out ICDRR at this time will produce the received data, and the RDRF flag is automatically cleared to 0 at the same time. Furthermore, the value of the acknowledgement field received during the ninth cycle of SCL clock is returned as the value set in the ACKBT bit of ICMR3. Save the received data into the FIFO and increment the pointer to the FIFO.

6. When the next value to be received will be the final byte, set the WAIT bit in ICMR3 to 1 (so that waiting is applied) before reading ICDRR. This causes the SCLn line to be held low from the falling edge of the ninth clock cycle after reception of the next data (i.e., the final byte), enabling issuance of a stop condition. However, when the ICMR3.RDRFS bit is 0 and the slave device must be notified that it is to end transfer for data reception after transfer of the next (final) byte, set the ACKBT bit in ICMR3 to 1 (NACK).

7. After reading out the byte before last from the ICDRR register, if the value of the ICSR2.RDRF flag is confirmed to be 1, write 1 to the SP bit in ICCR2 (stop condition issuance request) and then read the last byte from ICDRR. Save the received data bytes into the FIFO and increment the pointer to the FIFO. When ICDRR is read, the RIIC is released from the wait state and issues the stop condition after low-level output in the ninth clock cycle is completed or the SCL line is released from the low-hold state.

8. Upon detecting the stop condition, the RIIC automatically clears the MST and TRS bits in ICCR2 to "00b" and enters slave receiver mode. Furthermore, detection of the stop condition leads to setting of the STOP flag in ICSR2 to 1.

9. After checking that the ICSR2.STOP flag is 1, clear the ICSR2.NACKF and STOP flags to 0 for the next transfer operation.

The following two figures show the timings of the operations.

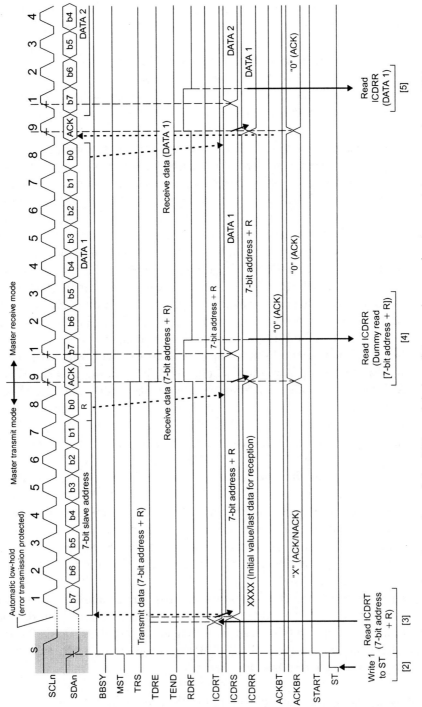

Figure 7.61 Operation of the RIIC module in master receiver mode. *Source: Hardware Manual, page 1526.*

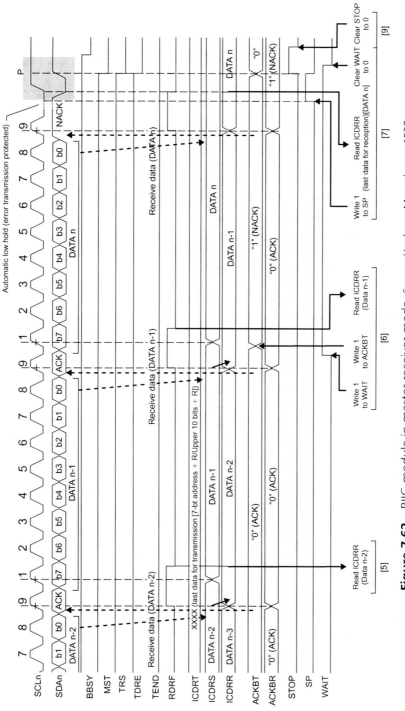

Figure 7.62   RIIC module in master receiver mode. Source: *Hardware Manual*, page 1527.

Advanced Section 7.5.3 helps demonstrate these concepts.

7.5 ADVANCED EXAMPLES

7.5.1 FIFO Data Structures for Transmission and Reception Using the UART Serial Communications Interface

Aim: Demonstration of the use of FIFOs towards transmission and reception.

Requirements: PC with High-performance Embedded Workshop 4.0 or 4.0+, Renesas Development Kit; PC with RS-232 serial port.

Details: In this example we demonstrate the use of FIFO data structures for transmission and reception to show how the communication interface operates using interrupts, and how the microcontroller manages to work on other tasks while communication proceeds normally. This example is based on the initialization codes of the **Basic Example 7.3.1** and is similar to the one detailed in **Section 7.4.1.**

Procedure: For this example, create a new workspace in HEW and fill the given lines of code in the corresponding files mentioned before the following code. Compile; build all files and Download to board as mentioned in Chapter 4. When downloaded, connect the RX62N development board to a standard PC with an RS-232 port configured at 115200 baud, no parity, and 1 stop bit to view the results on a HyperTerminal program or on a Serial Port Terminal.

Code: The following is the code related to the demonstration:

Setting up Interrupt Service Routines

Filename: vect.h

```
1. pragma interrupt (Excep_SCI2_RXI2(vect = 223))
2. void Excep_SCI2_RXI2(void);
3. #pragma interrupt (Excep_SCI2_TXI2(vect = 224))
4. void Excep_SCI2_TXI2(void);
```

Filename: intprg.c

```
1. #include "RX62N_SCI_UART.h"
2. #include <machine.h>
3. #include "vect.h"
4. #pragma Section IntPRG
5. void Excep_SCI2_RXI2(void){
```

```
6.      if(!Q_Enqueue(&rx_q, SCI2.RDR)){
7.      }
8. }
9. void Excep_SCI2_TXI2(void){
10.     if(!Q_Empty(&tx_q))
11.         SCI2.TDR = Q_Dequeue(&tx_q);
12. }
```

Setting up function definitions for operating on the queues:

Filename: RX62N_SCI_UART.h

```
1. #include "iodefine_RX62N.h"
2. #define Q_SIZE (32)
3. typedef struct {
4.     unsigned char Data[Q_SIZE];
5.     unsigned int Head;    //points to oldest data element
6.     unsigned int Tail;    //points to next free space
7.     unsigned int Size;    //quantity of elements in queue
8. } Q_T;
9. int Q_Empty(Q_T * q);
10. int Q_Full(Q_T * q);
11. int Q_Enqueue(Q_T * q, unsigned char d);
12. unsigned char Q_Dequeue(Q_T * q);
13. void Q_Init(Q_T * q);
14. void delay(long unsigned int n);
15. void init_switches();
16. void init_LEDs();
17. void init_UART0();
18. void d3_send_string(far char * s);
19. void demo3(void);
20. extern Q_T tx_q, rx_q;
```

Setting up all the function details related to the functioning of the UART and FIFO queues:

Filename: RX62N_SCI_UART.c

```
1. #include "RX62N_SCI_UART.h"
2. Q_T tx_q, rx_q;
3. int Q_Empty(Q_T * q){
```

```
 4.      return (q->Size == 0);
 5. }
 6. int Q_Full(Q_T * q){
 7.      return (q->Size == Q_SIZE);
 8. }
 9. int Q_Enqueue(Q_T * q, unsigned char d){
10.      if(!Q_Full(q)){
11.          q->Data[q->Tail++] = d;
12.          q->Tail %= Q_SIZE;
13.          q->Size++;
14.          return 1;
15.      }
16.      else return 0;
17. }
18. unsigned char Q_Dequeue(Q_T * q){
19.      unsigned char t = 0;
20.      if(!Q_Empty(q){
21.          t = q->Data[q->Head];
22.          q->Data[q->Head++] = 0;
23.          q->Head %= Q_SIZE;
24.          q->Size--;
25.      }
26.      return t;
27. }
28. void Q_Init(Q_T * q){
29.      unsigned int i;
30.      for(i = 0; i < Q_SIZE; i++)
31.          q->Data[i] = 0;
32.      q->Head = 0;
33.      q->Tail = 0;
34.      q->Size = 0;
35. }
36. void init_UART0(){
37.      MSTP(SCI2) = 0;
38.      IOPORT.PFFSCI.BIT.SCI2S = 1;
39.      PORT1.DDR.BIT.B2 = 0;
40.      PORT1.ICR.BIT.B2 = 1;
41.      PORT1.DDR.BIT.B3 = 1;
42.      SCI2.SCR.BYTE = 0;
43.      SCI2.SMR.BYTE = 0x00;
44.      SCI2.SCR.BIT.RIE = 1;
45.      SCI2.SCR.BIT.TIE = 1;
```

```
46.    IPR(SCI2,RXI2) = 1;
47.    IPR(SCI2,TXI2) = 1;
48.    IEN(SCI2, RXI2) = 1;
49.    IEN(SCI2, TXI2) = 1;
50.    SCI2.BRR = 12;
51.    SCI2.SCR.BYTE |= 0x30;
52. }
53. void d3_send_string(far char * s){
54.    while(*s){
55.        if(Q_Enqueue(&tx_q, *s))
56.            s++;
57.        else { }
58.    }
59.    if(IR(SCI2, TXI2) == 0){
60.        SCI2.TDR = Q_Dequeue(&tx_q);
61.    }
62. }
63. void demo3(void){
64.    char c;
65.    d3_send_string("Hello, interruptible world!\n\r");
66.    while(1){
67.        if(!Q_Empty(&rx_q)){
68.            c = Q_Dequeue(&rx_q);
69.            d3_send_string("Ouch!\n\r");
70.        }
71.    }
72. }
```

Main Program

Filename: Workspace_name.c

```
1. void main(){
2.    init_switches();
3.    init_LEDs();
4.    init_UART0();
5.    Q_Init(&tx_q);
6.    Q_Init(&rx_q);
7.    demo3();
8.    while(1)
9.        ;
10. }
```

7.5.2 Multiprocessor Communication Using Queues and the Renesas Serial Peripheral Interface

Aim: Demonstration of Multiprocessor Communication using queues and the RSPI for rapid communication between microcontrollers.

Requirements: PC with High-performance Embedded Workshop 4.0 or 4.0+, Two Renesas Development Kits.

Details: In the previous example, we demonstrated how communication takes place at a continuous pace using queues. In this example we demonstrate how to perform Multiprocessor communication at much higher speeds than those available with the SCI interface. Baud rates can reach maximum speeds of PCLK, which is the peripheral clock generated by the RX62N processor. Since the RSPI operates much faster than the SCI, it is an ideal serial bus for Multiprocessor communication as compared to the SCI and I^2C interface.

Procedure: For this example, create a new workspace in HEW and fill the given lines of code in the corresponding files mentioned before the following code. You now need to download two separate pieces of codes on to each board; one for the master device and one for the slave device. At the beginning of the main file for the master device, make sure that the "#define RSPI_Master_Device" is not commented out while the "#define RSPI_Slave_Device" is commented out. This will build the main example code for the master device. Once this example code has been built, download the module on to one board. For the slave device, make sure that the "#define RSPI_Slave_Device" is not commented where as the "#define RSPI_Master_Device" is commented out. This will build the main example code for the slave device. Once this example code has been built, download the module on to the other board. Make sure that you are not building both modules at the same time; i.e., "#define RSPI_Master_Device" and "#define RSPI_Slave_Device" are not defined at the same time, or else the code/device will not function.

Code: The following is the code related to the demonstration:

Setting Up Interrupt Service Routines

Filename: vect.h

```
1. #pragma interrupt (Excep_RSPI0_SPRI0(vect = 45))
2. void Excep_RSPI0_SPRI0(void);
3. #pragma interrupt (Excep_RSPI0_SPTI0(vect = 46))
4. void Excep_RSPI0_SPTI0(void);
```

Filename: intprg.c

```
1. void Excep_RSPI0_SPRI0(void){
2.    LED_Y = LED_ON;
```

```
3.     if(!SPI_Q_Enqueue(&rx_q, (0x00FF & RSPI0.SPDR.WORD.L))){
4.         LED_R = LED_ON;
5.     }
6.     LED_Y = LED_OFF;
7. }
8. void Excep_RSPI0_SPTI0(void){
9.     LED_G = LED_ON;
10.    if(!SPI_Q_Empty(&tx_q))
11.        RSPI0.SPDR.WORD.H = (0x00FF & SPI_Q_Dequeue(&tx_q));
12.    LED_G = LED_OFF;
13. }
```

Setting Up Function Definitions for Operating on the Queues
Filename: RX62N_RSPI.h

```
1. #include "iodefine_RX62N.h"
2. #define NULL (0)
3. #define SW1 (PORT4.PORT.BIT.B0)
4. #define SW2 (PORT4.PORT.BIT.B1)
5. #define SW3 (PORT4.PORT.BIT.B2)
6. #define SW1_EN (PORT4.DDR.BIT.B0)
7. #define SW2_EN (PORT4.DDR.BIT.B1)
8. #define SW3_EN (PORT4.DDR.BIT.B2)
9. #define Q_SIZE (32)
10. typedef struct {
11.    unsigned char Data[Q_SIZE];
12.    unsigned int Head;
13.    unsigned int Tail;
14.    unsigned int Size;
15. } Q_T;
16. int SPI_Q_Empty(Q_T * q);
17. int SPI_Q_Full(Q_T * q);
18. int SPI_Q_Enqueue(Q_T * q, unsigned char d);
19. unsigned char Q_Dequeue(Q_T * q);
20. void SPI_Q_Init(Q_T * q);
21. void SPI_delay(long unsigned int n);
22. void SPI_init_switches();
23. void SPI_init_LEDs();
24. void SPI_init_RSPI_Master();
25. void SPI_init_RSPI_Slave();
```

```
26. void SPI_d3_send_string(far char * s);
27. void SPI_demo3(void);
28. extern Q_T tx_q, rx_q;
```

Setting Up All the Function Details Related to the Functioning of the UART and FIFO Queues

Filename: RX62N_SCI_UART.c

```
1.  #include "iodefine_RX62N.h"
2.  #include "RX62N_RSPI.h"
3.  #include "RX62N_LED_Defs.h"
4.  Q_T tx_q, rx_q;
5.  void SPI_init_RSPI_Master(void){
6.     MSTP(RSPI0) = 0;
7.     IOPORT.PFGSPI.BIT.RSPIS = 0;
8.     IOPORT.PFGSPI.BIT.RSPCKE = 1;
9.     IOPORT.PFGSPI.BIT.SSL0E = 1;
10.    IOPORT.PFGSPI.BIT.MOSIE = 1;
11.    IOPORT.PFGSPI.BIT.MISOE = 1;
12.    PORTC.DDR.BIT.B7 = 0;
13.    PORTC.DDR.BIT.B6 = 1;
14.    PORTC.DDR.BIT.B5 = 1;
15.    PORTC.DDR.BIT.B4 = 1;
16.    PORTC.DR.BIT.B4 = 1;
17.    PORTC.DR.BIT.B7 = 1;
18.    PORTC.DR.BIT.B6 = 1;
19.    PORTC.DR.BIT.B5 = 1;
20.    RSPI0.SPPCR.BYTE = 0x00;
21.    RSPI0.SPBR.BYTE = 0x00;
22.    RSPI0.SPDCR.BYTE = 0x00;
23.    RSPI0.SPCKD.BYTE = 0x00;
24.    RSPI0.SSLND.BYTE = 0x00;
25.    RSPI0.SPND.BYTE = 0x00;
26.    RSPI0.SPCR2.BYTE = 0x00;
27.    IPR(RSPI0, SPTI0) = 1;   //Clear Transmit interrupt bit
28.    IEN(RSPI0, SPTI0) = 1;   //Enable Transmit interrupt bit
29.    IPR(RSPI0, SPRI0) = 1;   //Clear Transmit interrupt bit
30.    IEN(RSPI0, SPRI0) = 1;   //Enable Transmit interrupt bit
31.    RSPI0.SPCMD0.WORD = 0x0701;
32.    RSPI0.SPCR.BYTE = 0xE8;
```

```
33.     RSPI0.SSLP.BYTE = 0x00;
34.     RSPI0.SPSCR.BYTE = 0x00;
35. }
36. void SPI_init_RSPI_Slave(void){
37.     MSTP(RSPI0) = 0;
38.     IOPORT.PFGSPI.BIT.RSPIS = 0;
39.     IOPORT.PFGSPI.BIT.RSPCKE = 1;
40.     IOPORT.PFGSPI.BIT.SSL0E = 1;
41.     IOPORT.PFGSPI.BIT.MOSIE = 1;
42.     IOPORT.PFGSPI.BIT.MISOE = 1;
43.     PORTC.DDR.BIT.B7 = 1;
44.     PORTC.DDR.BIT.B6 = 0;
45.     PORTC.DDR.BIT.B5 = 0;
46.     PORTC.DDR.BIT.B4 = 0;
47.     PORTC.DR.BIT.B4 = 0;
48.     PORTC.DR.BIT.B7 = 1;
49.     PORTC.DR.BIT.B6 = 0;
50.     PORTC.DR.BIT.B5 = 0;
51.     RSPI0.SPPCR.BYTE = 0x04;
52.     RSPI0.SPBR.BYTE = 0x00;
53.     RSPI0.SPDCR.BYTE = 0x00;
54.     RSPI0.SPCKD.BYTE = 0x00;
55.     RSPI0.SSLND.BYTE = 0x00;
56.     RSPI0.SPND.BYTE = 0x00;
57.     RSPI0.SPCR2.BYTE = 0x00;
58.     RSPI0.SPCMD0.WORD = 0x0701;
59.     RSPI0.SPDR.WORD.L = 0xAA55;
60.     RSPI0.SPDR.WORD.H = 0x55AA;
61.     IEN(RSPI0, SPRI0) = 1;   //Enable Receive interrupt
62.     IEN(RSPI0, SPTI0) = 1;   //Enable Transmit interrupt
63.     IPR(RSPI0, SPRI0) = 1;
64.     IPR(RSPI0, SPTI0) = 1;
65.     RSPI0.SSLP.BYTE = 0x00;
66.     RSPI0.SPCR.BYTE = 0xA0;
67.     RSPI0.SPSCR.BYTE = 0x00;
68.     RSPI0.SPCR.BIT.SPE = 1;
69. }
70. int SPI_Q_Empty(Q_T * q){
71.     return (q->Size == 0);
72. }
```

```
73. int SPI_Q_Full(Q_T * q){
74.    return (q->Size == Q_SIZE);
75. }
76. int SPI_Q_Enqueue(Q_T * q, unsigned char d){
77.    if(!SPI_Q_Full(q)){
78.        q->Data[q->Tail++] = d;
79.        q->Tail %= Q_SIZE;
80.        q->Size++;
81.        return 1;
82.    }
83.    else return 0;
84. }
85. unsigned char SPI_Q_Dequeue(Q_T * q){
86.    unsigned char t = 0;
87.    if(!SPI_Q_Empty(q)){
88.        t = q->Data[q->Head];
89.        q->Data[q->Head++] = 0;
90.        q->Head %= Q_SIZE;
91.        q->Size—;
92.    }
93.    return t;
94. }
95. void SPI_Q_Init(Q_T * q){
96.    unsigned int i;
97.    for(i = 0; i < Q_SIZE; i++)
98.        q->Data[i] = 0;
99.    q->Head = 0;
100.    q->Tail = 0;
101.    q->Size = 0;
102. }
103. void SPI_delay(long unsigned int n){
104.    while(n—)
105.        ;
106. }
107. void SPI_init_switches(){
108.    SW1_EN = SW2_EN = SW3_EN = 0;   //inputs
109. }
110. void SPI_init_LEDs(){
111.    ENABLE_LEDS;
112.    ALL_LEDS_ON;
113. }
```

```
114. void SPI_d3_send_string(far char * s){
115.    while(*s){
116.        if(SPI_Q_Enqueue(&tx_q, *s))
117.            s++;
118.        if(IR(RSPI0, SPTI0) == 0){
119.            SCI2.TDR = SPI_Q_Dequeue(&tx_q);
120.        }
121.    }
122. void SPI_demo3(void){
123.    char c;
124.    SPI_d3_send_string("Hello, interruptible world!\n\r");
125.    while(1){
126.        if(!SPI_Q_Empty(&rx_q)){
127.            c = SPI_Q_Dequeue(&rx_q);
128.            (void)c;
129.            SPI_d3_send_string("Ouch!\n\r");
130.        }
131.    }
132. }
```

Main Program

Filename: Workspace_name.c

```
1. #include "iodefine_RX62N.h"
2. #include "RX62N_LED_Defs.h"
3. #include "RX62N_RSPI.h"
4. #define RSPI_SLAVE
5. #define RSPI_MASTER
6. void main(){
7.    SPI_init_switches();
8.    SPI_init_LEDs();
9.    #ifdef RSPI_MASTER
10.   SPI_init_RSPI_Master();
11.   #endif
12.   #ifdef RSPI_MASTER
13.   SPI_init_RSPI_Slave();
14.   #endif
15.   SPI_Q_Init(&tx_q);
16.   SPI_Q_Init(&rx_q);
```

```
17.    SPI_demo3();
18.    while(1)
19.       ;
20. }
```

7.5.3   Transfer of data between peripherals connected on the I²C bus using FIFOs

Aim: To demonstrate mass transfer of data between peripherals connected on the I²C bus.

Requirements: PC with High-performance Embedded Workshop 4.0 or 4.0+, Renesas Development Kits (YRDKRX62N) with on board I²C peripherals.

Details: In this example we will demonstrate how to use the I²C bus to transfer large amounts of data to the desired peripheral with minimum overhead. The device we will use is the ADXL345 and will be writing the default values to the ADXL345, specified in the device datasheet and reading the acceleration values for the X, Y, and Z values. The code also provides for a standard framework that can be used to access other devices using the RX62N microcontroller.

Procedure: For this example, create a new workspace in HEW and fill the given lines of code in the corresponding files mentioned before the code below. To use the following code for other peripherals make sure to specify the correct address and number of data bytes to read and write. The given following code is for the Analog Devices Accelerometer ADXL345 whose device sheet is found at http://www.analog.com/static/imported-files/data_sheets/ADXL345.pdf (Analog Devices, Inc.; *ADXL345 datasheet: 3-Axis, ±2 g/±4 g/±8 g/±16 g Digital Accelerometer, ADXL345*). A point to note is for the user to use the iodefine_RX62N.h header file instead of the standard iodefine.h file. Additional changes may be required if the two header files are switched.

Filename: riic.h

This file contains the most declarations and #define variables used by the RIIC module.

```
1.  #ifndef _RIIC_SETTING_DEF
2.  #define _RIIC_SETTING_DEF
3.  #define RIIC_CH0    //When use channel0, define "RIIC_CH0"
4.  #define RIIC_CH1    //When use channel1, define "RIIC_CH1"
5.  #ifdef RIIC_CH0
6.  #define RIIC RIIC0   //Replace I/O define
7.  #else
8.  #define RIIC RIIC1   //Replace I/O define
9.  #endif
10. #define RIIC_OK 0    //Return value for function "RiicMst"
```

```
11. #define RIIC_NG 1    //Return value for function "RiicMst"
12. #define RIIC_BUS_BUSY 2    //Return value for function "RiicMst"
13. void RiicIni(unsigned char, unsigned char);
14. unsigned char RiicStart(unsigned char, unsigned char*, unsigned
    long);
15. #endif    //_RIIC_SETTING_DEF
```

Filename: riic.c

This file contains definitions of functions that perform actions in response to calls from either the user or the interrupts.

```
1. void RiicIni(unsigned char in_SelfAddr, unsigned char in_Enable)
2. {
3.     #ifdef RIIC_CH0
4.     SYSTEM.MSTPCRB.BIT.MSTPB21 = 0;    //RIIC0(MSTPB21)
5.     #else
6.     SYSTEM.MSTPCRB.BIT.MSTPB20 = 0;    //RIIC1(MSTPB20)
7.     #endif
8.     RIIC.ICCR1.BIT.ICE = 0;    //RIIC disable
9.     RIIC.ICCR1.BIT.IICRST = 1;    //RIIC all reset
10.    RIIC.ICCR1.BIT.IICRST = 0;
11.    RiicMstCnt = 0;
12.    RiicMstNum = 0;
13.    if(in_Enable != 0){    //Initialise RIIC
14.        /* Self address setting */
15.        RIIC.SARU0.BIT.FS = 0;    //7bit address format
16.        RIIC.SARL0.BYTE = in_SelfAddr;    //Set self address
17.        RIIC.ICMR1.BIT.CKS = 7;    //IIC phi = PCLK/128 clock
18.        RIIC.ICBRH.BIT.BRH = 28;    //100kbps (PCLK = 50 MHz)
19.        RIIC.ICBRL.BIT.BRL = 29;
20.        RIIC.ICMR3.BIT.ACKWP = 1;    //Disable ACKBT protect
21.        RIIC.ICIER.BIT.RIE = 1;    //Edge interrupt
22.        RIIC.ICIER.BIT.TIE = 1;    //Edge interrupt
23.        RIIC.ICIER.BIT.TEIE = 0;    //Level interrupt
24.        RIIC.ICIER.BIT.NAKIE = 1;    //Level interrupt
25.        RIIC.ICIER.BIT.SPIE = 1;    //Level interrupt
26.        RIIC.ICIER.BIT.STIE = 0;    //Level interrupt
27.        RIIC.ICIER.BIT.ALIE = 0;    //Level interrupt
28.        RIIC.ICIER.BIT.TMOIE = 0;    //Level interrupt
```

```
29.        #ifdef RIIC_CH0    //RIIC channel0
30.        ICU.IPR[0x88].BYTE = 0x04;    //EEI0 interrupt level
31.        ICU.IPR[0x89].BYTE = 0x04;    //RXI0 interrupt level
32.        ICU.IPR[0x8A].BYTE = 0x04;    //TXI0 interrupt level
33.        ICU.IPR[0x8B].BYTE = 0x04;    //TEI0 interrupt level
34.        ICU.IER[0x1E].BIT.IEN6 = 1;    //EEI0 interrupt enable
35.        ICU.IER[0x1E].BIT.IEN7 = 1;    //RXI0 interrupt enable
36.        ICU.IER[0x1F].BIT.IEN0 = 1;    //TXI0 interrupt enable
37.        ICU.IER[0x1F].BIT.IEN1 = 1;    //TEI0 interrupt enable
38.        ICU.IR[246].BIT.IR = 0;    //EEI0 clear interrupt flag
39.        ICU.IR[247].BIT.IR = 0;    //RXI0 clear interrupt flag
40.        ICU.IR[248].BIT.IR = 0;    //TXI0 clear interrupt flag
41.        ICU.IR[249].BIT.IR = 0;    //TEI0 clear interrupt flag
42.        PORT1.ICR.BIT.B3 = 1;    //SDA0 setting
43.        PORT1.ICR.BIT.B2 = 1;    //SCL0 setting
44.        #else    //RIIC channel1
45.        ICU.IPR[0x8C].BYTE = 0x04;    //EEI1 interrupt level
46.        ICU.IPR[0x8D].BYTE = 0x04;    //RXI1 interrupt level
47.        ICU.IPR[0x8E].BYTE = 0x04;    //TXI1 interrupt level
48.        ICU.IPR[0x8F].BYTE = 0x04;    //TEI1 interrupt level
49.        ICU.IER[0x1F].BIT.IEN2 = 1;    //EEI1 interrupt enable
50.        ICU.IER[0x1F].BIT.IEN3 = 1;    //RXI1 interrupt enable
51.        ICU.IER[0x1F].BIT.IEN4 = 1;    //TXI1 interrupt enable
52.        ICU.IER[0x1F].BIT.IEN5 = 1;    //TEI1 interrupt enable
53.        ICU.IR[250].BIT.IR = 0;    //EEI1 clear interrupt flag
54.        ICU.IR[251].BIT.IR = 0;    //RXI1 clear interrupt flag
55.        ICU.IR[252].BIT.IR = 0;    //TXI1 clear interrupt flag
56.        ICU.IR[253].BIT.IR = 0;    //TEI1 clear interrupt flag
57.        PORT1.ICR.BIT.B3 = 1;    //SDA1 setting
58.        PORT1.ICR.BIT.B2 = 1;    //SCL1 setting
59.        #endif    //RIIC_CH0
60.        RIIC.ICCR1.BIT.ICE = 1;    //RIIC enable
61.    }
62.    else {    //Stop RIIC
63.        #ifdef RIIC_CH0
64.        SYSTEM.MSTPCRB.BIT.MSTPB21 = 1;    //RIIC0(MSTPB21)
65.        #else
66.        SYSTEM.MSTPCRB.BIT.MSTPB20 = 1;    //RIIC1(MSTPB20)
67.        #endif
68.    }
69. }
```

```
70.  unsigned char RiicStart(unsigned char in_addr, unsigned char
     *in_buff, unsigned long in_num)
71.  {
72.      if(in_num < 2){    //Check data number (include first byte
                            (address))
73.          return RIIC_NG;
74.      }
75.      if((RIIC.ICCR2.BYTE & 0xE0) != 0x00){
76.          return RIIC_BUS_BUSY;    //Bus busy
77.      }
78.      RIIC.ICCR2.BIT.ST = 1;    //Generate start condition
79.      RiicTrmAddr = in_addr;    //Set transmission address
80.      RiicMstBuff = in_buff;    //Set transmission buffer
81.      RiicMstCnt = 0;
82.      RiicMstNum = in_num;
83.      return RIIC_OK;
84.  }
85.  void RiicRDRF(void){
87.      volatile unsigned long cnt;
89.      if(RIIC.ICSR2.BIT.NACKF != 0){    //When receive NACK
90.          if(RIIC.ICCR1.BIT.SCLI == 0){
91.              for(cnt = RIIC_WAIT_VALUE; cnt! = 0; cnt--);
92.          }
93.          RIIC.ICCR2.BIT.SP = 1;    //Generate stop condition
94.          *RiicMstBuff = RIIC.ICDRR;    //Dummy read
95.          return;
96.      }
98.      if(RiicMstCnt >= RiicMstNum){    //After receive all data
99.          if(RIIC.ICCR1.BIT.SCLI == 0){
100.             for(cnt = RIIC_WAIT_VALUE; cnt != 0; cnt--);
101.         }
102.         RIIC.ICCR2.BIT.SP = 1;    //Generate stop condition
103.         RIIC.ICMR3.BIT.ACKBT = 0;    //Set ACK
104.         *RiicMstBuff = RIIC.ICDRR;    //Read data
105.         RiicMstBuff++;    //Add pointer
106.     }
107.     else if(RiicMstCnt == RiicMstNum -1){    //Next is last data
108.         RIIC.ICMR3.BIT.WAIT = 1;
109.         RIIC.ICMR3.BIT.ACKBT = 1;    //Set NACK
110.         *RiicMstBuff = RIIC.ICDRR;    //Read data
111.         RiicMstBuff++;    //Add pointer
```

```
112.    }
113.    else {    //Transfer next data
114.       *RiicMstBuff = RIIC.ICDRR;    //Read data
115.       RiicMstBuff++;    //Add pointer
116.    }
118.    RiicMstCnt++;    //Add internal counter
119. }
120. void RiicTDRE(void)
121. {
122.    volatile unsigned long cnt;
123.    if(RiicMstCnt >= RiicMstNum){    //After transfer all data
124.       #ifdef RIIC_CH0
125.       ICU.IER[0x1F].BIT.IEN0 = 0;    //TXI0
126.       #else
127.       ICU.IER[0x1F].BIT.IEN4 = 0;    //TXI1
128.       #endif
129.       RIIC.ICIER.BIT.TEIE = 1;    //TEND
130.    }
131.    else if(RiicMstCnt == 0){    //First byte
132.       #ifdef RIIC_CH0
133.       ICU.IER[0x1F].BIT.IEN0 = 0;    //TXI0
134.       #else
135.       ICU.IER[0x1F].BIT.IEN4 = 0;    //TXI1
136.       #endif
137.       RIIC.ICIER.BIT.TEIE = 1;    //TEND
139.       RIIC.ICDRT = RiicTrmAddr;    //Write slave address
140.    }
141.    else {    //Transfer next data
142.       if((RIIC.ICSR2.BIT.TEND == 1) &&
           (RIIC.ICCR1.BIT.SCLI == 0)){
143.          for(cnt = RIIC_WAIT_VALUE; cnt != 0; cnt--);
144.       }
145.       RIIC.ICDRT = *RiicMstBuff;    //Write next data
146.       RiicMstBuff++;    //Add pointer
147.    }
149.    RiicMstCnt++;    //Add internal counter
150. }
151. void RiicTEND(void)
152. {
153.    volatile unsigned long cnt;
154.    if(RiicMstCnt >= RiicMstNum){    //After transfer all data
```

```
155.        if(RIIC.ICCR1.BIT.SCLI == 0){    //
156.           for(cnt = RIIC_WAIT_VALUE; cnt != 0; cnt--);
157.        }
158.        RIIC.ICCR2.BIT.SP = 1;   //Generate stop condition
159.        return;
160.     }
161.     #ifdef RIIC_CH0
162.     ICU.IER[0x1F].BIT.IEN0 = 1;   //TXI0
163.     #else
164.     ICU.IER[0x1F].BIT.IEN4 = 1;   //TXI1
165.     #endif
166.     RIIC.ICIER.BIT.TEIE = 0;   //TEND
168.     if(RIIC.ICCR1.BIT.SCLI == 0){
169.        for(cnt = RIIC_WAIT_VALUE; cnt != 0; cnt--);
170.     }
171.     RIIC.ICDRT = *RiicMstBuff;   //Write first data
172.     RiicMstBuff++;   //Add pointer
173.     RiicMstCnt++;   //Add internal counter
174. }
175. void RiicSTOP(void){
176.     RIIC.ICSR2.BIT.STOP = 0;
177.     RIIC.ICSR2.BIT.NACKF = 0;
179.     #ifdef RIIC_CH0
180.     ICU.IER[0x1F].BIT.IEN0 = 1;   //TXI0
181.     #else
182.     ICU.IER[0x1F].BIT.IEN4 = 1;   //TXI1
183.     #endif
184.     RIIC.ICIER.BIT.TEIE = 0;    //TEND
185. }
186. void RiicNACK(void)
187. {
188.     volatile unsigned long cnt;
189.     #ifdef RIIC_CH0
190.     ICU.IER[0x1F].BIT.IEN0 = 0;   //TXI0
191.     #else
192.     ICU.IER[0x1F].BIT.IEN4 = 0;   //TXI1
193.     #endif
194.     RIIC.ICIER.BIT.TEIE = 0;   //TEND
196.     if(RIIC.ICCR1.BIT.SCLI == 0){
197.        for(cnt = RIIC_WAIT_VALUE; cnt != 0; cnt--);
198.     }
```

```
199.    RIIC.ICCR2.BIT.SP = 1;    //Generate stop condition
200. }
201. void RiicSTART(void){}
202. void RiicAL(void){}
203. void RiicTMO(void){}
```

Filename: vect.h

Add the following definition to vect.h to enable the working of the EEI0, RXI0, and TXI0 interrupts.

```
1. #pragma interrupt (Excep_RIIC0_EEI0(vect = 246))
2. void Excep_RIIC0_EEI0(void);
3. #pragma interrupt (Excep_RIIC0_RXI0(vect = 247))
4. void Excep_RIIC0_RXI0(void);
5. #pragma interrupt (Excep_RIIC0_TXI0(vect = 248))
6. void Excep_RIIC0_TXI0(void);
```

Filename: riic_int.c:

This file contains the definitions of the interrupts and what they should do whenever they occur.

```
 1. #include "..\iodefine_RX62N.h"
 2. #include "..\vect.h"
 3. #include "riic.h"
 4. void RiicSTART(void);
 5. void RiicAL(void);
 6. void RiicNACK(void);
 7. void RiicTMO(void);
 8. void RiicSTOP(void);
 9. void RiicRDRF(void);
10. void RiicTDRE(void);
11. void RiicTEND(void);
12. void Excep_RIIC0_EEI0(void){
13.     if((RIIC.ICIER.BIT.STIE != 0) && (RIIC.ICSR2.BIT.START != 0)){
14.         RiicSTART();
15.     }
16.     if((RIIC.ICIER.BIT.NAKIE != 0) &&
17.     (RIIC.ICSR2.BIT.NACKF != 0)){
18.         RiicNACK();
```

```
19.    }
20.    if((RIIC.ICIER.BIT.ALIE != 0) && (RIIC.ICSR2.BIT.AL != 0)){
21.        RiicAL();
22.    }
23.    if((RIIC.ICIER.BIT.TMOIE != 0) && (RIIC.ICSR2.BIT.TMOF != 0)){
24.        RiicTMO();
25.    }
26.    if((RIIC.ICIER.BIT.SPIE != 0) && (RIIC.ICSR2.BIT.STOP != 0)){
27.        RiicSTOP();
28.    }
29. }
30. void Excep_RIIC0_RXI0(void){
31.    RiicRDRF();
32. }
33. void Excep_RIIC0_TXI0(void){
34.    RiicTDRE();
35. }
36. void Excep_RIIC0_TEI0(void){
37.    RiicTEND();
38. }
39. void Excep_RIIC1_EEI1(void){
40.    if((RIIC.ICIER.BIT.STIE != 0) && (RIIC.ICSR2.BIT.START != 0)){
41.        RiicSTART();
42.    }
43.    if((RIIC.ICIER.BIT.NAKIE != 0) && (RIIC.ICSR2.BIT.NACKF != 0)){
44.        RiicNACK();
45.    }
46.    if((RIIC.ICIER.BIT.ALIE != 0) && (RIIC.ICSR2.BIT.AL != 0)){
47.        RiicAL();
48.    }
49.    if((RIIC.ICIER.BIT.TMOIE != 0) && (RIIC.ICSR2.BIT.TMOF != 0)){
50.        RiicTMO();
51.    }
52.    if((RIIC.ICIER.BIT.SPIE != 0) && (RIIC.ICSR2.BIT.STOP != 0)){
53.        RiicSTOP();
54.    }
55. }
56. void Excep_RIIC1_RXI1(void){
57.    RiicRDRF();
58. }
```

```
59. void Excep_RIIC1_TXI1(void){
60.     RiicTDRE();
61. }
62. void Excep_RIIC1_TEI1(void){
63.     RiicTEND();
64. }
```

Filename: main.c

This is the main file responsible for setting up the RIIC module correctly.

```
1. #include "iodefine_RX62N.h"
2. #include "iic\riic.h"
3. #define SELF_ADDRESS 0x10   //Self address (bit0 = 0. (R/W bit))
4. #define SLV_ADDRESS 0x3A    //Slave address (bit0 = 0. (R/W bit))
5. #define DATA_NUM (1 + 1)    //Date number ("+1" means first
                                  byte(slave address))
6. #define T_BUFF_SIZE (2)
7. #define R_BUFF_SIZE (7)
8. #define POWER_CTL_ADDR (0x2D)
9. #define POWER_CTL_VAL0 (0)
10. #define POWER_CTL_VAL1 (16)
11. #define POWER_CTL_VAL2 (8)
12. #define DATA_ADDRESS (0x32)
13. #define MST_WRITE 0x00   //Write bit (Don't change)
14. #define MST_READ 0x01    //Read bit (Don't change)
15. unsigned char MstTrmBuff[T_BUFF_SIZE];   //Buffer for
                                               transmission data
16. unsigned char MstRcvBuff[R_BUFF_SIZE] = {255};   //Buffer for
                                                       reception data
17. void main(void)
18. {
19.     unsigned long cnt,i;
20.     unsigned char rtn;
21.     SYSTEM.SCKCR.LONG = 0x00020100;   //ICLK = 100 MHz, BCLK =
                                            25 MHz, PCLK = 50 MHz
                                            (EXTAL = 12.5 MHz)
22.     for(cnt = 0; cnt < T_BUFF_SIZE; cnt++){
23.         MstTrmBuff[cnt] = 0xFF;
24.         MstRcvBuff[cnt] = 0xFF;
25.     }
```

```
26.     MstTrmBuff[0] = POWER_CTL_ADDR;
27.     MstTrmBuff[1] = POWER_CTL_VAL0;
28.     RiicIni(SELF_ADDRESS, 1);   //Initialise RIIC (Enable)
29.     rtn = RiicStart(SLV_ADDRESS | MST_WRITE, MstTrmBuff,
        DATA_NUM + 1);
30.     switch (rtn){   //Return value check
31.       case RIIC_OK:   //OK
32.          break;
33.       case RIIC_BUS_BUSY:   //Bus busy
34.          break;
35.       case RIIC_NG:   //Data number error
36.          break;
37.       default:   //Internal error
38.          while(1)
39.             ;
40.     }
41.     while(RIIC.ICCR2.BIT.BBSY != 1)    //Check Bus busy
42.        ;
43.     while(RIIC.ICCR2.BIT.BBSY != 0)    //Check Bus free
44.        ;
45.     MstTrmBuff[1] = POWER_CTL_VAL1;
46.     rtn = RiicStart(SLV_ADDRESS | MST_WRITE, MstTrmBuff,
        DATA_NUM+1);
47.     switch (rtn){    //Return value check
48.       case RIIC_OK:   //OK
49.          break;
50.       case RIIC_BUS_BUSY:   //Bus busy
51.          break;
52.       case RIIC_NG:   //Data number error
53.          break;
54.       default:   //Internal error
55.          while(1)
56.             ;
57.     }
58.     MstTrmBuff[1] = POWER_CTL_VAL2;
59.     while(RIIC.ICCR2.BIT.BBSY != 1)   //Check Bus busy
60.        ;
61.     while(RIIC.ICCR2.BIT.BBSY != 0)   //Check Bus free
62.        ;
63.     MstTrmBuff[0] = DATA_ADDRESS;
```

```
64.    rtn = RiicStart(SLV_ADDRESS | MST_WRITE, MstTrmBuff,
       DATA_NUM);
65.    switch (rtn){    //Return value check
66.      case RIIC_OK:   //OK
67.        break;
68.      case RIIC_BUS_BUSY:   //Bus busy
69.        break;
70.      case RIIC_NG:   //Data number error
71.        break;
72.       default:   //Internal error
73.         while(1)
74.           ;
75.    }
76.    while(RIIC.ICCR2.BIT.BBSY != 1)   //Check Bus busy
77.      ;
78.    while(RIIC.ICCR2.BIT.BBSY != 0)   //Check Bus free
79.      ;
80.    rtn = RiicStart(SLV_ADDRESS | MST_WRITE, MstTrmBuff,
       DATA_NUM);
81.    switch (rtn){    //Return value check
82.      case RIIC_OK:   //OK
83.        break;
84.      case RIIC_BUS_BUSY:   //Bus busy
85.        break;
86.      case RIIC_NG:   //Data number error
87.        break;
88.      default:   //Internal error
89.         while(1)
90.           ;
91.    }
92.    while(RIIC.ICCR2.BIT.BBSY != 1)   //Check Bus busy
93.      ;
94.    while(RIIC.ICCR2.BIT.BBSY != 0)   //Check Bus free
95.      ;
96.    rtn = RiicStart(SLV_ADDRESS | MST_READ, MstRcvBuff,
       DATA_NUM+6);
97.    switch (rtn){    //Return value check
98.      case RIIC_OK:   //OK
99.        break;
100.     case RIIC_BUS_BUSY:   //Bus busy
```

```
101.          break;
102.        case RIIC_NG:    //Data number error
103.          break;
104.        default:    //Internal error
105.          while(1)
106.             ;
107.      }
108.      while(RIIC.ICCR2.BIT.BBSY != 1)    //Check Bus busy
109.         ;
110.      while(RIIC.ICCR2.BIT.BBSY != 0)    //Check Bus free
111.         ;
112.      RiicIni(0, 0);    //Stop RIIC
113.      while(1)
114.         ;
115. }
```

7.6   RECAP

- The Serial Communications Interface can act as a Smart Card Interface and as a Universal Synchronous/Asynchronous Receiver and Transmitter.
- The UART is one of the oldest, simplest, and most frequently used techniques for half duplex serial communication that uses three wires at the most for data transfer.
- The SCI2 interface is available on the YRDKRX62N development board via an RS-232 level shifter.
- The Serial Peripheral Interface bus is a full duplex bus similar to the Universal Synchronous Receiver/Transmitter and is capable of data transfer at very high speeds.
- Each SPI device can act as either a master or a slave device. The master device is responsible for generating the clock cycles for synchronizing the data transfer.
- Slave Selection is always required prior to transfer of data on the SPI bus, otherwise data on the bus is void.
- Slave devices available aboard the YRDKRX62N on the SPI bus are the Graphical LCD module, Micro SD card interface, and the Micron/Numonyx Omneo P5Q Serial Flash Chip.
- I^2C is a two wire interface capable of talking to up to 128 devices connected on the same bus.
- The I^2C cycle consists of generation of a start condition, selecting a slave device, performing a data transfer, and sending a stop condition.

■ Devices available with the YRDKRX62N board that are connected on the I2C bus are accelerometer: ADXL345 (slave address: 0x3A) and the temperature sensor ADT7240 (slave address: 0x90).

■ The following table is a recap of Table 7.1 which summarizes the differences between the three protocols.

	SERIAL COMMUNICATION INTERFACE	RENESAS SERIAL PERIPHERAL INTERFACE	RENESAS INTER INTEGRATED CHIP BUS
Modes	USART/Smart Card interface	Four wire/Three wire mode	I2C mode or SM bus mode
Max Transfer Speed	1.92 Mbps with PCLK @ 50 Mhz	Up to 25 Mbps	Up to 1 Mbps
Max. number of devices/slaves connected per bus	1	8 SPI integrated channels for slave selection	127
Number of wires required for communication (not including ground)	2 to 3	3 to 4	2
Max. Length of wires	500 ft @ 9600 bps	10 feet with clock speed of few kHz	10 meters @ 100 kbps
Number of bits per unit transfer (excluding start and stop)	7 or 8	Up to 32 bits	8
Slave Selection method	Adressed during communication when in multiprocessor communication mode, else not available.	Using slave select line	Through addressing

7.7   REFERENCES

Analog Devices, Inc. *±0.25°C Accurate, 16-Bit Digital I2C Temperature Sensor, ADT7420 information and datasheet.* Norwood, MA: Analog Devices, Inc. 2011. Electronic publication. Accessed at http://www.analog.com/en/mems-sensors/digital-temperature-sensors/adt7420/products/product.html

Analog Devices, Inc. *ADXL345 datasheet: 3-Axis, ±2 g/±4 g/±8 g/±16 g Digital Accelerometer, ADXL345.* Norwood, MA: Analog Devices, Inc. 2009–2011. Electronic publication. Accessed at http://www.analog.com/static/imported-files/data_sheets/ADXL345.pdf

Becke, G., Borgert, C., Corrigan, S., Dehmelt, F., Feulner, M., Gonzalez, C., Groenebaum, M., Kabir, F., Kacprzak, A., Kinnaird, C., and Zipperer, J. *Comparing Bus Solutions; High-Performance Linear/Interface: An Application Report.* Texas Instruments. Revised February 2004. Electronic publication. Accessed at http://www.lammertbies.nl/download/ti-appl-slla067a.pdf

Electronic Industries Association, "EIA Standard RS-232-C Interface Between Data Terminal Equipment and Data Communication Equipment Employing Serial Data Interchange," August 1969. Reprinted in Telebyte Technology *Data Communication Library,* Greenlawn, NY, 1985. Print.

Hardware Manual, Renesas 32-Bit Microcomputer, RX Family/RX600 Series. Renesas Electronics America, Inc., 2010. Print.

Hwang, Enoch. *Digital Logic and Microprocessor Design with VHDL.* Thomson. ISBN 0–534–46593–5. 2006. Electronic Publication. Accessed at http://faculty.lasierra.edu/~ehwang/digitaldesign

Soltero, M., Zhang, J. and Cockril, C. Revised by Kevin Zhang, Clark Kinnaird, and Thomas Kugelstadt, 2010. *RS-422 and RS-485 Standards Overview and System Configurations, Application Report, SLLA070D.* Texas Instruments, Revised May 2010. Electronic publication. Accessed at http://focus.ti.com/lit/an/slla070d/slla070d.pdf

7.8   EXERCISES

1. Write a program to setup the Renesas serial communication interface to operate in the UART mode functioning at 9600 baud, odd parity, 2 Stop bits to transmit 8 bits of data with the LSB first.

2. Write a program to set up the Renesas Serial Peripheral Interface to transfer and receive 32 bit and 16 bit long data alternately as a single unit at 5 Mbps, with parity enabled in clock synchronous mode. The RSPI should function only as a master.

3. Write a program to maintain queues for multiprocessor communication using the Renesas Serial Peripheral Interface so as to perform data transfer between one master device and two slave devices. Mention algorithms for both. (Hint: Maintain six queues; two for each microcontroller).

4. Write a program to communicate with and to continuously obtain the values of the *X, Y,* and *Z* axis of the onboard ADXL345 accelerometer at 100 kbps.

5. Write a program to interface two microcontrollers that are monitoring temperatures and exchanging the observed temperature as strings with each other. Each board should display the observed temperature of itself and the other board on the graphical/character LCD. (Hint: Use FIFO type data structures).

Chapter Eight

Event Counters, Timers, and the Real Time Clock

8.1 LEARNING OBJECTIVES

In this chapter we show how timers work as event counters, as well as go into more advanced features. It is possible to cascade timers together when one timer does not provide the range needed. Using timers it is also possible to output a square wave with a controllable frequency and duty cycle. Additionally, the RX62N includes a Real Time Clock peripheral that can keep track of the current date and time. In this chapter we will cover the concepts behind these features and how to use them.

8.2 BASIC CONCEPTS

8.2.1 Timer and Event Counter

Timer

A timer in a microcontroller is a counter whose value can be read and written as a special-function register. When the timer is started, the value in the register increases or decreases each time it is clocked, and the rate at which the value changes is based upon the clock source provided to it. If the clock source for the timer is 10 MHz, then one count (increment or decrement) of the register would be equal to 0.1 μs. The timers may have a bit length of 8-bit (0–255), 16-bit (0–65535) and 32-bit (0–4294967295). For an 8-bit timer with a clock source of 10 MHz, the maximum time a timer can count depends on the maximum value a timer count register can hold; i.e., the maximum value in an 8-bit register is 255 (FFh). Therefore the maximum time for an 8-bit timer count is:

$$\frac{255}{10 \text{ MHz}} = 255 * 0.1 \ \mu\text{sec} = 25.5 \ \mu\text{sec}$$

Therefore, with an 8-bit timer you can measure a maximum of 25.5 μs, but what if you want to measure 100 μs with an 8-bit register? Should we count four times through an 8-bit timer? The answer is no. For this purpose the microcontroller has a prescaler, which is used to divide the external or internal clock source by a fixed integer. This increases the amount of time a timer can count without adding much hardware. The general division factor for the prescaler would be multiples of two. For example, if we have a division factor of thirty-two, then the maximum amount of time a timer can count with a 10 MHz clock source is:

$$\frac{255}{\frac{10 \text{ MHz}}{32}} = \left(255 * \frac{32}{10}\right) \mu\text{sec} = 816 \ \mu\text{sec}$$

As a result, the maximum amount of time a timer can count increases as the prescaler division factor increases.

A timer can also be used as an event counter. The function of the event counter is the same as the counter, but the event counter counts external events (indicated by signal transitions on an input pin or on overflows of another timer). For example, an event counter can be set up in a place where you need to automatically keep track of the number of people entering a building using a particular entrance. A person passing the entrance is tracked using an infrared sensor. The sensor is set up such that a person entering the building breaks an infrared light beam directed at the sensor, which changes its output from high to low as long as the beam is broken. The event counter can be set up to increment on the high to low transition of the sensor output, and in the end the count would give us the amount of people who entered the building using a selected entrance. We can also use the event counter to calculate the time intervals between two events.

Event Counter

The RX62N/RX621 group has two units (Unit 0, Unit 1) of 8-bit timers/counters. The 8-bit timer can be used in different operating modes: timer mode, event counter mode, and pulse output mode. The timer mode can also be used to generate interrupts at particular intervals, and two timers can be cascaded to use a 16-bit timer. In this chapter we cover the basic concepts of an event counter mode. The timer units can also generate a baud rate clock, which can be used for serial communication. Table 8.1 shows the functionality available from the timers.

The event counter of RX62N microcontroller is used detect the overflow of the timer. After detecting the overflow, another timer can be made to start counting. For example, the TMR0 (TMR2) can be made to start counting once the TMR1 overflows (TMR3). This feature is mainly used to cascade two timers. The overflow function can be used by setting the CSS [1:0] bits in TCCR to a value of three. (The description of timer registers can be found in Chapter 10.)

TABLE 8.1   Specification of Timers.

ITEM	DESCRIPTION
Count clock	▪ Internal clock: PCLK, PCLK/2, PCLK/8, PCLK/32, PCLK/64, PCLK/1024, PCLK/8192 ▪ External clock
Number of channels	8 bits × 4 channels (16 bits × 2 channels)
Compare match	▪ 8-bit mode (compare match A, compare match B) ▪ 16-bit mode (compare match A, compare match B)
Counter clear	Selected by compare match A or B, or an external reset signal.
Timer output	Output pulses with a desired duty cycle or PWM output
Cascading of two channels	▪ 16-bit count mode 16-bit timer using TMR0 for the upper 8 bits and TMR1 for the lower 8 bits (TMR2 for the upper 8 bits and TMR3 for the lower 8 bits) ▪ Compare match count mode TMR1 can be used to count TMR0 compare matches (TMR3 can be used to count TMR2 compare matches).
Interrupt sources	Compare match A, compare match B, and overflow
DTC activation	DTC can be activated by compare match A interrupts or compare match B interrupts.
Generation of trigger to start A/D converted conversion	Compare match A of TMR0 and TMR2*[1]
Capable of generating baud rate clock for SCI	Generates baud rate clock for SCI5 and SCI6.*[2]
Low power consumption facilities	Each unit can be placed in a module stop state.

Source: *Hardware Manual, Renesas 32-Bit Microcomputer, RX Family/RX600 Series.* Renesas Electronics America, Inc., 2010, page 20–1.

The RX62N has a TMR timer peripheral which provides two 8-bit timer units (Units 1 and 0), each comprising two counter channels. Each timer can be used as an independent timer, to count an external event, or as a pulse output device. The timer works by incrementing a register each time there is a 'count' within the device. The count is either triggered by a pulse from the internal peripheral clock, a scaled version of the clock, or an external count source. When this count overflows from its maximum value to zero and/or

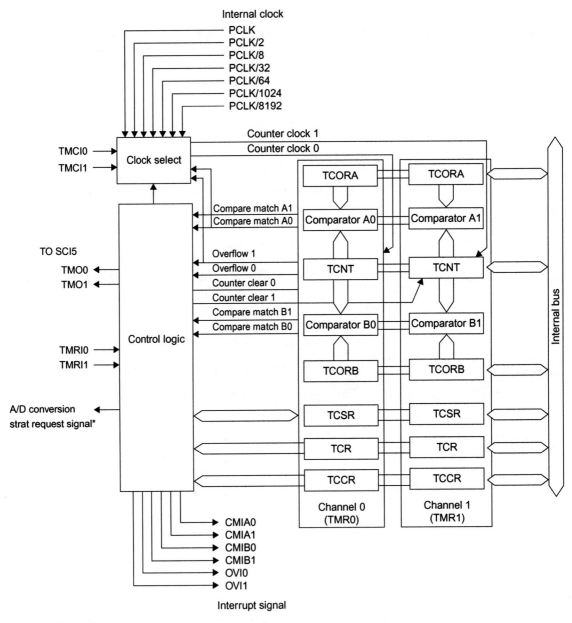

Figure 8.1 Block diagram of timer unit 0. Source: *Hardware Manual,* page 1110.

[Legend]
TCORA:	Time constant register A	TCSR:	Timer control/status register
TCNT:	Timer counter	TCR:	Timer control register
TCORB:	Time constant register B	TCCR:	Timer counter control register

Note: * Fore the corresponding A/D converter channels, see section 33, 12-Bit A/D Converter (S12AD), and section 34, 10-Bit A/SD Converter (ADa).

there is a compare match with one of the timer constant registers; an action is performed, such as toggling an output signal, or an interrupt is triggered. Before covering how the timer works more specifically we will briefly describe the 8-bit timer device's registers and how they work.

Figure 8.1 is a block diagram of timer unit 0; Unit 1 is identical except for naming differences (e.g., Timer2 in place of Timer0, and Timer3 in place of Timer1). Do not feel like you need to understand this entire diagram right away, we will cover the individual parts as we go along and by the end of this chapter it should all seem very simple. We will start by first covering the registers that are used when setting up a timer channel.

The legend in the bottom left of Figure 8.1 lists the registers you need to consider when setting up the 8-bit timer unit. For some registers we have an illustration included of the registers contents taken from the RX62N Hardware Manual. Make note of the register parts, as we will use these later when setting them up for specific features. Further details are available in the hardware manual if needed.

The TCNT (Timer Count) register holds the current timer value at any time after the timer has been configured. Whenever you want to know the value of the timer or counter you will read the value in this register. Also, when not currently operating the timer, you can load a value into this register and the timer will begin counting from that value when restarted. Note in Figure 8.2 that in the 16-bit mode TMR0.TCNT and TMR1.TCNT (TMR2.TCNT and TMR3.TCNT as well) cascade into one 16-bit register. This holds true for the timer constant registers as well.

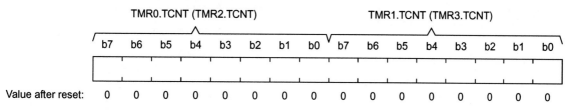

Figure 8.2 TCNT (Timer Count) register. Source: *Hardware Manual.*

The TCNT register is where the count is held. After the timer is started this register will increment every time a count is detected. If you want to know the current count, you can read this register. If the timer is stopped you can write a value to this register and it will begin counting from the written value when re-started.

Timer Control Register (TCR)

Address: TMR0.TCR 0008 8200h, TMR1.TRC 0008 8201h
TMR2.TCR 0008 8210h, TMR3.TCR 0008 8211h

	b7	b6	b5	b4	b3	b2	b1	b0
	CMIEB	CMIEA	OVIE	CCLR[1:0]		—	—	—
Value after reset:	0	0	0	0	0	0	0	0

BIT	SYMBOL	BIT NAME	DESCRIPTION	R/W
b2 to b0	—	(Reserved)	This bit is read as 0. The write value should always be 0.	R/W
b4, b3	CCLR[1:0]	Counter Clear*	b4 b3	R/W
			0 0: Clearing is disabled	
			0 1: Cleared by compare match A	
			1 0: Cleared by compare match B	
			1 1: Cleared by the external reset input	
			(Select edge or level by the TMRIS bit in TCCR.)	
b5	OVIE	Timer Overflow Interupt	0: Overflow interrupt requests (OVIn) are disabled	R/W
		Enable	1: Overflow interrupt requests (OVIn) are ensabled	
b6	CMIEA	Compare Match Interrupt	0: Compare match A interrupt requests (CMIAn) are disabled	R/W
		Enable A	1: Compare match A interrupt requests (CMIAn) are enabled	
b7	CMIEB	Compare Match Interrupt	0: Compare match B interrupt requests (CMIBn) are disabled	R/W
		Enable B	1: Compare match B interrupt requests (CMIBn) are enabled	

Note: * To use an external reset, set the Pn.DDR.Bi bit for the corresponding pin "0" and the Pn.ICR.Bi bit to "1".

Figure 8.3 TCR (Timer Control Register) description. Source: *Hardware Manual,* Section 20.2.4.

The TCCR controls where the timers count source comes from. Depending what value is set here will determine if the count comes from the internal peripheral clock, a pre-scaled peripheral clock, an external count source, or from another timer overflowing. This register also enables the timer's interrupts on the peripheral level. Keep in mind you must also enable to interrupts in the ICU (Interrupt Controls Unit) in order for an interrupt routine to be called.

Timer Counter Control Register (TCCR)

Address: TMR0.TCCR 0008 820Ah, TMR1.TCCR 0008 820Bh
TMR2.TCCR 0008 821Ah, TMR3.TCCR 0008 821Bh

b7	b6	b5	b4	b3	b2	b1	b0
TMRIS	—	—	CSS[1:0]		CKS[2:0]		

Value after reset: 0 0 0 0 0 0 0 0

BIT	SYMBOL	BIT NAME	DESCRIPTION	R/W
b2 to b0	CKS[2:0]	Clock Select*	See table 20.5.	R/W
b4, b3	CSS[1:0]	Clock Source Select	See table 20.5.	R/W
b6, b5	—	(Reserved)	These bits are always read as 0. The write value should always be 0.	R/W
b7	TMRIS	Timer Reset Input Select	0: Cleared at rising edge of the external reset	R/W
			1: Cleared when the external reset is high	

Note: * To use an external clock, set the Pn.DDR.Bi bit for the corresponding pin to "0" and the PnICR.Bi bit to "1". For details, see section 16, I/O Ports.

Figure 8.4 TCCR (Timer Counter Control Register) description. Source: *Hardware Manual,* Section 20.2.5.

The TCORA (Timer Constant Register A) and TCORB (Timer Constant Register B) are used to store constants to compare against the TCNT register. Every time the TCNT increments it is constantly being compared against either of these registers. When TCNT matches either of these registers, a compare match event occurs. Compare match events have many uses depending on what mode we are using the timer in.

The TCSR (Timer Control Status) register controls compare match output. Each timer has an output port assigned to it which is controlled via compare match events. This is one of many uses of the compare match events. When a compare match event occurs this register can set the output of the timer's port to 1 or 0, or toggle it. This register is used when we want the timer to control a pulse output.

CHANNEL	CSS[1:0]		CKS[2:0]			DESCRIPTION
	b4	b3	b2	b1	b0	
TMR0 (TMR2)	0	0	—	0	0	Clock input prohibited
					1	Uses external clock. Counts at rising edge*1.
				1	0	Uses external clock. Counts at falling edge*1.
					1	Uses external clock. Counts at both rising and falling edges*1.
	0	1	0	0	0	Uses internal clock. Counts at PCLK.
					1	Uses internal clock. Counts at PCLK/2.
				1	0	Uses internal clock. Counts at PCLK/8.
					1	Uses internal clock. Counts at PCLK/32.
			1	0	0	Uses internal clock. Counts at PCLK/64.
					1	Uses internal clock. Counts at PCLK/1024.
				1	0	Uses internal clock. Counts at PCLK/8192.
					1	Clock input prohibited
	1	0	—	—	—	Setting prohibited
	1	1	—	—	—	Counts at TMR1.TCNT (TMR3.TCNT) overflow signal*2
TMR1 (TMR3)	0	0	—	0	0	Clock input prohibited
					1	Uses external clock. Counts at rising edge*1.
				1	0	Uses external clock. Counts at falling edge*1.
					1	Uses external clock. Counts at both rising and falling edges*1.
	0	1	0	0	0	Uses internal clock. Counts at PCLK.
					1	Uses internal clock. Counts at PCLK/2.
				1	0	Uses internal clock. Counts at PCLK/8.
					1	Uses internal clock. Counts at PCLK/32.
			1	0	0	Uses internal clock. Counts at PCLK/64.
					1	Uses internal clock. Counts at PCLK/1024.
				1	0	Uses internal clock. Counts at PCLK/8192.
					1	Clock input prohibited
	1	0	—	—	—	Setting prohibited
	1	1	—	—	—	Counts at TMR0.TCNT (TMR2.TCNT) overflow signal*2

Notes: 1. To use an external clock, set the Pn.DDR.BI bit for the corresponding pin to "0" and the Pn.ICR.BI bit to "1". For details, see section 16, I/O Ports.
2. If the clock input of TMR0 (TMR2) is the overflow signal of the TMR1.TCNT (TMR3.TCNT) counter and that of TMR1 (TMR3) is the compare match signal of the TMR0.TCNT (TMR2.TCNT) counter, no incrementing clock is generated. Do not use this setting.

Figure 8.5   Clock input to TCNT and count condition. Source: *Hardware Manual,* Table 20.5.

Timer Counter/Status Register (TCSR)

Address: TMR0.TCSR 0008 8202h, TMR2.TCSR 0008 8212h

	b7	b6	b5	b4	b3	b2	b1	b0
	—	—	—	ADTE	OSB[1:0]		OSA[1:0]	
Value after reset:	x	x	x	0	0	0	0	0

Address: TMR1.TCSR 0008 8203h, TMR3.TCSR 0008 8213h

	b7	b6	b5	b4	b3	b2	b1	b0
	—	—	—	—	OSB[1:0]		OSA[1:0]	
Value after reset:	x	x	x	1	0	0	0	0

TMR0, TCSR, TMR2
[Legend] x: Undefined

BIT	SYMBOL	BIT NAME	DESCRIPTION	R/W
b1, b0	OSA[1:0]	Output Select A*1	b1 b0 0 0: No change when compare match A occurs 0 1: 0 is output when compare match A occurs 1 0: 1 is output when compare match A occurs 1 1: Output is inverted when compare match A occurs (toggle output)	R/W
b3, b2	OSB[1:0]	Output Select B*1	b3 b2 0 0: No change when compare match B occurs 0 1: 0 is output when compare match B occurs 1 0: 1 is output when compare match B occurs 1 1: Output is inverted when compare match B occurs (toggle output)	R/W
b4	ADTE	A/D Trigger Enable*2	0: A/D converter start requests by compare match A are disabled 1: A/D converter start requests by compare match A are enabled	R/W
b7 to b5	—	(Reserved)	These bits are always read as an indefinite value. The write value should always be 1.	R/W

Notes: 1. Timer output is disabled when the OSB[1:0] and OSA[1:0] bits are all 0. Timer output is 0 until the first compare match occurs after a reset.
2. For the corresponding A/D converter channels, see section 34, A/D Converter.

Figure 8.6   TCSR (Timer Control/Status Register) description. Source: *Hardware Manual,* Section 20.2.6.

That is a basic overview of the registers and what they do. Now that we know a bit about how the timer works we can start going into how we modify these registers to get the timer to go into its different modes of operation.

8.2.2   Cascading Timers

Sometimes when using a timer for an application you need a delay longer than is allowed when only using 8-bits. The RX62N allows both timer channels in either time unit to be cascaded into one 16-bit channel. Essentially every time the first timer overflows, the next timer will count. This multiplies the total time able to be counted by a factor of 2^8 (256). Originally we could only count from 0 to 255, now we can count to 65535.

So how do we calculate how long it will take for the timer to count to 0xFFFF (our max value)? First we consider the RX62N's main clock which is 24 MHz. This means every clock tick takes approximately 41.57 nanoseconds. We multiply by what division of the peripheral clock we are using, say 64, because the period for that clock is 64 times as long. Then we multiply by the number of ticks which is 0xFFFF or 65535. So when using PCLK/64 and a 16-bit counter, there will be approximately 174.76 ms between each overflow interrupt.

$$\frac{1}{24 \text{ MHz (peripheral clock)}} * \frac{64 \text{ (clock division)}}{1} * \frac{65535 \text{ (counts per interrupt)}}{1} = 174.76 \text{ ms.}$$

Table 8.2 lists the approximate time between interrupts for each clock division.

TABLE 8.2   Clock Division and Interrupt Times.

CLOCK DIVISION	TIMER PER COUNT	TIME BETWEEN OVERFLOW INTERRUPTS IN 16-BIT MODE
PLCK	41.67 ns	2.73 ms
PLCK/2	83.33 ns	5.41 ms
PCLK/8	333.33 ns	21.84 ms
PCLK/32	1.33 μs	87.38 ms
PCLK/64	2.67 μs	174.76 ms
PCLK/1024	42.67 μs	2.79 s
PCLK/8192	341.333 μs	22.37 s

NOTE:

It is possible in hardware setup to alter the speed of the PCLK, make sure to take note of this and alter your calculations accordingly. A basic HEW setup with no alterations will still have a PCLK of 24 MHz.

To set up a timer unit in 16-bit cascaded timer mode, set the bits in TMR0.TCCR.CSS[1:0] to 11b. This effectively sets the count source for Timer0 as Timer1. Whenever TCNT in Timer1 overflows, Timer0 will count once. In effect, this makes TMR0.TCNT and TMR1.TCNT combine into a single 16-bit register. The speed at which Timer1 can count is still determined in TMR1.TCCR.CSS and TMR1.TCCR.CKS. The settings for clearing the counter and interrupts are now controlled by the TMR0.TCR register; any settings in TMR1.TCR are ignored.

We have just covered how to cascade two 8-bit timer units to make one 16-bit timer. In the examples section we will give an example of how to set up a cascaded timer and an example of its usage.

8.2.3   Pulse Output Operation

Before covering how the RX62N 8-bit timer peripheral handles pulse outputs, we'll do a brief overview of pulse-width modulation concepts. There are three aspects of a wave we will concern ourselves with when dealing with pulse output operation: the period, frequency, and duty cycle. Any wave is basically a repeating pattern in output over time, such as a sine wave, square wave, or sawtooth wave. The period of the wave is defined as the time between repeats in the simplest form of the wave's pattern. In the case of a square wave, the period is the time between the rising edges of the positive output portion. The frequency is determined by how many periods there are of a wave in a second. We can determine frequency by the formula $f = \dfrac{\text{Number of Periods}}{\text{Length of Time}}$, yielding a value in Herz (Hz, periods/second). If we want to determine the period using the frequency we use the formula $T \text{ (period)} = \dfrac{1}{f(\text{Hz})}$. Duty cycle is defined as the percentage of the period during which the waveform is high. Duty cycle can be determined by the formula $\dfrac{\text{Time High}}{T \text{ (period)}} \times 100\%$.

Using the 8-bit timer peripheral we can output a square wave where the frequency and duty cycle are controlled by changing values in the registers we have already covered.

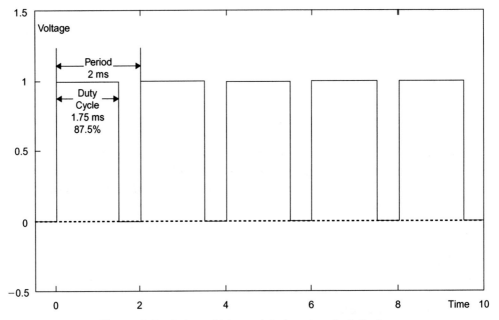

Figure 8.7 Pulse-width modulation signal attributes.

Pulse output mode is handy in applications such as interfacing the microcontroller to several types of motors. A servo motor usually uses a square wave input to determine the position or speed of the motor. Varying the duty cycle will vary the speed or position. When interfacing to a DC motor, the microcontroller almost always lacks the power output to drive the motor. A power amplifier must be used, most often an H-bridge. The H-bridge will take a square wave signal from the microcontroller and amplify it to whatever voltage and current levels are needed for the application. By varying the duty cycle of the wave we vary the average power that is delivered to the motor, making an efficient means of digitally controlling an analog device.

Now we will go over how to set up the RX62N in pulse output mode. First in pulse output mode, TCR.CCLR[1:0] is set to 01b. This will make TCNT clear to 0x00 every time a compare match A occurs. Now we set TCSR.OSA[1:0] to 10b and TCSR.OSB[0:1] to 01b. This will make the output from the timer channel change to 1 at the occurrence of compare match A and change back to 0 at the occurrence of compare match B.

Here is a brief overview of what happens on a single timer channel when set up in pulse output mode. TCNT begins to count up. Once it reaches the value of timer constant register A the first time, the pulse output becomes 1 and TCNT resets to 00h. TCNT restarts counting and upon reaching the value of timer constant register B, the output goes to 0. TCNT continues to count until it reaches the value of timer constant register A again. TCNT now resets to 00h again and the output goes back to 0. This process repeats, producing a square wave on the TCOn port (n being the number of the timer used). This is illustrated in Figure 8.8, TMOn being the waveform of the output pulse.

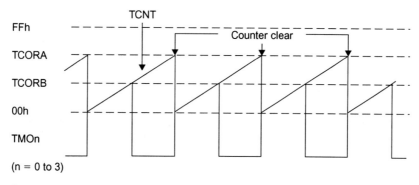

Figure 8.8   An example of pulse output. Source: *Hardware Manual,* Figure 20.3.

By altering the value of TCORA we change the frequency of the pulse output, and by altering TCORB without altering TCORA we alter the duty cycle of the wave. Take note that by altering TCORA without altering TCORB the duty cycle does not remain the same because the output is going low at the same amount of time after TCNT resets, but the time between when the pulse goes low and a compare match A occurrence has become longer.

We have just covered a basic overview of concepts to do with pulse output and how to control it on the RX62N. In the examples section we will show and explain a basic example of how to set up pulse output from one of the timer units.

8.3   REAL TIME CLOCK

The Real Time Clock is a separate unit unto itself. Without an independent Real Time Clock unit it would be necessary to cascade timers, set up variables, and use interrupt routines to track the time. Another advantage to a separate unit is that it takes less energy to keep running in low power modes. This unit makes keeping track of time much easier by keeping a separate binary coded decimal register for the years, months, date, day of the week, hours, minutes, and seconds. The unit also automatically tracks leap years. Using the Real Time Clock is as simple as setting the values for the date then setting it to start counting. The clock keeps count via a dedicated 32.768 KHz count source and outputs a 1 Hz clock.

8.3.1 RTC Registers

We will now cover all of the registers in the RTC and their functions.

64-Hz Counter (R64CNT)

Address: 0008 C400h

	b7	b6	b5	b4	b3	b2	b1	b0
	—	F1HZ	F2HZ	F4HZ	F8HZ	F16HZ	F32HZ	F64HZ

Value after reset: 0   x   x   x   x   x   x   x

[Legend] x: Undefined

BIT	SYMBOL	BIT NAME	DESCRIPTION	R/W
b0	F64HZ	64 Hz	Indicate the state between 64 Hz and 1 Hz.	R
b1	F32HZ	32 Hz		R
b2	F16HZ	16 Hz		R
b3	F8HZ	8 Hz		R
b4	F4HZ	4 Hz		R
b5	F2HZ	2 Hz		R
b6	F1HZ	1 Hz		R
b7	—	(Reserved)	This bit is always read as 0 and cannot be modified.	R

Figure 8.9 R64CNT (64 Hz Counter). Source: *Hardware Manual*, Section 22.2.1.

The second counter uses the 64 Hz counter (R64CNT) as its count source. This register can be read to determine time in the sub-seconds range.

RSECCNT is where the current count in seconds is read/written. Once the value is above fifty-nine it will reset to zero and the minute counter will increment.

The RMINCNT register is where the current value of the minutes is read/written. This counter behaves just like the second counter in that the hour counter will increment once it counts past fifty-nine and the minute counter will reset.

The RHRCNT register is where the current value in hours is read/written. The register counts from zero to twenty-three, then resets. When it resets, the day counter and day of the week counter are incremented.

RWKCNT holds the value of the current day of the week. It counts from zero to six, then resets.

Second Counter (RSECCNT)

Address: 0008 C402h

b7	b6	b5	b4	b3	b2	b1	b0
—		SEC10[2:0]				SEC1[3:0]	

Value after reset: 0   x   x   x   x   x   x   x

BIT	SYMBOL	BIT NAME	DESCRIPTION	R/W
b3 to b0	SEC1[3:0]	Ones Place of Seconds	Counts from 0 to 9 once per second. When a carry is generated, 1 is added to the tens place.	R/W
b6 to b4	SEC10[2:0]	Tens Place of Seconds	Counts from 0 to 5 for 60-second counting.	R/W
b7	—	(Reserved)	This bit is always read as 0. The write value should always be 0.	R/W

Figure 8.10   RSECCNT (Second Counter). Source: *Hardware Manual,* Section 22.2.2.

Minute Counter (RMINCNT)

Address: 0008 C404h

b7	b6	b5	b4	b3	b2	b1	b0
—		MIN10[2:0]			MIN1[3:0]		

Value after reset: 0   x   x   x   x   x   x   x

[Legend] x: Undefined

BIT	SYMBOL	BIT NAME	DESCRIPTION	R/W
b3 to b0	MIN1[3:0]	Tens Place of Minutes	Counts from 0 to 9 once per minute. When a carry is generated, 1 is added to the tens place.	R/W
b6 to b4	MIN10[2:0]	Ones Place of Minutes	Counts from 0 to 5 for 60-minute counting.	R/W
b7	—	(Reserved)	This bit is always read as 0. The write value should always be 0.	R/W

Figure 8.11   RMINCNT (Minute Counter). Source: *Hardware Manual,* Section 22.2.3.

Hour Counter (RHRCNT)

Address: 0008 C406h

	b7	b6	b5	b4	b3	b2	b1	b0
	—	—	HOUR10[1:0]		HOUR1[3:0]			

Value after reset: 0 0 x x x x x x

[Legend] x: Undefined

BIT	SYMBOL	BIT NAME	DESCRIPTION	R/W
b3 to b0	HOUR1[3:0]	Ones Place of Hours	Counts from 0 to 9 once per hour. When a carry is generated, 1 is added to the tens place.	R/W
b5, b4	HOUR10[1:0]	Tens Place of Hours	Counts from 0 to 2 once per carry from the ones place.	R/W
b7, b6	—	(Reserved)	These bits are always read as 0. The write value should always be 0.	R/W

Figure 8.12 RHRCNT (Hour Counter). Source: *Hardware Manual*, Section 22.2.4.

Day-of-Week Counter (RWKCNT)

Address: 0008 C408h

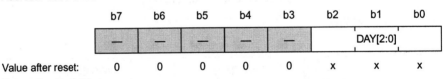

	b7	b6	b5	b4	b3	b2	b1	b0
	—	—	—	—	—	DAY[2:0]		

Value after reset: 0 0 0 0 0 x x x

[Legend] x: Undefined

BIT	SYMBOL	BIT NAME	DESCRIPTION	R/W
b2 to b0	DAY[2:0]	Day-of-Week Counting	000: Sunday	R/W
			001: Monday	
			010: Tuesday	
			011: Wednesday	
			100: Thursday	
			101: Friday	
			110: Saturday	
			111: (Setting Prohibited)	
b7 to b3	—	(Reserved)	These bits are always read as 0. The write value should always be 0.	R/W

Figure 8.13 RWKCNT (Day-of-Week Counter). Source: *Hardware Manual*, Section 22.2.5.

Date Counter (RDAYCNT)

Address: 0008 C40Ah

	b7	b6	b5	b4	b3	b2	b1	b0
	—	—	DAY10[1:0]		DAY1[3:0]			

Value after reset: 0 0 x x x x x x

[Legend] x: Undefined

BIT	SYMBOL	BIT NAME	DESCRIPTION	R/W
b3 to b0	DAY1[3:0]	Ones Place of Days	Counts from 0 to 9 once per day. When a carry is generated, 1 is added to the tens place.	R/W
b5, b4	DAY10[1:0]	Tens Place of Days	Counts from 0 to 3 once per carry from the ones place.	R/W
b7, b6	—	(Reserved)	These bits are always read as 0. The write value should always be 0.	R/W

Figure 8.14 RDAYCNT (Date Counter). Source: *Hardware Manual*, Section 22.2.6.

RDAYCNT holds the current value of the day of the month. The counter automatically accounts for the number of specifiable days in a month and leap years. When the count goes above the days of the current month it resets to zero and the month counter is incremented.

RMONCNT holds the value for the current month. It counts from one to twelve, and then resets. When it resets to zero, the year counter is incremented.

The RYRCNT register holds the current count of the years from zero to 9999.

For each counter register besides the 64 Hz Counter (R64CNT), there is a corresponding alarm register. Each of these is written to the same as the corresponding count register, other than the unused bit 7 which is now an enable bit; except in the case of the year alarm register which uses an entire word (it has a separate enable register named RYAREN). Whenever the values in each of the counters match the alarm registers with the enable bits set, the Real Time Clock alarm interrupt is triggered.

Take note that writing the decimal value of the number you want to input to these registers will not be input as the value you want. This is because the registers are not read as an 8-bit decimal value, but are instead split so that each 4-bit span is a binary encoded decimal digit. As a review of basic concepts of base 2 (binary) and base 16 (hexadecimal) numbers you will remember that a hexadecimal number can be used as shorthand for 4 bits of a binary number. As an example the hexadecimal 0x45 is equivalent to the binary

Month Counter (RMONCNT)

Address: 0008 C40Ch

	b7	b6	b5	b4	b3	b2	b1	b0
	—	—	—	MON10		MON1[3:0]		

Value after reset: 0   0   0   x   x   x   x   x

[Legend] x: Undefined

BIT	SYMBOL	BIT NAME	DESCRIPTION	R/W
b3 to b0	MON1[3:0]	Ones Place of Months	Counts from 0 to 9 once per month. When a carry is generated, 1 is added to the tens place.	R/W
b4	MON10	Tens Place of Months	Counts from 0 to 1 once per carry from the ones place.	R/W
b7 to b5	—	(Reserved)	These bits are always read as 0. The write value should always be 0.	R/W

Figure 8.15   RMONCNT (Month Counter). Source: *Hardware Manual,* Section 22.2.7.

Year Counter (RYRCNT)

Address: 0008 C40Eh

	b15	b14	b13	b12	b11	b10	b9	b8	b7	b6	b5	b4	b3	b2	b1	b0
	YEAR1000[3:0]				YEAR100[3:0]				YEAR10[3:0]				YEAR1[3:0]			

Value after reset: x   x   x   x   x   x   x   x   x   x   x   x   x   x   x   x

[Legend] x: Undefined

BIT	SYMBOL	BIT NAME	DESCRIPTION	R/W
b3 to b0	YEAR1[3:0]	Ones Place of Years	Counts from 0 to 9 once per year. When a carry is generated, 1 is added to the tens place.	R/W
b7 to b4	YEAR10[3:0]	Tens Place of Years	Counts from 0 to 9 once per carry from ones place. When a carry is generated in the tens place, 1 is added to the hundreds place.	R/W
b11 to b8	YEAR100[3:0]	Hundreds Place of Years	Counts from 0 to 9 once per carry from tens place. When a carry is generated in the hundreds place, 1 is added to the thousands place.	R/W
b15 to b12	YEAR1000[3:0]	Thousands Place of Years	Counts from 0 to 9 once per carry from hundreds place.	R/W

Figure 8.16   RYRCNT (Year Counter). Source: *Hardware Manual,* Section 22.2.8.

RTC Counter Register 1 (RCR1)

Address: 0008 C422h

	b7	b6	b5	b4	b3	b2	b1	b0
	—		PES[2:0]		—	PIE	CIE	AIE

Value after reset: 0   0   0   0   0   0   0   0

BIT	SYMBOL	BIT NAME	DESCRIPTION	R/W
b0	AIE	Alarm Interrupt Enable	0: An alarm interrupt is not requested	R/W
			1: An alarm interrupt is requested	
b1	CIE	Carry Interrupt Enable	0: A carry interrupt is not requested when a carry to the second counter occurred or a carry to the 64-Hz counter occurred during react access to the 64-Hz counter.	R/W
			1: A carry interrupt is requested when a carry to the second counter occurred or a carry to the 64-Hz counter occurred during read access to the 64-Hz counter.	
b2	PIE	Periodic Interrupt Enable	0: A periodic interrupt is not requested.	R/W
			1: A periodic interrupt is requested.	
b3	—	(Reserved)	This bit is always read as 0. The write value should always be 0.	R/W
b6 to b4	PES[2:0]	Periodic Interrupt Select	000: No periodic interrupts generated	R/W
			001: A periodic interrupt generated every $1/256$ second	
			010: A periodic interrupt generated every $1/64$ second	
			011: A periodic interrupt generated every $1/16$ second	
			100: A periodic interrupt generated every $1/4$ second	
			101: A periodic interrupt generated every $1/2$ second	
			110: A periodic interrupt generated every 1 second	
			111: A periodic interrupt generated every 2 seconds	
b7	—	(Reserved)	This bit is always read as 0. The write value should always be 0.	R/W

Figure 8.17   RCR1 (RTC Control Register). Source: *Hardware Manual,* Section 22.2.17.

RTC Counter Register 2 (RCR2)

Address: 0008 C424h

	b7	b6	b5	b4	b3	b2	b1	b0
	—	—	—	—	RTOOE	ADJ	RESET	START
Value after reset:	0	0	0	0	0	0	0	1

BIT	SYMBOL	BIT NAME	DESCRIPTION	R/W
b0	START	Start	0: Year, month, day-of-week, date, hour, minute, second, and 64-Hz counters, and prescaler are stopped.	R/W
			1: Year, month, day-of-week, date, hour, minute, second, and 64-Hz counters, and prescaler operate normally.	R/W
b1	RESET	Reset	0: Normal count operation or the initialization is completed	R/W
			1: Prescaler, 64-Hz counter, and alarm registers are initialized.	
b2	ADJ	30-Second Adjustment	0: Normal count operation or completion of 30-second adjustment	R/W
			1: During 30-second adjustment	
b3	RTOOE	RTOOUT Output Control	0: Clock signals are not output from the RTOOUT pin.	R/W
			1: Clock signals are output from the RTOOUT pin.	
b7 to b4	—	(Reserved)	These bits are always read as 0. The write value should always be 0.	R/W

Figure 8.18 RCR2 (RTC Control Register 2). Source: *Hardware Manual*, Section 22.2.18.

number 0b01000101. So if we were to write 0x45 to the seconds counter register, then 4 would be written to the tens span and 5 would be written to the ones span. The new count for the seconds register would be read as 45.

Keep in mind it is not a good idea to write to each span of the register individually as the counters update on each 128 Hz count. If your code writes a new value to the register during the same 128 Hz count it may not be acknowledged, even if is to different bits.

RCR1 enables and disables the three available RTC interrupts and the period of the periodic interrupt request. We will go over these interrupts in further detail in the advanced concepts section, for now we are most concerned with just understanding and initially setting up the Real Time Clock.

RCR2 controls the start and reset of the Real Time Clock. By writing a 1 or 0 to the START bit you start or stop the clock. By writing a 1 to the RESTART bit you will reset the 64 Hz counter, prescalers, and alarm registers to 0. Take note that these bits are updated in sync with the count source, so if you write to either of these bits it won't take effect until the next count of the RTC's 128 Hz clock. More details are available in the hardware manual. We will cover how to account for this in code examples.

8.3.2   Setting the RTC

Setting the Real Time Clock is relatively simple, as illustrated in Figure 8.19. After setting and waiting for the START bit in RCR2 to clear to 0, you set a 1 to the RESET bit. After this you can set the counter registers in any order. Then you set a 1 to the START bit in RCR2 to get the counter started again. Be sure to wait for the bit to set to 1 before you continue with any other operations on the RTC.

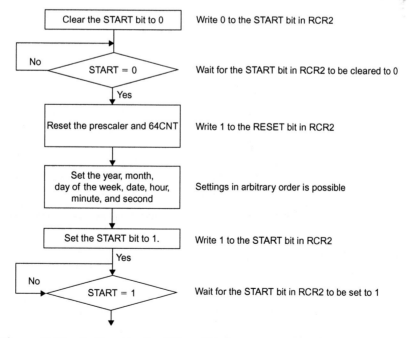

Figure 8.19 Setting the Real Time Clock. Source: *Hardware Manual,* Figure 22.2.

8.3.3   Reading the RTC

Reading the values in the RTC is a little tricky. If a carry request is performed from the 64 KHz clock to the second counter while a reading occurs, then the correct time won't be read. There are two ways to read the time that avoids this.

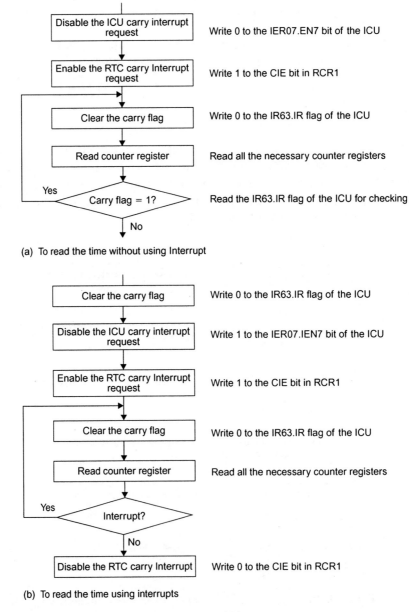

Figure 8.20   Reading 64 Hz Counter and Time. Source: *Hardware Manual,* Figure 22.4.

This flowchart from the RX62N manual illustrates the operation to take when reading the counter values using interrupts or not using interrupts. In the non-interrupt method you disable the carry interrupt in the ICU, but enable it in the RTC. Then you check the interrupt flag for the carry operation after reading the registers. If a carry has occurred, you clear the carry flag and start reading over again because the time has changed since reading started. When using the interrupt method you start the same, but instead of checking the carry flag you use the carry interrupt to indicate that a carry has occurred between the 64 Hz counter and the second count. The non-interrupt method is preferred as it takes less code.

8.4   BASIC EXAMPLES

Now that we have covered the basic concepts needed to understand how the timer works in these different modes, we will cover a few examples. For now we will demonstrate the initial setup of the clock and how to read from it.

8.4.1   Setting Up Cascaded Timers

For this demo we will be setting up Timer Unit 0 in cascaded timer mode by cascading Timer 0 and Timer 1 together. We will call an interrupt service routine every time this cascaded counter overflows from 0xFFFF to 0x0000. In the service routine we will put a call to a function that rotates the LEDs on the board. The resulting program will make the LEDs on the board blink in a rotating sequence at a speed determined by how we set up our timer.

We will start with a base HEW project that includes the iodefine.h file and other support headers for the RX62N. In this example we will use macros to control the LEDs, we will continue assuming you have defined a similar substitute for performing the action described by the macro.

The first thing to do in our main program is to declare our only global variable.

```
1. int Current_LED = 1;
```

We will use this variable to keep track of which LED is currently lit. We will cover how when we discuss the function that uses it.

Then we need to include our function prototypes. As you can see we will only use two function calls, one to set up the timer and another to blink the LEDs.

```
1. void InitTimer(void);
2. void Rotate_LED(void);
```

After our main() loop begins we will only need to include the macro for initializing the LEDs and our timer initialization function call. Our while(1) loop will be empty, as all operations will be handled in the timer interrupt. Note that this is generally bad programming practice and very uncommon; however, in some cases this is the correct solution.

```
1. void main(void){
2.    ENABLE_LEDS;
3.    InitTimer();
4.    while(1){}
5. }
```

Now comes the part we are most concerned with, the timer initialization. In this function we will set the timer registers for 16-bit cascaded mode.

```
1.  void InitTimer(void){
2.     IEN(TMR0,OVI0) = 1;    //Enable TMR0 Overflow interrupt in ICR
3.     IPR(TMR0,OVI0) = 2;    //Set priority level of interrupt
4.     MSTP(TMR0) = 0;    //Activate TMR0 unit
5.     MSTP(TMR1) = 0;    //Activate TMR1 unit
6.     TMR1.TCCR.BIT.CSS = 1;
7.     TMR1.TCCR.BIT.CKS = 4;    //Count source is PCLK/64 for TMR1
8.     TMR0.TCCR.BIT.CSS = 3;
9.     TMR0.TCR.BIT.CCLR = 1;    //Count source is TMR1 for TMR0
10.    TMR0.TCR.BIT.OVIE = 1;    //Overflow interrupt enabled
11. }
```

We start on lines 2–3 by enabling the Timer 0 overflow interrupt in the ICU and setting its priority level. Then on lines 4–5 we activate the Timer 0 and 1 units in the Module Stop Control Register (they are off by default). On lines 6–7 we set the count source for Timer 1 as the PCLK/64 input which is just the main clock divided by 64. On lines 9–10 we set the count source for Timer 0 as Timer 1. With the count source set, this will make Timer 0 count every time Timer 1 overflows. Now, with this set the two timers are cascaded. On line 14 we finish by setting the interrupt in the timer unit itself.

As we calculated earlier in our concepts, this setup will take the main clock of 24 MHz and divide it by 64. Then every 65535 counts of that the Timer 0 interrupt will occur and the interrupt routine will be called, thus rotating the current LED that is lit. This is calculated to be approximately every 174.76 ms. $\dfrac{1}{24\text{ MHz (main clock)}} * \dfrac{64\text{ (clock division)}}{1} *$ $\dfrac{65535\text{ (counts per interrupt)}}{1} = 174.76\text{ ms}$

The next function is used to light the LEDs on the board one at a time in a circular sequence. It uses the Current_LED variable to hold which Led is currently lit. Each time it is called, it increments the value, and as soon as it passes 12 it restarts at 1.

```
1.  void LED_Rotate(void){
2.    switch(Current_LED){
3.      case 1:
4.          ALL_LEDS_ON;
5.          LED6 = LED_OFF;
6.          break;
7.      case 2:
8.          ALL_LEDS_ON;
9.          LED12 = LED_OFF;
10.         break;
11.     case 3:
12.         ALL_LEDS_ON;
13.         LED3 = LED_OFF;
14.         break;
15.     case 4:
16.         ALL_LEDS_ON;
17.         LED9 = LED_OFF;
18.         break;
19.     case 5:
20.         ALL_LEDS_ON;
21.         LED5 = LED_OFF;
22.         break;
23.     case 6:
24.         ALL_LEDS_ON;
25.         LED11 = LED_OFF;
26.         break;
27.     case 7:
28.         ALL_LEDS_ON;
29.         LED2 = LED_OFF;
30.         break;
31.     case 8:
32.         ALL_LEDS_ON;
33.         LED8 = LED_OFF;
34.         break;
35.     case 9:
36.         ALL_LEDS_ON;
37.         LED4 = LED_OFF;
38.         break;
```

```
39.        case 10:
40.            ALL_LEDS_ON;
41.            LED10 = LED_OFF;
42.            break;
43.        case 11:
44.            ALL_LEDS_ON;
45.            LED1 = LED_OFF;
46.            break;
47.        case 12:
48.            ALL_LEDS_ON;
49.            LED7 = LED_OFF;
50.            break;
51.        default:
52.            ALL_LEDS_OFF;
53.            break;
54.    }
55.    Current_LED++;
56.    if(Current_LED == 13){
57.        Current_LED = 1;
58.    }
59. }
```

That is all of the code we need in the main program file. Now we need to define our interrupt and put a call to our LED_Rotate() function.

```
1. #pragma interrupt (Excep_TMR0_OV0I(vect = VECT_TMR0_OVI0))
2. void Excep_TMR0_OV0I(void);
3. //TMR0_OV0I
4. void Excep_TMR0_OV0I(void){ LED_Rotate();}
```

The first line of this code snippet defines an interrupt at the vector for Timer 0. Next it gives a function definition and the function itself. Inside the function is a call to the LED_Rotate() function. Make note that it is bad practice to include function calls inside of an ISR for many reasons. We will go over reasons why and workarounds for this later.

We have now successfully set up a 16-bit cascaded timer on the RX62N and used it to trigger an interrupt that rotates the board's LEDs. By modifying the count source of Timer 1 we can change the speed of this rotation. Later, in a more advanced example, we will cover how to take greater control of the timer and interrupt timing using the timer constant registers and compare match events.

8.4.2   Setting Up a Timer for Pulse Output

Now we will cover an example of setting up a timer for pulse output. This requires very little code to execute. Once we have set up the timer it will begin to output our desired pulse without any further intervention.

```
1.  void main(void);
2.  void InitTimer(void);
3.  void main(void){
4.      InitTimer();
5.      while(1){}
6.  }
7.  void InitTimer(void){
8.      MSTP(TMR0) = 0;    //Activate TMR0 unit
9.      TMR0.TCCR.BIT.CSS = 1;    //Count source is PCLK/8
10.     TMR0.TCCR.BIT.CKS = 2;
11.     TMR0.TCR.BIT.CCLR = 1;    //Timer resets at compare match A
12.     TMR0.TCSR.BIT.OSA = 2;    //1-output at compare match A
13.     TMR0.TCSR.BIT.OSB = 1;    //0-output at compare match B
14.     TMR0.TCORA = 0x55;    //Frequency
15.     TMR0.TCORB = 0x20;    //Duty cycle
16.     //Pulse outputs to TMo0, which is also P22/USB_DRPD
17.     //Can be monitored by touching a scope probe to the top
18.     //of resistor R46, near bottom right corner of ethernet
19.     //port. Port JN2 provides a ground.
20.  }
```

As can be seen here, we have no global variables to initialize and the only function we need is the function to set up the timer. In the timer initialization we first enable the 8-bit timer unit on Line 8. We set the count source for Timer 0 as PCLK/8 on Lines 9 and 10.

On line 11 we set the Timer 0 to clear every time a compare match A occurs. This allows us to alter how fast the timer resets with more control than just changing the count source.

On Lines 12 and 13 we set the timer output to go high every time there is a compare match A and to go low when there is a compare match B. This allows us to control the frequency using the timer constant register A, and the duty cycle using timer constant register B.

On Lines 14 and 15 we set the frequency and duty cycle by assigning a value to timer constant registers A and B. These are randomly chosen; we will worry about getting an exact frequency and duty cycle in the advanced concept section.

When running this code the pulse will be output on signal TMO0. By referencing the hardware manual and schematic we find that this is output to Pin 22/USB_DRPD on the board. There is no output pin to monitor this so we will have to observe the output waveform by touching a scope probe to the top of resistor R46 near the bottom right corner of the Ethernet port. You can get a ground reference by connecting to pin 2 on port JN1.

Figure 8.21   Resistor R46 location.

In this example we have set up a pulse output from Timer 0 and observed the output square wave. In a more advanced example later we will cover how to calculate and control the exact frequency of the wave and discuss how this relates to controlling external devices.

8.4.3   Setting and Reading from the Real Time Clock

In this example we will demonstrate how to set the time in the Real Time Clock. We will then continuously read the value in the RTC and display it on the LCD.

To start we will use a base project that has all of the included support files for the graphic LCD. The only needed font file is helvr10.c. Also included is the iodefine_RX62N.h file.

The first step in this example is to define our global variables.

```
1. char Year1000, Year100, Year10, Year1, Mon10, Mon1, Day10, Day1,
       Day, Hour10, Hour1, Min10, Min1, Sec10, Sec1;
```

These will all hold the value for each of the decimal places of the date values.

Next we insert the function prototypes for the functions we will write:

```
1. void InitTimer(void);
2. void DisplayTime(void);
3. void GetTime(void);
```

Now that all of that is defined we go into our main() program.

```
1. void main(void){
2.     int i;
3.
4.     InitTimer();
5.
6.     if(GlyphOpen(&G_lcd, 0) == GLYPH_ERROR_NONE){
7.         /* use Glyph full access direct functions */
8.         GlyphNormalScreen(G_lcd);
9.         GlyphSetFont(G_lcd, GLYPH_FONT_HELVR10);
10.        GlyphClearScreen(G_lcd);
11.        while(1){
12.            DisplayTime();
13.            for (i = 0; i < 100000; i++){}
14.        }
15.    } else {
16.    }
17.    GlyphClose(&G_lcd);
18. }
19. }
20.
21. GlyphClose(&G_lcd);
22. }
```

First we define the variable '*i*' in line 2. This is used to create a delay loop between writes to the LCD. Next we call our function initializing the timer in Line 4; this is where all of the code is that initializes and starts the Real Time Clock. The next few lines we won't cover in depth, but are merely to initialize the LCD. All of the code we are concerned with is in the while(1) loop. The function DisplayTime() is called which retrieves the time from the RTC and then sends it to be displayed on the LCD on Line 12. The for() loop on Line 13 is merely to create a delay so we aren't constantly writing to the LCD, which makes the display flicker. The else() clause on Line 15 would hold error handling code to executed in the event the LCD did not start up correctly. We also will not go into depth on the closing function on Line 17.

The next section of code we will consider is the InitTime() function.

```
1. void InitTimer(void){
2.     //Set date and time on RTC
3.
4.     RTC.RCR2.BIT.START = 0;    //Write 0 to start bit in RCR2
5.     while(RTC.RCR2.BIT.START == 1){}    //Wait for start bit to
                                            clear to 0
6.
7.     RTC.RCR2.BIT.RESET = 1;    //Write 1 to Reset bit in RCR2
8.
9.     RTC.RYRCNT.WORD = 0x2015;    //Set year, month, day of
10.    RTC.RMONCNT.BYTE = 0x10;    //week, date, hour, minute,
11.    RTC.RDAYCNT.BYTE = 0x21;    //second to 2015 Oct 21st
12.    RTC.RWKCNT.BYTE = 0x02;    //Tue 12:00:00
13.    RTC.RHRCNT.BYTE = 0x12;
14.    RTC.RMINCNT.BYTE = 0x00;
15.    RTC.RSECCNT.BYTE = 0x00;
16.
17.    RTC.RCR2.BIT.START = 1;    //Set start bit to 1 in RCR2
18.    while(RTC.RCR2.BIT.START == 0){}    //Wait for start bit to set
                                           to 1
19.
20.    //Set carry interrupt for use later when reading time from RTC
21.    IEN(RTC,CUP) = 0;    //Disable carry interrupt in ICU
22.    RTC.RCR1.BIT.CIE = 1;    //Enable carry interrupt in the RTC
23. }
```

Here we set up the Real Time Clock and initialize all of the count registers to the date we want. This follows the flowchart in Figure 8.19. Lines 4 and 5 clear and wait for the START bit in the RCR2 register to equal to 0. The wait is necessary because the bits in this register only update on every count of the 128 KHz clock in the RTC, and the program is executing at a much faster 24 MHz. Next the RESET bit in RCR2 is set to 1 on Line 7. This resets the RTC's prescaler clocks, 64 Hz counter, and alarm registers to 0. After this is done, from Line 9 through 15 the clock's count registers are set to the starting date and time desired. In this example the start time and date is 12:00 PM Tue, Oct 21, 2015. The next step is to start the clock. In Line 17 we write a 1 to the START bit in RCR2 and then wait for it to be set in Line 18. The code on Lines 21 and 22 disable the carry interrupt in the ICU, but enable it in the Real Time Clock peripheral. This allows us to monitor if there has been a carry from the 64 Hz counter to the second counter later on when we are reading the time. We will demonstrate this later in the example.

The next function is the DisplayTime() function. This function calls the GetTime function to update the value of the time in our global variables. It then writes them to the LCD using the sprintf() and BSP_Display() functions.

```
1.  void DisplayTime(void){
2.      char buffer[30];
3.      const char DayNames[7][4] = { "Sun", "Mon", "Tue", "Wed", "Thu",
        "Fri", "Sat"};
4.
5.      GetTime();
6.
7.      BSP_Display_String(LCD_LINE1, "RTC Example");
8.      sprintf((char *)buffer, "%d%d%d%d %d%d / %d%d",
9.      Year1000,
10.     Year100,
11.     Year10,
12.     Year1,
13.     Mon10,
14.     Mon1,
15.     Day10,
16.     Day1);
17.     BSP_Display_String(LCD_LINE2, buffer);
18.     BSP_Display_String(LCD_LINE3, DayNames[Day]);
19.     sprintf((char *)buffer, "%d%d:%d%d:%d%d",
20.     Hour10,
21.     Hour1,
22.     Min10,
23.     Min1,
24.     Sec10,
25.     Sec1);
26.     BSP_Display_String(LCD_LINE4, buffer);
27. }
```

In this function we first define two character arrays on Lines 2 and 3. The GetTime() function is called on line 5; this copies the values of the time and date into our global variable placeholders. On line 7 we write text to the first line of the display to show the program that is running. On Line 8 we use the sprintf() function to take date values and translate them into ASCII text, and then we place these in an array called buffer. On Line 17 we write these values to the second line of the screen using the BSP_Display_String function, and a pointer to the array holding the text to write. The day of the week is written to the screen on Line 18. On Line 19 we use sprintf() once again to write the time to an array of ASCII characters. On Line 26 we write this to line 4 of the display.

The last function we use is the GetTime() function.

```
 1. void GetTime(void)
 2. {
 3.    do {
 4.        IR(RTC,CUP) = 0;    //Clear the Carry Flag
 5.        Year1000 = RTC.RYRCNT.BIT.YEAR1000;
 6.        Year100 = RTC.RYRCNT.BIT.YEAR100;
 7.        Year10 = RTC.RYRCNT.BIT.YEAR10;
 8.        Year1 = RTC.RYRCNT.BIT.YEAR1;
 9.        Mon10 = RTC.RMONCNT.BIT.MON10;
10.        Mon1 = RTC.RMONCNT.BIT.MON1;
11.        Day10 = RTC.RDAYCNT.BIT.DAY10;
12.        Day1 = RTC.RDAYCNT.BIT.DAY1;
13.        Day = RTC.RWKCNT.BYTE;
14.        Hour10 = RTC.RHRCNT.BIT.HOUR10;
15.        Hour1 = RTC.RHRCNT.BIT.HOUR1;
16.        Min10 = RTC.RMINCNT.BIT.MIN10;
17.        Min1 = RTC.RMINCNT.BIT.MIN1;
18.        Sec10 = RTC.RSECCNT.BIT.SEC10;
19.        Sec1 = RTC.RSECCNT.BIT.SEC1;
20.    } while(IR(RTC,CUP) == 1);
21.    //If carry bit has been set since reading started,
          try again
22. }
```

This function follows procedure a in Figure 8.20: Reading 64 Hz Counter and Time. The interrupt has already been disabled in the ICU and enabled in the RTC peripheral by the TimerInit() function. Now when there is a carry from the 64 Hz counter to the seconds counter, the interrupt flag in the ICU will set but an interrupt will not trigger. Now we start this function by clearing the interrupt request flag for the carry interrupt. We then read all of the digits the RTC counter registers into separate variables from Lines 5 through 19.

After we have read the time we check and make sure the interrupt request flag for the carry interrupt hasn't been set. If it has, that means the seconds counter has incremented and the time held in our variables is no longer correct and we will need to call the function again. The GetTime() function will repeat itself until it successfully reads a time without the carry interrupt being requested.

Once all of this code is in our program we can compile it and load it onto our board. Once run, within a second the following text should appear on the graphical LCD screen.

```
Timer       Example
2015        10/21
Tue
12:00:00
```

The time will now be displayed as a clock until the program is paused in the debugger and/or power is removed from the board.

This example covered the basics of setting up and reading from the Real Time Clock by setting the time and then reading it and displaying it on the boards graphical LCD as it counts. In the advanced concepts section we will cover how to use the RTC interrupts such as the periodic and alarm interrupts.

8.5   ADVANCED CONCEPTS

By now we should have a basic grasp on how to set up and use the more advanced features of the 8-bit timers along with how to set up and read the real time clock. We have covered the basics in setting up a cascaded timer, the bare minimum set up of a pulse output signal, and how to set up and read the real time clock. Now we cover how to take more control of our timer count duration by using the timer counter registers. We will go into more detail on the pulse output operation by covering how to calculate and control our output frequency and duty cycle. Also, we will cover usage of the real time clocks alarm and periodic interrupts.

8.5.1   Using a Cascaded Timer with 16-Bit Timer Constant Registers

We have covered the basics of using a cascaded 16-bit timer and have given examples of a basic set up. However, this set up lacks a bit of control that an embedded designer would want. Currently, with what we know, we can only count in increments of 0xFFFF (65535). The only control we have over how fast the timer overflows is by altering the count source. This only leaves us with the capability to count to the lengths of time in Table 8. With the timer constant registers we can extend that functionality. We have taken note of this while setting up the timer in pulse output mode, and now will cover it in more depth.

Each timer channel offers three interrupts: the overflow interrupt, and two timer constant interrupts. If we set a value in either of the timer constant registers and enable these interrupts, the respective interrupt will be triggered when a compare match event occurs for that register. A compare match event will occur when the TCNT register matches the value in that timer constant register; i.e., compare match A when TCNT matches timer constant register A, and compare match B when TCNT matches timer constant register B. So now that gives us the ability to trigger interrupts at even more precise times. But we still have to wait for the timer to finish counting to 0xFFFF and overflow and then count back to the timer constant value before the interrupt is triggered again. This is imprecise and not practical in many situations. So, by setting in the TCR for the timer channel to reset on compare match A or B, we can control to a much higher degree the time the counter will count to.

This describes how the compare match counters work in 8-bit mode, but what about 16-bit mode? There is only a minor difference. When we place the timer channel into 16-bit mode, the TCNT, TCORA, and TCORB registers from the two timer channels in the unit span into one register. So now they each are practically one 16-bit register. We can still only write to them as their 8-bit entities; so when we calculate the values we want to enter into them, we just convert to hex and write the upper byte to the register of the channel with a higher number and the lower byte to the other. If we wanted a value of 0x1234 in TCORA of timer unit 1, we would enter 0x12 in TCORA of Timer 0, and 0x34 in TCORA of timer 1. For timer unit two we write the upper bytes to Timer 2's registers and the lower bytes to Timer 3's registers.

As an example we have a timer set up in 16-bit cascaded timer mode with a count source of 1/1028. If we wait for an overflow, that gives us an interrupt every 2.8 s. But what if we want to generate an interrupt every 1 s? First we calculate what fraction of 2.8 1 is, and then multiple 65535 by that: $\frac{1}{2.8} * 65535 = 23405$ (approximately). We enter this value into the timer constant register A and enable the compare match A interrupt. Of course, this is a 16 bit value, so we can't enter it at one time. So we convert it to hex and enter the upper byte into TMR0.TCORA and the lower byte into TMR1.TCORA. Now we still have the interrupt occurring every 2.8 s, but that's because the timer is still counting to 65535 before resetting. So we set the bit CCL bit in the TCR so the timer is clear by compare match A. Thus giving us an interrupt every 1 s on compare match A.

8.5.2   Calculating and Programming Pulse Frequency and Duty Cycle in Pulse Output Mode, and Controlling a Servo Motor

We have covered the concept of how pulse output works and demonstrated the basic register set up needed to get a pulse output. We did not go into much detail about calculating the frequency and duty cycle of our output wave. This is not too complex but has been saved for this section just to give time to get used to the concept of pulse output operation first. If you understand the concepts of pulse output operation and calculating timer speeds from the basic concepts section, this should be no problem.

For this example we will assume we are using the pulse output to control a servo motor. Common servo motors use a pulse input to determine how or where it moves to. Specifications vary by motor, as per frequency and duty cycle required. We will use specifications from an anonymously chosen motor for this example. In the case of this motor we need a 1 ms pulse to turn full left and a pulse of 2 ms to turn full right. Usually a frequency is not specified, however you want to have adequate space between your pulses for smooth operation; and also not have them too spaced apart, so that when the duty cycle is updated the servo reacts in a timely manner. 50 Hz (20 ms period) is a safe frequency for smooth operation.

For this example we will be using the timer in 16-bit cascaded mode as well as in pulse output mode. This gives us more precise control over the duty cycle while still allowing for a wide period between pulses (low frequency). This is not much more complicated than 8-bit pulse output.

Our first step is to choose a speed for our prescaler. If we look at Table 8.2: Clock Division and Interrupt Times we see that PCLK/8 (3 MHz) offers almost a 21.84 ms period between TCNT overflows. We will choose this prescaler, as choosing PCLK/32 (87.38 μs) will provide us with a much smaller resolution between a 1 ms pulse and a 2 ms pulse. Now we must calculate the values for the timer counter registers. First, we will calculate the values to place in timer constant register B to obtain a pulse of 1 ms and 2 ms. Then we must calculate the value to place in timer constant register A to obtain a 20 mS low signal after the pulse. Note that when we change the value of TCORB, the frequency of the wave still stays the same, so the time our wave is low is affected. However, since 1–2 ms is small compared to 20 ms, this is negligible and we don't have to worry about recalculating for TCORA.

To calculate the value for TCORB we divide 1 ms and 2 ms by the length of time between timer counts; $\frac{1 \text{ ms}}{333.33 \text{ ns}} = 3000$ and $\frac{2 \text{ ms}}{333.33 \text{ ns}} = 6000$. For the value in TCORA we add 20 ms to our maximum high period (2 ms) to get 22 ms, then divide this by the time for a clock tick, $\frac{22 \text{ ms}}{333.33 \text{ ns}} = 66000$. In this case it gives us a value greater than our range, which is 65535. Luckily we only max out 155 ns shorter than our desired time, which is acceptable because, once again, having a precise low period is not crucial with servo motors, only having a fair amount of low time for the control circuitry to acknowledge our high pulse. So in the case of this application it is fine to leave the value of TCORA at 0xFFFF.

So, in all practicality, when setting up a pulse output signal we are just calculating a timer length for the period of our wave and for each high duty cycle we desire, and then programing it into the timer constant registers. Also, keep in mind that with this example 1 ms and 2 ms are the maximum value pulses for our motor. If this were a 180 degree servo, 1 ms would put it at 0 degrees, and 2 ms at 180 degrees. If we wanted any position in between we would have to output a signal proportionally between 1 and 2 ms. 1.5 ms would place the servo at 90 degrees, 1.75 ms at 135 degrees and so on. In the case of a continuous rotation servo, 1 and 2 ms would be full forward and backward, and any pulse length in between would speed up or slow down the rotation; 1.5 ms would be a full stop.

8.5.3   Using the Real Time Clock's Alarm and Periodic Interrupts

The RX62N's real time clock peripheral includes three interrupts: the carry interrupt, periodic interrupt, and alarm interrupt. The carry interrupt we have used in a previous example, and is triggered every time there is a carry from the 64 KHz counter to the second counter. The periodic interrupt is an interrupt that can be set to occur on a regular interval determined by what we set in the RCR1 register. We can alter this interval by editing three bits in the register, allowing us seven options for interrupt intervals. The alarm interrupt gives us the ability to choose an exact time for an interrupt to occur. For each count register there is an alarm register. When enabled, once the values in all of the enabled registers match the real time clocks counter registers, an interrupt will be triggered. Besides triggering an interrupt routine the alarm interrupt also has the ability to wake the processor from low power modes.

Setting the periodic interrupt is simple in comparison to calculating and setting an 8-bit timer to do the same task. First we must make sure that the interrupt is disabled in the ICU. Then we set the periodic interrupt enable bit in RCR1 and set the periodic interrupt select bits to whichever interrupt period we desire. The options are 2 seconds, 1 second, ½ second, ¼ second, ¹⁄₁₆ second, ¹⁄₆₄ second, and ¹⁄₂₅₆ second. After clearing the request flag we enable the interrupt in the ICU and the ISR will begin triggering on the chosen interval.

Setting the alarm interrupt is a bit more complicated, but is illustrated in a flowchart in the RX62N hardware manual. We can set all of the alarm registers and have the interrupt only trigger at a specific date and time, or we can only enable certain registers so the interrupt triggers each time the counters match those particular alarm registers. Say we want an interrupt to trigger at thirty minutes of every hour; we will set the minute alarm register to thirty minutes, and then set the enable bit in the same register. After enabling and setting a priority level for the alarm interrupt, every time the value in the minute count register matches 30 the interrupt will occur.

First we make sure that the real time clock is running. Then we make sure the interrupt is not enabled in the ICU, so that it doesn't trigger accidentally while we are setting it. Now we are able to set all of the alarm registers to the time we desire the interrupt to be triggered at. Once done, we write a 1 to the alarm interrupt bit in the ICU. Using the periodic interrupt we will wait for the ¹⁄₆₄ second interrupt, this is to allow time for the alarm interrupt enable bit to be set. We then clear the alarm interrupt request flag in the ICU in case it has been set while we were setting the alarm. Our last step before the interrupt is ready to be

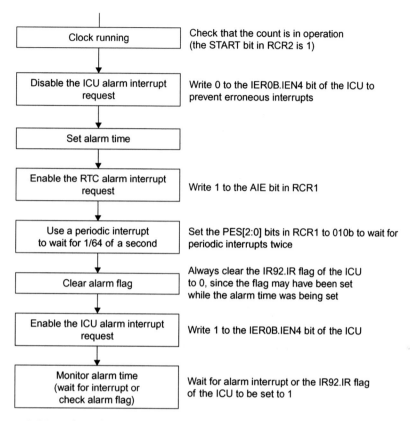

Figure 8.22   Alarm interrupt setting procedure. Source: *Hardware Manual,* Figure 22.5.

used is to enable the interrupt in the ICU. Now we can return to our normal program, and once the counters match the enabled alarm registers the interrupt will trigger.

8.6   ADVANCED EXAMPLES

Now that we have covered the more advanced concepts to using these features we will now go over examples implementing these concepts in code. The code will follow along with the examples in the earlier sections.

8.6.1   Using a Cascaded Timer with 16-Bit Timer Constant Registers

In this example our program will once again cause the LEDs on the board to blink in a rotating sequence, but this time with a 1s delay between blinks. We will implement this delay using a 16-bit cascaded timer and its interrupt.

We will be using the LEDs in these examples so the first part of our code will be the definitions for the LED ports. After the LED definitions, we declare our first global variable, which will keep track of which LED is currently lit. Also we set a global variable we will use to indicate whether the timer interrupt has triggered or not. This is known as a flag, and such usage will be covered in more depth in a later chapter.

```
1. int Current_LED = 1;
2. int TimerInterruptFlag = 0;
```

Next we have to declare our functions.

```
1. void main(void);
2. void InitTimer(void);
3. void Rotate_LED(void);
```

Our main() function doesn't contain much code. First we enable the LEDs with a macro on line 3, and then we call the timer setup function on line 4. Nothing happens in our while(1) loop until the TimerInterruptFlag variable is set by the interrupt. Note that the interrupt will run upon the timer triggering, and there will be some time delay between when the variable is set and the program returns to the main function and the LED is rotated. Because of this, the timing of the LED rotation won't be exactly one second, but that is acceptable because LEDs aren't time critical and can be off by a few milliseconds without hurting anything. It is bad programming practice to include the function call in the interrupt itself because it requires more time overhead in the ISR along with the need to save and restore all processor registers.

```
1. void main(void)
2. {
3.     ENABLE_LEDS;
4.     InitTimer();
5.
6.     while(1)
7.     {
8.         if(TimerInterruptFlag)
9.         {
10.             LED_Rotate();
11.             TimerInterruptFlag = 0;
12.         }
13.     }
14. }
```

The most important part of this example is our InitTimer() function. On lines 2 and 3 we enable and set a priority for the compare match A interrupt. We then enable timer unit 0 channels one and two (TMR0 and TMR1) on lines 5 and 6. On lines 8 and 9 the TMR1 count source is set to PCLK/1024, which gives us a count every 42.66 μs. This is done by writing the appropriate values to the TCCR register. Then on lines 11 and 12 we set the count source for TMR0 to TMR1, so now TMR0 counts once every time TMR1 overflows. Now we have a total of 2.8 s between timer overflows. In order to make the timer reset every 1 s we need to write the appropriate value to the TCORA(timer constant A) register and set the timer to reset on ever compare match A event. In Section 8.4.1 we calculated the needed value as 23405. We convert this into hex, separate it into a higher and lower byte, and then write the higher byte to TMR0 and the lower byte to TMR1 on lines 14 and 15. On line 17 we set the bit in the TCR that enables resets on compare match A event.

```
1. void InitTimer(void){
2.     IEN(TMR0,CMIA0) = 1;
3.     IPR(TMR0,CMIA0) = 3;
4.
5.     MSTP(TMR0) = 0;   //Activate TMR0 unit
6.     MSTP(TMR1) = 0;   //Activate TMR1 unit
7.
8.     TMR1.TCCR.BIT.CSS = 1;
9.     TMR1.TCCR.BIT.CKS = 5;   //Count source is PCLK/1024 for TMR1
10.
11.     TMR0.TCCR.BIT.CSS = 3;
12.     TMR0.TCR.BIT.CCLR = 1;   //Count source is TMR1 for TMR0
13.
14.     TMR0.TCORA = 0x5B;   //Set TCORA to 23405
15.     TMR1.TCORA = 0x6D;   //(0x5B6D hex)
16.
17.     TMR0.TCR.BIT.CMIEA = 1;
18. }
```

The only remaining code in our main C file is our LED_Rotate function which we have already covered.

The last code we need to consider is our interrupt. For this example, unlike our basic example, we will be using the compare match A interrupt.

```
1. #pragma interrupt (Excep_TMR0_CMI0A(vect = VECT_TMR0_CMIA0))
2. void Excep_TMR0_CMI0A(void);
3.
4. //TMR0_CMI0A
5. void Excep_TMR0_CMI0A(void){ LED_Rotate();}
```

If we look in the RX62N hardware manual we will see that the compare match A interrupt is at vector 174. This code defines an interrupt routine at that vector and places the LED_Rotate() function inside of it.

Now we have a program that once compiled and downloaded to the board will cause the LEDs to blink in a rotating sequence. The LEDs will advance at a rate of 1 per second as defined by our timer setup. This program demonstrates a timer function that makes use of a 16-bit cascaded timer with a compare match interrupt and reset on compare match event. This provides greater precision and a broader range of times to count.

8.6.2 Setting Up Pulse Output Mode to Control a Servo Motor

In this example we will use our calculations from Section 8.5.2 to write a program that will control our theoretical servo motor. We will be setting up a timer for the pulse output mode and then make two functions that will alter our timer setup such that the servo will rotate left or right.

Our program will only need the default iodefine_RX62N.h file, so we won't need any LED definitions or code for the graphical LCD.

We begin our main program by defining our function prototypes.

```
1. void main(void);
2. void InitTimer(void);
3. void Turn_Left(void);
4. void Turn_Right(void);
```

As you can see, once again we will only need a function to set up the timer initially, then we have two functions that when called will alter the timer setup to give us the needed pulse output to turn left or right.

```
 1. void main(void){
 2.     float i;
 3.
 4.     InitTimer();
 5.
 6.     while(1){
 7.
 8.         for(i = 0; i < 10000000; i++);
 9.         Turn_Left();
10.         for(i = 0; i < 10000000; i++);
11.         Turn_Right();
```

```
12.    }
13. }
```

Also, once again, our main program is very simple. We merely create the variable *i* as a method to create a delay. Once we call the function to initialize our timer we go into our while(1) loop. In that loop we repeatedly pause, call the function to turn left, pause again, then call the function to turn right. This represents a very simple method of setting up motor control in C. The for() loops merely create an arbitrary delay between the duty cycle changes which is long enough that we can observe the difference. In a normal program we would not make a delay this way; this is merely for the sake of demonstration.

```
1. void InitTimer(void){
2.     MSTP(TMR0) = 0;      //Activate TMR0 unit
3.     MSTP(TMR1) = 0;      //Activate TMR1 unit
4.
5.
6.     TMR1.TCCR.BIT.CSS = 1;
7.     TMR1.TCCR.BIT.CKS = 2;    //Count source is PCLK/64 for TMR1
8.
9.     TMR0.TCCR.BIT.CSS = 3;
10.    TMR0.TCR.BIT.CCLR = 1;    //Count source is TMR1 for TMR0
11.
12.    TMR0.TCR.BIT.CCLR = 1;    //Timer resets at compare match A
13.
14.    TMR0.TCSR.BIT.OSA = 2;    //1-output at compare match A
15.    TMR0.TCSR.BIT.OSB = 1;    //0-output at compare match B
16.
17.    TMR0.TCORA = 0xFF;    //Frequency
18.    TMR1.TCORA = 0xFF;
19.
20.    TMR0.TCORB = 0x00;    //Duty cycle
21.    TMR1.TCORB = 0x00;
22.
23.    //Pulse outputs to TMo0, which is also P22/USB_DRPD
24.    //Can be monitored by touching a scope probe to the top of
           resistor
25.    //R46, near bottom right corner of ethernet port. Port JN2
26.    //provides a ground.
27. }
```

Next in our code is our timer initialization function. This will set up the timer unit 0 channels one and two for the pulse output we desire. We will use the values we calculated earlier in Section 8.5.2. First we activate the timer channels on lines 2 and 3, because we cannot alter the registers in the unit until it is activated. Our next step is to set the Timer 1 count source to the PCLK/64 prescaler on lines 6 and 7. On lines 9 and 10 we set the count source for Timer 0 as Timer 1. We now have a 16-bit cascaded timer so any settings made for clearing in the Timer 0 TCR are effective for the entire cascaded unit. On line 12 we set the unit to reset on a compare match A event. We then set the timer output port to go to one output on compare match A events, and to zero on compare match B events. Remember that because the unit is now 16-bits, the timer constant registers are now spanned into single 16-bit registers, with the upper byte in the Timer 0 timer constant register and the lower byte in the Timer 1 timer constant registers. Any value we want to write to the compare match registers must first be converted to hex, and then the upper and lower bytes written to the appropriate registers. Lines 17 and 18 set our time count for compare match A events, thus setting the period and therefore frequency of our waveform. Lines 20 and 21 set our initial duty cycle to zero, so at this point our timer is set up but we are not yet outputting a waveform because the wave is constantly held low by the compare match B event at time count 0x0000.

```
1.  void Turn_Left(void){
2.
3.      TMR0.TCORB = 0x0B;    //Duty cycle
4.      TMR1.TCORB = 0xB8;
5.
6.  }
7.
8.  void Turn_Right(void){
9.
10.     TMR0.TCORB = 0x17;    //Duty cycle
11.     TMR1.TCORB = 0x70;
12.
13. }
```

Now all we need are our functions to turn left and right. These functions are very simple; they merely alter the values in the Timer constant B registers so that the duty cycle is either 1 ms or 2 ms. In the Turn_Left() function we write the value for 1 ms and in the Turn_Right() function we write the value for 2 ms.

After being compiled and downloaded to the board this program will initially not give an output, then begin to toggle the output between a 22 ms wave with 1 ms high pulse and 2 ms high pulse after an arbitrary delay created by the for() loops in our while(1) code.

8.6.3   Using the Real Time Clock's Alarm and Periodic Interrupts

This program example begins with the program we wrote in Section 8.3, so we already have a program that sets the real time clock, then reads it and displays the count. Initially the program will behave like our basic example: set the time, then begin counting, and display the time on the LCD. Then when the time reaches 12:00:15 the LEDs will be enabled by the alarm interrupt and begin to blink in a circular pattern at a rate determined by the periodic interrupt.

For review on the code we have already written refer to Section 8.3. In this section we will only focus on the parts we are adding to give the alarm and periodic interrupt functionality, which will not require the removal or modification of any old code.

```
1. void Set_Alarm(void);
2. void LED_Rotate(void);
```

Our first addition to the basic example is the addition of two new function prototypes. We are adding a function to set the alarm time and also we will be using our LED_Rotate function once again to make the LEDs rotate in a circular sequence.

```
1. void main(void){
2.     int i;
3.     ENABLE_LEDS;
4.     ALL_LEDS_OFF;
5.     DISABLE_LEDS;
6.
7.     InitTimer();
8.     Set_Alarm();
9.
10.    if(GlyphOpen(&G_lcd, 0) == GLYPH_ERROR_NONE){
11.        /* use Glyph full access direct functions */
12.        GlyphNormalScreen(G_lcd);
13.        GlyphSetFont(G_lcd, GLYPH_FONT_HELVR10);
14.        GlyphClearScreen(G_lcd);
15.        while(1){
16.            for(i = 0; i < 10000; i++);
17.            DisplayTime();
18.        }
19.    }
20.    else {}
21.
22.    GlyphClose(&G_lcd);
23. }
```

As you can see, our main function is the same save for some additions. The first addition is lines 4 through 6; this code enables the LEDs and turns them off, then disables them once again. Initially our program doesn't use the LEDs, so this makes sure LEDs left lit from previous running programs are turned off and then disables them so they won't be lit until re-enabled by the alarm interrupt. After this our only other addition is the Set_Alarm() function call on line 8 after we initialize the real time clock.

```
1. void Set_Alarm(void){
2.
3.     //Check clock running
4.     if(RTC.RCR2.BIT.START == 1){
5.
6.         //Disable ICU alarm interrupt
7.         IEN(RTC,ALM) = 0;
8.         IEN(RTC,PRD) = 1;
9.
10.        //Set alarm
11.        RTC.RSECAR.BYTE = 0x15;
12.        RTC.RMINAR.BYTE = 0x00;
13.        RTC.RHRAR.BYTE = 0x12;
14.        RTC.RWKAR.BYTE = 0x02;
15.        RTC.RDAYAR.BYTE = 0x21;
16.        RTC.RMONAR.BYTE = 0x10;
17.        RTC.RYRAR.WORD = 0x2015;
18.
19.        RTC.RSECAR.BIT.ENB = 0x01;
20.        RTC.RMINAR.BIT.ENB = 0x01;
21.        RTC.RHRAR.BIT.ENB = 0x01;
22.        RTC.RWKAR.BIT.ENB = 0x01;
23.        RTC.RDAYAR.BIT.ENB = 0x01;
24.        RTC.RMONAR.BIT.ENB = 0x01;
25.        RTC.RYRAREN.BIT.ENB = 0x01;
26.
27.        //Enable RTC alarm
28.        RTC.RCR1.BIT.AIE = 1
29.        while(RTC.RCR1.BIT.AIE == 0)    //Wait for it to be written
                                              before continuing
30.            ;
31.        //Use periodic interrupt to wait 1/64 second
32.        IR(RTC,PRD) = 0;
33.        RTC.RCR1.BIT.PES = 0x02;   //Set periodic interrupt to 1/64s
```

```
34.          while(IR(RTC,PRD) == 0)    //Wait for flag to be set
35.            ;
36.        //Clear alarm flag
37.        IR(RTC,ALM) = 0;
38.
39.        //Enable ICU alarm interrupt
40.        IEN(RTC,ALM) = 1;
41.        IPR(RTC,ALM) = 3;
42.          }
43.        else {
44.        //error handling code
45.        }
46.
47.    //Set up Periodic interrupt to trigger ISR every 0.5s
48.    RTC.RCR1.BIT.PES = 0x05;//Set periodic interrupt to 0.5s
49.    IR(RTC,PRD) = 0;    //Clear periodic interrupt flag
50.    IEN(RTC,PRD) = 1;    //Enable periodic interrupt in ICU
51.    IPR(RTC,PRD) = 4;    //Set priority level
52. }
```

Our most important addition to the basic program is our Set_Alarm() function. The code in this function follows the flowchart in Figure 8.22. First on line 4 we have an if statement that checks if the real time clock is counting, this is in case we call the function and have forgotten to initialize the real time clock or somehow the clock has ceased to count. On line 43 we have an else statement where error handling code would be put, but we will not worry about what to put there yet. The next step is to disable the alarm interrupt in the ICU; this ensures we aren't interrupted by the alarm while we are setting it. We also disable the periodic interrupt in the ICU since we are using it to set the alarm but do not want the ISR routine interrupting our configuration code. This is done on line 7.

With the periodic interrupt disabled, we can set the alarm registers for the time we want the alarm interrupt to occur; this is handled on lines 11 through 25. In this example we utilize all of the alarm registers and set it to occur fifteen seconds after the initial time set by the clock. Take note on lines 19–25 that we set the enable bit for each of the registers, otherwise they won't be compared. Also take note that because the year alarm register encompasses an entire word and doesn't have an extra bit set aside, there is a separate register we must set a 1 to in order to enable it, the RYRAREN register on line 25. After that we set the alarm enable bit in the RCR1 register on line 28. On line 29 we get stuck in a while loop until the bit gets set, because the RCR1 register only gets updated at the rate of the real time clocks internal clock. On line 32 through 34 we clear the periodic interrupt request flag and then set the periodic interrupt for $\frac{1}{64}$ of a second.

Then we have a while loop that will hold the program until the periodic interrupt sets the request flag again. After all of this we can be assured that the alarm interrupt enable bit has been set and we enable and set a priority for the alarm interrupt on lines 40 and 41. That is all of the code we need to set our alarm, but in this program example we are also using the periodic interrupt, so we include code to set that up for the rest of our program as well. On line 48 we set the periodic interrupt to occur at 0.5 second intervals. Then on lines 49 through 51 we clear the interrupt flag, and then enable it and set a priority level.

Also before the next snippet of code make sure to insert our LED_Rotate() function from previous examples. We won't cover it since we aren't covering any older code.

```
1.  //RTC PRD
2.  #pragma interrupt (Excep_RTC_PRD(vect = VECT_RTC_PRD))
3.  void Excep_RTC_PRD(void);
4.
5.  //RTC_ALM
6.  #pragma interrupt (Excep_RTC_ALM(vect = VECT_RTC_ALM))
7.  void Excep_RTC_ALM(void);
8.
9.  //RTC_PRD
10. void Excep_RTC_PRD(void){ LED_Rotate();}
11.
12. //RTC_ALM
13. void Excep_RTC_ALM(void){ ENABLE_LEDS;}
```

With any program using interrupt routines it is necessary to define where our interrupt is. On lines 2, 3, 6, and 7 we define the name of our interrupt service routines and their vectors, which are given in the *RX62N Hardware Manual* in Section 11.3. Then on lines 10 and 13 are our service routine functions. On line 10 is our periodic interrupt routine which will call our LED_Rotate() function, so once the LEDs are enabled they will blink in a rotating sequence at a rate of one LED per 0.5 s. On line 13 is our alarm interrupt function that contains our macro for enabling the LEDs, so no LEDs will light up from the periodic interrupts routine until the alarm interrupt enables them. Note once again this code includes a function call in an ISR for simplicity and illustration purposes, however, in an actual program this would be bad practice and should be avoided.

Once this program is built and downloaded to the board, at first it will seem the same as our basic example where it begins to display the time starting with when we set the clock to. Then after fifteen seconds the alarm interrupt will call and enable the LEDs. Afterwards the LEDs will blink in a circular sequence at a rate of one per 0.5 s for the duration of the programs running time.

8.7 RECAP

In this chapter we covered the capabilities of the 8-bit timer peripherals on the Renesas RX62N. We started with a brief overview of the timer concepts. Then we covered how to cascade two 8-bit timers into one 16-bit unit. We also covered pulse output operation that allows us to generate a steady frequency square wave whose duty cycle and frequency are maintained by the timer unit. Additionally we covered the Real Time Clock feature, which allows the RX62N to easily and accurately track the time and date. In the advanced concepts section we showed how to take more control of a cascaded timer by using the 16-bit timer constant register. We then went over how to calculate and precisely control frequency in pulse output mode, and gave an example of controlling a servo motor. For our final example we showed how to set up and use the Real Time Clock's alarm interrupt.

8.8 REFERENCES

Hardware Manual, Renesas 32-Bit Microcomputer, RX Family/RX600 Series. Renesas Electronics America, Inc., 2010. Print.

8.9 EXERCISES

1. What registers would you use when setting up the 8-bit timer unit 0 in cascaded mode?
2. Briefly describe three events that can happen when a compare match event occurs.
3. Explain the algorithm used and describe the purpose of the steps used when initially setting the RTC.
4. Give sample code that will set up a basic 1 KHz square wave with a 40% duty cycle.
5. Assume you have set up a 16-bit cascaded timer and now you want its interrupt to occur every 3 seconds. Name the registers you would write to, and the values you would write to them.
6. Assume you have set up a 16-bit cascaded timer for pulse output mode, what registers and what values would you write to them to get an output that is high for 3 ms and low for 18 ms?
7. Name two advantages to using the timer constant registers.
8. Give at least one advantage to using the periodic interrupt over setting up an 8-bit timer in order to get a 1 s recurring interrupt.
9. Besides triggering an ISR at the exact time specified by the real time clock alarm registers, what is another action the alarm interrupt performs?

Chapter Nine

Using Interrupts with Peripherals

9.1 ## 9.1 LEARNING OBJECTIVES

No doubt so far in this book you have seen interrupts mentioned several times. This book is only meant to touch on and explain concepts having to do with embedded systems and the peripherals of the RX62N, yet in the case of most peripherals covered so far it has been impossible to give even a brief overview without using interrupts in some way. In this chapter we will be covering more thoroughly exactly what interrupts are and how they work on a microcontroller. Using interrupts in an embedded application gives a greatly increased capacity for efficiency over a purely linear program.

In the basic concepts section we will give an in depth look at how an interrupt is triggered between a peripheral and the Interrupt Control Unit, and explain the process of setting up an interrupt and what is going on when we do so. In the advanced concepts section we will cover why keeping our code minimal in interrupts is important to prevent bugs. Also we will cover handling the passage of data from interrupts. After a brief overview of state machine programming design, we will pull all of this together by giving an example of a state machine whose state is controlled via interrupts.

9.2 BASIC CONCEPTS

Basic programs will read and execute in order from beginning to end in a mostly linear fashion save for control logic such as if() and while() loops. The problem with this is embedded systems are meant to interface with the real world, which does not often occur in such a predictable linear manner. Almost all embedded systems will depend on an external event and may even need to critically execute some given code immediately at that event, and we need a means to signal this in the program, stop what we are doing, handle another task, then return to the previous program execution. But how do we do that?

9.2.1 Using Interrupts for Tasks versus Other Methods

One method of gathering outside data into a program is via polling. For example, say you are getting ready for work in the morning and you want to brew a pot of coffee. The coffee takes at least five minutes to boil and then steep. If we were to act in a manner similar to polling we would set the water in the pot then watch (poll) it until it is boiling. That is five minutes of time that we are staring at a pot and not getting other things done that we could potentially be doing. Instead, we can set a kettle and then go about our routine and don't worry about 'processing' the coffee until the kettle whistles to signal the water is boiling. Once we are notified via this signal we 'interrupt' our routine to pour a cup and then return to what we were doing. There are also alternative methods of occasionally stepping back into the room to check if the water is boiling, which is similar to polling methods used for keypads. In more complex situations you will need to worry about multiple interrupts occurring; e.g., the dog wants out, the phone rings, someone knocks at the door. In a situation like this you will need some way to handle scheduling the interrupts and to make sure some lower priority interrupts don't interrupt more critical code that needs to execute faster. In these situations it is handy to use a Real Time Operating System, which is covered in a later chapter. For now we will start with the simple single interrupt method.

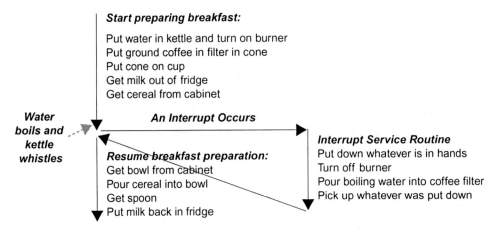

Figure 9.1 Preparing coffee flowchart.

9.3 INTERRUPTS

One good example of how interrupts are used is a robot with an IR sensor. Consider how the robot uses the IR sensor to detect and avoid obstacles. The robot continuously polls for a signal from the IR sensor, which tells the robot when an obstacle is close. The robot may be running lots of tasks, so if it gets stuck in a long process, the polling process is halted until the long task is executed. If the signal from the IR sensor occurs while the robot is processing, the robot will bump into the obstacle. Interrupts are an alternative to polling in these situations.

An interrupt is an external or internal event that takes the Program Counter (PC) from the current point of the code to a subroutine in the code called the Interrupt Service Routine (ISR) which has a higher priority of execution. The address to the ISRs is listed out in the

Interrupt Vector Table (IVT) which is defined in each processor memory. Whenever an interrupt occurs, the processor goes to the IVT and determines the location of the ISR; it then executes the subroutine present at that address. For example, consider the above situation of polling the signal from the sensor for detecting the obstacle. Instead of polling the signal, we can setup an interrupt which runs a subroutine whenever there is a change in the logic level. When a processor is running a long task we do not need to worry that we would lose the signal from the sensor as the interrupt is set up. The subroutine will be the ISR for the interrupt, and when the processor executes the ISR it means that an obstacle has occurred. So the function of the subroutine should be to avoid the obstacle, either change the path or stop the robot before bumping into the obstacle. The ISRs should contain very little code in them.

There are two types of interrupts: Maskable and Non-Maskable. Non-Maskable interrupts (NMI) are interrupts that cannot be ignored by the processor. When a non-maskable interrupt occurs, the processor should stop whatever it is executing and attend it first. The non-maskable interrupts are usually used for non-recoverable errors and serious hardware errors that need immediate attention. One example of a non-maskable interrupt is the reset pin.

The Interrupt Control Unit (ICU) receives signals from peripherals such as timers, ADCs, and external pins of the microcontroller. The interrupt sources available for the RX62N/RX621 group are listed in Table 9.1. The block diagram of the ICU is shown Figure 9.2. This chapter deals with the interrupts generated using software and the external pins of the microcontrollers.

The following registers are used to setup and read the status of the interrupts:

- Interrupt Request Register (IRR)
- Interrupt Request Enable Register (IER)
- Interrupt Priority Register (IPR)
- Fast Interrupt Register (FIR)
- Software Interrupt Activation Register (SWINTR)
- IRQ Control Register (IRQCR)
- Non-Maskable Interrupt Status Register (NMISR)
- Non-Maskable Interrupt Enable Register (NMIER)
- Non-Maskable Interrupt Clear Register (NMICLR)
- NMI Pin Interrupt Control Register (NMICR)

Interrupt Request Register n (IRn) (n = interrupt vector number)

The least significant bit of the interrupt request register indicates the status of a particular interrupt source. The value n of the interrupt request register corresponds to different interrupt sources in the vector table. For the interrupt sources and corresponding interrupt vector numbers, refer to the Interrupt Vector Table of the hardware manual (Table 11.4, *RX62N Group, RX621 Group Hardware Manual*).

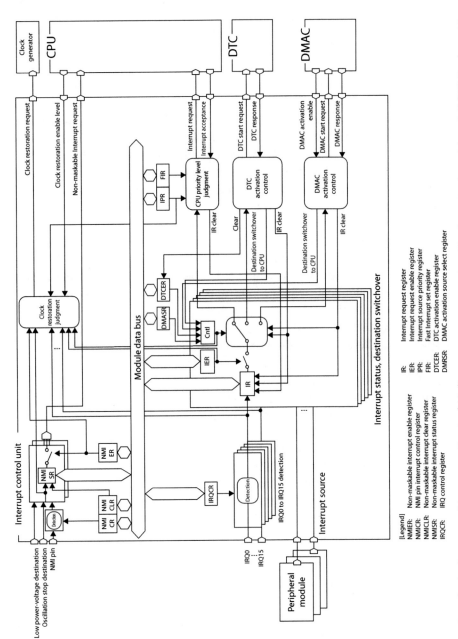

Figure 9.2 Block diagram of Interrupt Control Unit. Source: *RX62N Group, RX621 Group Hardware Manual: RX62N Hardware Manual*, Renesas Electronics America, Inc., 2010, page 11–2.

TABLE 9.1 Specifications of ICU.

ITEM		DESCRIPTION
Interrupts	Peripheral function interrupts	■ Interrupts from peripheral modules ■ Number of sources: 146 ■ Interrupt detection: Edge detection/level detection Edge detection or level detection is determined for each source of connected peripheral modules.
	External pin interrupts	■ Interrupts from pins IRQ15 to IRQ0 ■ Number of sources: 16 ■ Interrupt detection: Low level, falling edge, rising edge, both rising and falling edges One of these detection methods can be set for each source.
	Software interrupt	■ Interrupt generated by writing to a register ■ One interrupt source
	Interrupt priority	Specified by registers.
	Fast interrupt function	Faster interrupt processing of the CPU can be set only for a single interrupt source.
	DTC/DMACA control	■ The DTC and DMACA can be activated by interrupt sources. ■ Number of DTC activating sources: 102 (85 peripheral function interrupts + 16 external pin interrupts + 1 software interrupt) ■ Number of DMACA activating sources: 45(41 peripheral function interrupts + 4 external pin interrupts)
Non-maskable interrupts	NMI pin interrupts	■ Interrupt from the NMI pin ■ Interrupt detection: Falling edge/rising edge
	Power-voltage falling detection	Interrupt during power-voltage fall detection
	Oscillation stop detection	Interrupt during oscillation stop detection
Return from power-down modes		■ Sleep mode: Return is initiated by non-maskable interrupts or any other interrupt source. ■ All-module clock stop mode: Return is initiated by non-maskable interrupts, IRQ15 to IRQ0 interrupts, WDT interrupts, timer interrupts, USB resume interrupts, or RTC alarm interrupts. ■ Software standby mode: Return is initiated by non-maskable interrupts, IRQ15 to IRQ0 interrupts USB resume interrupts, or RTC alarm interrupts.

Source: *RX62N Group, RX621 Group Hardware Manual,* Table 11.1.

TABLE 9.2   Bit Description of Interrupt Request Register.

BIT	SYMBOL	BIT NAME	DESCRIPTION	R/W
b0	IR	Interrupt status flag	0: No interrupt request is generated	R/W*
b7 to b1	—	(Reserved)	These bits are read as 0. The write value should always be 0.	R/W

Note: *For edge-detected sources, only 0 can be written to this bit, which clears the flag, and writing 1 to the bit is prohibited. Writing is not possible if the source is level-detected.

Source: *RX62N Group, RX621 Group Hardware Manual,* Section 11.2.1.

IR Flag (Interrupt Status Flag)

When a particular interrupt request is generated, the corresponding vector number IR flag will be set to 1. The interrupt request detection can be set to edge detection or level detection for each interrupt by using the bits in IRQCRi ($i = 0$ to 15).

Interrupt Request Enable Register m (IERm) ($m = 02$ to 1Fh):

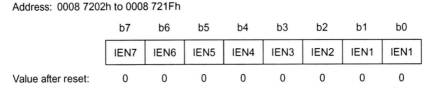

Address: 0008 7202h to 0008 721Fh

	b7	b6	b5	b4	b3	b2	b1	b0
	IEN7	IEN6	IEN5	IEN4	IEN3	IEN2	IEN1	IEN1
Value after reset:	0	0	0	0	0	0	0	0

Figure 9.3   Interrupt Request Enable Register. Source: RX62N Group, RX621 Group Hardware Manual, Section 11.2.2.

The Interrupt Request Enable Register (IERm) is used to enable and disable the interrupt requests to the CPU.

IENj bits (Interrupt Request Enable) ($j = 0$ to 7): When the IENj bit is set to 1, the CPU accepts that particular interrupt request and handles the interrupt. When this bit is set to 0, the CPU ignores that particular request. The m and j values in IERm and IENj are for enabling and disabling particular interrupts that can be referenced in the Interrupt Vector Table in the hardware manual (Table 11.4, *RX62N Group, RX621 Group Hardware Manual*).

External pin interrupt IRQ0 is referred using the IER register as IER08.IEN0.
The Timer1 overflow interrupt OVI1 is referred using the IER register as IER16.IEN

Interrupt Priority Register m (IPRm) (m = 00 to 8Fh)

The Interrupt Priority Register is used to set the priority for each interrupt source. The interrupt source should be disabled while setting the priority level. The possible priority levels are listed in Table 9.3. Each interrupt source has its own reserved IPR bits. For the IPR bits of each interrupt source, refer to the Interrupt Vector Table in the hardware manual (Table 11.4, *RX62N Group, RX621 Group Hardware Manual*). The interrupt sources with a higher priority than the priority level set by IPL [3:0] bits in PSW are accepted. If the interrupt priority level of two interrupts are the same and are requested at the same time, then the interrupt source with the smallest vector number will have the higher priority.

TABLE 9.3   Bit Description of Interrupt Priority Register.

BIT	SYMBOL	BIT NAME	DESCRIPTION	R/W
b3 to b0	IPR[3:0]	Interrupt Priority Level	b3 b0	R/W
		Select	0 0 0 0: Level 0 (interrupt prohibited)	
			0 0 0 1: Level 1	
			0 0 1 0: Level 2	
			:	
			1 1 1 1: Level 15 (highest)	
b7 to b4	—	(Reserved)	This bit is read as 0. The write value should always be 0.	R/W

Source: *RX62N Group, RX621 Group Hardware Manual,* Section 11.2.3.

Fast Interrupt Register (FIR)

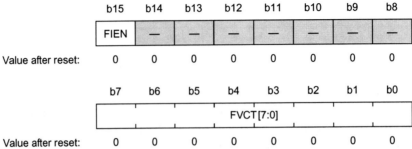

Figure 9.4 Fast Interrupt Register. Source: *RX62N Group, RX621 Group Hardware Manual*, Section 11.2.5.

This FIR register is used to set a particular interrupt source as a fast interrupt. The fast interrupt function cannot be used to trigger the peripherals like DTC, DMAC, etc. The fast interrupt function should not be set up for reserved interrupts in the interrupt vector table.

FVCT [7:0]: These bits are used to mention the interrupt vector number of the interrupt source, which should function as a fast interrupt.

FIEN: This bit should be set to 1 for the interrupt source mentioned in FVCT [7:0] to function as a fast interrupt.

Software Interrupt Activation Register (SWINTR)

TABLE 9.4 Bit Description of SWINTR.

BIT	SYMBOL	BIT NAME	DESCRIPTION	R/W
b0	SWINT	Software Interrupt	This bit is read as 0.	R/W*
		Activation	Writing 1 issues a software interrupt request.	
			Writing 0 to this bit has no effect.	
b7 to b1	—	(Reserved)	These bits are read as 0. The write value should always be 0.	R/W

Note: Only 1 can be written. This bit is read as 0.

Source: *RX62N Group, RX621 Group Hardware Manual*, Section 11.2.5.

The Software Interrupt Activation Register (SWINTR) is used to create a software interrupt request.

When the SWINT bit is set to 1, the interrupt occurs in vector 27 and the interrupt request for vector 27 is also set to 1. If the DTC Activation Enable Register 27 (DTCER) is set to 0, then a CPU interrupt is generated. If it is cleared to 0, then a DTC activation request is generated.

IRQ Control Register i (IRQCRi) (i = 0 to 15)

IRQ Control Register i (IRQCRi) (i = 0 to 15)

Address: 0008 7500h to 0008 750Fh

b7	b6	b5	b4	b3	b2	b1	b0
—	—	—	—	IRQMD[1:0]		—	—

Value after reset: 0 0 0 0 0 0 0 0

Figure 9.5 IRQ Control Register. Source: *RX62N Group, RX621 Group Hardware Manual,* page 336.

The IRQ Control Register (IRQCRi) is used to select the type of external interrupts, which are either edge detection or level detection. The IRQMD [1:0] bits in the IRQCR are used to set up the type of external interrupts. These settings should only be done when the interrupt is disabled and after the interrupt is set up. The interrupt request bit for the particular external interrupt should be cleared and the interrupt enable bit should be set to 1.

IRQMD [1:0]: The possible values for the IRQMD [1:0] bits and the corresponding setting for the interrupts are shown in Table 9.5.

Non-Maskable Interrupt Enable Register (NMIER)

The Non-Maskable Interrupt Enable Register (NMIER) is an 8-bit register that is used to enable or disable the NMI interrupts. The NMIER has control over three NMI interrupts: oscillation stop detection, power-voltage detection, and NMI pin interrupts.

Address: 0008 7581h

b7	b6	b5	b4	b3	b2	b1	b0
—	—	—	—	—	OSTEN	LVDEN	NMIEN

Value after reset: 0 0 0 0 0 0 0 0

Figure 9.6 Non-Maskable Interrupt Enable Register (NMIER). Source: *RX62N Group, RX621 Group Hardware Manual,* Section 11.2.10.

TABLE 9.5   Bit Description for IRQ Control Register.

BIT	SYMBOL	BIT NAME	DESCRIPTION	R/W
b1, b0	—	(Reserved)	These bits are read as 0. The write value should always be 0.	R/W
b3, b2	IRQMD[1:0]	IRQ Detection Sense Select	b3 b2	
			0 0: Low level	
			0 1: Falling edge	
			1 0: Rising edge	
			1 1: Rising and falling edges	
b7 to b4	—	(Reserved)	These bits are read as 0. The write value should always be 0.	R/W

Source: *RX62N Group, RX621 Group Hardware Manual*, Section 11.2.8.

NMIEN (Non-Maskable interrupt enable) bit: When this bit is set to 1, the interrupt request from the NMI pin will be sent to the CPU; otherwise the request will be ignored.

LVDEN (Power-voltage falling detection enable) bit: When this bit is set to 1, the power voltage falling detection interrupt request will be sent to the CPU; otherwise the request will be ignored.

OSTEN (Oscillation stop detection enable) bit: When this bit is set to 1, the oscillation stop detection interrupt request will be sent to the CPU; otherwise the request will be ignored.

NOTE:

For all of the bits described in Figure 9.6, writing "1" is accepted only once—subsequently writing 0 or 1 to these bits is disabled. In other words, we cannot disable the NMI interrupts after enabling them.

Non-Maskable Interrupt Status Register (NMISR)

The Non-Maskable Interrupt Status register is a read only 8-bit register. This register is used to read the status of three non-maskable interrupts: oscillation stop detection interrupt (OSTST), power-voltage falling detection interrupt (LVDST), and non-maskable pin interrupt (NMIST).

Address: 0008 7580h

	b7	b6	b5	b4	b3	b2	b1	b0
	—	—	—	—	—	OSTST	LVDST	NMIST
Value after reset:	0	0	0	0	0	0	0	0

Figure 9.7   Non-Maskable Interrupt Status Register (NMISR). Source: *RX62N Group, RX621 Group Hardware Manual*, Section 11.2.9.

Figure 9.7 shows the following about the Non-Maskable Interrupt Status Register:

- NMIST (NMI status flag) bit: This bit is set to 1 when the edge specified by the NMIMD bit in the NMICR occurs at the NMI pin. When this is bit is set to 1, the interrupt request from the NMI pin will be generated to the CPU. This bit is cleared to zero only when the NMICLR bit in NMICLR register is set to 1.
- LVDST (Power-voltage falling detection status flag) bit: This bit is set to "1" when the power-voltage falling detection interrupt is generated and is cleared to 0, and when the interrupt is cleared by the interrupt source.
- OSTST (Oscillation stop detection status flag) bit: This bit is set to 1 when the oscillation stop detection interrupt is generated and is cleared to 0, and when the OSTCLR bit in NMICLR register is set to 1.

Non-Maskable Interrupt Clear Register (NMICLR)

The Non-Maskable Interrupt Clear Register (NMICLR) is an 8-bit register that is used to clear the status flags of the NMI interrupts. The status flags of NMI pin and the oscillation stop detection interrupts can be cleared by this register.

Address: 0008 7582h

	b7	b6	b5	b4	b3	b2	b1	b0
	—	—	—	—	—	OSTCLR	—	NMICLR
Value after reset:	0	0	0	0	0	0	0	0

Figure 9.8   Non-Maskable Interrupt Clear Register (NMICLR). Source: *RX62N Group, RX621 Group Hardware Manual*, Section 11.2.11.

Figure 9.8 shows the following:

- NMICLR (NMI clear) bit: When this bit is set to 1, the NMIST flag in the NMISR register will be cleared to 0.

■   OSTCLR (OST clear) bit: When this bit is set to 1, the OSTST flag in the NMISR register will be cleared to 0.

NOTE:

We do not need to clear the NMICLR and the OSTCLR bits to 0. As soon as the corresponding status flag goes to 0, the NMICLR and the OSTCLR bits are also cleared to 0.

NMI Pin Interrupt Control Register (NMICR)

The NMI Pin Interrupt Control Register (NMICR) is an 8-bit register in which only one bit is used to set the type of edge detection of the interrupt to either the falling edge or the rising edge. The edge detection should be set before enabling the NMI interrupt.

Figure 9.9 illustrates how to address the NMI Pin Interrupt Control Register (NMICR). When this bit is set to 1, the interrupt request is generated on the rising edge input to the NMI pin. When this bit is cleared to 0, the interrupt request is generated on the falling edge input to the NMI pin.

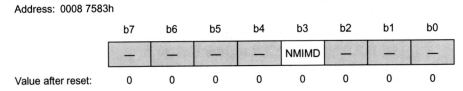

Figure 9.9   NMI Pin Interrupt Control Register (NMICR). Source: *RX62N Group, RX621 Group Hardware Manual,* Section 11.2.12.

9.3.1   Interrupt Vector Table

The Interrupt Vector Table (IVT) in an RX62N microcontroller has 256 interrupts, with each interrupt source occupying four bytes in the table. In total, the size of IVT is 1024 bytes (4 bytes × 256 sources). Each address space specifies the location of the interrupt service routine for the interrupt. When the CPU accepts an interrupt, it acquires the four byte address from the IVT and executes the code specified at that particular interrupt service routine. Refer to Table 11.4 located in the hardware manual of the RX62N microcontroller for the vector address for the interrupt sources.

9.3.2   Interrupt Operation

The interrupt control unit (ICU) performs the following operations while setting up the interrupts:

- Detecting the interrupts.
- Enabling and disabling the interrupts.
- Selecting the interrupt destination.
- Determining the priority.

The ICU first detects the interrupts. Detecting the interrupt requests is by way of either edge detection of the interrupt signal (edge triggered interrupts), or level detection of the interrupt signal (level triggered interrupts).

Edge Detection

The interrupt status flag is set to 1 when the microcontroller responds to the interrupt request, and the bit is cleared to 0 when the particular module or I/O pin interrupt request is accepted. Figure 9.10 shows how the interrupt status flag operates for edge triggered interrupts. The IR flag for the particular interrupt is set to 1 as soon as the interrupt signal goes high. If the interrupt is a CPU interrupt, the IR flag is cleared to 0 when the interrupt is accepted by the CPU. If the interrupt is a DMACA or DTC activation interrupt, the IR flag is cleared to 0 once the transfer by the DTC or DMACA has been completed.

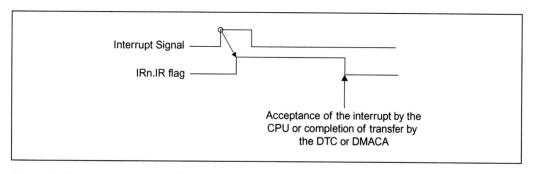

Figure 9.10   Interrupt status flag for edge triggered interrupts. Source: *RX62N Group, RX621 Group Hardware Manual*, page 11–40.

If the source of the interrupt generation is disabled and after the interrupt status flag goes high, the IR flag remains in the high state. For example after the IR flag for DTC activation interrupt goes high, if the DTC is disabled, then the IR flag of the DTC activation interrupt remains in the high state until the DTC is enabled and the transfer is done. Figure 9.9 shows how the IR flag operates when the source of the interrupt is disabled.

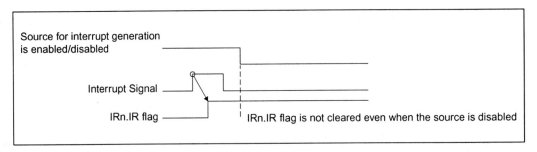

Figure 9.11 Interrupt status flag when the source of the interrupt is disabled. Source: *RX62N Group, RX621 Group Hardware Manual,* Figure 11.4.

Level Detection

The interrupt status flag remains set to 1 when the interrupt is requested and being sent to the destination. The bit is cleared to 0 when the source of the interrupt request is cleared. Figure 9.11 shows the operation of the IR flag for level-triggered interrupts. As shown in Figure 9.12, the IR flag remains in the high state until the source of the device requesting the interrupt is cleared.

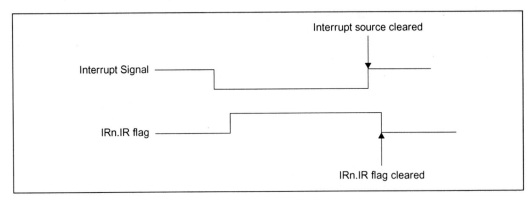

Figure 9.12 Interrupt status flag for level triggered interrupts. Source: *RX62N Group, RX621 Group Hardware Manual,* Figure 11.5.

The edge detection and the level detection of the interrupts can be selected using the IRQMD [1:0] bits in IRQ control register. When the level detection is selected for the interrupt requests, the interrupt status flag should not be cleared to 0.

After detecting the interrupts, the ICU checks to see if the interrupt is disabled or enabled. Enabling and disabling the interrupts can be performed by using the bits in IERm register. Refer to Table 11.4 of the hardware manual for information about the corresponding bit for each interrupt. If the interrupt is disabled, the ICU ignores the interrupt. If the interrupt is enabled, the ICU checks for the destination of the interrupt. The possible destinations for the interrupt would be the CPU, or DTC or DMACA activation. The destination for any interrupt is the CPU by default. The destination of the interrupt can be modified using the bits in the DTCER and DMRCR registers. For the interrupt vector number of a particular interrupt, refer to Table 11.4 of the hardware manual (Table 11.4, *RX62N Group, RX621 Group Hardware Manual*).

If two or more interrupts occur at the same time, the ICU fetches the interrupt requests based upon the interrupt priority set up by the IPR register. An interrupt selected as a fast interrupt will have the highest priority. After that, the highest value in the IPR [3:0] bits of IPRm will have the next highest priority. If interrupts with same priority level occur at the same time, the interrupt source with smallest vector number will have higher priority.

9.3.3 Setting Up an Interrupt for a Peripheral

All interrupts in the RX62N are handled via the Interrupt Control Unit (ICU). When setting up an interrupt there are two places where we make configuration settings, in the peripheral itself and in the ICU. When an interrupt occurs a signal is sent from the peripheral to the ICU, the ICU then processes the request and sends the interrupts to the CPU as needed.

Setting Up an Interrupt

The steps to set up an interrupt for a peripheral are as follows:

1. The peripheral or port pin must be enabled and configured.
2. Set an interrupt priority for the interrupt source (IPR macro) to a value greater than zero (zero = disabled).
3. Enable the interrupt in the peripheral (local enable bit).
4. Enable the interrupt in the ICU (IEN macro). (Conrad, J.)

NOTE:

The procedure is slightly different for setting an I/O pin as an interrupt; refer to section *Registers Set in the ICU for an Interrupt* under the definition for the IRQCRi register.)

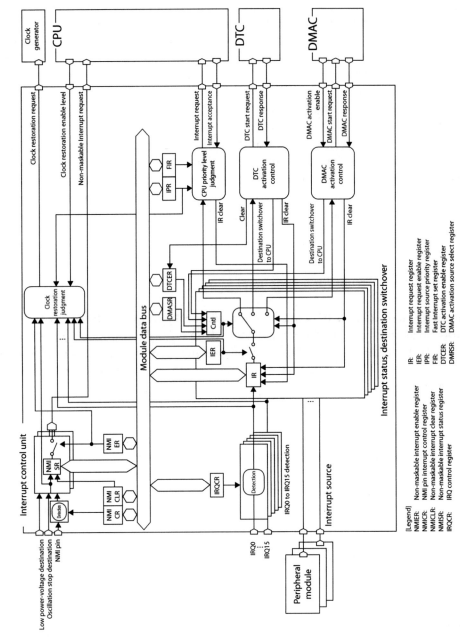

Figure 9.13 Interrupt Control Unit Block Diagram. Source: *RX62N Group, RX621 Group Hardware Manual*, Figure 11.1.

As can be seen, first off the peripheral must be enabled and configured; it can't signal an interrupt if it isn't on or configured to operate. The next steps don't necessarily need to be handled in the given order. A priority must be set for the interrupt in the ICU, you may have noticed in previous chapters we have done this using the IPR() macro. Using the provided macros from Renesas simplifies the process by only having us need to know the name of the peripheral and its interrupt in order to set its priority and enable it in the ICU. These can be found, along with the vector numbers for the interrupts, in the RX62N hardware manual or in Appendix A: Interrupt Vector Table of this text. We must also enable the interrupt in the peripheral itself. Where this is done is dependent on the peripheral, and could vary from setting an enable bit in a control register to a variety of settings in a separate register specifically for the interrupt. The interrupt must also be enabled in the ICU itself in order for the ICU to send it to the CPU.

Besides enabling the registers for the interrupt we need to define the Interrupt Service Routine to be used when the interrupt is triggered. The vector for each interrupt is available in the Interrupt Vector Table. In the case of the interrupts we will be using, the location the vector points to is variable and can be defined using a #pragma and another macro feature provided by Renesas. We put the code we want to run as an ISR in a subroutine, and then we define the subroutine as an interrupt and place a pointer to its memory address with the following code, where SUBROUTINE_NAME is the name of the subroutine and VECTORNUMBER is the number of the vector located in the Interrupt Vector Table.

```
1. #pragma interrupt (SUBROUTINE_NAME(vect = VECTORNUMBER))
2. void SUBROUTINE_NAME(void);
```

We place this code at the beginning of our program or in a separate .h file. Then we put the code for our ISR in the subroutine with the rest of our program's functions or in a separate .c file allocated for our interrupt code.

```
1. //Name of Interrupt
2. void SUBROUTINE_NAME(void){
3.     //ISR Code
4. }
```

Registers Set in the ICU for an Interrupt

Each of the following registers is not a single register, but a representation of a type of register. In the RX62N there are several of these. The one which services the interrupt we will use is determinable by looking in the Interrupt Vector Table. However, we need not worry about any details besides the abbreviation for the peripheral, the abbreviation for the interrupt, and the vector number, because everything is handled in the Renesas IR(), IPR(), and IEN() macros. We will cover the registers here just to help understand the interrupt process.

Interrupt Request Register n (IRn) (n = interrupt vector number)

Address: 0008 7010h to 0008 70FDh

	b7	b6	b5	b4	b3	b2	b1	b0
	—	—	—	—	—	—	—	IR
Value after reset:	0	0	0	0	0	0	0	0

BIT	SYMBOL	BIT NAME	DESCRIPTION	R/W
b0	IR	Interrupt status flag	0: No interrupt request is generated	R/W*
			1: An interrupt request is generated	
b7 to b1	—	(Reserved)	These bits are read as 0. The write value should always be 0.	R/W

Note: *For edge-detected sources, only 0 can be written to this bit, which clears the flag, and writing 1 to the bit is prohibited. Writing is not possible if the source is level-detected.

Figure 9.14   Interrupt Request Register. Source: *RX62N Group, RX621 Group Hardware Manual*, Section 11.2.1.

The Interrupt Request Register (shown in Figure 9.14) is merely a flag holder that indicates a request signal has been sent from the peripheral. When a signal is received in the ICU, the Interrupt Status Flag bit will be set to 1, and will return to 0 when the CPU accepts the interrupt. In the event that an interrupt is enabled in a peripheral and not in the ICU, this flag can still be set. It is possible to clear this register to 0 before an interrupt occurs by writing a 0 to it.

To clear a flag via the IR() macro we merely enter the code as:

```
1. IR("PERIPHERAL", "INTERRUPT") = 0;
```

Where PERIPHERAL is the abbreviation of the peripheral and INTERRUPT is the abbreviation for the interrupt name (available in the Interrupt Vector Table). To check a flag via the IR() macro we enter the code as:

```
1. VARIABLE = IR("PERIPHERAL", "INTERRUPT");
```

or

```
1. if(IR("PERIPHERAL", "INTERRUPT")) == 1){
2.     //Code if flag is set
3. }
```

Interrupt Request Register m (IERm) (m = 02h to 1Fh)

Address: 0008 7202h to 0008 721Fh

	b7	b6	b5	b4	b3	b2	b1	b0
	IEN7	IEN6	IEN5	IEN4	IEN3	IEN2	IEN1	IEN0
Value after reset:	0	0	0	0	0	0	0	0

BIT	SYMBOL	BIT NAME	DESCRIPTION	R/W
b0	IEN0	Interrupt Request Enable 0	0: Interrupt request is disabled	R/W
b1	IEN1	Interrupt Request Enable 1	1: Interrupt request is enabled	R/W
b2	IEN2	Interrupt Request Enable 2		R/W
b3	IEN3	Interrupt Request Enable 3		R/W
b4	IEN4	Interrupt Request Enable 4		R/W
b5	IEN5	Interrupt Request Enable 5		R/W
b6	IEN6	Interrupt Request Enable 6		R/W
b7	IEN7	Interrupt Request Enable 7		R/W
Note: Write 0 to the bit that corresponds to the vector number for reservation. These bits are read as 0.				

Figure 9.15   Interrupt Request Enable Register. Source: *RX62N Group, RX621 Group Hardware Manual,* Section 11.2.2.

The Interrupt request enable register (shown in Figure 9.15) enables whether the ICU will process the interrupt request flag once it is set by a signal from the peripheral. The address of the IEN register and the bit of the register that needs to be set for each interrupt is once again available in the Interrupt Vector Table, but we don't need to worry about that. We only need to know the IEN() macro, which operates just like the IR() macro.

To set or clear the bit corresponding to an interrupt in the IER register we only need to enter the following code, where PERIPHERAL and INTERRUPT are the abbreviations for the peripheral in the Interrupt Vector Table.

```
1. IEN("INTERRUPT", "PERIPHERAL") = 1;
2. //'1' to enable, or '0' to disable
```

Interrupt Request Register m (IPRm) (m = 00h to 8Fh)

Address: 0008 7300h to 0008 738Fh

	b7	b6	b5	b4	b3	b2	b1	b0
	—	—	—	—		IPR[3:0]		

Value after reset: 0 0 0 0 0 0 0 0

BIT	SYMBOL	BIT NAME	DESCRIPTION	R/W
b3 to b0	IPR[3:0]	Interrupt Priority Level Select	b3 b0	R/W
			0 0 0 0: Level 0 (interrupt prohibited)	
			0 0 0 1: Level 1	
			0 0 1 0: Level 2	
			:	
			1 1 1 1: Level 15 (highest)	
b7 to b4	—	(Reserved)	This bit is read as 0. The write value should always be 0.	R/W

Figure 9.16 Interrupt Priority Register. Source: *RX62N Group, RX621 Group Hardware Manual,* Section 11.2.3.

The Interrupt Priority Register (shown in Figure 9.16) allows the priority of the interrupt to be specified. A priority level from one to fifteen is allowed, fifteen being the highest. Interrupts with higher priority are handled first. If interrupts occur simultaneously with the same priority, the interrupt with the lower vector number is handled first. If a priority level isn't set, the interrupt will not be handled.

In case you are using an I/O pin to trigger an interrupt, you would use this register to determine how it is triggered. The number of the IRQ register for each I/O pin corresponds to the number of the interrupt request pin. Please refer to the RX62N schematic to determine where to connect to that pin physically. The only pins we are concerned with in this book are the pins connected to Switch 1, 2, and 3 which are IRQ pins; and 8, 9, and 10, respectively. Take note you must also enable the port as an input when using it to trigger an interrupt. It is important when setting up an I/O pin as an interrupt to do it in this order:

1. Clear the IEN bit.
2. Enable or confirm the I/O pin as an input.
3. Set the detection method in the IRQCR register.
4. Clear the IR flag.
5. Set the IEN bit.

Take note of Step 2. Alongside writing the ports data direction register to set it as an input, you must also write a 1 to the input buffer control register (ICR; *RX62N Group, RX621 Group Hardware Manual,* page 641) in the I/O registers. This must be done any time you are using an input pin to control a peripheral, in this case the peripheral is the ICU. You will have to refer to the schematic to see which port number and bit correspond to the IRQ input, and then write to that ICR bit. In the case of the three on board switches 1, 2, and 3, the ports are PORT4.0, PORT4.1 and PORT4.2 respectively. So for switch one you would write a 1 to PORT4.ICR.BIT.0.

9.3.4   How an Interrupt Operates

So, now that we know how to set up an interrupt and a bit of the inner workings of the ICU, we will briefly explain the process of what happens when an interrupt is triggered. When conditions are met in a peripheral to trigger an interrupt, the first process that happens is the sending of the request to, and the processing of that request by, the ICU.

1. Conditions met for interrupt in peripheral, peripheral flag set.
2. Signal sent to ICU, peripheral flag cleared.
3. IR flag set in ICU.
4. If the interrupt is enabled in the ICU and no higher priority interrupts are currently running, the interrupt is sent to the CPU.
5. Interrupt accepted by CPU, IR flag cleared.

Once the interrupt is sent to the CPU the following process occurs in the program:

1. Finish processing current instruction.
2. Save program counter and flags to memory.
3. Run interrupt service routine.
4. Restore program counter and flags from stack.
5. Resume main program.

The stack is a dynamically allocated resource that contains current working data to do with our program. If too many interrupts occur, the stack can fill up pretty quickly and may overflow. This can become a problem if not well monitored. Another reason to keep ISRs small and short is so that they get back to the main program quickly and don't interfere with other interrupts.

This, of course, is just a very basic overview of the process that occurs. The detailed order of this process and instructions used to perform it are more complex and processor specific. But hopefully this gives an overview and helps you understand the process involved with setting up and using interrupts.

9.4   BASIC EXAMPLES

9.4.1   Polling a Switch for Input versus Using an Interrupt

Aim: Demonstrate checking the status of a hardware switch via polling and with an interrupt.

Requirements: PC with High-performance Embedded Workshop 4.0 or 4.0+, RX62N Development kit.

Details: In this example, we will setup the RX62N processor to check the status of switch one (SW1). If the switch is pressed, the lit LED will rotate clockwise once until the switch is pressed again. We will first do this via a polling method, and then with an interrupt. We will compare and contrast the differences.

Procedure: First we will set up SW1 and check it with a polling method.

```
1.  #include "iodefine_RX62N.h"
2.
3.  //Function definitions
4.  void main(void);
5.  void LED_Rotate(void);
6.
7.  //Define global variables
8.  int Current_LED;
9.
10.
11. void main(void){
12.     ENABLE_LEDS
13.     ENABLE_SWITCHES
14.     Current_LED = 1;
15.
16.     while(1){
17.       if(SW1 == 0){
18.           LED_Rotate();
19.           while(SW1 == 0)    //Note that this code does not handle
                                   switch debouncing.
20.               ;
21.       }
22.     }
23. }
```

All of this should be familiar; the LED_Rotate function rotates the LEDs one step in a clock-wise sequence every time it is called. Current_LED is used to keep track of which LED is currently lit. For more reference on how to implement this function, refer to Chapter 8 where it is first used.

Lines 17 through 22 are where we check the status of SW1. SW1 is active low so once it is pressed the input will become a zero. Every time the program cycles through the while(1) loop it will check if SW1 is a zero yet. If it is a zero it will rotate the LED clockwise and then get stuck in the while (SW == 0); until the switch is released. Note that on line 19 there is a comment noting that this code does not account for debouncing. Debouncing accounts for how a switch will, for a brief time after being pressed, rapidly switch back and forth (or "bounce") between an ON and OFF position rather than cleanly switching between states. Usually this state is accounted for by calling a brief timer loop before checking ON or OFF, and indicating pressed or depressed. This method was left out in this example for simplicity.

Another method would be to replace lines 16 through 22 with the following code:

```
1. while(1){
2.    while(SW1 == 1);
3.    LED_Rotate();
4.    while(SW1 == 0)
5.       ;
6.    }
7. }
```

With this method, we avoid problem number one of the last method by pausing the program until the switch is pressed. This solves that problem, but now this makes problem number two even worse. The program will be hung up entirely and no other calculations will be performed until the switch is pressed and released each time the while(1) loop repeats. To solve both problems we will use an interrupt.

```
 1. #include "iodefine_RX62N.h"
 2.
 3. //Define SW1 interrupt
 4. #pragma interrupt(SW1_Int(vect = VECT_IRQ8))
 5. void SW1_Int(void);
 6.
 7. //Function definitions
 8. void main(void);
 9. void LED_Rotate(void);
10. void EnableIRQ8(void);
11.
```

```
12. //Define global variables
13. int Switch_Press = 0;
14. int Current_LED;
15.
16. void main(void)
17. {
18.     ENABLE_LEDS
19.     EnableIRQ8();
20.     Current_LED = 1;
21.
22.     while(1)
23.     {
24.        if(Switch_Press)
25.        {
26.            LED_Rotate();
27.            Switch_Press = 0;
28.        }
29.
30.     }
31. }
```

First take note of the addition on lines 3 through 5. SW1 is connected to IRQ8, if we look up IRQ8 in the Interrupt Vector Table we will see that it is at vector 72. This code defines the ISR for IRQ8 as SW1_Int and places a pointer to its memory address at vector 72, and also defines the function SW1_Int. Also on line 10 we define a new function EnableIRQ8 which is called on line 19 to perform all of the necessary operations to set up the switch to trigger an interrupt. In our while(1) loop nothing will happen unless the Switch_Press flag is set in the switches interrupt routine. If it does, the LED_Rotate function is called and the flag is reset to 0.

```
1. void EnableIRQ8(void){
2.     IEN( ,IRQ8) = 0;
3.     PORT4.ICR.BIT.B0 = 1;
4.     ICU.IRQCR[8].BIT.IRQMD = 0x01;
5.     ENABLE_SWITCHES
6.     IPR( ,IRQ8) = 0x03;
7.     IR( ,IRQ8) = 0;
8.     IEN( ,IRQ8) = 1;
9. }
```

You may notice this code follows the procedure defined for setting a switch for an interrupt in Section 9.3.3 in the description of the IRQCRi register. First, as a precaution we disable the interrupt in the ICU in case it has been enabled in our program. This is on line 2. Then on line 3 we write a 1 to the input control register on Port4.0, the port that SW1 is connected to. This passes a signal to the ICU when the switch is pressed. Then we set the triggering method for IRQ8 on line 4. The switch is active when low, and it goes from a one to zero when pressed, so we set the trigger as a falling edge. Line 5 is our macro to set up the switches as inputs. By default the ports are inputs when the program starts, and we have also already called this macro in the main program; but this is a precautionary measure in case we decide to put this function in other programs where this hasn't already been done. Now that all of this is done, all we have to do is set up the interrupt in the ICU by defining its priority level, clearing the request flag in case it has been generated during setup, and then enabling the interrupt on lines 7 through 9.

```
1. void SW1_Int(void)
2. {
3.     Switch_Press = 1;
4. }
```

Our last piece of code is for the SW1 Interrupt Subroutine. This sets the flag indicating the interrupt was triggered then returns to the main function. Because we set the trigger for the interrupt as a falling edge on the switch, it will only trigger when the button is pushed. Once the button is pushed, the subroutine is called and whatever code we want to address is executed. The switch is not ignored. Also, there is no waiting because the main program is halted for only as long as it takes to address the ISR. Though the setup is slightly more complex, the interrupt method is superior in efficiency.

9.4.2   Setting up the ADC with an Interrupt

Aim: Demonstrate using the interrupt with a peripheral.

Requirements: PC with High-performance Embedded Workshop 4.0 or 4.0+, RX62N Development kit, RX62N Graphical LCD Code package.

Details: In this example, we will set up the RX62N processor to read the value of the potentiometer. Our program will use an interrupt, a device interrupt as a trigger, and a subroutine. TMR0 will trigger the A/D conversion every one second. When the A/D conversion is done it will call a subroutine to store the conversion in a variable. The main program will use this variable to display the conversion value on the LCD.

Procedure: First we need to set up our definitions and global variables:

```
1.  #include "iodefine_RX62N.h"
2.
3.  //Glyph Includes
4.  #include <stdlib.h>
5.  #include <stdio.h>
6.  #include "src\Glyph\Glyph.h"
7.
8.  //Define interrupt for AD1
9.  #pragma interrupt (AD1_Interrupt(vect = VECT_AD1_ADI1))
10. void AD1_Interrupt(void);
11.
12. //Function definitions
13. void main(void);
14. void InitADC(void);
15. void InitTimer(void);
16. void LED_Rotate(void);
17. void BSP_Display_String(int8_t aLine, char *aText);
18. #define LCD_LINE1 0
19. #define LCD_LINE2 1
20. #define LCD_LINE3 2
21. #define LCD_LINE4 3
22.
23. //Define global variables
24. T_glyphHandle G_lcd;
25. int Current_LED;
26. int ADCResult = 0;
27. char buffer[30];
```

From line 1 to 6 we have included all I/O files for the RX62N and the LCD. On line 8 through 10 we define our interrupt function for the A/D conversion done interrupt, and place a pointer at its vector in the interrupt table. Notice in our function definitions on lines 13 to 17 that we have made a function for initializing the ADC and timer. Also note on line 26 that we have made the global variable ADCResult, where we will hold the value read from the A/D conversion. The array on line 27 will be used to store the ASCII conversion of the ADCResult that is sent to the LCD.

Next is our main function and while(1) loop:

```
1.  void main(void)
2.  {
```

```
3.      float i;
4.      InitADC();
5.      InitTimer();
6.
7.      if(GlyphOpen(&G_lcd, 0) == GLYPH_ERROR_NONE){
8.          /* use Glyph full access direct functions */
9.          GlyphNormalScreen(G_lcd);
10.         GlyphSetFont(G_lcd, GLYPH_FONT_HELVR10);
11.         GlyphClearScreen(G_lcd);
12.
13.         BSP_Display_String(LCD_LINE1, "ADC Int Example");
14.         BSP_Display_String(LCD_LINE2, "Potentiometer Value:");
15.
16.         while(1){
17.             for(i = 0; i < 100000; i++);
18.             sprintf(buffer, "%d", ADCResult);
19.             BSP_Display_String(LCD_LINE3, buffer);
20.         }
21.     }
22.     else {}
23.
24.     GlyphClose(&G_lcd);
25.
26. }
```

We create the variable *i* on line 3 to make our arbitrary delay loop on line 17. On lines 4 and 5 we call our functions to set up the timer and the AD converter. The code from lines 7 through 11 are initialization for the LCD. In lines 13 and 14 we display on the LCD some information concerning the program that is running. Then in our while(1) loop, repeatedly, after an arbitrary delay, we will convert our value from the A/D conversion to an ASCII string and write it to line 3 of the LCD. The rest of the code is LCD control code.

```
1. void InitADC(void){
2.      MSTP(AD1) = 0;
3.      AD1.ADCSR.BIT.ADIE = 1;
4.      AD1.ADCSR.BIT.ADST = 0;
5.      AD1.ADCSR.BIT.CH = 0x000;
6.
7.      AD1.ADCR.BIT.MODE = 0;
8.      AD1.ADCR.BIT.CKS = 3;
9.      AD1.ADCR.BIT.TRGS = 2;
```

```
10.    IPR(AD1,ADI1) = 0x03;
11.    IR(AD1,ADI1) = 0;
12.    IEN(AD1,ADI1) = 1;
13. }
```

This is our function to set up the AD converter to read the value from the potentiometer. We will set it up to do a single conversion every time it receives a trigger from TMR0. First we enable the peripheral on line 2. Then on line 3 we enable the interrupt in the A/D peripheral; this will trigger the interrupt service routine every time a conversion finishes. We set the conversion to not start yet on line 4, and then select channel AN4 on line 5. It is indicated in the RX62N schematic that AN4 corresponds to the pin that is connected to the potentiometer. On line 7 we set the mode to single conversion, so every time the converter is triggered it will do one conversion then stop. We select the clock source for the AD converter as the peripheral clock on line 8. On line 9 we select the trigger as a Compare Match A event on TMR0. Every time a Compare Match A event occurs in TMR0 a signal will be sent to the A/D converter. This requires some set up in TMR0 as well; we will see that code shortly. On lines 10 through 12 we have the code to set the priority level, clear the request flag, and then enable the interrupt in the ICU.

```
1. void InitTimer(void){
2.     MSTP(TMR0) = 0;
3.     MSTP(TMR1) = 0;
4.
5.     TMR1.TCCR.BIT.CSS = 1;
6.     TMR1.TCCR.BIT.CKS = 5;
7.
8.     TMR0.TCCR.BIT.CSS = 3;
9.     TMR0.TCR.BIT.CCLR = 1;
10.
11.    TMR0.TCORA = 0x5B;
12.    TMR1.TCORA = 0x6D;
13.
14.    TMR0.TCSR.BIT.ADTE = 1;
15. }
```

Here is our code to set up a 16-bit cascaded timer that resets and generates a Compare Match A signal every one second. The code from lines 3 through 13 configures the timer to generate a one second interval; details are in the timer chapter of this text. The only code we need to examine here is on line 14, where we set the unit to send a trigger to the A/D converter every time there is a Compare Match A or every one second.

```
1. void AD1_Interrupt(void){
2.    ADCResult = AD1.ADDRA;
3. }
```

Our last bit of code is our interrupt subroutine for the A/D conversion. Every time a conversion finishes this routine will interrupt to write the latest conversion value to our variable, and then the program will return to its previous task.

So, to review, this program begins by initializing the A/D converter and the TMR0. TMR0's interrupt routine is not enabled, but the Compare Match A interrupt in the peripheral will send a signal to the A/D converter every one second. Once triggered the A/D conversion will begin, and once finished it will trigger its own interrupt. This interrupts the main program for long enough to write the conversion value to a variable, then returns. Inside the main program there is a constant loop writing the A/D conversion to the LCD after a short delay. When run, the LCD screen should display "ADC Int Example" on line 1 of the LCD and "Potentiometer Value:" on line 2. On roughly one second intervals the screen should update with a new value for the potentiometer.

This example illustrates two uses of interrupts, and an alternative use of interrupt signals to triggering subroutines. By now you should be pretty familiar with the process of setting up an interrupt to trigger a subroutine as well as the concept of using them to trigger processes in other peripherals.

9.5   ADVANCED CONCEPTS

9.5.1   Minimizing the Amount of Code in Interrupts

In example 9.4.1, Polling a Switch for Input versus Using an Interrupt, it was pointed out that excessive function calls, or code in general, inside of an interrupt routine is bad. If a function call is made in an interrupt routine it requires that all the processor register information be stored to the stack, which makes the compiler blind to register usage. Also, as mentioned several times in this book, it just simply adds more time and over head to the interrupt, and we want to avoid this as much as possible.

So how do we do this? Often an ISR is used only to set flags or alter very small amounts of data. Then these flags or data are used to alter something in the main program. A flag can be a global variable that is toggled between one and zero. Once the program returns from the interrupt, some control statement will eventually use this as an indicator to change the program flow in some way.

For example, say we have a program that is constantly checking the value of a thermistor but we only want it to update the value on the LCD screen every second. We would set up a timer to interrupt periodically every second, and when it interrupts it writes a one to a variable named Timer_Flag. In our main program there is an if statement that checks the timer flag. When the Timer_Flag variable is 1 the function to write the value to the LCD is called. This way we still get the benefits of the interrupt, but keep our code in the interrupt minimal.

9.5.2   Brief Introduction to State Machines

In the next section we will cover how to make an interrupt controlled state machine. But first, in this section we need to give a brief overview of what a state machine is and how to program one. State machines are simply a method that makes it easier to abstract a process we want to perform in real life and convert it into a program.

So far we have thought of programs as sequential processes. One process is executed, then some others, repeat. Sometimes that flow is altered slightly due to something happening, such as an interrupt or control loops, but with an embedded system we still will restart in our while(1) loop eventually and the program will repeat and execute the same processes again. With state machines we think of our program as having 'states.' In each state there is a different flow of operations to perform. Depending on some change in data or a triggering event, the state will change. The program will continue to perform the functions in this state until conditions are met to go into another state. We will implement the state machine by making a variable to represent the current state of the machine, and then using a switch statement to check that variable in the while(1) loop. If the variable is changed the state will change, otherwise the code in the current state will continue to run repeatedly. We can also make states that perform one task and then immediately switch to another state without to another state by default.

In order to better understand a state machine, let's imagine a vending machine as a state machine. The vending machine can be in a 'state' depending on what task it needs to perform at the current moment. In each state the program is focused on a particular function such as accepting money, returning change, or vending drinks. In the case of the coin return state, it will return the proper amount of coins and then by default return to the Accept Money state. The same for the vend state, which automatically goes to the Coin Return state (which we assume simultaneously checks to see if coins are needed to be returned at all). In the case of the Accept Money state, the state will not change until a selection is made or the coin return button is pressed. In the case of the Check Correct Change state it will immediately go to either state 4 or 1, depending on if the right amount of change was deposited for the selection. This is how a state machine works on a very basic level. A full implementation of a vending machine state machine would require many more states such as "jammed coin," "machine tilt," "coolant problem," "out of order," etc. In order to address the real world well embedded systems must get very intricate. This is just a simple illustrative example.

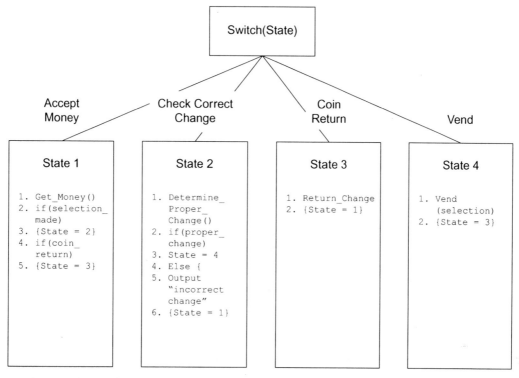

Figure 9.17   Vending machine state machine example.

9.5.3   State Machines and Using Them with Interrupts

So now that we know what a basic state machine looks like, we are going to demonstrate how to implement one effectively using interrupts to switch states. You'll notice in the vending machine examples that different actions triggered a state change, such as coin_return or selection made. These actions were represented as a variable of some sort and were checked by an If statement; if these variables were a one or higher the state was changed. Do these variables look familiar to something else we talked about in this chapter? These are simply the flags we talked about in Section 9.5.1, Minimizing the Amount of Code in Interrupts. So by setting flags with an interrupt we can have code in our states check these flags and change states based on input. Once again let's use an example to illustrate.

For this example let's use the RX62N. We will make a state machine that will have three states. In one state the machine will rotate the LEDs in a circular sequence. In the second state we will display the value of the potentiometer on the LCD. In the third state the LCD will display the number of seconds elapsed since the program has started. Each time switch

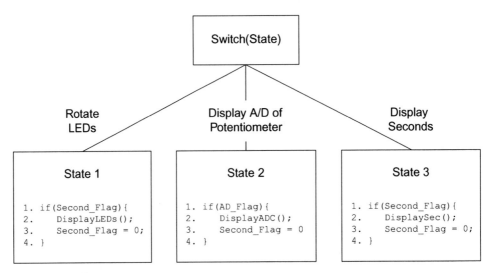

Figure 9.18 RX62N state machine example with interrupts.

one is pressed the board will cycle to the next state, once it goes beyond state three it will return to state one. We will make it that each state performs its actions at one second intervals.

With state machines this implementation is very simple. We only need three states as specified. The flag indicating which state is currently active is rotated using the ISR for switch one, defaulting to state one on start. Every second the timer will interrupt and set a flag that a second has passed, this flag will trigger actions in States 1 and 3. Note that the DisplayLEDs function in State 1 will include a function call to rotate the LEDs as well as display information on the LCD, thus rotating the LEDs. In the case of State 2 we are using the A/D converter, so we will use a flag set by its own ISR to trigger this state's actions. This will occur on roughly one second intervals since the A/D itself will be set to be triggered by a signal from the Timer device. This is a full, very basic state machine that uses interrupts to switch states. We will give a coding example of this in the advanced examples section.

9.6   ADVANCED EXAMPLES

9.6.1   Using an ADC Interrupt with Flags to Process Data

Aim: Demonstrate using flags with an interrupt to minimize the time spent in an ISR.

Requirements: PC with High-performance Embedded Workshop 4.0 or 4.0+, RX62N Development kit.

Details: In this example, we will set up the A/D converter once again to perform a conversion, except in this example the A/D will trigger an interrupt when the conversion is done. This interrupt will set a flag that is checked in the main code to trigger, writing the new data to the LCD.

Procedure: The code is mostly the same as our example in Section 9.4.2, Setting up the ADC with an Interrupt, except with modifications so that it now operates around the A/D interrupt. Our variable and function prototypes are mostly the same.

```
1.  #include "iodefine_RX62N.h"
2.
3.  //Glyph Includes
4.  #include <stdlib.h>
5.  #include <stdio.h>.
6.  #include "src\Glyph\Glyph.h"
7.
8.  //Define interrupt for AD1
9.  #pragma interrupt (AD1_Interrupt(vect = VECT_AD1_ADI1))
10. void AD1_Interrupt(void);
11.
12. //Function definitions
13. void main(void);
14. void InitADC(void);
15. void InitTimer(void);
16. void LED_Rotate(void);
17. void BSP_Display_String(int8_t aLine, char *aText);
18. #define LCD_LINE1 0
19. #define LCD_LINE2 1
20. #define LCD_LINE3 2
21. #define LCD_LINE4 3
22.
23. //Define global variables
24. T_glyphHandle G_lcd;
25. int Current_LED;
26. int ADCResult = 0;
27. char AD_Flag = 0;
28. char buffer[30];
```

The only difference here is we have added the AD_Flag variable on line 27. It is initialized to zero to indicate the interrupt has not been triggered yet.

```
1.  void main(void){
2.      ENABLE_LEDS
3.      InitADC();
4.      InitTimer();
5.
6.      if(GlyphOpen(&G_lcd, 0) == GLYPH_ERROR_NONE){
7.          /* use Glyph full access direct functions */
8.          GlyphNormalScreen(G_lcd);
9.          GlyphSetFont(G_lcd, GLYPH_FONT_HELVR10);
10.         GlyphClearScreen(G_lcd);
11.
12.         BSP_Display_String(LCD_LINE1, "ADC Int Flag Example");
13.         BSP_Display_String(LCD_LINE2, "Potentiometer Value:");
14.
15.         while(1){
16.             if(AD_Flag){
17.                 ADCResult = AD1.ADDRA;
18.                 sprintf(buffer, "%d", ADCResult);
19.                 BSP_Display_String(LCD_LINE3, buffer);
20.                 AD_Flag = 0;
21.             }
22.         }
23.     }
24.     else{}
25.
26.     GlyphClose(&G_lcd);
27.
28. }
```

Our main code has only been modified so all code to do with reading the A/D conversion value and writing it to the LCD has been placed in an If statement. When the AD_Flag variable becomes a 1 or higher this will cue the code to execute, then the flag will be reset to 0. The code will not execute again until the flag has been set to 1 again.

We won't cover the InitADC or InitTimer functions again as they are identical to a previous example. We are once again setting a one second interval timer. The timer generates a Compare Match A signal after one second that resets the timer and sends a signal to the AD converter to start converting. Once done, the A/D converter will trigger its own interrupt that will call an ISR.

```
1.  void AD1_Interrupt(void){
2.      AD_Flag = 1;   //Set A/D conversion flag
3.  }
```

Now the A/D conversion ISR will set the flag to one, indicating the conversion is done.

Conclusion: We have effectively altered our old program to use an interrupt and a flag to indicate data is ready from an external device. The flag now triggers the execution of a large amount of code in the main program. Keeping this code out of the interrupt service routine improves responsiveness for other ISRs.

9.6.2   A Simple State Machine Controlled by Interrupts

Aim: Demonstrate a state machine whose state is altered by an interrupt.

Requirements: PC with High-performance Embedded Workshop 4.0 or 4.0+, RX62N Development kit, RX62N Graphical LCD Code package.

Details: In this example, we will set up a state machine on the RX62N. When SW1 is pressed, the machine will rotate states. In State 1 the LEDs will blink clockwise at a rate of one LED per second. In State 2 the LCD will display the current ADC reading across the board's potentiometer every second. In State 3 the LCD will display the number of seconds elapsed since the program started. If the switch is pressed again the state will rotate back to State 1.

Procedure: First we once again need to set up our definitions and global variables:

```
1.  #include "iodefine_RX62N.h"
2.
3.  //Glyph Includes
4.  #include <stdlib.h>
5.  #include <stdio.h>
6.  #include "src\Glyph\Glyph.h"
7.
8.  //Define SW1 interrupt
9.  #pragma interrupt (SW1_Int(vect = VECT_IRQ8))
10. void SW1_Int(void);
11.
12. //Define interrupt for TMR0 Compare Match A
13. #pragma interrupt (TMR0_CompareMatchA_Interrupt
    (vect = VECT_TMR0_CMIA0))
14. void TMR0_CompareMatchA_Interrupt(void);
15.
16. //Define interrupt for AD1
```

```
17. #pragma interrupt (AD1_Interrupt(vect = VECT_AD1_ADI1))
18. void AD1_Interrupt(void);
19.
20. //Function definitions
21. void main(void);
22. void InitADC(void);
23. void InitTimer(void);
24. void EnableIRQ8(void);
25. void LED_Rotate(void);
26. void DisplaySec(void);
27. void DisplayADC(void);
28. void DisplayLEDs(void);
29. void BSP_Display_String(int8_t aLine, char *aText);
30. #define LCD_LINE1 0
31. #define LCD_LINE2 1
32. #define LCD_LINE3 2
33. #define LCD_LINE4 3
34.
35. //Define global variables
36. T_glyphHandle G_lcd;
37. int Current_LED;
38. int State = 1;
39. int Second_Flag;
40. int AD_Flag;
41. int SecCount;
42. int ADCResult = 0;
43. char buffer[30];
```

For this example we will use three ISRs. One each for the switch interrupt, the A/D conversion interrupt, and the TMR0 interrupt. These are defined on lines 8 through 18. On lines 22 to 24 we define our functions to set up each of these peripherals. We have also defined functions to call to display these on lines 26 through 28. On line 38 we create our state variable; altering this variable will alter which state we are in. On lines 39 to 40 we create flags for each interrupt, so when the interrupt is triggered the ISRs will set these flags, and then the main program will use these to trigger code to handle the events. On line 41 we create a global variable that counts the number of seconds the program has run.

Now we have our main program code, which is very simple.

```
1. void main(void){
2.     ENABLE_LEDS
3.     InitADC();
```

```
4.      InitTimer();
5.      EnableIRQ8();
6.
7.      if(GlyphOpen(&G_lcd, 0) == GLYPH_ERROR_NONE){
8.          /* use Glyph full access direct functions */
9.          GlyphNormalScreen(G_lcd);
10.         GlyphSetFont(G_lcd, GLYPH_FONT_HELVR10);
11.         GlyphClearScreen(G_lcd);
12.
13.         BSP_Display_String(LCD_LINE1, "State Machine");
14.
15.         while(1){
16.             switch(State){
17.                 case 1:
18.                     if(Second_Flag){
19.                         DisplayLEDs();
20.                         Second_Flag = 0;
21.                     }
22.                     break;
23.                 case 2:
24.                     if(AD_Flag){
25.                         DisplayADC();
26.                         AD_Flag = 0;
27.                     }
28.                     break;
29.                 case 3:
30.                     if(Second_Flag){
31.                         DisplaySec();
32.                         Second_Flag = 0;
33.                     }
34.                     break;
35.                 default:
36.                     //In the off chance that the State variable is set
                           to something other than 1 through 3
37.                     //we will be informed via this default state.
38.                     BSP_Display_String(LCD_LINE1, "Error");
39.                 break;
40.             }
41.         }
42.     }
43.     else{}
44.
```

```
45.     GlyphClose(&G_lcd);
46.
47. }
```

First on lines 2 through 5 we call our macros and functions to enable the LEDs and each of our peripherals (the A/D, timer and SW1). After the code to set up the LCD we enter our while(1) loop, where the only code we have is our state machine. This is implemented via a switch statement that uses the state variable to control it. In State 1 we will check the Second_Flag; every time it is set we will call the DisplayLEDs function which will update the LCD to display our state and then rotate the LEDs. In State 2 we check the A/D conversion finish flag, as the A/D conversion itself is trigger by the timer interrupt and we don't want to write the A/D value until the conversion is finished. When the flag is set, we will call the DisplayADC function which updates the LCD for the state and displays the conversion of the voltage across the potentiometer. In State 3 we check the second flag and once it is set we call the DisplaySec function, which updates our LCD for the state and displays the number of seconds elapsed on the screen.

Now we will go over out peripheral setup functions.

```
 1. void InitADC(void){
 2.     MSTP(AD1) = 0;
 3.     AD1.ADCSR.BIT.ADIE = 1;
 4.     AD1.ADCSR.BIT.ADST = 0;
 5.     AD1.ADCSR.BIT.CH = 0x000;
 6.
 7.     AD1.ADCR.BIT.MODE = 0;
 8.     AD1.ADCR.BIT.CKS = 3;
 9.     AD1.ADCR.BIT.TRGS = 2;
10.
11.     IPR(AD1,ADI1) = 0x03;
12.     IR(AD1,ADI1) = 0;
13.     IEN(AD1,ADI1) = 1;
14. }
15.
16. void InitTimer(void){
17.     MSTP(TMR0) = 0;
18.     MSTP(TMR1) = 0;
19.
20.     TMR1.TCCR.BIT.CSS = 1;
21.     TMR1.TCCR.BIT.CKS = 5;
22.
```

```
23.     TMR0.TCCR.BIT.CSS = 3;
24.     TMR0.TCR.BIT.CCLR = 1;
25.
26.     TMR0.TCORA = 0x5B;
27.     TMR1.TCORA = 0x6D;
28.
29.     TMR0.TCSR.BIT.ADTE = 1;
30.     TMR0.TCR.BIT.CMIEA = 1;
31.
32.     IPR(TMR0,CMIA0) = 3;
33.     IR(TMR0,CMIA0) = 0;
34.     IEN(TMR0,CMIA0) = 1;
35.
36. }
37.
38. void EnableIRQ8(void){
39.     IEN( ,IRQ8) = 0;
40.     PORT4.ICR.BIT.B0 = 1;
41.     ICU.IRQCR[8].BIT.IRQMD = 0x01;
42.     ENABLE_SWITCHES
43.     IPR( ,IRQ8) = 0x03;
44.     IR( ,IRQ8) = 0;
45.     IEN( ,IRQ8) = 1;
46. }
```

Each of these peripherals is set up as in previous examples so we won't have to review the code extensively. AD1 is set up to be triggered every time TMR0 sends it a Compare Match A signal, once triggered it will convert the voltage across the board's potentiometer and then trigger its ISR. TMR0 will generate a Compare Match A signal and trigger its ISR every second. SW1 will trigger its ISR every time it is pressed via IRQ8.

```
1. void DisplayLEDs(void)
2. {
3.     LED_Rotate();
4.     BSP_Display_String(LCD_LINE2, "State 1");
5.     BSP_Display_String(LCD_LINE3, "Rotating LEDs");
6.     BSP_Display_String(LCD_LINE4, " ");
7. }
8.
9. void DisplayADC(void){
```

```
10.      ADCResult = AD1.ADDRA;
11.      sprintf(buffer, "%d", ADCResult);
12.      BSP_Display_String(LCD_LINE2, "State 2");
13.      BSP_Display_String(LCD_LINE3, "Potentiometer Value:");
14.      BSP_Display_String(LCD_LINE4, buffer);
15. }
16.
17. void DisplaySec(void){
18.      sprintf(buffer, "%d", SecCount);
19.      BSP_Display_String(LCD_LINE2, "State 3");
20.      BSP_Display_String(LCD_LINE3, "Seconds Count:");
21.      BSP_Display_String(LCD_LINE4, buffer);
22. }
```

Our display functions are quite similar. As said before, each one updates the LCD and performs necessary actions based on which interrupt it is related to. The DisplayLEDs function calls the LED_Rotate function. The DisplayADC function updates the variable that contains the conversion result, and converts it to ASCII before sending it to the LCD. The DisplaySec function merely converts the seconds count variable to ASCII as the variable is updated in the ISR.

Now we will cover our interrupt functions themselves.

```
1. //Timer 0 Compare Match A Interrupt
2. void TMR0_CompareMatchA_Interrupt(void){
3.      Second_Flag = 1;
4.      SecCount++;
5. }
6.
7. //AD1 Conversion Finished Interrupt
8. void AD1_Interrupt(void){
9.      AD_Flag = 1;
10. }
11.
12.
13. //SW1 Interrupt
14. void SW1_Int(void){
15.      State++;
16.      if(State >= 4){
17.          State = 1;
18.      }
19. }
```

Each ISR is kept very simple. The TMR0 ISR merely sets the second flag and increments the count of the number of seconds. The AD1 interrupt only sets its flag. The SW1 interrupt increments the state, if it is 4 or greater the state is reset to 1.

Once compiled and run the state machine should start off in State 1. The LEDs will once again rotate on a one second interval with the state displayed on the LCD. Once SW1 is pressed, the state will increment to State 2 where the A/D conversion result from the potentiometer will update on the LCD every one second along with the state information. When SW1 is pressed again, the seconds count will be displayed on the screen along with State 3's info.

9.7   RECAP

In this chapter we have made a broad overview of the interrupt features on the RX62N and how they can be used with the different peripherals. We started by covering reasons for using an interrupt for tasks as compared to other techniques. Then we covered the full process of setting up an interrupt as it may apply to any peripheral. In the advanced concepts section we went over the reasons for keeping code minimal in interrupts. Then an example of a full implementation of interrupts was presented by introducing state machines and then describing a state machine controlled purely by peripheral interrupts.

9.8   REFERENCES

Conrad, James. ECGR 4101 Class Lecture; Topic: "Interrupts, and Using Them in C." Charlotte, NC: Department of Electrical and Computer Engineering, University of North Carolina at Charlotte; July, 2010. Lecture.

RX62N Group, RX621 Group Hardware Manual: RX62N Hardware Manual. Renesas Electronics America, Inc., Feb, 2010. Print.

9.9   EXERCISES

1. You want to set up one of the switches on the RX62N board to trigger an interrupt. List the registers you need to modify and the values you need to assign to them.
2. List at least three advantages of using an interrupt to signal data ready from a device rather than polling.
3. List at least five examples of an application where using an interrupt to signal data from a processor peripheral would greatly speed up a program.

4. Choose one of these examples and write pseudocode explaining how you would program this. Include descriptions of the interrupt function, your interrupt initialization function, and your main function.

5. Explain how you would use a flag to signal and process data from a device with an interrupt.

6. Why would you use a flag to signal processing of the data in the main program instead of placing all of the code in the interrupt?

7. What advantages does a state machine approach have over a purely sequential approach to embedded programming?

8. Give some examples of where a state machine would be a good choice of design approach.

9. Choose one of those examples and make a simple state machine design such as the one in Section 9.5.2, Brief Introduction to State Machines.

Chapter Ten

Floating Point Unit and Operations

10.1   LEARNING OBJECTIVES

All microprocessors can store and operate on integers. However, often we wish to operate on real numbers. We can represent these values with fixed-point or floating-point approaches. Fixed-point math is nearly as fast as integer math. Its main drawback is that the designer must understand the sizes of the smallest and largest data values in order to determine the appropriate fixed-point representation. Floating-point math automatically adjusts the scaling to account for large and small values.

Generally floating-point math is emulated in software, but some microprocessors have special hardware called a Floating Point Unit (FPU) for executing these operations natively, greatly increasing the speed. Though the FPU varies with the microcontroller, or with different families of microcontrollers, we will be discussing the FPU in the RX62N microcontroller and comparing it with the software emulation of a FPU on the QSK62P board.

In this chapter the reader will learn:

- The Instruction Set Architecture (ISA) of the RX62N Floating Point Unit
- Differences between a fixed point and a floating point operation
- Handling floating point exceptions

10.2   BASIC CONCEPTS

10.2.1   Floating Point Basics

Floating Point Representation

Before taking a look at the FPU in the RX62N, let's look at the basics of floating point.
Consider a floating point number, say 241.32478_{10}. It denotes the following.

10^2	10^1	10^0		10^{-1}	10^{-2}	10^{-3}	10^{-4}	10^{-5}
2	4	1	.	3	2	4	7	8

Figure 10.1   Decimal floating point representation.

The number in the box is the significand, 10 is the base and the power to which 10 is raised is the exponent.

We can represent the above number in exponential form as 2.4132478×10^2.

Consider a binary number, say 1011.0110_2. The number can be represented as:

2^3	2^2	2^1	2^0		2^{-1}	2^{-2}	2^{-3}	2^{-4}
1	0	1	1	.	0	1	1	0

Figure 10.2 Binary floating point representation.

We can represent the above binary number in exponential form as 1.0110110×2^3.

From the above notations, we can generalize the floating point expression as:

$$(-1)^{\text{sign}} \times \text{Significand} \times \text{Base}^{\text{Exponent}}$$

Though the decimal floating point representation is simple, it cannot be used by microcontrollers to work on floating point numbers. Since they work on binary digits, the IEEE 754 Floating Point Standard was introduced to represent decimal numbers as binary numbers.

IEEE 754 Floating Point Standard

In order to standardize floating point arithmetic, the IEEE 754 floating point standard was first introduced in 1985. Though the current version of IEEE 754 is IEEE 754–2008, it includes the original information in IEEE 754–1985 as well.

The binary floating point numbers represented by IEEE 754 are in sign magnitude form where the most significant bit is the sign bit followed by the biased exponent and significand without the most significant bit. The field representation of IEEE 754 is as follows.

Figure 10.3 IEEE 754 floating point representation.

The IEEE 754 defines four formats for representing floating point values.

- Single-Precision (32 bit)
- Double Precision (64 bit)

- Single Extended Precision ($\geq$ 43 bit, not commonly used)
- Double Extended Precision ($\geq$ 79 bit, not commonly used)

The IEEE 754 Floating Point Standard

Though the number of bits varies in each precision, the format for representing the floating point number is the same. The format for representing a floating point number according to IEEE 754 is as follows.

$$(-1)^{sign} \times (1 + \text{Significand}) \times 2^{\text{Exponent-Bias}}$$

Since we will not be using Single Extended Precision and Double Extended Precision, we will look at Single Precision and Double Precision in detail.

Single Precision (32 bits)

Single Precision consists of 4 bytes (or) 32 bits, where the 32 bits are divided into the following fields.

Figure 10.4   IEEE 754 single precision floating point representation.

In order to obtain the Single Precision representation, a few general steps are to be followed.

- Convert the decimal into a binary number.
- Express the binary number in normalized exponential notation. Since we are representing binary numbers, the power will be raised to 2, which is the base.
- Since we need to represent the exponent as an 8 bit binary number, we add 127 to the exponent in the normalized notation if the number we need to represent is positive.
- If the number we need to represent is negative, we subtract the exponent in the normalized notation from 127.
- Having done that, we add the significand bits by extending it to 23 bits.

EXAMPLE 1

A decimal number can be represented as a Single Precision number as follows. Consider a number, say 10.0_{10}

$$10.0_{10} = 1010 \times 2^0 \text{ or } 1.010 \times 2^3$$

In the above number 1.010×2^3, the significand is 010 as the number before the decimal point will always be 1. Since the significand here does not have a specific pattern of repetition, the 23 bit significand field will be the significand appended with zeroes at the end. From the above number:

Sign Bit: 0 (Since the number is positive).

Exponent: $127 + 3 = 130$. For simplification, let's split 130 as $128 + 2$. As 128 is nothing but 8-bit or 10000000_2

$$128_{10} + 2_{10} = 10000000_2 + 00010_2 = 10000010_2$$

Significand: 0100 0000 0000 0000 0000 000 (010 appended with zeroes)

From the Single Precision field representation, we can represent this number as:

1 bit	8 bits	23 bits
0	10000010	0100 0000 0000 0000 0000 000

Figure 10.5 Example 1; single precision conversion.

EXAMPLE 2

Consider a negative floating point number, say -0.1_{10}.

$$-0.1_{10} = 0.000110011 \times 2^0 \text{ or } 1.10011 \times 2^{-4}$$

In the binary number 1.**10011,** the 0011 pattern is repeated. Since the number has a pattern which gets repeated, the significand is 1 followed by a pattern of 0011.

Therefore, from the above number:

Sign Bit: 1 (Since the number is negative)

Exponent: $127 - 4 = 123$

Since 123 is less than 128, we cannot adopt the technique used in Example 10.1.

We know $123_{10} = 0111\ 1011_2$

Significant: 1001 1001 1001 1001 1001 100

From the Single Precision field representation, we can represent this number as,

Figure 10.6 Example 2; single precision conversion.

Double Precision (64 bits)

Double Precision consists of 8 bytes (or) 64 bits, where the 64 bits are divided into the following fields.

Figure 10.7 IEEE 754 double precision floating point representation.

Obtaining the Double Precision numbers, follow the same steps we adopted for Single Precision numbers but with different bits.

In order to obtain the Double Precision representation, the following steps are adopted:

- Convert the decimal into a binary number.
- Express the binary number in normalized exponential notation. Since we are representing binary numbers, the power will be raised to 2, which is the base.
- Since we need to represent the exponent as an 11 bit binary number, we add 1023 to the exponent in the normalized notation if the number we need to represent is positive.
- If the number we need to represent is negative, we subtract the exponent in the normalized notation from 1023.
- Having done that, we add the significand bits which is 52 bits wide.

EXAMPLE 3

Consider Example 10.1. To represent the number 10_{10} to a Double Precision number, we do the following.

$$10 = 1010 \times 2^0 \text{ or } 1.010 \times 2^3$$

In the above number 1.010×2^3, the significand is 010 as the number before the decimal point will always be 1. Since the significand here does not have a specific pattern of repetition, the 52 bit significand field will be the significand appended with zeroes at the end.

From the above number,

Sign Bit: 0 (Since the number is positive).

Exponent: $1023 + 3 = 1026_{10} = 10000000010_2$
Significand: 0100 0000 0000 0000 0000 0000 0000 0000 0000 0000 0000 0000 0000
(010 appended with zeroes)
From the Double Precision field representation, we can represent this number as:

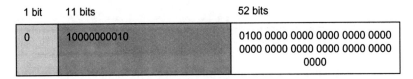

Figure 10.8   Example 3; double precision conversion.

EXAMPLE 4

Consider Example 10.2. To represent the number -0.1_{10} to a Double Precision number, we do the following:

$$-0.1 = 0.00011 \times 2^0 \text{ or } 1.10011 \times 2^{-4}$$

Therefore, from the above number,

Sign Bit: 1 (Since the number is negative)

Exponent: $1023 - 4 = 1019$
$1019_{10} = 01111111011_2$

Significand: 1001 1001 1001 1001 1001 1001 1001 1001 1001 1001 1001 1001 1010

From the Double Precision field representation, we can represent this number as:

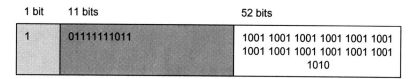

1 bit	11 bits	52 bits
1	01111111011	1001 1001 1001 1001 1001 1001 1001 1001 1001 1001 1001 1001 1010

Figure 10.9   Example 4; double precision conversion.

10.2.2 Pipelining Basics

In order to understand the floating point operations in microcontrollers and the difference between fixed point and floating point operations, it is necessary to take a look at the some of the basics of pipelining.

Pipelining is the technique adopted for increasing the instruction throughout and reducing the number of clock cycles required to execute an instruction by microprocessors. It is a method of realizing temporal parallelism, an assembly line processing technique. The instruction is broken down into a sequence of sub-tasks, each of which can be executed concurrently with other stages in the pipeline. The basic instruction cycle consists of five stages:

- Instruction Fetch
- Instruction Decode
- Execute
- Memory Access
- Write Back

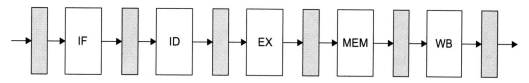

Figure 10.10   A basic pipeline.

Instruction Fetch

- The Instruction Fetch (IF) cycle fetches the current instruction from the memory into the program counter (PC).
- It updates the PC to the next sequential instruction.

Instruction Decode

- The Instruction Decode cycle (ID) decodes the instruction and reads the registers corresponding to the specified register source.
- It performs an equality test of registers for a possible branch.
- The decoding is done in parallel with reading registers.

Execution

The Execution (EX) cycle does the following:

- Memory Reference—Calculates effective address.
- Register—Register Operation—ALU performs the operation specified by the ALU opcode on the values read from the register file.
- Register-Immediate Operation—Operation specified by the ALU on the value read from the register and the sign-extended immediate.

Memory Access

The Memory Access (MEM) cycle does the following operations:

- Load—A read operation performed by the memory using the calculated effective address.
- Store—A write operation performed by the memory from the register read from the register file using the effective address.

Write-Back

- The Write-Back (WB) cycle writes the result into the register file, whether it comes from the memory system (load) or from the ALU (ALU instruction).

10.2.3 Floating Point in RX62N

In order to handle floating point operations, RX62N has the following:

- A Floating Point Unit
- Floating Point Instructions
- Floating Point Registers
- Floating Point Exceptions

Floating Point Unit

The Floating Point Unit (FPU) in RX62N operates on Single Precision floating point operands (32-bit) and the data-types and floating point exceptions conform to the IEEE 754 standard. This implementation facilitates the FPU to operate directly on the CPU registers rather than the dedicated register sets, thereby avoiding extra load/store operations and improving the performance. Figure 10.11 shows the floating point unit architecture in RX62N.

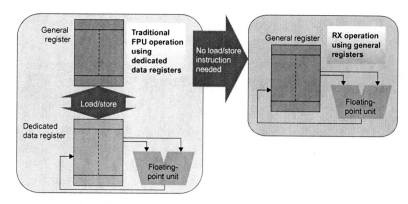

Figure 10.11 Architecture used by RX62N with dedicated registers for floating point operations.

Floating Point Registers

The RX62N uses a single floating point register, Floating-Point Status Word (FPSW) to indicate the results of the floating-point operations. It is a 32-bit register consisting of flags, bits representing modes for rounding off floating point numbers, exception enable/disable bits and reserved bits. Figure 10.12 shows the FPSW bits and Table 10.1 shows the bit definitions for the FPSW.

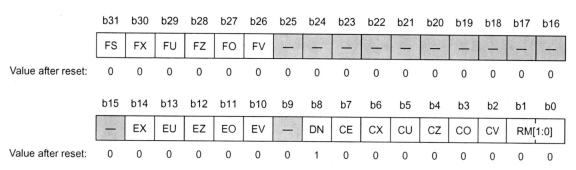

Figure 10.12 Floating-point status word. Source: *Software Manual, Renesas 32-Bit Microcomputer, RX Family/RX600 Series,* Renesas Electronics America, Inc., 2010, Section 2.2.2.8.

TABLE 10.1 Floating-Point Status Word Bit Definition.

BIT	SYMBOL	BIT NAME	DESCRIPTION	R/W
b1, b0	RM[1:0]	Floating-point rounding-mode setting bits	b1 b0 0 0: Round to the nearest value 0 1: Round towards 0 1 0: Round towards $+\infty$ 1 1: Round towards $-\infty$	R/W
b2	CV	Invalid operation cause flag	0: No invalid operation has been encountered. 1: Invalid operation has been encountered.	R/(W)[*1]
b3	CO	Overflow cause flag	0: No overflow has occurred. 1: Overflow has occurred.	R/(W)[*1]
b4	CZ	Division-by-zero cause flag	0: No division-by-zero has occurred. 1: Division-by-zero has occurred.	R/(W)[*1]
b5	CU	Underflow cause flag	0: No underflow has occurred. 1: Underflow has occurred.	R/(W)[*1]
b6	CX	Inexact cause flag	0: No inexact exception has been generated. 1: Inexact exception has been generated.	R/(W)[*1]
b7	CE	Unimplemented processing cause flag	0: No unimplemented processing has been encountered. 1: Unimplemented processing has been encountered.	R/(W)[*1]
b8	DN	0 flush bit of denormalized number	0: A denormalized number is handled as a denormalized number.	R/W
			1: A denormalized number is handled as 0.[*2]	R/W
b9	—	Reserved	When writing, write 0 to this bit. The value read is always 0.	R/W

Source: *Software Manual, Renesas 32-Bit Microcomputer, RX Family/RX600 Series,* Renesas Electronics America, Inc., 2010, Section 2.2.2.8.

Floating Point Instructions

The RX62N uses eight floating point instructions to perform floating point operations. All floating point instructions work on single precision floating point operands conforming to IEEE754 standard. The floating point instructions are as follows:

FADD

Function: Adds two floating point operands and stores the result in the register file.
Operations performed: Immediate-Register and Register-Register.
Number of cycles taken: Four.

FADD Operation:

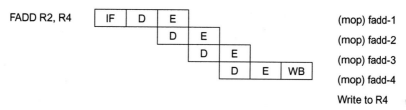

Figure 10.13   FADD Operation (Register-Register, Immediate-Register). Source: *Hardware Manual, Renesas 32-Bit Microcomputer, RX Family/RX600 Series,* Renesas Electronics America, Inc., 2010, Figure 2.19.

FSUB

Function: Subtracts the second floating point operand from the first floating point operand and stores the result in the register file.
Operation performed: Immediate-Register, Register-Register.
Number of cycles taken: Four.

FSUB Operation:

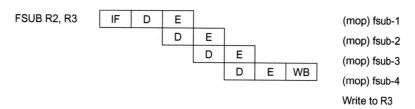

Figure 10.14   FSUB Operation (Register-Register, Immediate-Register). Source: *Hardware Manual.*

TABLE 10.1   Floating-Point Status Word Bit Definition.—Continued

BIT	SYMBOL	BIT NAME	DESCRIPTION	R/W
b10	EV	Invalid operation exception enable bit	0: Invalid operation exception is masked.	R/W
			1: Invalid operation exception is enabled.	
b11	EO	Overflow exception enable bit	0: Overflow exception is masked.	R/W
			1: Overflow exception is enabled.	
b12	EZ	Division-by-zero exception enable bit	0: Division-by-zero exception is masked.	R/W
			1: Division-by-zero exception is enabled.	
b13	EU	Underflow exception enable bit	0: Underflow exception is masked.	R/W
			1: Underflow exception is enabled.	
B14	EX	Inexact exception enable bit	0: Inexact exception is masked.	R/W
			1: Inexact exception is enabled.	
b25 to b15	—	Reserved	When writing, write 0 to these bits. The value read is always 0.	R/W
b26	FV[3]	Invalid operation flag	0: No invalid operation has been encountered.	R/W
			1: Invalid operation has been encountered.[8]	
b27	FO[4]	Overflow flag	0: No overflow has occurred.	R/W
			1: Overflow has occurred.[8]	
b28	FZ[5]	Division-by-zero flag	0: No division-by-zero has occurred.	R/W
			1: Division-by-zero has occured	
b29	FU[6]	Underflow flag	0: No underflow has occurred.	R/W
			1: Underflow has occurred.[8]	
b30	FX[7]	Inexact flag	0: No inexact exception has been generated.	R/W
			1: Inexact exception has been generated.[8]	
b31	FS	Floating-point error summary flag	This bit reflects the logical OR of the FU, FZ, FO, and FV flags.	R

FCMP

Function: Compares the floating point operands and updates the status register based on the results. The difference between FSUB and FCMP is that, FCMP does not store the result anywhere.

> *Operation performed:* Immediate-Register, Register-Register.
> *Number of cycles taken:* Four.

> *FSUB Operation:*

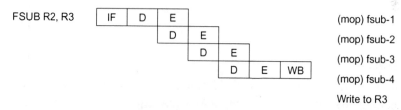

Figure 10.15 FSUB Operation (Register-Register, Immediate-Register). Source: *Hardware Manual.*

Floating Point Exceptions

The floating point exceptions are basically exceptions which arise due to inappropriate floating point operations. According to IEEE 754 standard, there are five floating-point exceptions as follows:

- Overflow
- Underflow
- Inexact
- Division-by-zero
- Invalid Operation

Overflow

This exception occurs when the result of a floating-point operation is too large. Under such circumstances, the result cannot be represented as a single-precision floating point number (32 bit) or a double precision floating point number (64 bit).

- The limits for signed single precision floating point numbers are 3.4E − 38 to 3.4E + 38.

- The limits for unsigned single precision floating point numbers are 0 to 6.8E38.
- The limits for signed double precision floating point numbers are $1.7E - 308$ to $1.7E + 308$.
- The limits for unsigned double precision floating point numbers are 0 to $3.4E + 308$.

If the result exceeds these limits, an overflow exception is raised.

Underflow

This exception occurs when the result is too small to be represented as a normalized floating-point number.

Inexact

This exception occurs when the result is not a single-precision floating point number. Rounding off the result and using it as a single-precision floating point number may cause this exception.

Divide-By-Zero

This exception occurs when a floating point number is divided by zero.

Invalid Operation

This exception occurs when the result is ill-defined. For example, an operation leading to a result which is $\pm\infty$ (Infinty) or NaN (Not a number) could cause this exception.

For example, $1.0 / 0.0 = +\infty$, $0.0 / 0.0 = $ NaN.

10.3   BASIC EXAMPLES

10.3.1   Operations Explaining Floating Point Exceptions

Before working on the RX62N's FPU, it is important to take a look at the operations causing Floating Point Exceptions, so that they can be handled efficiently. The Floating-point error summary flag (FS) notifies the programmer that an error (overflow, underflow, invalid operation, inexact, or division-by-zero) has occurred.

EXAMPLE 1

Overflow Exception

Consider the following example:

```
1. float a, c;
2. a = 999999969999999923.235;
3. c = a * 9999999999999969999999923.235;
```

The above operation causes an Overflow exception. To observe this exception, the contents of the FPSW can be viewed.

Click on the  (Registers icon) in the CPU Toolbox.

Figure 10.16   CPU toolbox.

For the above example, the FPSW was C8000100, where the Radix is Hexadecimal.

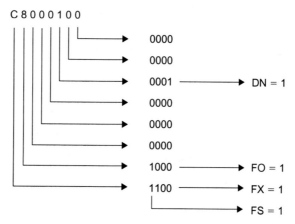

Figure 10.17   Example 1; FPSW.

From the above example:

- DN = 1, where a denormalized number is handled as 0.
- FO = 1, where an overflow exception has occurred.
- FX = 1, where an inexact exception has been generated.
- FS = 1, where the logical OR of the exception flags, except inexact exception, is 1; meaning an overflow/underflow/divide-by-zero/invalid operation exception flag has been set.

EXAMPLE 2

Underflow Exception

Consider the following example:

```
1. float a, c;
2. a = 0.000000000000000000000000000000005623;
3. c = a * 0.000000000000000000000000001235431435234;
```

The above operation causes an Underflow Exception. The FPSW has the following value.

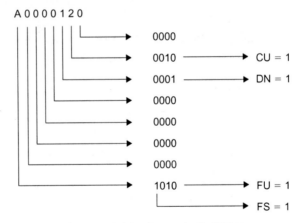

Figure 10.18   Example 2; FPSW.

From the above example:

- CU = 1, where an underflow operation has occurred.
- DN = 1, where a denormalized number is handled as 0.

- FU = 1, where an underflow exception has occurred and the underflow flag has been set.
- FS = 1, where the logical OR of the exception flags, except inexact exception, is 1; meaning an overflow/underflow/divide-by-zero/invalid operation exception flag has been set.

EXAMPLE 3

Divide-by-Zero Exception

Consider the following example:

```
1. float a, c;
2. a = 1.2;
3. c = a / 0;
```

The above code returns a divide-by-zero exception and the FPSW has the following value.

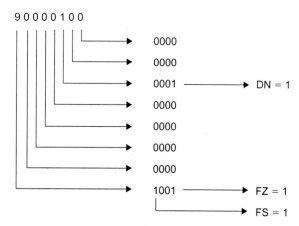

Figure 10.19   Example 3; FPSW.

From the above example:

- DN = 1, where a denormalized number is handled as 0.
- FZ = 1, where Division-by-zero flag has been set.
- FS = 1, where the Floating-point error summary flag has been set.

EXAMPLE 4

Invalid Operation

Consider the following example:

```
1. float c;
2. c = 0.0 / 0.0;
```

The above code returns an Invalid Operation and the FPSW has the following value.

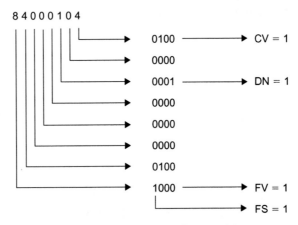

Figure 10.20   Example 4; FPSW.

From the above example:

- CV = 1, where an invalid operation has occurred.
- DN = 1, where a denormalized number is handled as 0.
- FV = 1, where an invalid operation exception has occurred and the invalid operation flag has been set.
- FS = 1, where the the floating-point error summary flag has been set.

10.4   ADVANCED CONCEPTS OF RX62N FLOATING POINT UNIT

10.4.1   FPSW in Detail

In order to perform complex floating point operations and handle floating point exceptions, a detailed knowledge about the FPSW is important. The bits in the FPSW can be categorized as follows:

Rounding-Modes

Using the RM bits in the FPSW, the floating point value or the result can be rounded to 0, $+\infty$, $-\infty$ or the nearest value. The bits b0 and b1 in the RM represent the rounding-mode. By default, the values are rounded towards the nearest absolute value. Consider Table 10.2, for RM bit definitions.

TABLE 10.2 RM Bit Definitions in FPSW.

BIT	SYMBOL	BIT NAME	DESCRIPTION
b1, b0	RM[1:0]	Floating-point rounding-mode setting bits	b1 b0
			0 0: Round to the nearest value
			0 1: Round towards 0
			1 0: Round towards $+\infty$
			1 1: Round towards $-\infty$

Source: *Software Manual*, page 24.

- Round to the nearest value: With this rounding-mode, the inexact value or the inexact result is rounded to the nearest absolute value. If two absolute values are equally close, the result is the one with the even alternative.
- Round towards 0: With this rounding mode, the inexact value or the inexact result is rounded to the smallest available absolute value in the direction of zero.
- Round towards $+\infty$: The inexact value is rounded to the nearest available value in the direction of $+\infty$.
- Round towards $-\infty$: The inexact value is rounded to the nearest available value in the direction of $-\infty$.

Cause Flags

In order to handle the floating point exceptions and floating point exceptions that are generated upon detection of unimplemented processing, the cause flags are used. When a cause flag is set to 1, it means a corresponding exception has occurred. The bit that has been set to 1 is cleared to 0 when an FPU instruction is executed.

The Cause Flags in the FPSW are:

- Invalid Operation Exception Cause Flag (CV)
- Overflow Exception Cause Flag (CO)

- Underflow Exception Cause Flag (CU)
- Divide-By-Zero Exception Cause Flag (CZ)
- Inexact Exception Cause Flag (CX)
- Unimplemented Processing Cause Flag (CE)

Exception Flags

The Exception Flags are used to indicate the occurrence of exceptions. If the exception flag is set to 1, it means the corresponding error has occurred. The exception flags available in the FPSW are:

- Invalid Operation Flag (FV)
- Overflow Flag (FO)
- Underflow Flag (FU)
- Division-by-zero flag (FZ)
- Inexact Flag (FX)

Exception Handling Enable Bits

When any of the five floating point exceptions occur, the bit decides whether the CPU will start handling the exception. When the bit is set to 0, the exception handling is masked. When the bit is set to 1, exception handling is enabled.

The Exception Handling bits in the FPSW are:

- Invalid Operation Exception Enable bit (EV)
- Overflow Exception Enable bit (EO)
- Underflow Exception Enable bit (EU)
- Divide-by-zero Exception Enable bit (EZ)
- Inexact Exception Enable bit (EX)

Denormalized Number Bit

A denormalized number is a number of the form $1 \times \alpha^{-n}$, where α is the base of the number (2 for decimal numbers and 10 for binary numbers) and n is the exponent.

When the denormalized number bit (DN) is set to 1, a denormalized number is handled as 0. When the DN bit is set to 0, the denormalized number is handled as a denormalized number.

From the basic examples, it can be seen that the DN bit is set to 1 when an Overflow, Underflow, Invalid Operation, or a Divide-by-zero exception occurs. This denotes that the result of the operation cannot be handled as a denormalized number.

Floating Point Error Summary Flag

The Floating Point Error Summary flag (FS) bit represents the logical OR of the following Exception flags:

- Invalid Operation Exception
- Overflow Exception
- Underflow Exception
- Divide-by-Zero Exception

Since the occurrence of inexact operation is common and is taken care of by the RM bits under certain circumstances, the FS bit does not reflect the occurrence of an inexact operation.

Reserved Bits

The reserved bits are restricted for the programmer, as they are used by the microcontroller itself. The reserved bits have a value of 0.

10.4.2 Floating Point Exception Handling Procedure

Though the floating-point exceptions appear similar to other exceptions, the handling routine for the floating-point exceptions vary slightly from that of other instructions. Floating-point exceptions are of the lowest priority and handling the exceptions can be classified as follows:

- Acceptance of the exception
- Hardware pre-processing
- Processing of the user-written code
- Hardware post-processing

Acceptance of the Exception

When a floating-point exception occurs, the CPU suspends the execution of the current instruction and stores the PC value of the instruction that is generated by the exception on the Stack. It is for this reason; the floating-point instruction is of instruction canceling type.

Hardware Pre-Processing

The following steps take place during hardware pre-processing:

- Preserving the PSW
  The value of the PSW is stored in the stack.
  PSW → Stack
- Updating the PSW
  The following bits are updated:
  □   I → 0
  □   U → 0
  □   PM → 0
- Preserving the PC
  The value of the PC is stored in the stack.
  PC → Stack
- Updating the PC
  The PC is updated with branch-destination address fetched from the vector address FFFFFFE4h in the fixed vector table. The processing is then shifted to the exception handling routine.

Processing of User-Written Program Code

The following steps take place while processing user-written code.

- Preserving general purpose registers
  The contents of the general purpose registers are stored in the stack.
  General purpose registers → Stack
- User code execution
  Corresponding user code is executed. In general, the code is inserted in the Excep_FloatingPoint() interrupt/function.
- General Purpose registers restoration
  The contents of the general purpose registers are stored in the stack.
  Stack → General purpose registers
- RTE Execution
  After restoring the contents of the general-purpose registers, the Return from Exception (RTE) is executed. This marks the end of exception handling. Following this step will be hardware post-processing.

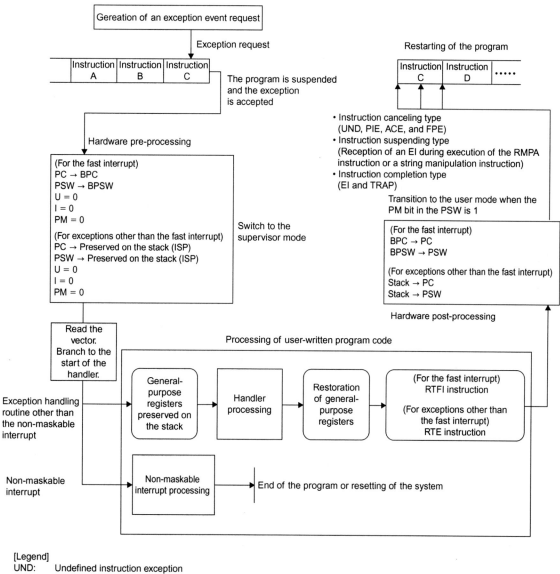

Figure 10.21   Exception handling procedure. Source: *Software Manual*, page 258.

Hardware Post-Processing

The following steps take place during hardware post-processing:

- Restoring PC
  The contents of the PC are restored from the Stack.
  Stack → PC.
- Restoring PSW
  The contents of the PC are restored from the Stack.
  Stack → PC.

Following the exception handling routine, the program is restarted. Figure 10.21 explains the exception handling procedure.

10.5   ADVANCED EXAMPLES _____

10.5.1   Fixed-Point and Floating-Point Operation Time Calculation

This example calculates the time taken for a single fixed-point operation and the time taken for a single floating point operation based on switch presses. For example, if Switch 1 is pressed, an Integer operation is carried out and the time taken for the operation is displayed.

In order to calculate the operation time, we need a timer. Let's say we are using Timer 0 (TMR0), with a clock source of PCLK/2 (to be more precise). In order to calculate the time taken, we initialize the timer and reset the Timer Counter (TCNT). The following would be the function to initialize the timer.

```
1. void Init_Timer(void)
2. {
3.    MSTP(TMR0) = 0;    //Activate TMR0
4.    TMR0.TCCR.BIT.CSS = 1;    //Count source is PCLK/2
5.    TMR0.TCCR.BIT.CKS = 1;
6.    TMR0.TCNT = 0x00;    //Reset TCNT
7. }
```

We will also need a function to reset the timer, which will deactivate the timer unit and reset the timer counter.

```
1. void Reset_Timer(void)
2. {
3.    MSTP(TMR0) = 1;    //Deactivate TMR0
4.    TMR0.TCNT = 0x00;    //Reset TCNT
5. }
```

The following code would be the main function:

```
1.  void main(void)
2.  {
3.      char str[30];
4.      int i;
5.      long int int1, int2, int3;
6.      float float1, float2, float3;
7.      double double1, double2, double3;
8.
9.      int1 = 2; int2 = 3;
10.     float1 = 2.0; float2 = 3.0;
11.     double1 = 2.0; double2 = 3.0;
12.
13.     ENABLE_LEDS;
14.     if(GlyphOpen(&G_lcd, 0) == GLYPH_ERROR_NONE){
15.         /* use Glyph full access direct functions */
16.         GlyphNormalScreen(G_lcd);
17.         GlyphSetFont(G_lcd, GLYPH_FONT_6_BY_13);
18.         GlyphClearScreen(G_lcd);
19.     }
20.     while(1)
21.     {
22.         if(SW1 == 0)    //If SW1 pressed
23.         {
24.             Init_Timer();
25.             for(i = 0; i < 10; i++)
26.                 int3 = (int1 * int2);
27.             sprintf((char *)str, "C:%d", TMR0.TCNT);
28.             Reset_Timer();
29.             BSP_Display_String(LCD_LINE3, str);
30.         }
31.
32.         else if(SW2 == 0)
33.         {
34.             Init_Timer();
35.             for(i = 0; i < 10; i++)
36.                 float3 = (float1 * float2);
37.             sprintf((char *)str, "C:%d", TMR0.TCNT);
38.             Reset_Timer();
39.             BSP_Display_String(LCD_LINE3, str);
```

```
40.        }
41.
42.        else if(SW3 == 0)
43.        {
44.            Init_Timer();
45.            for(i = 0; i < 10; i++)
46.                double3 = (double1 * double2);
47.            sprintf((char *)str, "C:%d", TMR0.TCNT);
48.            Reset_Timer();
49.            BSP_Display_String(LCD_LINE3, str);
50.        }
51.
52.        else
53.        {
54.            sprintf((char *)str, "Press any Switch");
55.            BSP_Display_String(LCD_LINE1, str);
56.            sprintf((char *)str, "to continue!");
57.            BSP_Display_String(LCD_LINE2, str);
58.        }
59.    }
60.
61.    GlyphClose(&G_lcd);
62. }
```

In the previous code, consider the snippet from Line 22 to Line 30:

```
22. if(SW1 == 0)    //If SW1 pressed
23. {
24.    Init_Timer();
25.    for(i = 0; i < 10; i++)
26.        int3 = (int1 * int2);
27.    sprintf((char *)str, "C:%d", TMR0.TCNT);
28.    Reset_Timer();
29.    BSP_Display_String(LCD_LINE3, str);
30. }
```

Line 24 initiates the timer and starts counting. Line 25 and line 26 perform integer multiplication for ten iterations. Since the time taken for iteration would be less, we consider ten iterations and divide the result by ten. Similar to the above code snippet, the multiplication operation is performed for float and double, and the value of the counter is found.

From the above code, it was found that the operations performed take the following time:

Int

Timer Count = 80

$$\text{Time Taken} = \frac{\text{Timer Count}}{\left(10 \times \dfrac{\text{PCLK}}{2}\right)}$$

Since we use $\dfrac{\text{PCLK}}{2}$ clock and we perform ten iterations, we divide the timer count by 10 and $\dfrac{\text{PCLK}}{2}$ (PCLK = 16.5 MHz here).

Therefore,

$$\text{Time Taken} = \frac{80}{\left(10 \times \dfrac{16.5}{2}\right)} = 0.9696 \text{ microseconds}$$

Float

Timer Count = 90

Therefore,

$$\text{Time Taken} = \frac{90}{\left(10 \times \dfrac{16.5}{2}\right)} = 1.0909 \text{ microseconds}$$

Double

Timer Count = 90

Therefore,

$$\text{Time Taken} = \frac{90}{\left(10 \times \dfrac{16.5}{2}\right)} = 1.0909 \text{ microseconds}$$

From the above example, the time taken for a floating point operation in the RX62N processor was found to be 1.0909 micro-seconds.

To observe the floating point instructions, one could follow the **Source Address** and view the corresponding Disassembly by clicking the 🖾 (View Disassembly) icon.

For example, consider the following figure.

| 266 | FFFFCFFA | | | f(i - 0; i < 10; i++) |
| 227 | FFFFD006 | | | float3 = (float1 * float2); |

Figure 10.22   Code snippet in view source tab.

The above code generates the following assembly code after building/compilation:

FFFFD006	ED0E0C		MOV.L	30H[R0],R14
FFFFD009	AB0D		MOV.L	34H[R0],R5
FFFFD00B	FC8FF5E		FMUL	R5,R14
FFFFD00E	E70E0E		MOV.L	R14,38H[R0]
FFFFD011	ED0E08		MOV.L	20H[R0],R14
FFFFD014	621E		ADD	#1H,R14
FFFFD016	E70E08		MOV.L	R14,20H[R0]
FFFFD019	ED0E08		MOV.L	20H[R0],R14
FFFFD01C	61AE		CMP	#0AH,R14
FFFFD01E	29E8		BLT.B	0FFFFD006H

Figure 10.23   Assembly code in view disassembly tab.

10.5.2   Matrix Multiplication Time Calculation

Similar to the above example, let's examine the time taken to calculate a simple 3×3 matrix.

In order to choose between int, float, and double, let's use the following code for user-friendliness:

```
1. void Init_Display()
2. {
3.     char str[30];
4.     sprintf((char *)str, "Matrix Mult");
5.     BSP_Display_String(LCD_LINE1, str);
6.
7.     sprintf((char *)str, "SW1: Int");
```

```
8.      BSP_Display_String(LCD_LINE2,str);
9.
10.     sprintf((char *)str, "SW2: Float");
11.     BSP_Display_String(LCD_LINE3,str);
12.
13.     sprintf((char *)str, "SW3: Double");
14.     BSP_Display_String(LCD_LINE4,str);
15. }
```

The previous code allows the user to choose the operation to perform. Pressing SW1 performs matrix multiplication with integer variables, whereas pressing SW2 and SW3 performs matrix multiplication using single precision and double precision floating point variables.

```
16. void int_Multiply(int matA[3][3], int matB[3][3], int
    matC[3][3],)
17. {
18.     int i, j, k;
19.     for(i = 0; i < 3; i++)
20.         for(j = 0; j < 3; j++)
21.             for(k = 0; k < 3; k++)
22.                 matC[i][j] += matA[i][k] * matB[k][j];
23. }
24.
25. void float_Multiply(float matA[3][3], float matB[3][3], float
    matC[3][3])
26. {
27.     int i, j, k;
28.     for(i = 0; i < 3; i++)
29.         for(j = 0; j < 3; j++)
30.             for(k = 0; k < 3; k++)
31.                 matC[i][j] += matA[i][k] * matB[k][j];
32. }
33. void dbl_Multiply(double matA[3][3], double matB[3][3], double
    matC[3][3])
34. {
35.     int i, j, k;
36.     for(i = 0; i < 3; i++)
37.         for(j = 0; j < 3; j++)
38.             for(k = 0; k < 3; k++)
39.                 matC[i][j] += matA[i][k] * matB[k][j];
40. }
```

In the previous code, lines 16 through 23 perform matrix multiplication using integers, lines 24 through 31 perform matrix multiplication using single-precision floating-point numbers, and lines 32 through 39 perform matrix multiplication using double precision floating-point numbers.

We use the Init_Timer() and Reset_Timer() functions discussed in the previous example to activate and deactivate the timer unit.

The main function would be as follows:

```
41. void main(void)
42. {
43.     char str[30];
44.     int i, j;
45.     int Timer_Count;
46.     float time;
47.     int int_matA[3][3], int_matB[3][3];
48.     int int_matC[3][3],
49.     float float_matA[3][3], float_matB[3][3];
50.     float float_matC[3][3],
51.     double dbl_matA[3][3], dbl_matB[3][3];
52.     double dbl_matC[3][3],
53.     for(i = 0; i < 3; i++)
54.         for(j = 0; j < 3; j++)
55.             int_matA[i][j] = j * 2;
56.     for(i = 0; i < 3; i++)
57.         for(j = 0; j < 3; j++)
58.             int_matB[i][j] = (9 - j) * 2;
59.     for(i = 0; i < 3; i++)
60.         for(j = 0; j < 3; j++)
61.             float_matA[i][j] = j * 1.1;
62.     for(i = 0; i < 3; i++)
63.         for(j = 0; j < 3; j++)
64.             float_matB[i][j] = (9 - j) * 1.1;
65.     for(i = 0; i < 3; i++)
66.         for(j = 0; j < 3; j++)
67.             dbl_matA[i][j] = j * 1.1;
68.     for(i = 0; i < 3; i++)
69.         for(j = 0; j < 3; j++)
70.             dbl_matB[i][j] = (9 - j) * 1.1;
71.     if(GlyphOpen(&G_lcd, 0) == GLYPH_ERROR_NONE){
72.         /* use Glyph full access direct functions */
73.         GlyphNormalScreen(G_lcd);
74.         GlyphSetFont(G_lcd, GLYPH_FONT_6_BY_13);
```

```
 75.        GlyphClearScreen(G_lcd);
 76.    }
 77.    Init_Display();
 78.    while(1)
 79.    {
 80.        if(SW1 == 0)
 81.        {
 82.            GlyphClearScreen(G_lcd);
 83.            Init_Timer();
 84.            int_Multiply(int_matA, int_matB, int_matC);
 85.            Timer_Count = TMR0.TCNT;
 86.            Reset_Timer();
 87.            sprintf((char *)str, "Count:%d", Timer_Count);
 88.            BSP_Display_String(LCD_LINE3, str);
 89.            Timer_Count = 0;
 90.        }
 91.        if(SW2 == 0)
 92.        {
 93.            GlyphClearScreen(G_lcd);
 94.            Init_Timer();
 95.            float_Multiply(float_matA, float_matB, float_matC);
 96.            Timer_Count = TMR0.TCNT;
 97.            Reset_Timer();
 98.            sprintf((char *)str, "Count:%d", Timer_Count);
 99.            BSP_Display_String(LCD_LINE3,str);
100.            Timer_Count = 0;
101.        }
102.        if(SW3 == 0)
103.        {
104.            GlyphClearScreen(G_lcd);
105.            Init_Timer();
106.            dbl_Multiply(dbl_matA, dbl_matB, dbl_matC);
107.            Timer_Count = TMR0.TCNT;
108.            Reset_Timer();
109.            sprintf((char *)str, "Count:%d", Timer_Count);
110.            BSP_Display_String(LCD_LINE3, str);
111.            Timer_Count = 0;
112.        }
113.    }
114.    GlyphClose(&G_lcd);
115. }
```

In the above code lines 52 through 69 initialize the matrices in corresponding data-type. When switch 1 is pressed, the code enters line 79. The integer matrix multiplication is performed at line 83 and the corresponding count is measured as the previous example.

From the previous example, the following results were observed:

Int
Timer Count = 112

$$\text{Time Taken} = \frac{111}{\left(10 \times \frac{16.5}{2}\right)} = 1.3454 \text{ microseconds}$$

Float
Timer Count = 197

$$\text{Time Taken} = \frac{197}{\left(10 \times \frac{16.5}{2}\right)} = 2.3878 \text{ microseconds}$$

Double
Timer Count = 198

$$\text{Time Taken} = \frac{198}{\left(10 \times \frac{16.5}{2}\right)} = 2.4 \text{ microseconds}$$

From the example, time taken to perform matrix multiplication of two 3×3 matrices was found. Also, a slight difference in time taken to perform single-precision and double-precision floating point matrix multiplication operation was observed.

10.6   RECAP

In this chapter, the Floating Point Unit (FPU) used in the Renesas RX62N was analyzed in detail, where the floating point instructions, floating point exceptions and floating point registers were discussed.

By applying this knowledge about the FPU, the RX62N board can be used in signal processing, image processing applications, and applications that require precise round-off (for example, in applications involving currency, floating-point rounding off errors should be considered in order to value currency as $$.cc where "$$" denotes the dollar value and "cc" denotes the cent value) with an understanding of the time-memory tradeoff between a microcontroller with an FPU and one without an FPU.

10.7   REFERENCES

Hardware Manual, Renesas 32-Bit Microcomputer, RX Family/RX600 Series. Renesas Electronics America, Inc., 2010. Print.

Software Manual, Renesas 32-Bit Microcomputer, RX Family/RX600 Series. Renesas Electronics America, Inc., 2010. Print.

10.8   EXERCISES

1. Write a C program to identify different Floating Point Exceptions.
2. Consider the following operations:

   Addition: 2.0 + 3.0
   Multiplication: 2.0 * 3.0
   Division: 2.0/3.0

   Do different operations involving floating-point (addition, multiplication, and division) take the same time to complete? Justify your answer. Use single-precision floating point numbers for the operations. Use Switch 1 (SW1), Switch 2 (SW2), and Switch 3 (SW3) to perform Addition, Multiplication, and Division respectively and display the time taken as the result.
3. Write a C program on the RX62N to calculate the time taken to perform the operations stated in problem 10.7.2. Use single-precision floating point numbers for the operations.
4. Implement problem 10.7.3 using double precision floating point numbers. Does it take the same time as single precision floating point numbers? Justify your answer.
5. Identify the floating point instructions involved in single precision and double precision operations in problems 10.7.3 and 10.7.4 from the disassembly. Do they look alike? Explain your answer.

6. Write a C program on the RX62N to calculate the time taken to perform the inverse of the given matrix A. (Note: The inverse of the matrix should be calculated in a different function other than "main.")

$$A = \begin{matrix} 1 & 2 & 0 \\ 3 & 6 & -1 \\ 1 & 2 & 1 \end{matrix}$$

7. Multiply the inverted A matrix with B matrix given below. Identify the floating point exceptions involved. (Note: Matrix Multiplication should be done in a different function other than "main.")

$$B = \begin{matrix} 0.001 & 2.400 & 0.120 \\ 3.143 & 2.743 & 4.901 \\ 0.917 & -0.008 & -2.001 \end{matrix}$$

Chapter Eleven

Watchdog Timer and Brown-Out Detector

11.1 LEARNING OBJECTIVES

Embedded systems are expected to work correctly. However, it is very difficult (even impossible) to completely test a system in all possible environments. Hence embedded system designers usually rely on a **watchdog timer (WDT)** to reset the processor if the program runs out of control. They also use a brown-out (or low-voltage) detector to hold the processor in reset if the supply voltage is too low for correct operation.

This chapter presents information on:

- Basic watchdog timer concepts
- How application software and the WDT should interact
- How to configure the RX62N WDT
- Concepts for the brown-out detector

11.2 BASIC CONCEPTS OF WATCHDOG TIMER

Many embedded systems are built to operate without an operator, so there should be a mechanism that monitors the system for unexpected errors due to some hardware fault, an unusual endless loop, or other fatal software bug. The watchdog timer serves the purpose of automatically monitoring and recovering the system from such situations.

The watchdog timer is an internal hardware timer peripheral in the CPU or an external device which resets the processor if it is not reset within a given period of time. The application software needs to periodically reset the watchdog timer. If the application software does not do this soon enough, the WDT overflows and the overflow signal is used to reset the system. So, the watchdog timer can only help the system recover from faults which prevent the timely refresh of the WDT.

In a multitasking system, it is a best practice to have each task check in with a task which monitors system-wide task progress. This monitor task will only reset the WDT if **all tasks** are making adequate progress.

One should **never** build a system in which the WDT is reset automatically by a task or ISR which operates autonomously of the rest of the system. This defeats the purpose of the WDT.

11.2.1 Watchdog Timer (WDT)

The Watchdog timer in RX62N microcontroller is an 8-bit timer which outputs an overflow signal (WDTOVF), if the timer overflow occurs during general program flow, and it can also be set up to reset the processor whenever the overflow signal occurs. The watchdog timer can also be used as an interval timer which generates an interrupt each time the counter overflows.

11.2.2 Register Descriptions

The registers used for the watchdog timer are listed in Table 11.2. The Timer control/status register (TCSR) is used for selecting the timer operation and clock source for the timer. The Timer counter (TCNT) contains the count value for the timer. The Reset control/status register (RSTCSR) is used to reset the timer. Window A and Window B registers are used for writing data into TCNT, TCSR and RSTCSR.

TABLE 11.1   Specifications of WDT.

ITEM	SPECIFICATIONS
Count clocks	PCLK/4, PCLK/64, PCLK/128, PCLK/512, PCLK/2048, PCLK/8192, PCLK/32768, and PCLK/131072
Number of channels	8 bits × 1 channel
Count clear	Write to TCNT
Operating modes	Switchable between watchdog timer mode and interval timer mode
Watchdog timer mode	Outputs a WDTOVF# signal when the counter overflows.
	Selectable whether or not to internally reset the RX62N/RX621 at the same time.
Interval timer mode	Generates an interval timer interrupt (WOVI) when the counter overflows.

Source: *Hardware Manual, Renesas 32-Bit Microcomputer, RX Family/RX600 Series.* Renesas Electronics America, Inc., 2010, Table 23.1.

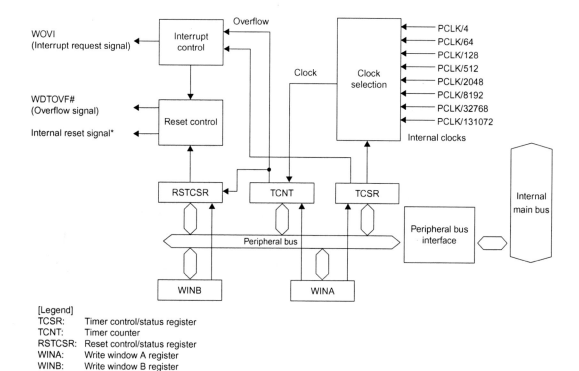

[Legend]
TCSR: Timer control/status register
TCNT: Timer counter
RSTCSR: Reset control/status register
WINA: Write window A register
WINB: Write window B register

Note:* An internal reset signal can be generated depending on the register setting.

Figure 11.1   Block diagram of the WDT. Source: *Hardware Manual, Renesas 32-Bit Microcomputer, RX Family/RX600 Series,* Renesas Electronics America, Inc., 2010, Figure 23.1.

TABLE 11.2   WDT Registers.

REGISTER NAME	SYMBOL	VALUE AFTER RESET	ADDRESS	ACCESS SIZE
Timer control/status register	TCSR	x8h	0008 8028h[*1]	8
Timer counter	TCNT	00h	0008 8029h[*1]	8
Reset control/satus register	RSTCSR	1Fh	0008 802Bh[*1]	8
Write window A register	WINA	—	0008 8028h[*2]	16
Write window B register	WINB	—	0008 802Ah[*2]	16

Notes: 1. Read-only register
        2. Write-only register

Source: *Hardware Manual,* Table 23.3.

Window A Register (WINA): WINA is a 16-bit write-only register which is used to write the data into Timer Counter (TCNT) register and Timer Control/Status register (TCSR). To write to this register, use word access. The address of the WINA register is 0008 8082h.

Window B Register (WINB): WINB is a 16-bit write-only register and is used to write the data into Reset Control/Status register (RSTCSR). To write to this register, use word access. The address of WINB register is 0008 802Ah.

Timer Counter Register (TCNT)

The timer counter register (TCNT) is an 8-bit register which contains the maximum up-count value for the internal clock. To write any value into TCNT register, data should be written into WINA register by word access. The value of the register after reset would be 00h. The address of the TCNT register is 0008 8029h.

The following is a code snippet to write data into the TCNT register:

```
1. void write_TCNT (void){
2.    WINAL* = count_value;
3.    WINAH* = 0x5Ah;
4. }
```

Explanation of the Code

Line 2:   WINAL = count_value;
           The count value for the timer is set in the lower byte of the WINA register.

Line 3:   WINAH = 0x5Ah;
           To write the required data into the TCNT register, the upper byte of the WINA register is set to 5Ah.

Timer Control/Status Register (TCSR)

Timer Control/Status Register is an 8-bit register which is used to select the clock source for the timer and type of operation of the timer.

---

*In the code snippets, for easy explanation of settings for WINA and WINB registers, they are not used through word access. WINAL/WINBL is the lower byte of the word and WINAH/WINBH is the upper byte of the word. The actual way of setting the registers will be in the code examples.

Address: 0008 8028h

b7	b6	b5	b4	b3	b2	b1	b0
—	TMS	TME	—	—	CKS[2:0]		

Value after reset: 0   0   0   0   0   0   0   0

[Legend] x: Undefined

Figure 11.2   Timer Control/Status Register (TCSR). Source: *Hardware Manual,* page 23–4.

Bit Description of TCSR

CKS [2:0] Bits: These bits are used to select the clock input to the timer in timer mode.

TME Bit (Timer Enable): This bit is used to start or stop the counting. When the bit is set to 1, TCNT starts counting. When the bit is cleared to 0, TCNT stops counting and is initialized to 00h.

TMS Bit (Timer Select): This bit is used to select the operation of WDT as a Watchdog timer or Interval timer. When this bit is cleared to 0, Interval timer mode is selected and as the TCNT overflows, an interval timer interrupt is generated. When this bit is set to 1, Watchdog timer mode is selected and as the TCNT overflows WDTOVF signal goes high.

The importance of using the clock source:

Problem 1: Design an embedded system using RX62N microcontroller with a delay of 326.4 μs to a watchdog timer. (Given PCLK = 50 MHZ)

Solution: The highest possible value the Timer count register (TCNT) can count up to 255 (FFh). So the delay we get with PCLK as the clock source is:

$$\text{Delay} = \frac{255}{(\text{PCLK})} = (255 / 50)\ \mu s = 5.1\ \mu s$$

So with a maximum value in the TCNT register we only get a delay of 5.1 μs. To increase the delay the clock source frequency should be decreased.

Because 326.4 μs/5.1 μs = 64, the clock source frequency should be reduced to $1/64$ of the original clock source PCLK.

If PLCK/64 is used as a clock source:

$$\text{Delay} = (255/(\text{PLCK}/64)) = ((255 * 64)/\text{PCLK}) = ((255 * 64)/50)\ \mu s = 326.4\ \mu s$$

TABLE 11.3 Bit Description of TCSR.

BIT	SYMBOL	BIT NAME	DESCRIPTION	R/W
b2 to b0	CKS[2:0]	Clock select	b2 b0	R/W
			0 0 0: PCLK/4 (cycle: 20.4 μs)	
			0 0 1: PCLK/64 (cycle: 326.4 μs)	
			0 1 0: PCLK/128 (cycle: 652.8 μs)	
			0 1 1: PCLK/512 (cycle: 2.6 ms)	
			1 0 0: PCLK/2048 (cycle: 10.4 ms)	
			1 0 1: PCLK/8192 (cycle: 41.8 ms)	
			1 1 0: PCLK/32768 (cycle: 167.1 ms)	
			1 1 1: PCLK/131072 (cycle: 668.5 ms)	
			Note: The overflow cycle for PCLK = 50 MHz is indicated in parentheses.	
b4, b3	—	(Reserved)	These bits are always read as 1. The write value should always be 1.	R/W
b5	TME	Timer enable	0: TCNT stops counting and is initialized to 00h.	R/W
			1: TCNT starts counting.	
b6	TMS	Timer Mode Select	0: Interval timer mode	R/W
			When TCNT overflows, an interval timer interrupt (WOVI) is requested.	
			1: Watchdog timer mode	
			When TCNT overflows, WDTOVF# is output.	
b7	—	(Reserved)	If read, an undefined value will be read. The write value should always be 1.	R/W

Source: *Hardware Manual,* page 23–4.

The following is a code snippet to start the timer in WDT mode with a clock source of $\frac{1}{64}$:

To write data to the TCSR register, data should be written into the WINA register by word access.

```
1. void write_TCNT (void){
2.    WINAL = data;
3.    WINAH = 0xA5h;
4. }
```

Explanation of the Code

Line 2: `WINAL = data;`

The value in data variable to—the timer counting in WDT mode with a clock source of $\frac{1}{64}$—is F9h, so data = F9h.

Line 3: `WINAH = 0xA5h;`

To write the required data into the TCNT register, the upper byte of the WINA register is set to A5h.

Reset Control/Status Register (RSTCSR)

Reset Control/Status Register is an 8-bit register which is used to control the internal reset signal when TCNT overflows and to select the type of internal reset signal. After the reset signal from the RES pin or a deep software standby reset, the register value is set to 1Fh but the value does not change when the WDT internal reset signal occurs.

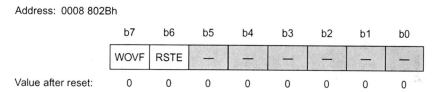

Address: 0008 802Bh

	b7	b6	b5	b4	b3	b2	b1	b0
	WOVF	RSTE	—	—	—	—	—	—
Value after reset:	0	0	0	0	0	0	0	0

Figure 11.3   Reset Control/Status Register. Source: *Hardware Manual,* page 23–5.

Bit Description of RSTCSR

RSTE Bit (Reset Enable): This bit is used to enable or disable the internal reset of the microcontroller when TCNT overflows in watchdog timer mode. When the bit is set to 1, the internal reset of the microcontroller will be enabled.

WOVF Flag (Watchdog Timer Overflow): This bit is used to check the overflow of TCNT in watchdog timer mode. This bit cannot be set to 1 in interval timer mode. The WOVF flag is set to 1 when the TCNT overflows (changed from FFh to 00h) in watchdog timer mode. WOVF flag should be cleared to 0 by the software when it is read as 1.

The following is a code snippet to start the timer in WDT mode with a clock source of $\frac{1}{4}$, LSI internally reset and writing 0 to the WOVF flag:

To write data to the TCSR register, data should be written into the WINA register by word access. To write data to the RSTCSR data should be written into the WINB register by word access.

```
1. void write_RSTCSR (void){
2.     WINAL = data;
3.     WINAH = 0xA5h;
4.     WINBL = data1;
5.     WINBH = 0x5Ah;
6.     while((RSTCSR&0x80) != 0x80)
7.         ;
8.     WINBL = data2;
9.     WINBH = 0x5Ah;
10. }
```

Explanation of the Code

Line 2: `WINAL = data;`
> The value in data variable to start counting the timer in WDT mode with a clock source of $1/4$ is F8h.

Line 3: `WINAH = 0x5Ah;`
> To write the required data into the TCNT register, the upper byte of the WINA register is set to 5Ah.

Line 4: `WINBL = data1;`
> The value in the data1 variable to make the microcontroller reset internally is 5Fh.

Line 5: `WINBH = 0x5Ah;`
> To write the required data into the RSTCSR, the upper byte of the WINB register is set to 5Ah.

Line 7: `while((RSTCSR&0x80) != 0x80);`
> The program waits here until the WOVF flag is set.

Line 8: `WINBL = data2;`
> When the WOVF flag is set, the program comes out of the while loop and clears the WOVF flag. To clear the flag, a value of 00h is written in the lower byte of the WINB register through the local variable data2. data2 = 00h.

Line 9: `WINBH = 0x5Ah;`
> To write into RSTCR, the upper byte of the WINB register should be set to a value of A5h.

11.2.3 Operation of WDT

Watchdog Timer Mode: To use the watchdog timer mode, the TMS bit and the TME bit should be set to 1. In watchdog timer mode, the TCNT overflows either when a system goes unresponsive due to a software bugs or any other error. When the TCNT overflows, the WDTOVF signal goes high for 257 cycles of PCLK when the RSTE bit in RSTCSR is set to 1, and WDTOVF signal goes high for 256 cycles of PCLK when RSTE is cleared to 0. This signal can be used to reset the MCU internally in watchdog timer mode. TCNT overflows must be prevented in the software by rewriting the value of TCNT to 00h before overflow occurs. If TCNT overflows and the RSTE bit in RSTCSR is set to 1, the internal reset signal that resets the RX62N/RX621 and the WDTOVF signal are generated at the same time. If the external reset from the RES pin and the reset from the WDT occur at the same time, the RES pin gets the highest priority and the WOVF flag in RSTCSR is cleared to 0. The software should rewrite the TCNT value to 00h before the overflow occurs.

Figure 11.4 shows an example of how the WDT operates. At the first arrow the TMS and TME bit are set to 1. At the next three arrows, the WDT is refreshed. WDT overflow occurs at WOVF arrow point so the internal reset signal goes high for 1027 cycles and the WDTOVF signal toggles for 257 or 256 cycles depending on the RSTE bit in RSTCSR.

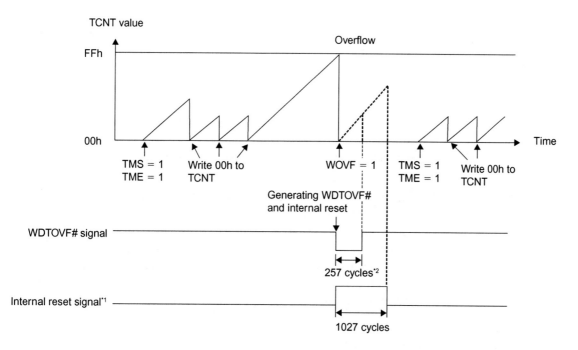

Notes: 1. An internal reset signal is generated if TCNT overflows when the RSTE bit in RSTCSR is set to 1.
2. The WDTOVF# signal is output for 256 cycles when RSTE bit in RSTCSR is set to 0.

Figure 11.4 Watchdog timer mode operation. Source: *Hardware Manual,* page 23–7.

11.3 BASIC CODE EXAMPLES

11.3.1 Example 1: Setting Up Watchdog Timer Mode

In this example code a subroutine is provided with the watchdog timer set up for a delay time of FFh; i.e., equal to 5.1 μs. (PCLK = 50 MHZ)

```
1. void Init_WDT(void){
2.    WDT.WRITE.WINA = 0x5A00;    //Writing data into TCNT
3.    WDT.WRITE.WINB = 0x5A5F;    //Writing data into RSTCSR
4.    WDT.WRITE.WINA = 0xA5FD;    //Writing data into TCSR
5. }
```

Explanation of the Code

Line 2: `WDT.WRITE.WINA = 0x5A00;`
A value of 00h is written into the TCNT register. Since we cannot directly write value into TCNT register, WINA register is used to write the value. To write data into the TCNT register, the upper byte of the word of WINA register should be set to 5Ah and then the data is written to the lower byte of the word of WINA register.

Line 3: `WDT.WRITE.WINB = 0x5A5F;`
A value of 5F is written into the RSTCSR using WINB register. To write data into the RSTCSR the upper byte of the word of WINB register should be set to 5Ah, and then the data is written to the lower byte of the word of WINB register. The internal reset enable (RSTE) pin is set to 1 to reset the microcontroller on the overflow of the watchdog timer.

Line 4: `WDT.WRITE.WINA = 0xA5FD;`
A value of FD is written into TCSR using the WINA register. To write data into the TCSR the upper byte of the word of the WINA register should be set to 5Ah and then the data is written to the lower byte of the word of the WINA register. The CKS [2:0] bits are set to a value of 7 selecting the prescaler division factor as 131072 with clock source as PCLK. The TMS bit in this register is set to 1 to select the watchdog timer mode, and the timer start enable bit is set to 1 to start counting.

11.3.2 Example 2: Application of a Watchdog Timer

Consider a software bug which leads the program into an infinite loop. This example shows how the watchdog timer brings the program out of the infinite loop.

```
1. void main(){
2.     int i;
3.     ENABLE_LEDS;
4.     while(1){
5.         Init_WDT(void);
6.         ALL_LEDS_OFF();
7.         for(i = 0; i < 10000000; i++){
8.             i--;
9.         }
10.        ALL_LEDS_ON();
11.        WDT.WRITE.WINA = 0x5A00;    //Clearing data into TCNT
12.    }
13. }
```

In the above program, the LEDs should switch on and switch off with some delay, but due to the software bug the program enters into an infinite loop which eventually causes the overflow of the watchdog timer—and the overflow causes the internal reset of the microcontroller. If there is no infinite loop, the count of the watchdog timer is reset frequently to prevent the overflow.

Explanation of the Code

Line 3:   `ENABLE_LEDS;`
This macro enables the LEDs.

Line 5:   `Init_WDT(void);`
Calls the subroutine to initialize the watchdog timer, which resets the system as the overflow occurs.

Line 6:   `ALL_LEDS_OFF();`
Switches off all the LEDs.

Lines 7–9: These are the lines with the bug which takes the program into an infinite loop. We start the loop, decrement the counter variable, and then increment the counter variable—the counter variable will not be anything other than -1 or 0.

Line 10:   `ALL_LEDS_ON();`
Switches on all the LEDs.

Line 11:   `WDT.WRITE.WINA = 0x5A00;`
This line is used to clear the value of TCNT periodically if the program executes without the infinite loop. If this line is not executed then the TCNT is not cleared to zero, which forces the overflow of the watchdog timer.

11.4 ADVANCED CONCEPTS OF THE WATCHDOG TIMER

11.4.1 Interval Timer Mode

To use WDT as an interval timer mode, set the TMS bit to 0 and the TME bit to 1 in TCSR. In interval timer mode, a timer interrupt WOVI is generated each time the TCNT overflows. As the TCNT overflows periodically, the timer interrupt is an interval timer interrupt.

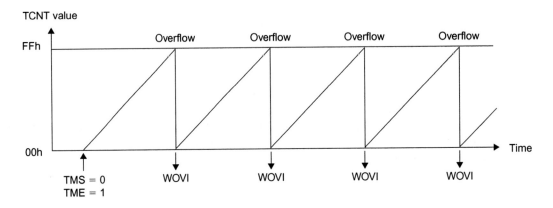

WOVI: An interval timer interrupt request is generated.

Figure 11.5 Interval timer mode operation. Source: *Hardware Manual*, page 23–8.

11.4.2 Independent Watchdog Timer (IWDT)

The independent watchdog timer (IWDT) is a watchdog timer for use independent of the conventional watchdog timer, which is for detecting programs with runaway execution and system crashes (*Hardware Manual*, page 1184). The IWDT is a 14-bit down counter which resets the system if an underflow of the timer count value occurs. The timer count value must be refreshed before the counter underflows.

Registers Used to Set Up IWDT: Table 11.5 shows the list of registers used to set up the IWDT.

IWDT Refresh Register (IWDTRR): The IWDT refresh register (IWDTRR) is used to refresh the timer down count value of the IWDT. The down count value of the IWDT is refreshed by passing 00h and FFh as a sequence to the IWDTRR. After the writing of FFh to IWDTRR, refreshing the down counter takes up to four cycles of the signal for counting.

TABLE 11.4   Specification of IWDT.

ITEM	SPECIFICATIONS
Clock for counting	OCOCLK, OCOCLK/16, OCOCLK/32, OCOCLK/64, OCOCLK/128, OCOCLK/256
Counter operation	Counting down by a 14-bit down-counter
Conditions for starting the counter	Counting can be started by refreshing the down-counter (write FFh after 00h has been written to the IWDTRR register).
Conditions for stopping the counter	■ Pin reset (the down-counter and other registers return to their initial values) ■ Generation of an underflow
Window facility	A refresh-permitted period and fresh-prohibited period may be set.
Reset-output sources of the IWDT	Underflow of the down-counter
Reading the value of the IWDT counter	The value reached in counting by the down-counter can be read out from a register (the IWDTSR).

Source: *Hardware Manual,* Table 24.1.

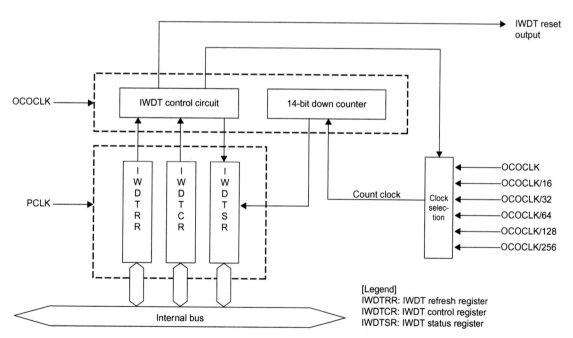

Figure 11.6   Block diagram of IWDT. Source: *Hardware Manual,* figure 24.1.

TABLE 11.5 List of Registers.

REGISTER NAME	SYMBOL	VALUE AFTER RESET	ADDRESS	ACCESS SIZE
IWDT refresh register	IWDTRR	FFh	0008 8030h	8
IWDT control register	IWDTCR	3303h	0008 8032h	16
IWDT status register	IWDTSR	0000h	0008 8034h	16

Source: *Hardware Manual*, Table 24.2.

After the counter value has been refreshed and the reset signal has been generated and released, the timer starts to count down from the value set up in the TOPS [1:0] bits in IWDT Control Register (IWDTCR).

IWDT Control Register (IWDTCR): The IWDTCR is a sixteen bit register in which only six bits are used for setting up the IWDT. The IWDT Control register (IWDTCR) is used to specify the time-out period for the down count of the timer. The time-out period in the bits TOPS [1:0] can only be changed between the release from the reset state and the first time the counter is refreshed. The writing to the IWDTCR is locked otherwise, because we don't want to change the time out period of the timer after the counting has started. The writing is only unlocked by the reset signal generated by the IWDT.

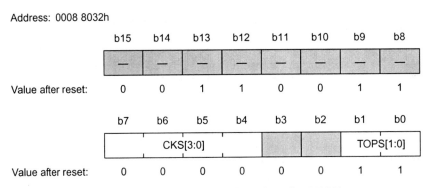

Figure 11.7 IWDT Control Register (IWDTCR).

Bit Description for IWDTCR

TOPS [1:0]: These bits in the IWDTCR are used to select the time-out period for the down count of the timer. The different possible values of the time-out period are 1024, 4096,

TABLE 11.6 Bit Description for IWDTCR.

BIT	SYMBOL	BIT NAME	DESCRIPTION	R/W
b1, b0	TOPS[1:0]	Time-out period selection	b1 b0	R/W
			0 0: 1024 cycles (03FFh)	
			0 1: 4096 cycles (0FFFh)	
			1 0: 8192 cycles (1FFFh)	
			1 1: 16384 cycles (3FFFh)	
b3, b2	—	(Reserved)	These bits are read as 0. The write value should be 0.	R/W
b7 to b4	CKS[3:0]	Clock selection	b7 b4	R/W
			0 0 – –: OCOCLK	
			0 1 0 0: OCOCLK/16	
			0 1 0 1: OCOCLK/32	
			0 1 1 0: OCOCLK/64	
			0 1 1 1: OCOCLK/128	
			1 – – –: OCOCLK/256	
b9, b8	—	(Reserved)	These bits are read as 1. The write value should be 1.	R/W
b11, b10	—	(Reserved)	These bits are read as 0. The write value should be 0.	R/W
b13, b12	—	(Reserved)	These bits are read as 1. The write value should be 1.	R/W
b15, b14	—	(Reserved)	These bits are read as 0. The write value should be 0.	R/W

Source: *Hardware Manual.*

8192 and 16384. The number of cycles for the time-out period is determined by the clock source selected by the CKS [3:0] bits.

CKS [3:0]: These bits are used to select the clock source for the IWDT. A minimum of 1024 cycles to a maximum of 4194304 cycles time-out period of the LOCO signal can be selected with the combination of TOPS [1:0] and CKS [3:0] bits. The different combinations of the time-out period is shown in Table 11.7.

TABLE 11.7 Different Combinations of TOPS [1:0] and CKS [3:0], with Corresponding Number of Cycles of the LOCO Signal.

CKS[3:0]				TOPS[1:0]		COUNT CLOCK	TIME-OUT PERIOD (NUMBER OF CYCLES)	CYCLES OF THE LOCO SIGNAL
0	0	—	—	0	0	OCOCLK	1024	1024
				0	1		4096	4096
				1	0		8192	8192
				1	1		16384	16384
0	1	0	0	0	0	OCOCLK/16	1024	16384
				0	1		4096	65536
				1	0		8192	131072
				1	1		16384	262144
0	1	0	1	0	0	OCOCLK/32	1024	32768
				0	1		4096	131072
				1	0		8192	262144
				1	1		16384	524288
0	1	1	0	0	0	OCOCLK/64	1024	65536
				0	1		4096	262144
				1	0		8192	524288
				1	1		16384	1048576
0	1	1	1	0	0	OCOCLK/128	1024	131072
				0	1		4096	524288
				1	0		8192	1048576
				1	1		16384	2097152
1	—	—	—	0	0	OCOCLK/256	1024	262144
				0	1		4096	1048576
				1	0		8192	2097152
				1	1		16384	4194304

Source: *Hardware Manual,* Table 24.3.

IWDT Status Register (IWDTSR): The IWDTSR is a sixteen bit register which contains the underflow information and the counter value of the down counter. This register is initialized only by the IWDT reset source.

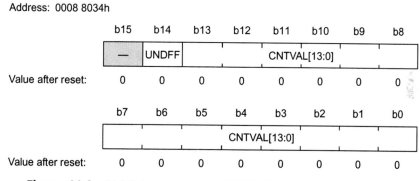

Address: 0008 8034h

b15	b14	b13	b12	b11	b10	b9	b8
—	UNDFF			CNTVAL[13:0]			

Value after reset: 0   0   0   0   0   0   0   0

b7	b6	b5	b4	b3	b2	b1	b0
			CNTVAL[13:0]				

Value after reset: 0   0   0   0   0   0   0   0

Figure 11.8   IWDT Status Register (IWDTSR). Source: *Hardware Manual.*

Bit Description of IWDTSR

CNTVAL [13:0]: These bits of IWDTSR can be read to check the count value of the down counter.

UNDFF: This bit of IWDTSR shows the state of underflow. If this bit is set to 1, the down counter has underflowed. If this bit is cleared to 0, the down counter has not underflowed.

Operation of Independent Watchdog Timer

The TOPS [1:0] bits of IWDTCR are used to select the time out period of the IWDT. The writing to IWDTCR is unlocked only after the reset from the IWDT. When the IWDT is refreshed, the timer counts down from the value set in the TOPS [1:0] bits.

In the normal execution of the program, the IWDT is refreshed at regular intervals. If the refresh of the IWDT does not occur, that shows that the program has entered into an infinite loop, has gotten stuck in a long process, or is not working in the desired manner. The underflow flag is set to 1 and the reset source from the IWDT is activated to reset the system. After the output of the reset signal, the down counter is initialized and the writing to the IWDTCR is unlocked. After the system has been re-booted, counting down is again started by refreshing the counter. Figure 11.9 shows an example of the operation of the IWDT.

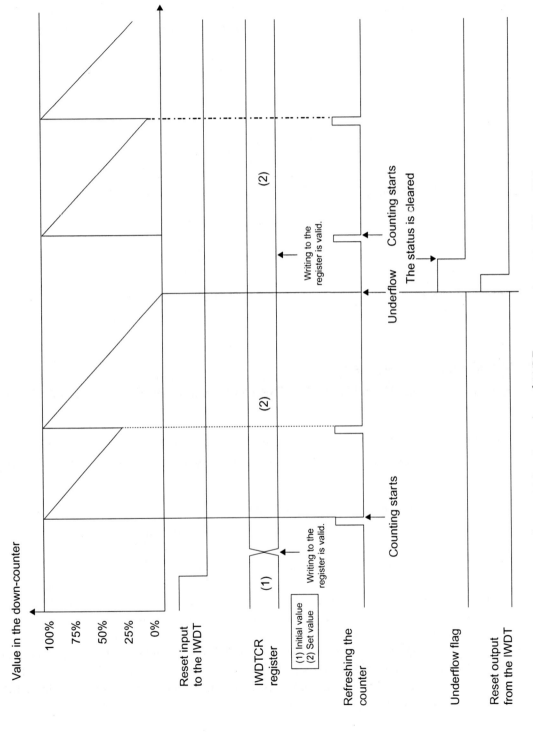

Figure 11.9   Operation of IWDT. Source: *Hardware Manual,* Figure 24.2.

11.5   COMPLEX EXAMPLES

11.5.1   Example 1: Interval Timer Mode of a Watchdog Timer

In the next example of code a subroutine has been provided for setting up the WDT as an interval timer. This function should be called before the main function to initialize the WDT in interval timer mode. The interval timer has been set up for a clock with a prescaler division factor of 8192 and an interrupt occurs as the timer overflows. Therefore, code can be added to the ISR if needed.

```
1. void init_WDT_intervaltimer(){
2.     IEN(WDT,WOVI) = 0;
3.     IPR(WDT,WOVI) = 3;
4.     IEN(WDT,WOVI) = 1;
5.     WDT.WRITE.WINA = 0x5AFF;    //Writing data into TCNT
6.     WDT.WRITE.WINB = 0x5A1F;    //Writing data into RSTCSR
7.     WDT.WRITE.WINA = 0xA53D;    //Starting the timer
8. }
```

Explanation of the Code

Line 2: `IEN (WDT, WOVI) = 0;`
When setting the priority level for an interrupt, the interrupt source should be disabled. So this instruction disables the WDT overflow interrupt (WOVI).

Line 3: `IPR (WDT, WOVI) = 3;`
This instruction sets a priority level of 3 to the WDT overflow interrupt (WOVI).

Line 4: `IEN (WDT, WOVI) = 1;`
This instruction enables the WDT overflow interrupt.

Line 5: `WDT.WRITE.WINA = 0x5AFF;`
This instruction writes the timer count value to the timer counter register (TCNT) of WDT through WINA register.

Line 6: `WDT.WRITE.WINB = 0x5A1F;`
This instruction writes a value of 1Fh to RSTCSR register. The internal reset enable bit (RSTE) in RSTCSR is disabled.

Line 7: `WDT.WRITE.WINA = 0xA53D;`
This instruction is used to write the 3Dh value to the TCSR register. The CKS [2:0] bits are set to 101b for a prescaler division factor of 8192. The timer mode select (TMS) bit is cleared to 0, which selects the interval timer mode of WDT. The timer enable (TME) bit is set to 1 which starts the timer.

11.5.2 Example 2: Setting Up of IWDT

The following is the subroutine to set up the watchdog timer for a clock source of OCOCLK/16 with a time out period of 4096 cycles. The IWDT down counts from the value set up by the bits in IWDTCR register and as the underflow occurs the system will reset.

```
1. void Init_IWDT(void){
2.    IWDT.IWDTCR.BIT.CKS = 4;
3.    IWDT.IWDTCR.BIT.TOPS = 1;
4. }
```

We can also use a single instruction by writing a word into the IWDTCR register.

```
IWDT.IWDTCR.WORD = 0x3340;
```

Explanation of the Code

Line 2:   `IWDT.IWDTCR.BIT.CKS = 4;`
This line is used to set up the value for CKS [3:0] bits in IWDTCR register; for selecting a prescaler division factor of 16 for clock source OCOCLK, a value 0100b should be written to CKS [3:0] bits.

Line 3:   `IWDT.IWDTCR.BIT.TOPS = 1;`
This line is used to set up the value for TOPS [1:0] bits in IWDTCR register. For selecting a timeout period of 4096 cycles, a value 01b should be written to TOPS [1:0] bits.

11.6   BROWNOUT CONDITION

11.6.1 How Brownout Occurs

A brownout condition in a microcontroller occurs when the supply voltage for the microcontroller temporarily goes below a threshold value (Vdet). Below this threshold value, the microcontroller may malfunction. There is also a blackout condition in which the microcontroller will have a total loss of electricity. In a brownout condition, some operations may work but in a blackout condition none of the operations will be active.

11.6.2 Automatically Detecting a Brownout Condition

The main purpose of automatically detecting the brownout condition is to prevent the corruption of processor critical information. Whenever the brownout condition is detected, the internal reset from the voltage detection circuit should keep the processor in reset condition until the voltage increases above the threshold value (Vdet).

The RX62N MCU group provides two low-voltage detection (LVD) circuits based on analog comparators. Each compares the supply voltage Vcc against a fixed reference voltage (Vdet1 or Vdet2). If the supply voltage is not above the reference voltage, the LVD can reset the processor or generate an interrupt, based on the LVD configuration. Because there are two LVD comparators, one can be configured to warn of a likely impending power failure (when Vdet2 is reached) using an interrupt. This will trigger the saving of critical data and putting outputs into safe states (e.g. turning off motors). The second LVD can be configured to reset the processor when Vdet1 is reached.

11.7   RECAP

A watchdog timer is one of the tools in the microcontroller, which gets the system out of unexpected errors or infinite loops. The watchdog timer count is refreshed frequently so that the overflow does not occur in the general flow of the program. When the overflow occurs, it implies that the timer count has been not refreshed and the program is not functioning in the way it should. So the watchdog timer resets the system whenever it overflows. The RX62N/RX621 group has two watchdog timers, WDT and IWDT. The WDT can be used in watchdog timer mode and interval timer mode. The registers are used to set up the WDT and IWDT. WINA and WINB registers are used to write data to WDT registers. To refresh the timer count for IWDT, two length sequence 00h and FFh should be written to the timer counter register of IWDT.

11.8   REFERENCES

Hardware Manual, Renesas 32-Bit Microcomputer, RX Family/RX600 Series. Renesas Electronics America, Inc., 2010. Print.

11.9   EXERCISES

1. List the registers used to set up the WDT and describe the importance of the registers.
2. List the registers used to set up the IWDT and describe the importance of the registers.
3. What registers used to write data into RSTCR, TCNT, and TCSR registers with pseudo code?
4. Draw a flowchart explaining when and how a WDT resets the system.

5. What is the maximum interval time of the WDT in interval timer mode? Show with calculations.

6. Write pseudo code to reset the microcontroller when a brownout condition occurs (use the pins available on the microcontroller to detect the brownout condition).

7. Write the Code to set up the WDT in watchdog timer mode with a 167.1 ms clock, with no internal reset, and to start the counting of the timer.

8. Write the Code to refresh the timer counter register of the IWDT.

9. Write the Code to set up the WDT to reset the microcontroller every 1s.

10. Write the Code to set up the IWDT to reset the microcontroller every 1s.

11. Write a program to create a software bug, and reset the microcontroller using IWDT when the bug occurs.

Chapter Twelve

Designing Responsive and Real-Time Systems

12.1 LEARNING OBJECTIVES

Most embedded systems have multiple independent tasks running at the same time. Which activity should the microprocessor perform first? This decision determines how **responsive** the system is, which then affects how determines how fast a processor we must use, how much time we have for running intensive control algorithms, how much energy we can save, and many other factors. In this chapter we will discuss how the microprocessor schedules its tasks.

12.2 MOTIVATION

Consider an embedded system which controls a doorbell in a house. When a person at the front door presses the switch, the bell should ring inside the house. The system's **responsiveness** describes how long it takes from pressing the switch to sounding the bell. It is easy to create a very responsive embedded system with only one task. The scheduling approach shown below is an obvious and simple approach.

```
1. void main (void){
2.    init_system();
3.    while(1){
4.       if(switch == PRESSED){
5.          Ring_The_Bell();
6.       }
7.    }
8. }
```

Our doorbell is very responsive. In fact, we like it so much that we decide to add in a smoke detector and a very loud beeper so we can be warned about a possible fire. We also add a burglar detector and another alarm bell. This results in the code shown on the next page.

```
1. void main (void){
2.    init_system();
3.    while(1){
4.       if(switch == PRESSED){
5.          Ring_The_Doorbell();
6.       }
7.       if(Burglar_Detected() == TRUE){
8.          Sound_The_Burglar_Alarm();
9.       }
10.      if(Smoke_Detected() == TRUE){
11.         Sound_The_Fire_Alarm();
12.      }
13.   }
14. }
```

Going from one task to three tasks has complicated the situation significantly.[1] How should we share the processor's time between these tasks?

- How long of a delay are we willing to accept between smoke detection and the fire alarm sounding? And the delay between the switch being pressed and the doorbell sounding?
- Should the system try to detect smoke or burglars while the doorbell is playing?
- Should the doorbell work while the smoke alarm is being sounded? What about when the burglar alarm is sounding?
- Which subsystem should the processor check first: the doorbell, the smoke detector, or the burglar detector? Or should it just alternate between them?
- Should the doorbell switch be checked as often as the smoke and burglar detectors, or at a different rate?
- What if the person at the door presses the switch again before the doorbell finishes sounding? Should that be detected?

Now that we have to share the processor, we have to worry about how long the bell rings and the alarms sound. If we use a doorbell ringtone which lasts for thirty seconds, then Ring_The_Bell will take at least thirty seconds to run. During this time, we won't know if our house is burning or being robbed. Similarly, what if the firemen come when the alarm is sounding? How quickly should the doorbell respond in that case?

---

[1] In fact, any number of tasks greater than one complicates the situation!

12.3   SCHEDULING FUNDAMENTALS

This example reveals the two fundamental issues in scheduling for responsive systems.

- If we have multiple tasks ready to run, which one do we run first? This decision defines the **ordering** of task execution.
- Do we allow one task to interrupt or **preempt** another task (or even itself)?

Both of these decisions will determine the system's **responsiveness** (measured by response time):

- How long will it take for the **most important** task to **start running? To finish running?** Does this depend on how long any other tasks take to run, and how often they run?
- How long will it take for the **least important** task to **start running? To finish running?** We expect it will depend on how long all the other tasks take to run, and how often they run.
- If we allow tasks to preempt each other, then a task may start running very soon but finish much later, after multiple possible preemptions.

These response times in turn affect many performance-related issues, such as these:

- How fast must the processor's clock rate be to ensure that nothing happens "late"?
- How much time do we have available for running compute-intensive algorithms?
- How much energy can we save by putting the processor to sleep?
- How much power can we save by slowing down the processor?

Figure 12.1 shows a visual representation of some arbitrary scheduling activity. Task *A* is released (becomes ready to run) at the first vertical bar. There is some **latency** between the release and when the task starts running, due to other processing in the system and scheduler overhead. Similarly, there is a **response time** which measures how long it takes task *A* to complete its processing. Some scheduling approaches allow a task to be preempted (delayed) after it has started running, which will increase the response time.

12.3.1   Task Ordering

The first factor affecting response time is the **order in which we run tasks.** We could always follow the same order by using a **static** schedule. The code shown for the Doorbell/

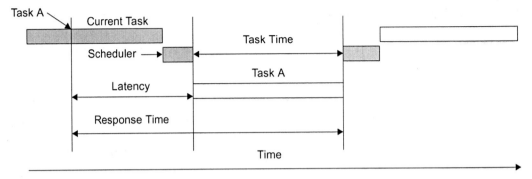

Figure 12.1 Diagram and definitions of scheduler concepts.

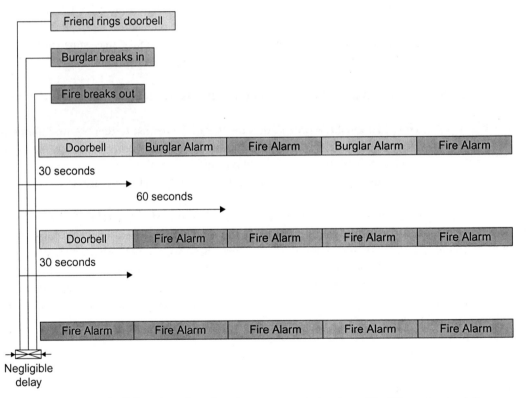

Figure 12.2 Doorbell/fire alarm/burglar alarm system behavior with different scheduling approaches.

Fire Alarm/Burglar Alarm uses a static schedule. Figure 12.2a shows an interesting case. If a burglar broke in and a fire broke out just after someone pressed the switch to ring the doorbell; we wouldn't find out about the burglar for almost thirty seconds and the fire for about sixty seconds. We probably do not want these large delays for such critical notifications.

We can change the order based on current conditions (e.g., if the house is on fire) using a **dynamic** schedule. An obvious way to do this is to reschedule after finishing each task. A dynamic schedule lets us improve the responsiveness of some tasks at the price of delaying other tasks. For example, let's prioritize fire detection over burglar detection over the doorbell.

```
1.  void main (void){
2.     init_system();
3.     while(1){
4.        if(Smoke_Detected() == TRUE){
5.           Sound_The_Fire_Alarm();
6.        } else if (Burglar_Detected() == TRUE) {
7.           Sound_The_Burglar_Alarm();
8.        } else if (switch == PRESSED) {
9.              Ring_The_Doorbell();
10.       }
11.    }
12. }
```

Notice how this code is different—there are **else** clauses added, which change the schedule to a dynamic one. As long as smoke is detected, Sound_The_Fire_Alarm() will run repeatedly. The burglar alarm and doorbell will be ignored until no more smoke is detected. Similarly, burglar detection will disable the doorbell. This is shown in Figure 12.2b.

This **strict prioritization** may or may not be appropriate for a given system. We may want to ensure some **fairness,** perhaps by limiting how often a task can run. Later in this chapter we present a periodic table-based approach which is much better than this hard-coded design.

12.3.2 Task Preemption

The second aspect to consider is whether one task can **preempt** another task. Consider our thirty-second doorbell ringtone—the task Ring_The_Doorbell will **run to completion** without stopping or yielding the processor.

What if a burglar breaks the window a split second after an accomplice rings the doorbell? In this worst-case scenario, we won't find out about the burglar (or a possible fire) for thirty seconds.[2] Let's say we'd like to find out within one second. We have several options:

- Limit the maximum duration for the doorbell ringtone to one second.
- Add another microprocessor which is dedicated to playing the doorbell ringtone. This will raise system costs.
- Break the Ring_The_Doorbell function into thirty separate pieces (e.g., with a state machine or separate functions), each of which takes only one second to run. This code will be hard to maintain.
- Allow the smoke and burglar detection code to preempt Ring_The_Doorbell. We will need to use a more sophisticated task scheduler which can (1) preempt and resume tasks, and (2) detect events which trigger switching and starting tasks. We will not need to break apart any source code. This will make code maintenance easier. However, we introduce the vulnerability to race conditions for shared data, and we also will need more memory (enough to hold each task's stack simultaneously).

Let's apply this preemption option to our system. We assign the highest priority to fire detection, then burglar detection, and then the doorbell. Now we have the response timeline shown in Figure 12.2c. The system starts sounding the doorbell after the switch is pressed, but as soon as the fire is detected, the scheduler preempts the Ring_The_Doorbell and starts running Sound_The_Fire_Alarm. We find out about the fire essentially immediately, without having to wait for the doorbell to finish sounding.

As with the previous example, we have strict prioritization without control of how often tasks can run. As long as smoke is detected, Sound_The_Fire_Alarm() will run repeatedly. The burglar alarm and doorbell will be ignored until no more smoke is detected. Similarly, burglar detection will disable the doorbell.

12.3.3 Fairness and Prioritization

These examples all show one weakness of our system: prioritizing some tasks over others can lead to starvation of lower priority tasks (they may never get to run). For some systems this is acceptable, but for others it is not. Here are two ways of providing some kind of fairness:

- We can allow multiple tasks to share the same priority level. If both tasks are ready to run, we alternate between executing each of them (whether by allowing each task to run to completion, or by preempting each periodically).

---

[2] Imagine what Thomas Crown, James Bond, or Jason Bourne could do in that time!

▪ We can limit how often each task can run by defining the task frequency. This is the common approach used for designers of real-time systems. Note that we can still allow only one task per priority level.

12.3.4 Response Time and Preemption

For the two non-preemptive examples in Figure 12.2, notice how the response time for the fire alarm and the burglar alarm depends on **how long the doorbell sounds.** However, for the preemptive approach those response times are **independent** of how long the doorbell sounds. This is the major benefit of a preemptive scheduling approach: it makes a task's response time essentially **independent** of all processing by lower priority tasks.[3] Instead, only **higher priority** tasks can delay that task.

In Figure 12.3 we present these relationships in a graph. Tasks and ISRs are nodes, while edges (or arcs) are timing dependences. For example, the edge from B to C indicates

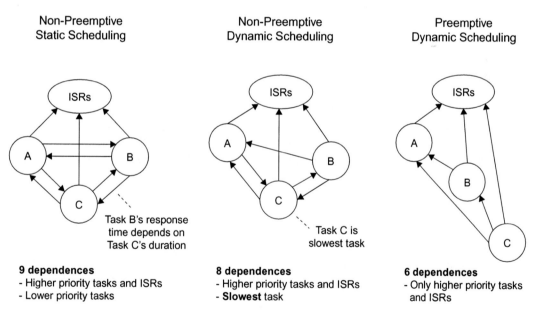

Figure 12.3 Timing dependences of different scheduling approaches.

---

[3] There are exceptions when tasks can communicate with each other with semaphores and other such mechanisms, but that is beyond the scope of this introductory text.

that task B's response time depends on task C's duration. We can now compare timing dependences for these three classes of scheduler.

- With the non-preemptive static scheduler, each task's response time depends on the duration of all other tasks and ISRs, so there are nine dependences.[4]
- With the non-preemptive dynamic scheduler, we assign priorities to tasks (A > B > C). In general, a task no longer depends on lower priority tasks, so we have more timing independence and isolation. This accounts for six dependences. The exception is the **slowest** or longest duration task, which is C in this example. If task C has started running, it will delay any other task, regardless of priority. So the higher priority tasks A and B each have a dependence edge leading to task C in Figure 12.3, which results in a total of eight dependences.
- With the preemptive dynamic scheduler, we also prioritize the tasks (A > B > C). Because a task can preempt any lower priority task, the slowest task no longer matters. Each task can be preempted by an ISR, so there are three dependence edges to begin with. Task A cannot be preempted by B or C, so it adds no new edges. Task B can be preempted by task A, which adds one edge. Finally, task C can be preempted by task A or B, which adds two more edges. As a result we have only six dependences. Most importantly, these dependence edges **all point upwards.**[5] This means that in order to determine the response time for a task, we only need to consider **higher priority tasks.** This makes the analysis much easier.

The real-time system research and development communities have developed extensive precise mathematical methods for calculating worst-case response times, determining if deadlines can ever be missed, and other characteristics of a system. These methods consider semaphores, task interactions, scheduler overhead, and all sorts of other complexities of practical implementations. We do not discuss them here as they are beyond the scope of this text.

12.3.5 Stack Memory Requirements

The non-preemptive scheduling approaches do not require as much data memory as the preemptive approaches. In particular, the non-preemptive approach requires only **one call stack,** while a preemptive approach typically requires **one call stack per task.**[6]

---

[4] Of course, if task code can disable interrupts, then there will be three more edges leading from the ISRs back to the tasks! That would be a total of twelve dependences, which is quite a few to handle.

[5] This is called a DAG or directed acyclic graph.

[6] There are several ways to reduce the number of stacks needed for preemptive scheduling, but they are beyond the scope of this text.

The function call stack holds a function's state information such as return address and limited lifetime variables (e.g., automatic variables, which only last for the duration of a function). Without task preemption, task execution does not overlap in time, so all tasks can share the same stack. Preemption allows tasks to preempt each other at essentially any point in time. Trying to reuse the same stack space for different tasks would lead to corruption of this information on the stack. For example, task B is running. Function B3 in task B calls function B4. The scheduler then preempts task B to run the higher priority task A, which was running function A2. Function A2 completes and it expects to return to function A1, which called A2. However, the call stack has function B3's information on the stack, so task A will start executing function B3! And so the system fails to operate correctly.

As a result of these memory requirements for preemptive scheduling approaches, there are many cost-sensitive embedded systems which use a non-preemptive scheduler to minimize RAM sizes and therefore costs.

12.3.6 Interrupts

Interrupts are a special case of preemption with dedicated hardware and compiler support. They can be added to any of these scheduling approaches in order to provide faster, time-critical processing. In fact, for many systems **only** interrupt service routines are needed for the application's work. The main loop is simply an infinite loop which keeps putting the processor into a low-power idle mode.

When designing a system which splits between ISRs and task code, one must strike a balance. The more work which is placed in an ISR, the slower the response time for other processing (whether tasks or other ISRs[7]). The standard approach is to perform time-critical processing in the ISR (e.g., unloading a character from the UART received data buffer) and deferring remaining work for task code (pushing that character in a FIFO from which the task will eventually read). ISR execution duration affects the response time for other code, so it is included in the response time calculations described in Section 12.3.4 and in Figure 12.3.

There are many good texts which suggest approaches for architecting ISRs; please see the references list.

---

[7] It is possible to make ISRs interruptable, but this introduces many new ways to build the system wrong. Hence it is discouraged.

12.4   TASK MANAGEMENT

12.4.1   Task States

A task will be in one of several possible states. The scheduler and the task code itself both affect which state is active. With a **non-preemptive dynamic scheduler,** a task can be in any one of the states[8] shown in Figure 12.4a:

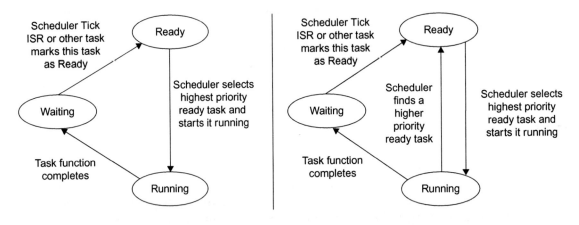

Non-preemptive Dynamic Scheduler   Preemptive Dynamic Scheduler

Figure 12.4   Task states and transitions for different schedulers.

- **Waiting** for the scheduler to decide that this task is ready to run. For example, a task which asked the scheduler to delay it for 500 ms will be in this state for that amount of time.
- **Ready to start running** but not running yet. There may be a higher-priority task which is running. As this task has not started running, no automatic variables have been initialized, and there is no activation record.
- **Running** on the processor. The task **runs to the completion** of the task function, at which point the scheduler resumes execution and the task is moved to the waiting state. Automatic variables have been initialized, and there is at least one activation record on the stack frame for this task. A single processor system can have only one task in this state.

---

[8] We consider preemption by an ISR as a separate state. However, since it operates automatically and saves and restores system context, we consider it as a separate enhancement to the RTC scheduler and leave it out of our diagrams. In fact, the scheduler relies on a tick ISR to track time and move tasks between certain states.

Consider a task which needs to write a block of data to flash memory. After issuing a write command to the flash memory controller, it may take some significant amount of time (e.g., 10 ms) to program the block. We have two options with a non-preemptive kernel:

■ Our task can use a busy wait loop until the flash block programming is complete. The task remains in the **running** state while programming. This approach delays other processing and wastes processor cycles.

■ We can break the task into a state machine so that task state one issues the write command, task state two checks to see if the programming is done, and task state three continues with the task's processing. The task executes task state two each time it is called as long as programming is not done. The task spends most of its time **waiting,** with occasional brief periods **running** when executing the code for task state two. This approach complicates program design but is practical for smaller systems. However, it grows unwieldy for complex systems.

Allowing tasks to **preempt** each other reduces response time and simplifies application design. With preemption, each task need not be built with a run-to-completion structure. Instead, the task can yield the processor to other tasks, or it can be preempted by a higher-priority task with more urgent processing. For example, our task can tell the scheduler "I don't have anything else to do for the next 10 ms, so you can run a different task." The scheduler then will save the state of this task, and swap in the state of the next highest priority task which is ready to run. This introduces another way to move from running to waiting, as well as a way to move from running to ready. We examine these in detail next.

12.4.2 Transitions between States

We now examine the ways in which a task can move between the various states. These rules govern how the system behaves, and therefore set some ground rules for how we should design our system.

■ The transition from **ready to running:**
  □ In a non-preemptive system, when the scheduler is ready to run a task, it selects the highest priority ready task and moves it to the running state, typically by calling it as a subroutine (as there is no context to restore).
  □ In a preemptive system, when the kernel is ready to run a task, it selects the highest priority ready task and moves it to the running state by restoring its context to the processor.

■ The transition from **running to waiting:**
  □ In a non-preemptive system, the only way a task can move from running to waiting is if it **completes** (returns from the task function). At this point there is

no more execution context for the task (return addresses, automatic variables), so there is no data to save or restore.

- □ In a preemptive system, the task can yield the processor.[9] For example, it can request a delay ("Hey, RTOS! Wake me up in at least 10 ms!") or it can wait or **pend** on an event ("Hey, RTOS! Wake me up when I get a message in my mailbox called foo!"). This makes application programming much easier, as mentioned before. At this point there still is execution context, so the kernel must save it for later restoration.

- ▨ The transition from **waiting to ready:**
  - □ In a non-preemptive system such as the RTC scheduler above, the timer tick ISR moves the task by setting the run flag. Alternatively, another task can set the run flag to request for this task to run.
  - ⊔ In a preemptive system, the kernel is notified that some event has occurred. For example, time delay has expired, or a task has sent a message to the mailbox called foo. The kernel knows which task is waiting for this event, so it moves that particular task from the waiting state to the ready state.

- ▨ The transition from **running to ready:**
  - □ In a non-preemptive system this transition does not exist, as a task cannot be preempted.
  - □ In a preemptive system, when the kernel determines a higher priority task is ready to run, it will save the context of the currently running task, and move that task to the ready state.

12.4.3 Context Switching for Preemptive Systems

In preemptive systems, some of these state transitions require the scheduler to save a task's execution context and restore another task's context to ensure programs execute correctly. This is called **context switching** and involves accessing the processor's general-purpose registers.

Figure 12.5 shows a view of a processor and its memory as it is executing task A in a system with two tasks (A and B). The CPU uses the program counter PC to fetch the next instruction to execute, and various pointer registers refer to locations in memory such as the task's stack, etc. The CPU also has general purpose registers which are used to hold the programs data and intermediate computation results.

In order to perform a context switch from task A to task B correctly, we must first copy all of this task-specific processor register information to a storage location (e.g., task

---

[9] What happens if the task function finishes executing depends on the RTOS. The task could move to the waiting state, or to a terminated state.

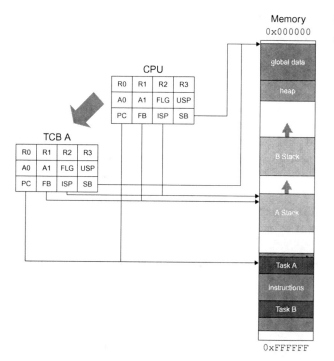

Figure 12.5 Saving task A's context from the CPU.

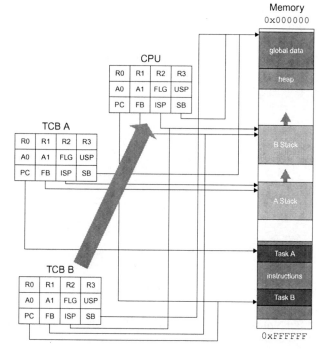

Figure 12.6 Restoring task B's context to the CPU.

control block (TCB) A). Second, we must copy all of the data from TCB B into the CPU's registers. This operation is shown in Figure 12.6. Now the CPU will be able to resume execution of task B where it left off.

12.5   SHARING DATA SAFELY

Preemption among tasks introduces a vulnerability to data race conditions. Now a task can be considered to be as bug-prone and difficult to debug as an ISR! The system can fail in new ways when:

- Multiple tasks or ISRs share data,[10] or
- Multiple instances of a function can execute concurrently.

In order to prevent these failures we need to be careful when designing our system.

12.5.1   Data Shared Objects

If a data object is accessed by code which can be interrupted (is not *atomic*), then there is a risk of data corruption. *Atomic* code is the smallest part of a program that executes without interruption. Generally a single machine instruction is atomic,[11] but sequences of instructions are not atomic unless interrupts are disabled.

Consider an example where task A starts modifying object O. Task B preempts it before it finishes. At this point in time object O is corrupted, as it is only partially updated. If task B needs to read or write O, the computation results will be incorrect and the system will likely fail.

```
1. unsigned time_minutes, time_seconds;
2. void task1 (void){
3.    time_seconds++;
4.    if(time_seconds >= 60){
5.       time_minutes++;
6.       time_seconds = 0;
7.    }
8. }
```

------

[10] Hardware registers which change outside of the program's control also introduce problems but we do not discuss them further here.

[11] Some instruction sets have long instructions (e.g., string copy, block move) which can be interrupted, in which case those instructions are not atomic.

```
 9. void task2 (void){
10.    unsigned elapsed_sec;
11.    elapsed_seconds = time_minutes * 60 + time_seconds;
12. }
```

Here is a more specific example. Our shared object is a pair of variables which measure the current time in minutes and seconds. Task1 runs once per second to increment the seconds, and possibly the minutes as well. Task2 calculates how many total seconds have elapsed since time zero. There are data races possible:

- If task1 is preempted between lines 4 and 5 or lines 5 and 6, then when task2 runs it will only have a partially updated version of the current time, and elapsed_ seconds will be incorrect.
- If task2 is preempted during line 11, then it is possible that timeinutes is read **before** task1 updates it and time_seconds is read **after** task 1 updates it. Again, this leads to a corrupted elapsed_seconds value.

12.5.2 Function Reentrancy

Another type of shared data problem comes with the use of non-reentrant functions. In this case, the problem arises from multiple instances of the **same function** accessing the same object. Consider the following example:

```
 1. void task1 ( ){
 2.    . . . . . . . . . . . . . . .
 3.    swap(&x, &y);
 4.    . . . . . . . . . . . . . .
 5. }
 6. void task2 ( ){
 7.    . . . . . . . . . . . . . .
 8.    swap(&p, &q);
 9.    . . . . . . . . . . . . . .
10. }
11. int Temp;
12. void swap (*i, *j ){
13.    Temp = *j;
14.    *j = *i;
15.    *i = Temp;
16. }
```

Suppose task1 is running and calls the swap function. After line 13 is executed, task2 becomes ready. If task2 has a higher priority, task1 is suspended and task2 is serviced. Later, task1 resumes to line 14. Since Temp is a shared variable, it is not stored in the TASK subroutine shared data stack. When task1 line 15 is executed, variable x (of task1 pointed by variable pointer i) gets the wrong value. Such function executions should not be suspended in between or shared by more than one task. Such functions are called **non-reentrant.** The code which can have multiple simultaneous, interleaved, or nested invocations which will not interfere with each other is called reentrant code. These types of code are important for parallel processing, recursive functions or subroutines, and for interrupt handling. An example of a reentrant code is as follows:

```
1. void swap (*i, *j ){
2.    static int Temp;
3.    Temp = *j;
4.    *j = *i;
5.    *i = Temp;
6. }
```

Since the variable Temp is declared within the function, if any other task interrupts the execution of the swap function, the variable Temp will be stored in the corresponding task's stack and will be retrieved when the task resumes its function. In most cases, especially in a multi-processing environment, the non-reentrant functions should be eliminated. A function can be checked for its reentrancy based on these three rules:

1. A reentrant function may not use variables in a non-atomic way unless they are stored on the stack of the calling task or are the private variables of that task.
2. A reentrant function may not call other functions which are not reentrant.
3. A reentrant function may not use the hardware in a non-atomic way.

12.5.3 High-Level Languages and Atomicity

We can identify **some but not all** non-atomic operations by examining high-level source code. Since the processor executes machine code rather than a high-level language such as C or Java, we can't identify all possible non-atomic operations just by examining the C source code. Something may seem atomic in C but actually be implemented by multiple machine instructions. We need to examine the assembly code to know for sure. Let's examine the following function and determine whether it is reentrant or not:

EXAMPLE 1

```
1. static int event_count;
2. void event_counter (void){
3.    ++event_count;
4. }
```

Example 1 in assembly language:

```
1. MOV.L #0000100CH, R4
2. MOV.L [R4], R5
3. ADD #1H, R5
4. MOV.L R5, [R4]
5. RTS
```

Consider example 1, and then apply the first rule. Does it use shared variable `event_count` in an atomic way? The `++event_count` operation is not atomic, and that single line of C code is implemented with three lines of assembly code (lines two through four). The processor loads R4 with a pointer to event_count, copies the value of event_count into register R5, adds 1 to R5, and then stores it back into memory. Hence, example 1 **is non-reentrant.**

However, what if the processor instruction set supports in-place memory operations? The RX architecture does not, but many others do. In that case, the assembly code could look like this:

Example 1 in assembly language, compiled for a different processor architecture:

```
1. MOV.L #0000100CH, A0
2. ADD #1H, [A0]
3. RTS
```

This code **is reentrant,** since there is only one instruction needed to update the value of the event count. Instruction 1 is only loading a pointer to the event count, so interrupting between 1 and 2 does not cause a problem.

EXAMPLE 2

```
1. void add_sum (int *j){
2.    ++(*j);
3.    DisplayString(LCDLINE1, Int_to_ascii(*j));
4. }
```

Now consider example 2. Even though `line 2` in this example is not atomic, the `variable *j` is task's private variable, hence rule 1 is not breached. But consider `line 3`. Is the function `DisplayString` reentrant? That depends on the code of `DisplayString`, which depends on the user. Unless we are sure that the `DisplayString` function is reentrant, example 2 is considered to be non-reentrant. So every time a user codes a function, he has to make sure the function is reentrant to avoid erroneous results.

12.5.4 Shared-Data Solutions and Protection

In the previous section, we discussed the problems of using shared data in a RTOS environment. In this section we shall study some methods to protect the shared data. The solutions provided in this section may not be ideal for all applications. The user must judge which solution may work best for the application.

Disable Interrupts

One of the easiest methods is to disable the interrupts during the critical section of the task. Disabling the interrupts may not take more than one machine cycle to execute, but will increase the worst case response time of all other code, including other interrupt service routines. Once the critical section, or shared variable section, of the code is executed, the interrupt masking be restored to its previous state (either enabled or disabled). The user must be cautious while disabling or enabling interrupts, because if interrupts are disabled for too long, the system may fail to meet the timing requirements. See Chapter 9, Using Interrupts with Peripherals, to find out how to disable and restore interrupt masking state. A simple example of disabling interrupts is as follows:

```
 1. #define TRUE 1
 2. #define FALSE 0
 3. static int error;
 4. static int error_count;
 5. void error_counter ( ){
 6.    if(error == TRUE){
 7.       SAVE_INT_STATE;
 8.       DISABLE_INTS;
 9.       error_count++;
10.       error = FALSE;
11.       RESTORE_INT_STATE;
12.    }
13. }
```

Disabling and restoring the interrupt masking state requires only one or a few machine cycles. Disabling interrupts must take place only at critical sections to avoid increasing response time excessively. Also, while restoring the interrupt masking state the user must keep in mind the need to enable only those interrupts that were active (enabled) before they were disabled. Determining the interrupt masking status can be achieved by referring to the **interrupt mask register.** The Interrupt mask register keeps track of which interrupts are enabled and disabled.

Use a Lock

Another solution is to associate every shared variable with a lock variable, which is also declared globally. If a function uses the shared variable, then it sets the lock variable and once it has finished process, it resets the lock variable. Every function must test the lock variable before accessing it. If the lock variable is already set, the task should inform the scheduler to be rescheduled once the variable becomes available. Since only one variable has to be checked every time before accessing the data, using lock variables simplifies the data structure and I/O devices access. Consider the following example for using a lock:

```
1.  unsigned int var;
2.  char lock_var;
3.  void task_var ( ){
4.     unsigned int sum;
5.     if(lock_var == 0){
6.        lock_var = 1;
7.        var = var + sum;
8.        lock_var = 0;
9.     }
10.    else {
11.       /* message to scheduler to check var
12.       and reschedule */
13.    }
14. }
```

Since it takes more than one clock cycle to check whether a variable is available and use a lock on it, the interrupts have to be disabled. Once again when the lock has to be released, the interrupts should be disabled since locking and releasing the variable is a critical part of the code. Interrupts must be enabled whenever possible to lower the interrupt service response time. If the variable is not available, the scheduler is informed about the lock and the task goes into a waiting state.

Microprocessors such as the Renesas RX support Bit Test and Set instructions can perform a test and set in one atomic machine instruction, and therefore do not require an interrupt disable/enable lock around semaphore usage.

The challenge with this approach is determining what to do in lines 11 and 12 if there is no scheduler support. There may be no easy way to tell the scheduler to reschedule this task when the lock variable becomes available again.

RTOS-Provided Semaphore

Most operating systems provide locks to shared variables through the use of *semaphores*. A semaphore is a mechanism that uses most of the multitasking kernels to protect shared data and to synchronize two tasks. A semaphore is very much similar to the variable lock process explained in the Section 12.4.3. The main difference is that the OS takes care of initializing and handling the locks, so the implementation is much more likely to be correct than if you try to create your own lock.

There are two types of semaphores—*binary semaphores* and *counting semaphores*. Binary semaphores take two values, 0 or 1. A counting semaphore takes a value between 0 and $2^N - 1$, where N is the number of bits used for the semaphore. In this book we consider only the binary semaphore. A semaphore usually has three tasks: *initialization/create, wait,* and *signal.*

A non-zero number or value is assigned to the semaphore once it is created. At this point no task is waiting for the semaphore. Once a task requires a data, the task performs a *wait* operation on the semaphore. The OS checks the value of the semaphore; for example, if the semaphore is available (semaphore value is non-zero), the OS changes the value of the semaphore to zero and assigns the semaphore to the task. If the semaphore value is zero during the wait operation, the task that requested the *wait* operation is placed on the semaphore's waiting list. Once the semaphore becomes available based on the priority of the tasks waiting for it, the OS decides which task to assign to the semaphore.

The tasks added to the semaphore's waiting list wait only for a certain amount of time. If the time expires, the task sends an error code to the semaphore seeking function and resumes its work. When the task has attained the semaphore and all its operations are complete, the task performs a *signal* operation, announcing that the semaphore is free. The OS checks if any other task is waiting for the semaphore and then transfers the semaphore to the task without changing the semaphore's value. If no task is waiting for the semaphore, the semaphore is incremented to a non-zero number. The wait operation is also referred to as *Take* or *Pend* or *P* and signal operation is referred to as *Release* or *Post* or *V.* The following example shows how wait and signal operations are performed:

```
1. typedef int semaphore;
2. float temp;
3. semaphore var_temp
4. void Task1 (void){
```

```
 5.      wait (var_temp);
 6.      temp = (9/5)(temp + 32); /* Celsius into Fahrenheit */
 7.      Signal (var_temp);
 8. }
 9. void Task2 (void){
10.      wait(var_temp);
11.      temp = ADDR0; /* Read ADC value from thermistor */
12.      temp = ADCtotemp_conversion();
13.      Signal (var_temp);
14. }
```

In the previous example two tasks share the variable `temp`. The `Task2` subroutine reads the temperature value from a thermistor and saves it on `temp`, while `Task1` converts the temperature from Celsius to Fahrenheit. Just before the tasks enter the critical section, they request the semaphore and only then perform the operation on the shared variable.

RTOS-Provided Messages

The RTOS provides other mechanisms besides semaphores for allowing tasks to communicate, such as message queues and mailboxes. It may be possible to structure your program to use messages to pass information rather than sharing data objects directly. We leave further discussion of this approach to the many RTOS-oriented books and articles already available.

Disable Task Switching

If no other method seems to work, one unattractive option is to disable the scheduler. If the scheduler is disabled, the task switching does not take place and the critical sections or shared data can be protected by other tasks. This method is counter-productive; disabling the scheduler increases response times and makes analysis much more difficult. This is considered bad practice and must be properly justified; hence consider this method as a last resort.

12.6 NONPREEMPTIVE DYNAMIC SCHEDULER

12.6.1 Concepts

We will now examine a flexible nonpreemptive scheduler for periodic and aperiodic tasks. We call it the RTC (run-to-completion) scheduler. This simple tick-based scheduler is quite flexible and offers the following major benefits:

- We can configure the system to run each task with a given period (e.g., every 40 ms) measured in time ticks. This simplifies the creation of multi-rate systems.

- We can define task priorities, allowing us to design the system's response (which tasks are executed earlier) when there are multiple tasks ready to run.
- We can selectively enable and disable tasks.

This scheduler has three fundamental parts.

- **Task Table:** This table holds information on each task, including:
  - □ The address of the task's root function.
  - □ The period with which the task should run (e.g., 10 ticks).
  - □ The time delay until the next time the task should run (measured in ticks).
  - □ A flag indicating whether the task is ready to run.
- **Tick ISR:** Once per time tick (say each 1 millisecond) a hardware timer triggers an interrupt. The interrupt service routine decrements the time delay (**timer**) until the next run. If this reaches zero, then the task is ready to release, so the ISR sets its **run** flag.
- **Task Dispatcher:** The other part of the scheduler is what actually runs the tasks. It is simply an infinite loop which examines each task's run flag. If it finds a task with the **run** flag set to 1, the scheduler will clear the **run** flag back to 0, execute the task, and then go back to examining the **run** flags (starting with the highest-priority task in the table).

Figure 12.7 shows a simple example of how this works with three tasks. Task 1 becomes active every twenty time intervals, and takes one time interval to complete. Task 2 is active every ten time intervals, and takes two time intervals to complete. Task 3 becomes active every five time intervals and takes one time interval to complete.

If more than one task becomes ready simultaneously (as seen at elapsed time ten), the higher priority task is serviced first. When the higher priority task finishes, the next highest ready task is executed. This repeats until there are no ready tasks.

Another example of a run-to-completion dynamic scheduling with interrupts is shown in Figure 12.8. A new task, Task 4, is added, which becomes active every three time intervals and runs for one time interval.

As shown in Figure 12.8, at time = 20, tasks T1, T2, T3 all become active and T2 is run based on priority. At time = 21, task T4 becomes active and is scheduled to run at time = 22. T1 runs at time = 23, but before T3 gets a chance to run, T4 becomes active again and gains the processor. At time = 25, T3 misses a turn since T3 becomes active again and the T3 is serviced as if it were active only once. This is an example of an overload situation which leads to one of the tasks missing its turn.[12]

---

[12] We could use a counter rather than a flag for the run variable, to allow for processing backlogs. In this case the ISR would increment run rather than set it, and the scheduler function would decrement it rather than clear it. This could be useful in some situations, but it would complicate the analysis.

	Priority		Length		Frequency
Task 1	2		1		20
Task 2	1		2		10
Task 3	3		1		5

	0	1	2	3	4	5	6	7	8	9	10	11	12	13	14	15	16	17	18	19	20	21	22	23	24	25
Elapsed time	0	1	2	3	4	5	6	7	8	9	10	11	12	13	14	15	16	17	18	19	20	21	22	23	24	25
Task executed						T3					T2		T3			T3					T2	T1	T3			T3
Task T1	20	19	18	17	16	15	14	13	12	11	10	9	8	7	6	5	4	3	2	1	20	19	18	17	16	15
Task T2	10	9	8	7	6	5	4	3	2	1	10	9	8	7	6	5	4	3	2	1	10	9	8	7	6	5
Task T3	5	4	3	2	1	5	4	3	2	1	5	4	3	2	1	5	4	3	2	1	5	4	3	2	1	5
Run T1																					W	W	R			
Run T2											R										R					
Run T3						R					W	W	R			R					W	W	W	R		R

R = Running on processor   W = Ready and waiting for processor

Figure 12.7   Simple run-to-completion dynamic scheduling.

	Priority		Length		Frequency
Task 1	2		1		20
Task 2	1		2		10
Task 3	3		1		5
Task 4	0		1		3

	0	1	2	3	4	5	6	7	8	9	10	11	12	13	14	15	16	17	18	19	20	21	22	23	24	25
Elapsed time	0	1	2	3	4	5	6	7	8	9	10	11	12	13	14	15	16	17	18	19	20	21	22	23	24	25
Task executed				T4		T3	T4			T4	T2		T4	T3		T4	T3		T4		T2		T4	T1	T4	T3
Task T1	20	19	18	17	16	15	14	13	12	11	10	9	8	7	6	5	4	3	2	1	20	19	18	17	16	15
Task T2	10	9	8	7	6	5	4	3	2	1	10	9	8	7	6	5	4	3	2	1	10	9	8	7	6	5
Task T3	5	4	3	2	1	5	4	3	2	1	5	4	3	2	1	5	4	3	2	1	5	4	3	2	1	5
Task T4	3	2	1	3	2	1	3	2	1	3	2	1	3	2	1	3	2	1	3	2	1	3	2	1	3	2
Run T1																					W	W	W	R		
Run T2											R										R					
Run T3						R					W	W	W	R		W	R				W	W	W	W	W	R
Run T4				R		R				R			R			R			R		W	R			R	

R = Running on processor   W = Ready and waiting for processor

Figure 12.8   Complex run-to-completion dynamic scheduling.

	Priority	Length	Frequency
Task 1	2	1	20
Task 2	1	2	10
Task 3	3	1	5
Task 4	0	2	3

	0	1	2	3	4	5	6	7	8	9	10	11	12	13	14	15	16	17	18	19	20	21	22	23	24	25	26	27	28	29	30
Elapsed time	0	1	2	3	4	5	6	7	8	9	10	11	12	13	14	15	16	17	18	19	20	21	22	23	24	25	26	27	28	29	30
Task executed				T4	T4	T3	T4	T4		T4	T4	T2	T2	T4	T4	T4	T4	T3	T4	T4	T2	T2	T4	T4	T4	T4	T1	T4	T4	T3	T4
Task T1	20	19	18	17	16	15	14	13	12	11	10	9	8	7	6	5	4	3	2	1	20	19	18	17	16	15	14	13	12	11	10
Task T2	10	9	8	7	6	5	4	3	2	1	10	9	8	7	6	5	4	3	2	1	10	9	8	7	6	5	4	3	2	1	10
Task T3	5	4	3	2	1	5	4	3	2	1	5	4	3	2	1	5	4	3	2	1	5	4	3	2	1	5	4	3	2	1	5
Task T4	3	2	1	3	2	1	3	2	1	3	2	1	3	2	1	3	2	1	3	2	1	3	2	1	3	2	1	3	2	1	3
Run T1																					W	W	W	W	W	W	R				
Run T2										W	R										R										W
Run T3					R					W	W	W	W	W	W	W	R				W	W	W	W	W	W	W	W	W	R	W
Run T4				R			R			R			W	R		R			R			W	R		R			R			R

R = Running on processor   W = Ready and waiting for processor

Figure 12.9 Overload example of run-to-completion dynamic scheduling.

Figure 12.9 shows a complex overloaded example where the scheduler fails to service every task that is ready.

12.6.2 Implementation

Task Table

A scheduler uses a table to store information on each task. Each task has been assigned a timer value. A task becomes active at regular intervals based on this value. This timer value is decremented each tick by the timer tick ISR. Once the timer value reaches zero, the task becomes ready to run. To reset this value after it has reached zero, an initial Timer Value variable is used to store the time at which the task has to be active. Two variables, enabled and run, are used to signal when a task is enabled and when it is ready to run. Variables enabled and run are used to indicate to the scheduler if a task is enabled and if it is ready to run. The function pointer *task indicates to the scheduler which function to perform.

The task's priority is defined by its position within this array. Entry 0 has the highest priority; whenever the scheduler needs to find a task to run, it begins at entry 0 and then works its way through the table.

The scheduler's task table is defined as follows:

```
1.  #define MAX_TASKS 10
2.  #define NULL ((void *)0)
3.  typedef struct {
4.      int initialTimerValue;
5.      int timer;
6.      int run;
7.      int enabled;
8.      void (* task)(void);
9.  } task_t;
10. task_t GBL_task_table[MAX_TASKS];
```

Before running the scheduler, the application must initialize the task table as follows:

```
1.  void init_Task_Timers(void){
2.      int i;
3.      /* Initialize all tasks */
4.      for(i = 0; i < MAX_TASKS; i++){
5.          GBL_task_table[i].initialTimerValue = 0;
6.          GBL_task_table[i].run = 0;
7.          GBL_task_table[i].timer = 0;
8.          GBL_task_table[i].enabled = 0;
9.          GBL_task_table[i].task = NULL;
10.     }
11. }
```

Managing Tasks

Once the initialization is completed, tasks must be added to the task structure. The new tasks can be added before starting the scheduler or during the scheduler's execution time. When adding a task, the following must be specified: the time interval in which the task has to be active, its priority, and the function on which the task has to operate. The following code shows how adding a task is added:

```
1.  int Add_Task(void (*task)(void), int time, int priority){
2.      /* Check for valid priority */
3.      if(priority >= MAX_TASKS || priority < 0)
4.          return 0;
5.      /* Check to see if we are overwriting an already scheduled
        task */
6.      if(GBL_task_table[priority].task != NULL)
```

```
7.        return 0;
8.     /* Schedule the task */
9.     GBL_task_table[priority].task = task;
10.    GBL_task_table[priority].run = 0;
11.    GBL_task_table[priority].timer = time;
12.    GBL_task_table[priority].enabled = 1;
13.    GBL_task_table[priority].initialTimerValue = time;
14.    return 1;
15. }
```

We can remove an existing task:

```
1. void removeTask(void (* task)(void)){
2.    int i;
3.    for(i = 0; i < MAX_TASKS; i++){
4.        if(GBL_task_table[i].task == task){
5.            GBL_task_table[i].task = NULL;
6.            GBL_task_table[i].timer = 0;
7.            GBL_task_table[i].initialTimerValue = 0;
8.            GBL_task_table[i].run = enabled = 0;
9.            return;
10.        }
11.    }
12. }
```

We can also selectively enable or disable a task by changing its **enabled** flag:

```
1. void Enable_Task(int task_number){
2.    GBL_task_table[task_number].enabled = 1;
3. }
4.
5. void Disable_Task(int task_number){
6.    GBL_task_table[task_number].enabled = 0;
7. }
```

Finally, we can change the period with which a task runs:

```
1. void Reschedule_Task(int task_number, int new_timer_val){
2.    GBL_task_table[task_number].initialTimerValue =
3.    new_timer_val;
4.    GBL_task_table[task_number].timer = new_timer_val;
5. }
```

Tick Timer Configuration and ISR

A run-to-completion dynamic scheduler uses a timer to help determine when tasks are ready to run (are released). A timer is set up to generate an interrupt at regular intervals. Within the interrupt service routine the timer value for each task is decremented. When the timer value reaches zero, the task becomes ready to run. In this code we have configured the 8-bit timer to generate an interrupt every 0.5 milliseconds. For details on how to set up a timer see Chapter 8.

```
1. void Init_RTC_Scheduler(void){
2.     IEN(TMR0,CMIA0) = 0;
3.     IPR(TMR0,CMIA0) = 3;
4.     MSTP(TMR0) = 0;
5.     TMR0.TCNT = 0x00;
6.     TMR0.TCORA = 78;
7.     TMR0.TCSR.BYTE = 0xE2;
8.     IEN(TMR0,CMIA0) = 1;
9.     TMR0.TCCR.BYTE = 0x0C;
10.    TMR0.TCR.BYTE = 0x48;
11. }
```

In the next example Timer 0 is set to compare the match mode with timer constant A. An interrupt occurs every 0.5 millisecond. The timer is configured in a continuous mode and resets every time a compare match is made.

```
1. void Excep_TMR0_CMI0A(void){
2.     int i;
3.     for(i = 0; i < MAX_TASKS; i++){
4.         if(GBL_task_table[i].task != NULL) &&
5.         (GBL_task_table[i].enabled == 1) &&
6.         (GBL_task_table[i].timer > 0))
7.         {
8.             if(--GBL_task_table[i].timer == 0){
9.                 GBL_task_table[i].run = 1;
10.                GBL_task_table[i].timer =
11.                GBL_task_table[i].initialTimerValue;
12.            }
13.        }
14.    }
15. }
```

Scheduler

The scheduler looks for ready tasks starting at the top of the table (highest priority task). It runs every ready task it finds, calling it as a function (in line 16).

```
1.  void Run_RTC_Scheduler(void){
2.      int i;
3.      /* Loop forever */
4.      while(1){
5.          /* Check each task */
6.          for(i = 0; i < MAX_TASKS; i++){
7.              /* check if valid task */
8.              if(GBL_task_table[i].task != NULL){
9.                  /* check if enabled */
10.                 if(GBL_task_table[i].enabled == 1){
11.                     /* check if ready to run */
12.                     if(GBL_task_table[i].run == 1){
13.                         /* Reset the run flag */
14.                         GBL_task_table[i].run = 0;
15.                         /* Run the task */
16.                         GBL_task_table[i].task();
17.                         /* break out of loop to start at entry 0 */
18.                         break;
19.                     }
20.                 }
21.             }
22.         }
23.     }
24. }
```

12.6.3 Example Application using RTC Scheduler

Let's use the RTC scheduler to create a toy with red and green LEDs flashing at various frequencies. The grnLED task toggles a green LED (on board LED 6) every one second, and the redLED task toggles a red LED (on board led 12) every 0.25 seconds. The grn_redLED task toggles one red LED and one green LED (on board led 7 and led 8 respectively) every 0.5 seconds.

The tasks and the main program are shown below:

```
1.  void grnLED(void){
2.      if(LED3 == LED_ON)
```

```
3.          LED3 = LED_OFF;
4.      else
5.          LED3 = LED_ON;
6.  }
7.  void redLED(void){
8.      if(LED4 == LED_ON)
9.          LED4 = LED_OFF;
10.     else
11.         LED4 = LED_ON;
12. }
13. void grn_redLED(void){
14.     if(LED5 == LED_ON)
15.         LED5 = LED9 = LED_OFF;
16.     else
17.         LED5 = LED9 = LED_ON;
18. }
19. void main(void){
20.     ENABLE_LEDS;
21.     init_Task_Timers();
22.     Add_Task(grnLED,10000,0);
23.     Add_Task(redLED,2500,1);
24.     Add_Task(grn_redLED,5000,2)
25.     Init_RTC_Scheduler();
26.     Run_RTC_Scheduler();
27. }
```

12.7   REFERENCES

Simon, David E. *An Embedded Software Primer.* Indianapolis: Addison-Wesley Professional, 1999. Print.

Labrosse, J. *MicroC/OS II: The Real-Time Kernel,* 2nd Ed. Lawrence, KS: Newnes, 2002. Print.

Labrosse, J., Ganssle, J., Oshana, R., Walls, C., Curtis, K., Andrews, J., Katz, D., Gentile, R., Hyder, K., and B. Perrin. *Embedded Software: Know it All.* Burlington, MA: Newnes, 2008. Print.

Labrosse, J. *MicroC/OS-III: The Real-Time Kernel, or a High Performance, Scalable, ROMable, Preemptive, Multitasking Kernel for Microprocessors, Microcontrollers & DSPs.* Weston, FL: Micrium Press, 2009. Print.

12.8   EXERCISES

1. For some task sets, changing from static to dynamic task ordering in a scheduler will provide a major response time improvement for the highest priority task, while for other task sets it will not. Give an example of each and explain the difference.

2. For some task sets, adding preemption to a scheduler will provide a major response time improvement for the highest priority task, while for other task sets it will not. Give an example of each and explain the difference.

3. Write C code to implement run-to-completion dynamic scheduling without interrupts to poll the following tasks:
   a. If switch 1 is pressed Toggle the RED LEDs.
   b. If switch 2 is pressed read the temperature value from the onboard thermistor and display on LCD.
   c. If switch 3 is pressed read the potentiometer value and display on the LCD.
   d. If no switch is pressed Toggle the GREEN LEDs.

4. Write an algorithm which implements the below functionality using run-to-completion dynamic scheduling with interrupts:
   a. Toggle RED LEDs every 0.5 seconds.
   b. Toggle GREEN LEDs every 0.25 seconds.
   c. Read temperature value from onboard thermistor and display on LCD every 1.0 seconds.
   d. Read potentiometer value and display on LCD every 2.5 seconds.

5. Write a C code to implement round-robin with interrupts algorithm to perform the following tasks:
   a. Toggle RED LEDs every 0.5 seconds.
   b. Toggle GREEN LEDs every 0.25 seconds.
   c. Read temperature value from onboard thermistor and display on LCD every 1.0 seconds.
   d. Read potentiometer value and display on LCD every 2.5 seconds.

6. Fill in the following table to show which tasks the processor will execute and when, as well as scheduler table contents. Assume that timer tick interrupts occur every 1 millisecond, all tasks take 1.2 milliseconds to complete, and initialTimerValue for tasks A, B, and C are 2, 4, and 5 respectively. Note that the entries in the table in column "Right before n" (e.g., timer, run, enabled) show the variable's value right before the timer tick interrupt occurs. This means that a task will run on the tick when its timer reaches 0 (but show the value after the tick and after the ISR executes). Assume task A has the highest priority, followed by task B, and then C.

TASK NAME		RIGHT BEFORE N	N	N + 1	N + 2	N + 3	N + 4	N + 5	N + 6	N + 7	N + 8	N + 9	N + 10	N + 11	N + 12	N + 13
A	timer	2														
	run	0														
	enabled	1														
B	timer	3														
	run	0														
	enabled	1														
C	timer	1														
	run	0														
	enabled	1														
	Activity	—														

7. Fill in the table in Exercise 4, if timer tick interrupts occur every 0.5 milliseconds and all tasks take 1.25 milliseconds to complete.

Appendix A

Interrupt Vector Table

Priority	Source of Interrupt Generation	Name	Vector No.	Vector Adress Offset	Form of Detection	Selectable Interrupt Request Destination			Sstb Return	Sacs Return	IER	IPR
						CPU	DTC	DMA				
High	—	Reserved	0	0000	—	×	×	×	×	×	—	—
	—	Reserved	1	0004	—	×	×	×	×	×	—	—
	—	Reserved	2	0008	—	×	×	×	×	×	—	—
	—	Reserved	3	000C	—	×	×	×	×	×	—	—
	—	Reserved	4	0010	—	×	×	×	×	×	—	—
	—	Reserved	5	0014	—	×	×	×	×	×	—	—
	—	Reserved	6	0018	—	×	×	×	×	×	—	—
	—	Reserved	7	001C	—	×	×	×	×	×	—	—
	—	Reserved	8	0020	—	×	×	×	×	×	—	—
	—	Reserved	9 to 15	0024 to 003C	—	×	×	×	×	×	—	—
	Bus error	BUSERR	16	0040	Level	o	×	×	×	×	IER02. IEN0	IPR00
	—	Reserved	17	0044	—	×	×	×	×	×	IER02. IEN1	—
	—	Reserved	18	0048	—	×	×	×	×	×	IER02. IEN2	—
	—	Reserved	19	004C	—	×	×	×	×	×	IER02. IEN3	—
	—	Reserved	20	0050	—	×	×	×	×	×	IER02. IEN4	—
	FCU	FIFERR	21	0054	Level	o	×	×	×	×	IER02. IEN5	IPR01
		Reserved	22	0058	—	×	×	×	×	×	IER02. IEN6	—
		FRDYI	23	005C	Edge	o	×	×	×	×	IER02. IEN7	IPR02
	—	Reserved	24	0060	—	×	×	×	×	×	IER03. IEN0	—
	—	Reserved	25	0064	—	×	×	×	×	×	IER03. IEN1	—
	—	Reserved	26	0068	—	×	×	×	×	×	IER03. IEN2	—
	ICU	SWINT	27	006C	Edge	o	o	×	×	×	IER03. IEN3	IPR03
	CMT Unit 0	CMI0	28	0070	Edge	o	o	o	×	×	IER03. IEN4	IPR04
Low		CMI1	29	0074	Edge	o	o	o	×	×	IER03. IEN5	IPR05

o: Selectable ×: Not Selectable

Source: RX62N Group, RX621 Group Hardware Manual, page 342-355.

Priority	Source of Interrupt Generation	Name	Vector No.	Vector Adress Offset	Form of Detection	Selectable Interrupt Request Destination			Sstb Return	Sacs Return	IER	IPR
						CPU	DTC	DMA				
High	CMT Unit 1	CMI2	30	0078	Edge	○	○	○	×	×	IER03. IEN6	IPR06
		CMI3	31	007C	Edge	○	○	○	×	×	IER03. IEN7	IPR07
	Ether	EINT	32	0080	Level	○	×	×	×	×	IER04. IEN0	IPR08
	USB0	D0FIFO0	36	0090	Edge	○	○	○	×	×	IER04.IEN4	IPR0C
		D1FIFO0	37	0094	Edge	○	○	○	×	×	IER04.IEN5	IPR0D
		USBI0	38	0098	Edge	○	×	×	×	×	IER04.IEN6	IPR0E
	USB1	D0FIFO1	40	00A0	Edge	○	○	○	×	×	IER05. IEN0	IPR10
		D1FIFO1	41	00A4	Edge	○	○	○	×	×	IER05. IEN1	IPR11
		USBI1	42	00A8	Edge	○	×	×	×	×	IER05. IEN2	IPR12
	RSPI0	SPEI0	44	00B0	Level	○	×	×	×	×	IER05. IEN4	IPR14
		SPRI0	45	00B4	Edge	○	○	○	×	×	IER05. IEN5	
		SPTI0	46	00B8	Edge	○	○	○	×	×	IER05. IEN6	
		SPII0	47	00BC	Level	○	×	×	×	×	IER05. IEN7	
	RSPI1	SPEI1	48	00C0	Level	○	×	×	×	×	IER06. IEN0	IPR15
		SPRI1	49	00C4	Edge	○	○	○	×	×	IER06. IEN1	
		SPTI1	50	00C8	Edge	○	○	○	×	×	IER06. IEN2	
		SPII1	51	00CC	Level	○	×	×	×	×	IER06. IEN3	
	—	Reserved	52	00D0	—	×	×	×	×	×	IER06. IEN4	—
	—	Reserved	53	00D4	—	×	×	×	×	×	IER06. IEN5	—
	—	Reserved	54	00D8	—	×	×	×	×	×	IER06. IEN6	—
	—	Reserved	55	00DC	—	×	×	×	×	×	IER06. IEN7	—
	CAN0	ERS0	56	00E0	Edge	○	×	×	×	×	IER07. IEN0	IPR18
		RXF0	57	00E4	Edge	○	×	×	×	×	IER07. IEN1	
		TXF0	58	00E8	Edge	○	×	×	×	×	IER07. IEN2	
		RXM0	59	00EC	Edge	○	×	×	×	×	IER07. IEN3	
		TXM0	60	00F0	Edge	○	×	×	×	×	IER07. IEN4	
	RTC	PRD	62	00F8	Edge	○	×	×	×	×	IER07. IEN6	IPR1E
		CUP	63	00FC	Edge	○	×	×	×	×	IER07. IEN7	IPR1F
	External pins	IRQ0	64	0100	Edge/level	○	○	○	○	○	IER08. IEN0	IPR20
Low		IRQ1	65	0104	Edge/level	○	○	○	○	○	IER08. IEN1	IPR21

Priority	Source of Interrupt Generation	Name	Vector No.	Vector Adress Offset	Form of Detection	Selectable Interrupt Request Destination			Sstb Return	Sacs Return	IER	IPR
						CPU	DTC	DMA				
High		IRQ2	66	0108	Edge/level	○	○	○	○	○	IER08. IEN2	IPR22
		IRQ3	67	010C	Edge/level	○	○	○	○	○	IER08. IEN3	IPR23
		IRQ4	68	0110	Edge/level	○	○	×	○	○	IER08. IEN4	IPR24
		IRQ5	69	0114	Edge/level	○	○	×	○	○	IER08. IEN5	IPR25
		IRQ6	70	0118	Edge/level	○	○	×	○	○	IER08. IEN6	IPR26
		IRQ7	71	011C	Edge/level	○	○	×	○	○	IER08. IEN7	IPR27
		IRQ8	72	0120	Edge/level	○	○	×	○	○	IER09. IEN0	IPR28
		IRQ9	73	0124	Edge/level	○	○	×	○	○	IER09. IEN1	IPR29
	External pins	IRQ10	74	0128	Edge/level	○	○	×	○	○	IER09. IEN2	IPR2A
		IRQ11	75	012C	Edge/level	○	○	×	○	○	IER09. IEN3	IPR2B
		IRQ12	76	0130	Edge/level	○	○	×	○	○	IER09. IEN4	IPR2C
		IRQ13	77	0134	Edge/level	○	○	×	○	○	IER09. IEN5	IPR2D
		IRQ14	78	0138	Edge/level	○	○	×	○	○	IER09. IEN6	IPR2E
		IRQ15	79	013C	Edge/level	○	○	×	○	○	IER09. IEN7	IPR2F
	—	Reserved	80 to 87	0140 to 015C	—	×	×	×	×	×	—	—
	—	Reserved	88	0160	—	×	×	×	×	×	IER0B. IEN0	—
	—	Reserved	89	0164	—	×	×	×	×	×	IER0B. IEN1	—
	USB_resume	USBR0	90	0168	Level	○	×	×	○	○	IER0B. IEN2	IPR3A
		USBR1	91	016C	Level	○	×	×	○	○	IER0B. IEN3	IPR3B
	RTC	ALM	92	0170	Edge	○	×	×	○	○	IER0B. IEN4	IPR3C
		Reserved	93	0174	—	×	×	×	×	×	IER0B. IEN5	—
		Reserved	94	0178	—	×	×	×	×	×	IER0B. IEN6	—
		Reserved	95	017C	—	×	×	×	×	×	IER0B. IEN7	—
	WDT	WOVI	96	0180	Edge	○	×	×	×	○	IER0C. IEN0	IPR40
		Reserved	97	0184	—	×	×	×	×	×	IER0C. IEN1	—
	AD0	ADI0	98	0188	Edge	○	○	○	×	×	IER0C. IEN2	IPR44
	AD1	ADI1	99	018C	Edge	○	○	○	×	×	IER0C. IEN3	IPR45
	—	Reserved	100	0190	—	×	×	×	×	×	IER0C. IEN4	—
	—	Reserved	101	0194	—	×	×	×	×	×	IER0C. IEN5	—
Low	S12AD	ADI12_0	102	0198	Edge	○	○	○	×	×	IER0C. IEN6	IPR48

Priority	Source of Interrupt Generation	Name	Vector No.	Vector Adress Offset	Form of Detection	Selectable Interrupt Request Destination			Sstb Return	Sacs Return	IER	IPR
						CPU	DTC	DMA				
High	—	Reserved	103 to 113	019C to 01C4	—	×	×	×	×	×	—	—
↑	MTU0	TGIA0	114	01C8	Edge	○	○	○	×	×	IER0E. IEN2	IPR51
		TGIB0	115	01CC	Edge	○	○	×	×	×	IER0E. IEN3	
		TGIC0	116	01D0	Edge	○	○	×	×	×	IER0E. IEN4	
		TGID0	117	01D4	Edge	○	○	×	×	×	IER0E. IEN5	
		TCIV0	118	01D8	Edge	○	×	×	×	×	IER0E. IEN6	IPR52
		TGIE0	119	01DC	Edge	○	×	×	×	×	IER0E. IEN7	
		TGIF0	120	01E0	Edge	○	×	×	×	×	IER0F. IEN0	
	MTU1	TGIA1	121	01E4	Edge	○	○	○	×	×	IER0F. IEN1	IPR53
		TGIB1	122	01E8	Edge	○	○	×	×	×	IER0F. IEN2	
		TCIV1	123	01EC	Edge	○	×	×	×	×	IER0F. IEN3	IPR54
		TCIU1	124	01F0	Edge	○	×	×	×	×	IER0F. IEN4	
	MTU2	TGIA2	125	01F4	Edge	○	○	○	×	×	IER0F. IEN5	IPR55
		TGIB2	126	01F8	Edge	○	○	×	×	×	IER0F. IEN6	
	MTU2	TCIV2	127	01FC	Edge	○	×	×	×	×	IER0F. IEN7	IPR56
		TCIU2	128	0200	Edge	○	×	×	×	×	IER10. IEN0	
	MTU3	TGIA3	129	0204	Edge	○	○	○	×	×	IER10. IEN1	IPR57
		TGIB3	130	0208	Edge	○	○	×	×	×	IER0E. IEN2	
		TGIC3	131	020C	Edge	○	○	×	×	×	IER10. IEN3	
		TGID3	132	0210	Edge	○	○	×	×	×	IER10. IEN4	
		TGIV3	133	0214	Edge	○	×	×	×	×	IER10. IEN5	IPR58
	MTU4	TGIA4	134	0218	Edge	○	○	○	×	×	IER10. IEN6	IPR59
		TGIB4	135	021C	Edge	○	○	×	×	×	IER10. IEN7	
		TGIC4	136	0220	Edge	○	○	×	×	×	IER11. IEN0	
		TGID4	137	0224	Edge	○	○	×	×	×	IER11. IEN1	
		TCIV4	138	0228	Edge	○	○	×	×	×	IER11. IEN2	IPR5A
	MTU5	TGIU5	139	022C	Edge	○	○	×	×	×	IER11. IEN3	IPR5B
		TGIV5	140	0230	Edge	○	○	×	×	×	IER11. IEN4	
		TGIW5	141	021C	Edge	○	○	×	×	×	IER10. IEN7	
Low	MTU6	TGIA6	142	0238	Edge	○	○	○	×	×	IER11. IEN6	IPR5C

Priority	Source of Interrupt Generation	Name	Vector No.	Vector Adress Offset	Form of Detection	Selectable Interrupt Request Destination			Sstb Return	Sacs Return	IER	IPR
						CPU	DTC	DMA				
High		TGIB6	143	023C	Edge	o	o	x	x	x	IER11. IEN7	
		TGIC6	144	0240	Edge	o	o	x	x	x	IER12. IEN0	
	MTU6	TGID6	145	0244	Edge	o	o	x	x	x	IER12. IEN1	IPR5C
		TCIV6	146	0248	Edge	o	x	x	x	x	IER12. IEN2	IPR5D
		TGIE6	147	024C	Edge	o	x	x	x	x	IER12. IEN3	
		TGIF6	148	0250	Edge	o	x	x	x	x	IER12. IEN4	
	MTU7	TGIA7	149	0254	Edge	o	o	o	x	x	IER12. IEN5	IPR5E
		TGIB7	150	0258	Edge	o	o	x	x	x	IER12. IEN6	
		TCIV7	151	025C	Edge	o	x	x	x	x	IER12. IEN7	IPR5F
		TCIU7	152	0260	Edge	o	x	x	x	x	IER13. IEN0	
	MTU8	TGIA8	153	0264	Edge	o	o	o	x	x	IER13. IEN1	IPR60
		TGIB8	154	0268	Edge	o	o	x	x	x	IER13. IEN2	
		TCIV8	155	026C	Edge	o	x	x	x	x	IER13. IEN3	IPR61
		TCIU8	156	0270	Edge	o	x	x	x	x	IER13. IEN4	
	MTU9	TGIA9	157	0274	Edge	o	o	o	x	x	IER13. IEN5	IPR62
		TGIB9	158	0278	Edge	o	o	x	x	x	IER13. IEN6	
		TGIC9	159	027C	Edge	o	o	x	x	x	IER13. IEN7	
		TGID9	160	0280	Edge	o	o	x	x	x	IER14. IEN0	
		TCIV9	161	0284	Edge	o	x	x	x	x	IER14. IEN1	IPR63
	MTU10	TGIA10	162	0288	Edge	o	o	o	x	x	IER14. IEN2	IPR64
		TGIB10	163	028C	Edge	o	o	x	x	x	IER14. IEN3	
		TGIC10	164	0290	Edge	o	o	x	x	x	IER14. IEN4	
		TGID10	165	0294	Edge	o	o	x	x	x	IER14. IEN5	
		TCIV10	166	0298	Edge	o	o	x	x	x	IER14. IEN6	IPR65
	MTU11	TGIU11	167	029C	Edge	o	o	x	x	x	IER14. IEN7	IPR66
		TGIV11	168	02A0	Edge	o	o	x	x	x	IER15. IEN0	
		TGIW11	169	02A4	Edge	o	o	x	x	x	IER15. IEN1	
	POE	OEI1	170	02A8	Level	o	x	x	x	x	IER15. IEN2	
		OEI2	171	02AC	Level	o	x	x	x	x	IER15. IEN3	
Low		OEI3	172	0280	Level	o	x	x	x	x	IER15. IEN4	

Priority	Source of Interrupt Generation	Name	Vector No.	Vector Adress Offset	Form of Detection	Selectable Interrupt Request Destination CPU	DTC	DMA	Sstb Return	Sacs Return	IER	IPR
High		OEI4	173	02B4	Level	○	×	×	×	×	IER15. IEN5	
	TMR0	CMIA0	174	02B8	Edge	○	○	×	×	○	IER15. IEN6	IPR68
		CMIB0	175	02BC	Edge	○	○	×	×	○	IER15. IEN7	
		OVI0	176	02C0	Edge	○	×	×	×	○	IER16. IEN0	
	TMR1	CMIA1	177	02C4	Edge	○	○	×	×	○	IER16. IEN1	IPR69
		CMIB1	178	02C8	Edge	○	○	×	×	○	IER16. IEN2	
		OVI1	179	02CC	Edge	○	×	×	×	○	IER16. IEN3	
	TMR2	CMIA2	180	02D0	Edge	○	○	×	×	○	IER16. IEN4	IPR6A
		CMIB2	181	02D4	Edge	○	○	×	×	○	IER16. IEN5	
		OVI2	182	02D8	Edge	○	×	×	×	○	IER16. IEN6	
	TMR3	CMIA3	183	02DC	Edge	○	○	×	×	○	IER16. IEN7	IPR6B
		CMIB3	184	02E0	Edge	○	○	×	×	○	IER17. IEN0	
		OVI3	185	02E4	Edge	○	×	×	×	○	IER17. IEN1	
	—	Reserved	186	02E8	—	×	×	×	×	×	IER17. IEN2	
	—	Reserved	187	02EC	—	×	×	×	×	×	IER17. IEN3	
	—	Reserved	188	02F0	—	×	×	×	×	×	IER17. IEN4	
	—	Reserved	189	02F4	—	×	×	×	×	×	IER17. IEN5	
	—	Reserved	190	02F8	—	×	×	×	×	×	IER17. IEN6	
	—	Reserved	191	02FC	—	×	×	×	×	×	IER17. IEN7	
	—	Reserved	192	0300	—	×	×	×	×	×	IER18. IEN0	
	—	Reserved	193	0304	—	×	×	×	×	×	IER18. IEN1	
	—	Reserved	194	0308	—	×	×	×	×	×	IER18. IEN2	
	—	Reserved	195	030C	—	×	×	×	×	×	IER18. IEN3	
	—	Reserved	196	0310	—	×	×	×	×	×	IER18. IEN4	
	—	Reserved	197	0314	—	×	×	×	×	×	IER18. IEN5	
	DMACA	DMAC0I	198	0318	Edge	○	○	×	×	×	IER18. IEN6	IPR70
		DMAC1I	199	031C	Edge	○	○	×	×	×	IER18. IEN7	IPR71
		DMAC2I	200	0320	Edge	○	○	×	×	×	IER19. IEN0	IPR72
		DMAC3I	201	0324	Edge	○	○	×	×	×	IER19. IEN1	IPR73
Low	EXDMAC	EXDMAC0I	202	0328	Edge	○	○	×	×	×	IER19. IEN2	IPR74

Priority	Source of Interrupt Generation	Name	Vector No.	Vector Adress Offset	Form of Detection	Selectable Interrupt Request Destination			Sstb Return	Sacs Return	IER	IPR
						CPU	DTC	DMA				
High		EXDMAC1I	203	032C	Edge	○	○	×	×	×	IER19. IEN3	IPR75
		Reserved	204	0330	—	×	×	×	×	×	IER19. IEN4	
		Reserved	205	0334	—	×	×	×	×	×	IER19. IEN5	
	—	Reserved	206	0338	—	×	×	×	×	×	IER19. IEN6	
	—	Reserved	207	033C	—	×	×	×	×	×	IER19. IEN7	
	—	Reserved	208	0340	—	×	×	×	×	×	IER1A. IEN0	
	—	Reserved	209	0344	—	×	×	×	×	×	IER1A. IEN1	
	—	Reserved	210	0348	—	×	×	×	×	×	IER1A. IEN2	
	—	Reserved	211	034C	—	×	×	×	×	×	IER1A. IEN3	
	—	Reserved	212	0350	—	×	×	×	×	×	IER1A. IEN4	
	—	Reserved	213	0354	—	×	×	×	×	×	IER1A. IEN5	
	SCI0	ERI0	214	0358	Level	○	×	×	×	×	IER1A. IEN6	IPR80
		RXI0	215	035C	Edge	○	○	○	×	×	IER1A. IEN7	
		TXI0	216	0360	Edge	○	○	○	×	×	IER1B. IEN0	
		TEI0	217	0364	Level	○	×	×	×	×	IER1B. IEN1	
	SCI1	ERI1	218	0368	Level	○	×	×	×	×	IER1B. IEN2	IPR81
		RXI1	219	036C	Edge	○	○	○	×	×	IER1B. IEN3	
		TXI1	220	0370	Edge	○	○	○	×	×	IER1B. IEN4	
		TEI1	221	0374	Level	○	×	×	×	×	IER1B. IEN5	
	SCI2	ERI2	222	0378	Level	○	×	×	×	×	IER1B. IEN6	IPR82
		RXI2	223	037C	Edge	○	○	○	×	×	IER1B. IEN7	
		TXI2	224	0380	Edge	○	○	○	×	×	IER1C. IEN0	
		TEI2	225	0384	Level	○	×	×	×	×	IER1C. IEN1	
	SCI3	ERI3	226	0388	Level	○	×	×	×	×	IER1C. IEN2	IPR83
		RXI3	227	038C	Edge	○	○	○	×	×	IER1C. IEN3	
		TXI3	228	0390	Edge	○	○	○	×	×	IER1C. IEN4	
		TEI3	229	0394	Level	○	×	×	×	×	IER1C. IEN5	
	—	Reserved	230	0398	—	×	×	×	×	×	IER1C. IEN6	—
		Reserved	231	039C	—	×	×	×	×	×	IER1C. IEN7	
Low	—	Reserved	232	03A0	—	×	×	×	×	×	IER1D. IEN0	—

Priority	Source of Interrupt Generation	Name	Vector No.	Vector Adress Offset	Form of Detection	Selectable Interrupt Request Destination			Sstb Return	Sacs Return	IER	IPR
						CPU	DTC	DMA				
High		Reserved	233	03A4	—	×	×	×	×	×	IER1D. IEN1	
↑	SCI5	ERI5	234	03A8	Level	○	×	×	×	×	IER1D. IEN2	IPR85
		RXI5	235	03AC	Edge	○	○	○	×	×	IER1D. IEN3	
		TXI5	236	03B0	Edge	○	○	○	×	×	IER1D. IEN4	
		TEI5	237	03B4	Level	○	×	×	×	×	IER1D. IEN5	
	SCI6	ERI6	238	03B8	Level	○	×	×	×	×	IER1D. IEN6	IPR86
		RXI6	239	03BC	Edge	○	○	○	×	×	IER1D. IEN7	
		TXI6	240	03C0	Edge	○	○	○	×	×	IER1E. IEN0	
		TEI6	241	03C4	Level	○	×	×	×	×	IER1E. IEN1	
	—	Reserved	242	03C8	—	×	×	×	×	×	IER1E. IEN2	—
		Reserved	243	03CC	—	×	×	×	×	×	IER1E. IEN3	—
		Reserved	244	03D0	—	×	×	×	×	×	IER1E. IEN4	—
		Reserved	245	03D4	—	×	×	×	×	×	IER1E. IEN5	—
	RIIC0	ICEEI0	246	03D8	Level	○	×	×	×	×	IER1E. IEN6	IPR88
		ICRXI0	247	03DC	Edge	○	○	○	×	×	IER1E. IEN7	IPR89
		ICTXI0	248	03E0	Edge	○	○	○	×	×	IER1F. IEN0	IPR8A
		ICTEI0	249	03E4	Level	○	×	×	×	×	IER1F. IEN1	IPR8B
	RIIC1	ICEEI1	250	03E8	Level	○	×	×	×	×	IER1F. IEN2	IPR8C
		ICRXI1	251	03EC	Edge	○	○	○	×	×	IER1F. IEN3	IPR8D
		ICTXI1	252	03F0	Edge	○	○	○	×	×	IER1F. IEN4	IPR8E
		ICTEI1	253	03F4	Level	○	×	×	×	×	IER1F. IEN5	IPR8F
	—	Reserved	254	03F8	—	×	×	×	×	×	IER1F. IEN6	IPR90
Low	—	Reserved	255	03FC	—	×	×	×	×	×	IER1F. IEN7	IPR91

Index

Product Development from Start to Success™

Product Development Engineering

Since 1990, we have designed some of the most exciting technologies for Fortune 500 and small companies alike in the medical, video and portable wireless markets. We specialize in product development services from start to success, including electrical, software, mechanical and industrial design services.

We transform your product idea, marketing requirement, or product specification into a marketable product that's profitable.

Paragon has been developing products around Renesas seminconductors since its inception.

At Paragon Innovations, we get excited about technology.

Medical

* Infusion pumps
* Pulse oximeters
* Electroporation devices
* Surgical lasers
* Continuous Cardiac Output Monitor
* Insulin pumps
* Breathalyzers
* Wireless & bar coding devices
* Smart phone medical applications
* Pneumothorax detection
* Ear effusion

Wireless/Portable

* Insulin pumps
* Gas compressor lubrication monitor
* GPS based tracking devices
* GSM telephony
* CDMA telephony
* Electroporation devices
* Panasonic PDA
* Breathalyzers
* Weather stations
* Automotive OBD-II Products

Video

* Video projectors
* Extreme off axis projection
* Rear Projection HDTV
* Video compression
* Video scaling
* Set top box
* Flight Information Display Systems
* Airline Video Docking Systems (VDOCKS)
* LED displays

How often do you experience this?

What the client explained

What the system architect specified

What the project manager understood

What the engineer developed

What the third-party contractor defined

How the project got documented

What actually was manufactured

What was billed

How it was maintained

What the client actually needed

Lightning Source UK Ltd.
Milton Keynes UK
UKOW030613200313

207860UK00004B/157/P